W9-APV-835

BARRON'S

HOW TO PREPARE FOR THE

AP®

Advanced Placement Exam

UNITED STATES HISTORY

7TH EDITION

William O. Kellogg
Former Head of the History Department
St. Paul's School
Concord, New Hampshire
President, World Affairs Council of New Hampshire

BARRON'S

® AP and Advanced Placement Program are registered trademarks of the College Entrance Examination Board, which was not involved in the production of and does not endorse this book.

Dedication

To all those students who have made teaching United States history a pleasure. May they inspire others.

© Copyright 2004, 2000 1996, 1993, 1988, 1983, 1977
by Barron's Educational Series, Inc.

All rights reserved.
No part of this book may be reproduced in any form, by photostat,
microfilm, xerography, or any other means, or incorporated into
any information retrieval system, electronic or mechanical,
without the written permission of the copyright owner.

All inquiries should be addressed to:
Barron's Educational Series, Inc.
250 Wireless Boulevard
Hauppauge, New York 11788
http://www.barronseduc.com

Library of Congress Catalog Card No. 2003062814

International Standard Book No. 0-7641-2338-6

Library of Congress Cataloging-in-Publication Data
Kellogg, William O.
    How to prepare for the AP, United States history advanced placement
examination / William O. Kellogg. — 7th ed.
      p.   cm.
    At head of title: Barron's
    Includes bibliographical references and index.
    ISBN 0-7641-2338-6
     1. United States—History—Examinations, questions, etc.
I. Title: Barron's how to prepare for the AP, United States history
advanced placement examination. II. Title.

E178.25.K44 2004
973—dc22   2003062814

PRINTED IN THE UNITED STATES OF AMERICA
9 8 7 6 5

Contents

Preface to the Seventh Edition

Writing, rewriting, and editing this book on the Advanced Placement examination has been most interesting and educational for me. I only hope it proves to be the same for the students and teachers who will use it to further their study and understanding of that always intriguing subject: the history of the American people.

Although the material included in the book is mine and I am responsible for the emphasis and interpretations, more than 4,000 St. Paul's students during the past 40 years have strongly influenced my understanding and method of presenting American history. They, together with the many colleagues with whom I have worked both at St. Paul's and elsewhere, have my heartfelt thanks for providing ideas and the stimulating atmosphere that have made teaching such an exciting endeavor. Special thanks go to several students who wrote responses to questions for this text. They have provided an important student voice.

I would also like to express my gratitude to my typist of the first and second editions, Judy Morin, who had an uncanny ability to decipher scratchings, turning them into words and to follow arrows making words into sentences. Without her this manuscript would never have emerged, and she is greatly missed. My special thanks go to my daughter, Elli Kellogg Blackwell, who has taken over where Judy began as decipherer and typist. My thanks also go to the several editors at Barron's who have helped with the seven editions. Their patience, advice, and insights are greatly appreciated.

WILLIAM O. KELLOGG
June 2003

PART ONE

INTRODUCTION

Using This Book

Three Ways to Use This Book

This book was written to help students prepare for the Advanced Placement examination. It can be used three different ways. First, it can be used as a supplement to a regular course in United States history. The student wishing to take the Advanced Placement examination and not enroll in an advanced course can use this book to provide depth of coverage. If the student writes the essays and answers the multiple-choice questions, he or she will be well prepared for the Advanced Placement examination. In addition, supplemental readings are suggested in the bibliography and these can be pursued as the student wishes.

The second way this book may be used is as part of an Advanced Placement course. The teacher can assign chapters in the book to supplement work in class or a student can pick those chapters where he or she needs help. The suggested essay topics in each chapter can be assigned at the teacher's discretion.

The third way the book may be used is by a student who has already had a course in American history and wishes to simply review before attempting the Advanced Placement examination. A student using the book in this way should start by taking the Model A Advanced Placement examination to find areas of weakness in the information he or she already has and then develop a review plan.

To the Student

A careful study of this book will provide you with the skills needed on the Advanced Placement examination. Writing the practice essays will help prepare you for that important part and answering the multiple-choice questions will remind you of just how much you already know. Part Five presents a chronological summary of American history that will be covered on the Advanced Placement examinations. It will help your review. The Model Advanced Placement examination will, if taken in a situation similar to the examination, provide you a rehearsal, which is extremely valuable.

While it is important that you move at your own pace in working through the book, it is also important that you at least skim the material in each chapter. Do not skip chapters, because there is important information included in each one.

To the Teacher

This book can be used to supplement work in class. If you are teaching a regular section of American history, the book can provide the supplementary stimulation needed to prepare a few interested students to take the Advanced Placement examination. You may in this case wish to suggest additional reading, but it is not necessary, as this book will help those students prepare for the exam. If you are teaching an Advanced Placement course, the book can be broken up in segments and assigned as you find appropriate. The chronological material in Part Five provides a good overview of important issues in our history. The essays in Part Three provide much factual information.

Organization of This Book

Part One presents an introduction to this book and to the Advanced Placement examination.

Part Two introduces skills needed in the study of history and presents a method of writing essays. The Seven Steps method has proven very helpful for students preparing for the essays on the Advanced Placement examination or writing any essays.

Part Three is organized around periods of time in American history and in each chapter the important issues of the period are listed. Each chapter focuses on a different type of essay question. Each type is analyzed and sample answers are included. Also in Part Three different types of multiple-choice questions are introduced and analyzed. Included in each chapter are five sample essay questions and 12 multiple-choice questions dealing with the time period or with preceding time periods. This is not to suggest that only these types of questions will be asked on that particular era of American history. As you work through Part Three, your knowledge of American history will be broadened.

Part Four presents two sample Advanced Placement examinations. Also included are suggestions on how to take the examination and how to do the final review before the exam.

As mentioned above, Part Five of this book includes a chronological outline of important events in American history. Although this book is not meant as a complete textbook, using this section should stimulate the recall of important issues and developments in American history. It can provide a good last-minute review of American history before taking the exam, or it can be used to supplement your chronological study of American history in a standard textbook. Part Five also includes a date line. The book ends with a Glossary and an Index.

This volume was designed to be used in a flexible way. It can be read straight through, or different sections can be chosen to help your review and in-depth study. It has proven very helpful to many students of American history, and it has been used in a variety of courses throughout the country.

The Advanced Placement Examination

Advanced Placement examinations are offered in a wide range of subject areas. The structure of each of these examinations differs somewhat, and therefore all information offered in this book regarding Advanced Placement examinations refers only to the examination in United States history, which is often referred to as the American history examination.

Grading

Advanced Placement examinations are offered annually in May. Final grades are reported on a five-point scale as follows:

5   extremely well qualified
4   well qualified
3   qualified
2   possibly qualified
1   no recommendation

In granting credit or advanced placement, many colleges honor grades of 3 or higher. The policies of colleges vary: some automatically grant credit or advanced academic standing; others respond individually to each situation. The United States history examination essays are read by college and high school consultants meeting in June. Grades are reported in July.

The College Board presents a number of AP Scholar Awards to students obtaining a 3 or better on three AP course examinations. The AP program will send your AP grade to the colleges of your choice. More than 1,400 colleges give credit for AP work. You should check with the colleges that interest you to check their AP policies. The College Board also has information.

Many high school juniors take the AP United States history exam. Having your grade and the fact that you took an AP exam reported to the college may help your admission opportunities.

The Types of Questions

The United States History AP examination consists of three types of questions: the multiple-choice question, the document-based essay question (often abbreviated as DBQ), and the standard essay question. Both types of essay questions are referred to as free response questions. In evaluating the examination, essay answers account for 50 percent of the grade. It is thus clear that writing skills are extremely important in achieving a good score on the Advanced Placement examination. Minor adjustments have been made to the format of the examination over the years. **Students now have 2 hours and 10 minutes in which to answer one DBQ and two standard essay questions.** If you use old examinations for practice, it is important to realize they may not follow the format of the current examination.

The Multiple-Choice Questions

In 1996 the time allotted for multiple-choice questions was also changed. **Students now have 55 minutes to answer 80 multiple-choice questions.**

The following questions are typical of those that appear on the examination:

1. "A well-regulated militia being necessary to the security of a free state, the right of the people to keep and bear arms shall not be infringed."

   All of the following are true in relation to the above quotation EXCEPT
   (A) It is the second amendment to the U.S. Constitution
   (B) It is considered part of the Bill of Rights
   (C) The "right to bear arms" has been a major political issue in post-World War II United States
   (D) The National Guard of each state is an example of a "well-regulated militia"
   (E) The statement assumes that all people will serve in the military

2. Among the scandals connected with the Grant administration are
   (A) Credit Mobilier and Watergate
   (B) Teapot Dome and the Whiskey Ring
   (C) the Whiskey Ring and Credit Mobilier
   (D) Iran-Contra and Teapot Dome
   (E) Monica Lewinsky and Watergate

3. Which of the following is true about the concept of neutrality?
   (A) Its aim is to avoid involvement in foreign wars.
   (B) It has been successfully applied by the United Nations.
   (C) It has been an important concept since the Monroe Doctrine.
   (D) It prolonged the fighting in World War II.
   (E) It was the basis of U.S. policy in Central America in the 19th century.

   Questions in the multiple-choice section of the exam will be based on recall of information and analysis as well as on interpretation of information such as political cartoons, tables and charts, maps, or documents presented in the question. These latter questions are often referred to as "stimulus" questions. The multiple-choice section of the examination will draw on information from social and intellectual history, including possibly a question or two on literature and art as they relate to history, as well as the more traditional areas of political, diplomatic, and economic history. There will be further information on multiple-choice questions in Part Three.

Scoring the Multiple-Choice Question

In scoring the multiple-choice section of the AP examination, one-fourth of a point is taken off for each incorrect answer. Therefore, you should not guess blindly at answers but rather analyze the choices. If at least one of the five choices can be eliminated, then you may wish to pick an answer from the remaining four options. Statistically you have at least an even chance, and if you can eliminate two or more choices, you have a better than even chance, of gaining a point. As the sample multiple-choice questions in each chapter are analyzed, practice eliminating incorrect choices.

Answers to Sample Questions

1. E   2. C   3. A

The Document-Based Essay Question (DBQ)

The essay or free response section of the examination consists of two parts: the document-based question and the standard essay questions. The DBQ will be based on documents but not necessarily famous documents such as the Constitution. The documents may include writings by well-known individuals, or individuals representative of their time, journals, Supreme Court decisions, other important national documents, or newspaper articles, and when appropriate will include visual representation such as pictures, charts, graphs, maps, or cartoons. There is no limit to the type of document that may be used.

The document-based question is designed to test your analytical skills **as well as** your ability to relate the material to the major issues of the time period covered by the DBQ. These major issues form what is referred to by the historians who develop the Advanced Placement examination as the "mainstream" of American history. You must be able to introduce ideas and information from this "mainstream" in your DBQ answer. For example, the question might be on the intricacies of U.S. foreign policy between 1795 and the outbreak of the war in 1812. The documents included would reflect the various aspects of this foreign policy and might include selections from treaties, the XYZ correspondence, or the embargo of 1807. You would then be expected to interpret these documents and show how they relate to the "mainstream" developments of those years. For instance, you should be able to express the views of the Federalists and the Anti-Federalists, of John Adams and Thomas Jefferson, of New Englanders and frontier settlers on the issues raised by the documents. You must include such information from the "mainstream" of American history in your DBQ answer if you wish to achieve a good grade. Your answer cannot be based simply on the documents.

The DBQ is discussed in greater detail in Part Three, Chapter 5, where a sample question is included, and in Part Two, Section C, where information is presented on what to look for when creating a DBQ that will help you in your analysis and study of documents. There are also sample DBQs included in the model exams found in Part Four.

The Standard Essay Question

The second part of the essay section presents two groups of two questions each for a total of four questions. You are to answer two questions—one from each group. You should choose the questions about which you know the most and pick your facts carefully to support your opinion on the particular subject. In each chapter of Part Three, a different type of essay question is presented and analyzed and sample answers presented. The examples are chosen from different periods in American history. **A great deal of American history is included in these sample essay answers, and although some of it is not presented well, there are no factual errors in these answers, and therefore these sample answers provide a helpful review of American history.** Thus, as you work through this book you will be studying both American history chronologically and different types of essay and multiple-choice questions.

The fact that a particular type of question is included in a chapter on the Civil War period does *not* mean that all questions on the exam dealing with the Civil War will be of that type. Of course, any type of question can be asked on any period. This combination of chronology and questions has proven to be an effective and efficient way to review American history while preparing for the Advanced Placement examination. Be sure to read all of Part Three. Study carefully each of the question types.

Following are three essay questions similar to those that appear on the Advanced Placement examination:

1. "The English founded colonies in the new world to escape oppression in England." Evaluate this statement.

2. Analyze how TWO of the following prepared the way for the United States to emerge as a world leader in the latter half of the 20th century.

   The Spanish American War
   Woodrow Wilson's Fourteen Points
   The Lend-Lease Act

3. Describe and evaluate the significance of the abolitionist movement in bringing about the Civil War.

Time Allotment on the Exam

The United States history exam is 3 hours and 5 minutes in length. You are given 55 minutes to answer 80 multiple-choice questions. You are then allotted 2 hours and 10 minutes for the free response or essay section. This is divided so that you have 15 minutes to read and analyze the DBQ and 45 minutes to write it. You will then have 70 minutes to answer two of the four essay questions. It is suggested you spend 5 minutes reading and making notes on the two questions you will answer and 30 minutes writing each answer. Thus you have a total of 105 minutes of writing and 25 minutes of reading and analysis on the essay section for a total of 2 hours and 10 minutes.

Content Covered on the Exam

The AP exam has traditionally been given in May, and this will continue. Since this mid-May date falls at a time when many high school courses have not yet completed their chronological study, the AP exam has placed less emphasis on the period since the Reagan presidency. No essay questions will deal exclusively with the last 25 years but there can be multiple-choice questions specifically on these years. Also, since a number of schools today devote little time to colonial history and concentrate on the period after 1754, the AP exam has placed less emphasis on pre-1754 American history than on later history, although students should have an understanding of the interaction between Native American culture and that of the European settlers in the colonial period and the differences and similarities between the British colonies as well as some knowledge of pre-Columbian culture and the development of Hispanic culture in the Southwest. On the multiple-choice section of the exam approximately one-sixth of the questions come from the period prior to 1789, approximately one-half of the questions deal with the period from 1790 to 1914, and approximately one-third of the questions deal with the period from 1915 to the present.

Fifty percent of multiple-choice questions come from 1790–1915.

Recently the United States History Development Committee, which is responsible for designing the AP exam, prepared a 33-item outline of what might be included in an AP course covering the "mainstream" of American history. The outline reads like the table of contents of any standard two-volume textbook of American history. The first three items refer to settlement, the growth of the English colonies, and colonial life before 1754. The last two items refer to the presidencies of Nixon and his successors. Thus, 28 items provide an outline of the years that are the focus of the exam. Such an outline, which follows the "mainstream" of United States history, would include the following periods:

The Road to Independence
The American Revolution and Its Aftermath
The Constitution
The New Republic
The Jeffersonian Revolution
Early Nationalism
Sectional Differences
Age of Jackson
Manifest Destiny
The Establishment of an American Culture
Coming of the Civil War
Civil War
Reconstruction
The Passing of the Frontier
Social Darwinism and American Industrial Growth
The Growth of the City
The Emergence of a New South
The Gilded Age and the Populist Movement
The Emergence of the United States as a World Power
The Progressive Era
World War I and Its Aftermath
The 1920s and the Great Crash
The Depression and the New Deal
Twentieth-Century Literature and the Arts
The Coming of World War II
World War II and Its Aftermath
The Cold War
The Truman and Eisenhower Presidencies
The Civil Rights Movement and Social Reform
The Vietnam War
Watergate and the Nixon–Ford Presidencies

The Development Committee makes it very clear that the outline it has developed is meant only as a suggestion as to what might be covered in an AP course and the above list simply suggests those topics covered in the typical chronological survey of American history. **Since 1996 the Development Committee has placed a heavier emphasis on social history and change than in the past as a response to what is being emphasized in the colleges.**

The exam breaks down as 35 percent on political activity, 35 percent on social history, 15 percent on diplomatic history and foreign policy, 10 percent on economic change, and 5 percent on cultural and intellectual developments.

The Advanced Placement program has always emphasized and acknowledged the independence of each classroom teacher in designing an advanced-level course. Any publication on the subject of Advanced Placement history curriculum will offer only general guidelines.

In designing your study, whether you are a teacher or a student studying on your own, all periods of American history should be considered. However, you should give extra time to several of the periods mentioned above. In considering which periods to emphasize you should keep in mind that political institutions and behavior account for approximately 35 percent of the questions on both the multiple-choice and essay sections of the examination. Another 35 percent of the questions deal with social history. The remaining part of the exam will be divided among diplomatic history (15 percent), economic history (10 percent), and intellectual history (5 percent). The essay questions may require relating two or more of these types of issues, such as specific economic implications of the foreign policy moves or the political response to economic crises.

In recent years there has been strong emphasis on chronology as the organizing principle for advanced courses. In the 1960s many courses were designed around topics or themes. Survey courses that cover the "mainstream" of American history can be successfully organized around chronology or themes. Samples of such themes are

American expansion, both on the continent and overseas, and its social and economic impact on the nation

The changing role of government throughout our history

Economic changes both in business and labor practices and attitudes

Slavery, immigration, and the role of minorities in American life

The cause of major wars and their effect—economic, political, and social

The growth of an American culture in the 19th century and its flowering in the 20th century

One should include in any investigation of American history material peripheral to the political chronology. When considering literature, one should study it as it reflects changing attitudes and values in American history and not only as a work of literary art. The same holds true for any consideration of art and philosophy. Gender, ethnic and racial differences, socioeconomic conflicts, as well as changing historiographic interpretations of major developments in the mainstream of American political history should be considered, although historiography will not be questioned directly on the examination. Of course, not all of this material can be included in a one-year course so choices must be made. There are many literary anthologies, TV documentaries, and collections of documents that can help you gain the understanding you need.

Summary of the Content of the Exam

This description of exam content may seem confusing: Just realize that no two courses in Advanced Placement American history will be the same; thus you must decide what areas to concentrate on. The core or 70 percent of the exam will cover social and political history with items from diplomatic, economic, and intellectual history making up the other 30 percent. You need to consider the major events in the "mainstream" of the nation's history. You can do this by studying either chronology or themes. There will be less emphasis on the period prior to 1754 and after 1980 than on the other periods, with approximately half the multiple-choice questions covering material between 1790 and 1914.

Getting College Credit for AP Work

Colleges have very different ways of awarding placement and credit based on the AP exams, and you should have the correct information. The College Entrance Examination Board (CEEB—often referred to as the College Board) has some information. You should speak to your college advisor and/or write to colleges to which you are applying for specific information on their Advanced Placement policies. Some colleges give credit for grades of 3 and above; others require higher grades. All students considering taking AP examinations should seek this information from colleges that interest them.

The Achievement Examination in United States History (SAT)

A student who is well prepared to take the May U.S. History AP exam is also prepared to take the U.S. History Achievement Test (SAT II) later in May. This test is different in its emphasis, consisting of multiple-choice questions only. To do well on the SAT, a quick review of the multiple-choice questions in this book would be helpful. The multiple-choice questions on the SAT are similar to those in this book.

CLEP Examination

Several years ago the College Entrance Examination Board introduced the College Level Examination Program (CLEP) to provide a method for students to gain college credit for work and life experience outside the classroom. Some high school students have used the exam to gain college credit. However, the Advanced Placement Program is designed for such students and is the exam you should plan to take. Information on the CLEP Exam can be obtained from the College Board.

Publications of the College Board

It is most important that you, your teacher, or your guidance counselor check with the CEEB for the latest details on AP exams. Each year there may be minor changes. The program and test dates, and testing centers can change. You must apply to take the exam and there is a fee. For the latest information, check with the guidance department of your high school or write directly to

The Advanced Placement Program
The College Board
45 Columbus Avenue
New York, New York 10023-6992

In addition to specific information on the AP and CLEP programs and on testing dates, the CEEB publishes a variety of pamphlets, videos, and CDs that can help you. Information on them may be obtained on the Internet at the College Board web site or by contacting the AP program office in Princeton, N.J. The address is

The Advanced Placement Program
Dept. E-22
P.O. Box 6670
Princeton, New Jersey 08541-6670
The CEEB web site is *www.collegeboard.org/ap* and the address of their online store is *http://cbweb2.collegeboard.org/shopping/.*

Helpful Hints for Studying United States History

In studying any subject there are certain study techniques and approaches that make understanding the material easier for the student. However, many students approach all subjects with the same methods and become frustrated when they fail to achieve success in one area with techniques that proved successful in other subjects. For example, the study of history requires a great deal of reading, but if you read history the way you read a novel, you will not find success, since you may miss many of the important details you must know.

Each student studying history will develop his or her own very personal approaches to material. Part Two introduces a number of study techniques that students of history have found valuable.

Reading Skills

Approaches to Reading

Any student planning to take the Advanced Placement examination should be a good reader, since he or she will have to read extensively, quickly, and with understanding. Many students read all written material in the same manner—they start at the beginning and go to the end. In a novel or in other literary works and in pleasure reading, this is a satisfactory approach, but another method is more beneficial when you are attempting to learn the details presented in the written material and when the subject is strange or unfamiliar to you. This method is to pre-read the material.

Pre-Reading

In pre-reading one looks over the material (book, chapter, document) quickly, reading titles and subheadings when they occur and, when they do not, reading the first sentence of paragraphs to get the sense of what will be presented in the reading. Often one will find review questions or a summary at the end of a chapter, and these should be read as part of the pre-reading. Once you have looked over the reading, you should have a good idea of what it is about. You should have some questions of your own. These questions should be written down.

If there are questions in the book, these should be noted. These questions should guide your reading.

Reading the Material

As you read, you should interact with the material. Keep in mind the questions you have developed. Take notes (see below) to help you answer them. Stop after a section and ask yourself, "What was the main point I just read?" Write it down. Remember that the writer is an individual with ideas and a point he or she wants you to believe. You need, in reading, to know what the ideas are, but you must also decide if you believe them and how the writer has used evidence to convey them. You must ask, "Is the evidence correct? Is it complete? What might have been left out?"

Finding the Evidence

Many students consider history to be nothing but facts. Actually, history is what writers have done with the facts, the evidence from the past. What we have in a history book or a document is what the author thought was important. Not every fact or every bit of evidence from the past is included, any more than we include everything we have done, or thought, when we write a letter. When you read history, you must consider what evidence or facts might have been left out because of the author's viewpoint.

Analyzing Authors' Viewpoints

History is a very personal subject. Every writer has his or her own ideas about the relationship of different happenings, the importance of certain individuals, the motivations behind various actions, and the significance of each event. No two historians will agree entirely on their interpretations and the evidence they use. For example, if you are reading one of the *Federalist Papers* written by James Madison, it is important to realize Madison's biases in favor of the Constitution, of education, and of wealth and his biases against the poorer and less educated. When you see Madison quoted in a text, you will want to keep these points in mind. Likewise, if you are reading Charles Beard, one of the great American historians of the first half of the 20th century, you will want to be aware of his biases. If you are not aware, you might accept without question Beard's interpretation of the Constitution as a document written by wealthy men for the protection of their own wealth. Knowing that Beard was an economic historian and that he interpreted history, as does a Marxist, in terms of economic pressures and class divisions based on wealth, you might not accept all Beard has to present. Charles Beard made many important points in his famous book, *The Economic Interpretation of the Constitution*, but many of his assumptions have been questioned or tempered by later scholars, such as Richard Brown, who based their interpretations on other assumptions, some of which are also being questioned.

The point is that historians interpret events based on their personal viewpoints and the student must learn what these viewpoints or biases are as well as learn the evidence the historian presents. Further reading may make you aware of how much evidence was left out or overlooked by the author of a particular book. This will lead you to develop and identify your own viewpoints or biases.

Identifying Biases

There are many ways to identify biases. Such simple devices as the date of publication and the place of residence of an author will give some insights. Prefaces, biographical sketches, and reviews will also provide information. The most important way to discover bias, however, is through a careful reading of the material. For instance, the words chosen to describe the slave in America may reveal certain attitudes. Is he Sambo, a *shuffling* character who *benefited* from his *master's* religion? Or was he an *exploited* worker—more exploited than those in the factories of England since he could never be *free*? Such words reveal a lot about the author, as will the manner in which various events are described. As a test of author's biases, try reading about the same event in several different books. Most historians in considering Lincoln's signing of the Emancipation Proclamation would include the same so-called hard facts or evidence, such as the date (1863), document (Emancipation Proclamation), and events (the signing ceremony). How each uses these facts to explain Lincoln's reasons for signing reveals the author's bias. Textbooks compared this way can reveal a great deal.

Not only do writers have biases; everyone has them. You must be aware of these—and particularly your own biases and prejudices—as you study. Also, do not overlook the fact that I, the author, have biases that are incorporated in this text. Can you identify some of them?

Biases and prejudices are not necessarily bad, although we often use the word *prejudice* negatively. They are simply a part of being human and thus are a part of history. The greater your awareness of the biases of the authors you read, and of your own, the greater your understanding of events will be.

Post-Reading

The final step of effective reading is to post-read. Look back at the questions you developed in your pre-reading and be sure you can answer them. This amounts to a review of the chapter. If you are taking a history course, you will want to do this reviewing as close to the class meeting time as possible. If you are studying independently, you will want to look over your questions and the answers you developed at regular intervals. If you have good notes on the material you study, you will find it very helpful to read these during the week before you take the Advanced Placement exam. You will find it exceedingly difficult to review all the reading you do in an advanced level course the week before the exam, so your notes will be most important.

Reading "Nonverbal" Material

Documentary films and videos as well as those created for entertainment, CD-ROMs, charts, graphs, maps, cartoons, paintings, and songs can all be used as sources for historical research. In viewing such sources it is important to apply your reading skills. You may not be able to skim through a film, but you can read about it before seeing it and develop questions. You can look at selected sections of videos after viewing them. Computer information and CD-ROM sources can be printed out or reviewed. For all these sources you should analyze the author's views and biases. If the author, artist, producer, or director is not identified, seek information about the company that produced the item. The maker of a video, the painter of a portrait, and the creator of a chart all have something they personally wish to convey. Be aware of that as you use these sources.

Underlining

Many students who own books develop techniques of underlining or making marginal notes in the books to identify the information that will answer the questions they have developed. This can be a very helpful technique, but one should limit the amount of underlining that is done. Too much underlining is worse than none, since it defeats the purpose, which is to clearly mark those items in a book that you think are important to remember. Underlinings, slash marks through important sentences, and circles around key words are all helpful techniques. Each student fortunate enough to own his or her history books will develop a technique that will make reviewing written material easy and will enable the student to answer questions developed in pre-reading.

Summary

In studying for a history course or exam, you should first pre-read all material. While doing this you should develop questions that will provide the focus for your reading. You should then read the material. Be aware as you read (or look) of the author's viewpoints and biases. Finally, before class or before going on to the next reading, you should review the material by checking the answers you have prepared for the questions you developed in your pre-reading. You will also want to review your answers to questions before any test and especially before taking the AP exam.

Note-taking Skills

Collecting Information to Answer Your Questions

Note taking is an important skill for every history student to develop. There are several approaches one may follow. Students should try different methods and use those with which they are most comfortable.

As suggested above, one method of note taking is to develop questions about your reading and then take notes to develop answers. The evidence might be written on a page under the question or on your computer. This method allows the student to restructure the material in a book into patterns that he or she has developed. If you follow this method, you will have put yourself into the role of the historian, collecting and reordering factual information to provide answers to questions of interest to you. If you consider the question as a sort of thesis and the factual information you put in your notes as the data to prove it, this method of note taking will be excellent practice for writing essays as presented in Part Three.

Many students today use the note-taking technique called "mapping" in which a key word or idea is put in the center of the page and circled. Then, relevant ideas are grouped along lines running out from the circle. The technique, often used in brainstorming, allows the student to reorganize material around key points.

Outlining

Another valuable method of note taking is outlining. In this approach the student simply summarizes or condenses the information in the book. The summary does not reorder the information, but retains the important data in a short version that can be referred to for review or before the exam. The student is not involved in being the historian in preparing such notes, but will have at hand a brief version of the information he or she needs to discuss issues or to prove given hypotheses.

Where to Keep Notes

Many students will keep their notes in a notebook. A looseleaf book is suggested since you can add or rearrange pages. This can be helpful. A few students will take notes on index cards. This is a valuable technique when writing a research paper, but can become rather burdensome when simply taking notes on a text. Some students take their notes on the computer using hypercard or a technique they develop such as using the questions you develop.

Time Line

In addition to taking notes on the general content of the material read, there are several types of specialized note taking that can be invaluable to the student of history. The first involves making a time line. Dates are important in history since they provide the key to the cause-and-effect relationship that is at the heart of understanding history in the Western world. Unless you know the chronological order in which events happened, you cannot explain the relationships among them. Therefore, as you read it would be wise to keep a list of major events and the date on which each occurred. This can be a simple list in which you merely record the date and the name of the event. For instance, a time line can be as simple as the following:

1763 — Treaty of Paris
     — Proclamation Line

1764 — Grenville Program
     — Sugar Act

1765 — Stamp Act
     — Stamp Act Congress
     — Boycott

1766 — Stamp Act Repealed
     — Declaratory Act

You can make your time line more complex by adding the day and month of each event, which is sometimes very important, by adding the names of people and places, and even going so far as to briefly describe each event, person, or place.

Part Five includes a simple time line. You may wish to add to this one or make your own as you study. If you make your own, emphasize what is important to you and not what someone else has decided you should learn. This is an important part of any study—to make the information yours.

Lists of Individuals

A second specialized type of note taking is that of keeping a list of important individuals. Your notes might group them by activity, such as political leaders, business leaders, reformers, inventors, and the like, or by time periods. Part Five includes such lists but you should make your own lists as you study.

Building Vocabulary

Every discipline has its own vocabulary. We often do not realize this as we study English or history, since most of the vocabulary is familiar to us from our daily usage. However, there are many words that are used in special ways in history. As you study, you should develop a list of words with which you were not familiar when you began your study. In the list, after each word you should write a definition. Such a list is a glossary. A short glossary is included at the end of the book but you should develop your own word list.

Many words used in history change their meaning during the course of time. You must be aware of the *shifting use* of words as well as of their meanings today. For instance, a person labeled as a *liberal* in 1830, in 1912, in 1968, and in 2004 might stand for very different points of view. As you read, be certain you can identify these shifting meanings of such a word.

Also, many terms or phrases used in history refer to much more than is meant by the word alone. For instance, the word *frontier* has different meanings and different connotations depending upon how it is used. If by *frontier* one means the edge of unsettled land, you react in one way. However, if you mean *frontier* as understood by the very important American historian Frederick Jackson Turner, then you need to react in many other ways. *Frontier* is simply one example of many words that have particular meanings for history.

Key Phrases

Historians also have adopted many phrases used by politicians and others through the years to convey certain concepts. For instance, the New Frontier of President Kennedy has a specialized meaning with which you should be familiar. Keep a list of such phrases as you study; you will find them to be invaluable in aiding your understanding of American history. Many questions on the examination will assume a knowledge of such phrases and words.

The sample multiple-choice questions in Chapter 8 deal with vocabulary. By the time you get to those questions you should have developed your own vocabulary list and thus should find these questions easy. Of course, all questions dealing with history require knowledge of the vocabulary of history. Thus, you need to add new words to your vocabulary notes as you study.

Summary

When studying history, it is very important to take notes on the material. Each student should practice taking notes in different ways to find one that works best for him or her. However, all students should keep their own time lines, lists of individuals and key phrases, and glossary. Reorganizing the evidence presented under questions of significance to you leads you to act as an historian and is strongly recommended as a study skill.

What Sources to Use

When students or teachers first look at the amount of material available in the field of United States history, both in hardcover editions and in paperbacks, on video and film and now on CD-ROMs and the Internet, they are often overwhelmed. The quantity, much of it of high quality by important people and outstanding historians, is so discouraging that the teacher or student often retreats to a safe textbook within the covers of which will be found brief presentations of all the important events of American history, at least as understood by one or several authors. It is hoped that the users of this book will not fall into that trap, but rather will use a variety of sources for the study of American history. A textbook is often a fine starting place, but for the truly interested student-scholar, it should be only that—a starting place. Documents, cartoons, videos, even well-written novels of a period will supply depth of understanding to your study and will provide important evidence for the answers to your questions. With the greater emphasis on social history on the exam, such supplemental sources will be even more important.

Bibliography

At the end of this section is a bibliography of texts, general works, and special reference books illustrating the type of works you should consult in your study. Each of the review chapters contains a bibliography of special works dealing with the period covered. In no way could a student in a one-year course be expected to use all these works, but they are included to serve as examples of the type of material one might use to supplement his or her study. Many of the works in these chapter bibliographies cover one aspect of the period, such as the Great Crash of 1929. Students should pursue special interests of this type as they study the main pattern of United States history.

Textbooks, General Works, and Special Reference Works

There are many textbooks from which to choose. A major consideration is length. A brief text will provide the basic structure and allow time for extensive special research. The texts mentioned at the end of the chapter are a sampling of those often used in AP classes.

Under General Works are listed a sampling of sources that trace one aspect of United States history such as diplomatic or intellectual. Students should consult at least one such work to learn how historians approach specialized topics. The Special Reference Works list a few of the encyclopedias and document collections available. These works can be very helpful when investigating a particular question.

Journals and Magazines

You may wish to consult some of the learned history journals that carry articles on recent research. Consulting such journals is a good supplement to your regular study. At least one or two of these journals should be available in your school library or in the local public library. They supplement any study of American history and they provide insights into new interpretations of past events. The articles are often written by well-known historians and this provides an opportunity to learn who they are.

Historiography and Changing Interpretations

Historiography, which includes the methodology or way historians work and write, must be understood by each student of history. As stated above, each historian has his or her own viewpoints and biases. From time to time, these personal views change but more importantly, interpretations of past events change both over time and with new authors. Such change has been referred to as revisionist history. It is always going on. While these changing interpretations have not been specifically tested on the AP exam in recent years, it would be wise to be aware of some of them and of the historians who represent the changing views. For instance, in the past 50 years there have been new interpretations of the start of the American Revolution (Bernard Bailyn, *Pamphlets of the American Revolution*), Lincoln (David Donald, *Lincoln Reconsidered*), slavery in the South (R. W. Fogel and S. L. Engerman, *Time on the Cross*), the Cold War (Louis J. Halle, *Cold War as History*), and the Vietnam War (Stanley Karnow, *Vietnam: A History* and Robert McNamara, *In Retrospect: the Tragedy and Lessons of Vietnam*). In addition, the work of specific historians who presented strong theses such as Charles Beard's *Economic Interpretations of the Constitution* and Frederick Jackson Turner's *Significance of the Frontier in American History* have been challenged. As you read books from the bibliographies and articles in journals, keep this in mind. When you can, identify an interpretation with an author.

Internet, Videos, and CD-ROMs

The Internet, videos, and CD-ROMs provide a wide range of helpful information for students of United States history. As a relatively new and rapidly changing and expanding resource, it is difficult to remain abreast of the most valuable sources since the quality of such resources can vary immensely. For the Internet, .edu web sites are more likely to be accurate and helpful, but that is not always true. The Library of Congress web site as well as state and university sites are important ones to check. The issue in using all three resources is time. The Web can absorb one for hours, and videos and most CD-ROMs must be viewed in real time and cannot be skimmed as printed material can be. Also, web sites and addresses change. Therefore, no sites have been listed. However, it you are comfortable on the Internet, you should use search engines to find specific information, especially documents, relevant to your study.

Summary

The works listed in the bibliographies are meant to be suggestions for further study. There are other works that would serve as well, but it would be overwhelming to list them all. These are merely examples of the types of works you might use and those that reflect the author's personal prejudices.

If you are studying independently in preparation for the Advanced Placement examination, your first step should be to decide if you will pick a text from the bibliography, or use several different reference works for your study. If you are in an Advanced Placement or regular class, the teacher will have already made this choice.

Textbooks

There are innumerable textbooks on United States history. Among those that might be used in an advanced-level course are the following:

Bailey, T. A., and David M. Kennedy. *The American Pageant*. Boston: Houghton Mifflin, 2001. (An old favorite of many teachers.)

Blum, John, et al. *The National Experience: A History of the United States*. New York: International Thomson Pub. (A standard college-level textbook.

Kellogg, W. O. *American History: The Easy Way*. Hauppauge, NY: Barron's Educational Series, Inc., 2003. (A brief overview of American history that serves well as a text and can be supplemented by specialized works.)

Norton, M. B. et al. *A People and a Nation: A History of the United States*. Boston: Houghton Mifflin, 2002, 1991. (The textbook emphasizes the social history of the nation.)

Zinn, Howard. *A People's History of the United States: 1492 to the Present*. New York: Harper/Collins, 2003. (Another text that emphasizes social history.)

General Works

Bailey, T. A. *Diplomatic History of the American People*. New York: Prentice Hall College Div., 1980.

Corwin, Edward S. *The Constitution and What It Means Today, 14th Edition*. Princeton: Princeton University Press, 1979.

Curti, Merle. *The Growth of American Thought*. New Brunswick, NJ: Transaction Pubs., 2003.

Friedman, Lawrence. *Crime and Punishment in American History*. New York: Basic Books, 1994.

Karsten, Peter *(ed.) The Military in America: From the Colonial Era to the Present*. New York: Free Press, 1986.

Page, Jake. *In the Hands of the Great Spirit: The 20,000 Year History of the American Indians*. New York: Free Press, 2003.

Quarles, Benjamin. *The Negro in the Making of America*. New York: Touchstone, 1996.

Special Reference Works

Adams, J. T. *(ed.) Atlas of American History*. New York: Macmillan, 1985.

American Council of Learned Societies, Garraty, J. A. *(ed.) Dictionary of American Biography*. 7 volumes plus supplements. New York: Macmillan, 1981.

Carruth, Gordon *(ed.) Encyclopedia of American Facts and Dates*. New York: HarperCollins, 1997.

Cayton, M. K. et al. *Encyclopedia of American Culture and Intellectual History*. New York: Charles Scribner's Sons, 2001.

———. *Encyclopedia of American Social History*. New York: Charles Scribner's Sons, 1993.

Cullen-DuPont, Kathryn. *The Encyclopedia of Women's History in America*. Boulder, CO: Capo Press, 1998.

Deconde, A. *(ed.) Encyclopedia of American Foreign Policy*. New York: Charles Scribner's Sons, 2002.

Evans, J. M. *(ed.) Two Thousand Notable American Women*. Raleigh, NC: American Biographic Institute, 1991.

Freidel, Frank, et al. *(eds.) Harvard Guide to American History*. Cambridge, MA: Belknap Press, 1980.

Gambone, M. D. *Documents of American Diplomacy: From the American Revolution to the Present*. Westport, CT: Greenwood Publishing Group, 2001.

Garraty, J. A. *(ed.) American National Biography*. 24 volumes plus supplement. New York: Oxford University Press, 1999, 2002.

Gilbert, Marin, and Martin Gilbert. *The Routledge Atlas of American History: From the First Exploration to the Present Day*. New York: Routledge, 2003.

Gonick, Larry. *Cartoon History of the United States*. New York: HarperCollins, 1991.

Heffner, Richard *(ed.) A Documentary History of the United States*. New York: Signet, 2002.

Hofstadter, Richard and Beatrice. *Great Issues in American History: From Reconstruction to the Present Day 1864–1981*. New York: Random House, 1982.

Kutler, Stanley. *Dictionary of American History*. 10 volumes. New York: Charles Scribner's Sons, 2003.

Levy, Leonard, and Louis Fisher. *Encyclopedia of the American Presidency*. New York: Simon and Schuster Trade, 1993.

Maddex, R. L. *The U.S. Constitution A to Z (C. Q.'s Ready Reference Encyclopedia of American Government)*. Washington, DC: C. Q. Press, 2002.

McCoy, D. R. (*ed.*) *American Presidency Series.* Multivolume. Lawrence, KS: University of Kansas Press.

Magill, F. N. (*ed.*) *Great Events from History: North American Series 15000 B.C.–1996.* 4 volumes. Pasadena, CA: Salem Press, Inc., 1997.

Morris, R. B. (*ed.*) *Encyclopedia of American History.* New York: HarperCollins, 1995.

Pious, R. M. *Presidency of the United States (Oxford Student Companions to American Government).* New York: Oxford University Press, 2002.

Porter, Glenn (*ed.*) *Encyclopedia of American Economic History.* New York: Macmillan, 1980.

Salzman, Jack (*ed.*) *African-American Culture and History: A Student's Guide.* New York: Macmillan Library Reference, 2000.

Journals and Magazines
American Heritage Magazine
American Historical Review
Foreign Affairs
Journal of American History

Seven Steps to Make Essay Writing Easy

Why the Essay Technique Is Important

A good essay style is the key to success on the Advanced Placement United States History examination. This may appear to be an extreme statement, but it is true; *essays count 50 percent of your AP grade.*

You may be well trained at analyzing documents, and you may have mastered the factual content of American history, but if you cannot express yourself in writing, the reader of your exam paper will never know how much you understand and how much work you have done. In this 3 hour and 5 minute examination, you will have 2 hours and 10 minutes in which to organize and write three essays. The first, the DBQ, is a required question in which you must analyze the given documents and incorporate in your answer both your analysis of them and information from the "mainstream" of American history. The other two are to be chosen from four options presented to you and you will have 60 minutes to write both answers and 10 minutes to analyze and take notes on the questions. In the grading formula the three essays count for 50 percent of the grade. To arrive at this 50 percent, the DBQ is given a weight of 45 and the two essays 27.5 each. So you can see how important it is to do well on the essays if you want to get a good grade on the examination.

Because of this, in Chapters 1–8 in Part Three we will consider different types of essay questions used on the Advanced Placement examination. There are many ways in which essay questions may be phrased and it is important to understand how they differ.

The Essay Question

The term *essay* is often used to mean a composition or a piece of writing in which a question is answered. However, by definition an essay is more. It is a literary, analytical composition expressing the writer's viewpoint on a single subject. An essay is not a rambling piece of writing that answers a question.

An essay is
1. literary
2. analytical or interpretive
3. on a single subject
4. the personal viewpoint of the author

All four of these points are important for you to understand about the essay, but the idea that the essay presents a personal viewpoint is most significant. We will refer to this personal viewpoint as the thesis[1] of the essay, and we want you to develop your personal opinion on each essay topic presented in this book.

---

[1]The *American Heritage Dictionary* defines *thesis* as "1. a proposition . . . that is maintained by argument. 2. a dissertation advancing an original point of view as a result of research."

Your thesis will distinguish your essay answer from those of other students and how well you convince the reader that your view is correct will determine the grade you receive for your essay.

The *Evaluate This Statement* Question

Essay questions may be phrased in many different ways using such key words as *evaluate, compare, contrast, analyze,* and *assess.* As an introduction to essay writing, we will first look at an *Evaluate This Statement* question. In the *Evaluate This Statement* question the test designer presents a statement that may or may not be controversial. The word *Evaluate* is crucial in this type of question. The student must be prepared to judge the validity of the statement, to weigh the pros and cons, and to reject or accept the truth of the statement after analysis. Therefore, you must first read the statement and be certain that you understand what it says, then you decide what your opinion on the statement is—that is the evaluation. Your opinion provides your thesis, which you must prove using evidence you can recall.

This *Evaluate This Statement* essay question deals with the geography of the colonial regions. Two sample introductory paragraphs are presented and then analyzed. Next, two complete essay answers to the question are presented and analyzed. From these analyses some general guides for the writing of essays are presented. You should follow these guidelines throughout your study.

Sample Question

> "The geographic conditions of the three major areas of English settlement in America—New England, the mid-Atlantic region, and the South—were the primary factors in determining the differences in the colonial way of life in these three areas." Evaluate this statement.

Sample Introduction 1

Virginia had a fairly mild climate and fertile soil in the tidewater area where many rivers supplied transportation to the plantations. The mid-Atlantic region also had fertile soil, but it lacked the rivers into the interior to aid transportation and the winters were less mild. With cold winters and hot summers, New England was climatically the least attractive of the three colonial regions, and the soil was very rocky. Therefore, New Englanders turned to business and the sea in order to make a living.

Sample Introduction 2

Geography is an important factor in the lives of all people. However, to say that geography accounts for the differences in the colonial way of life in the three areas of English settlement—New England, the mid-Atlantic, and the South—is an exaggeration. The relations with the mother country, the different reasons for settlement, and especially the different types of settlers had a major impact on the colonial way of life.

Comments on Sample Introduction 1

Sample Introduction 1 is a poor, ineffective response to the given question. It clearly illustrates the greatest problem students have in writing essay answers—the problem of analysis of the question. Under the pressure of limited time, students too often begin their writing without considering what they are being asked, how they should organize their response, and what their opinion (their thesis) is on the topic. Such a response can lead to disaster on the Advanced Placement examination. Let us look at this introduction and see what the student has done.

The student has immediately grabbed the idea of three regions and focused on an example of one, Virginia, and in the first sentence has proceeded to present three items of information connected with geography—climate, soil, rivers. The student demonstrates good factual information, referring to "tidewater" Virginia and to the plantation economy. In the second and third sentences, general information is presented about the two other regions. There is a structure to the paragraph, to these three sentences, and to the way they are constructed. You might wonder, therefore, why this paragraph is being criticized as an introduction. The problem, of course, is that the writer has not indicated what the question is. There is no evaluation and no personal view or thesis presented. The writer does not understand the purpose of an introduction to an essay.

Rules for an Introductory Paragraph

An effective introductory paragraph must answer two questions:

1. What is the topic? (for example, a statement of the topic or issue under consideration or, simply, the question rephrased)
2. What is the author's opinion on the topic? (for example, the author's thesis)

An excellent introductory paragraph will also contain

3. a rather broad, attention-catching comment on the topic
4. limited factual information because the facts should be saved for the body of the essay

The most effective introductory or opening paragraphs have the thesis as the last sentence of the paragraph, and the earlier sentences present the question and the broad comment on the general topic. Now with these guides in mind look at the last sentence of Sample Introduction 1 and decide what thesis or personal opinion this student is presenting. Is this sentence the thesis of the essay? Reread the paragraph. Is there a statement of what the author believes or is trying to prove anywhere in the paragraph? Can you tell what the topic is? If you cannot determine that the topic is a comparison of the geographic features of New England, the South, and the mid-Atlantic states, and you can find no personal opinion stated, you would agree with the author. This illustration should impress upon you the importance of that first step in writing any essay—*analyzing the question.*

Comments on Sample Introduction 2

Now consider Sample Introduction 2. What factors distinguish Introduction 2 from Introduction 1? Can you determine what the topic under consideration is for the second introduction? Can you determine what that writer's opinion is on the topic?

Sample Introduction 2 is one type of effective introductory paragraph for an essay. In the first sentence a broad comment on the general topic of the question—geographic influences in history—is introduced. This catches your attention. The specific topic is presented in the second sentence, and the author's personal opinion, or the thesis of the essay, is presented in the last half of that sentence and in the third sentence. This introduction answers the two questions that should be dealt with in every essay in the introductory paragraph.

Now let us look at the body or remainder of the two sample answers to this same essay question. As you read the body of sample essays 1 and 2, first pay particular attention to the organizational structure used by each writer. Second, consider the way specific information is used in each essay.

Sample Essay 1

The Pilgrims were the first settlers in New England. They farmed, taught by the Indian Squanto, and as a result of their production, they celebrated the first Thanksgiving. The later Puritan settlers based their life around the church and lived very strict and limited lives. Because they believed that God rewarded those who worked hard, the Puritans were very industrious. Boston became a thriving seaport and many merchants were soon involved in the triangular trade with England or Africa, the West Indies, and Boston, trading slaves, sugar, and rum. Lumber for ships of the English navy also made fortunes for many Bostonians.

Tobacco was the crop that produced the wealth of Virginia. Rice and indigo were important in South Carolina as fortunes were made there in the 18th century by plantation owners. The southerners sold their crops to England and in return imported fine English furniture and china. Some of the plantations in Virginia, such as Westover, rivaled the finest English homes and showed that the southern colonies had come a long way from the log houses of Jamestown. The Virginia plantation owners imported blacks from Africa to work the tobacco fields as slaves, while the owners developed the first legislative body in America in the House of Burgesses.

Pennsylvania, in the mid-Atlantic region, had its own system of government. The colony was the private estate of William Penn. He ruled it as such, but because he was a Quaker, he allowed religious toleration in the colony. Pennsylvania prospered, with many small farms producing staple crops. When Ben Franklin came to Philadelphia, he worked as a printer, showing how advanced Philadelphia was as a city. The city was well planned with straight streets and fine buildings.

In this paper I have tried to show how different the colonies were. Virginia was the best place to live because it was easiest to make a living on the plantations. New England and Pennsylvania were not as good, although many people in both colonies made money in trade.

Sample Essay 2

The majority of settlers in New England came there for religious reasons—the Pilgrims to separate from the Church of England and the Puritans to purify the church. Later settlements such as those founded by Roger Williams and Anne Hutchinson were established essentially for religious reasons. This fact colored the colonists' outlook on life and led to such events as the great preaching of Cotton Mather in the Massachusetts Bay Colony and the Salem witch trials. The emphasis upon religion and the Bible required that people could read and led to public-supported schools and the founding of Harvard College. The Puritan view of life held that work was essential and success God-given. Therefore, the New Englanders were driven to seek employment and use their abundant resource—lumber—and experience with the sea to become sailors and merchants in the triangular trade. New Englanders sold rum in Africa, brought slaves to the West Indies, and imported sugar or molasses to New England for the production of rum.

English mercantilist policies, incorporated in various Acts of Trade and Navigation, such as the Molasses Act, attempted to control this trade. The attempts led to antagonisms between England and New England. The struggle between the two affected colonial life, and the basis for the antagonism may be traced to religious differences. Of course, geography provided the harbors and the lumber for ships involved in the triangular trade and for the British navy, but it was their religion that was most important in setting the lifestyle of New Englanders.

Virginia's plantation-based lifestyle was representative of the South. One might consider that soil and climate determined it. That is partly true, but what was crucial in Virginia was the London Company's motivation in founding the colony—to make a profit. Until tobacco was discovered and a market was found in England, Virginians struggled. Once a money-making product was found—it could as easily have been gold, which would have greatly changed the lifestyle—Virginia's future was determined. Slaves, large farms or plantations, a close connection with England—sons were sent there for education and plantation homes such as Westover were built on Georgian models—all developed as a result of economic motivation and the finding of a cash product. Geography may have determined the product, but the type of people and their contacts with England helped determine the lifestyle.

Pennsylvania, in the mid-Atlantic region, was founded at a time of economic prosperity, which allowed the colony to grow rapidly. William Penn, a Quaker, was an idealist who believed in religious toleration. This attracted numerous Germans to the colony. Many became small farmers in the rich valleys—a geographic factor—but it was Philadelphia that typified the colony. Here, merchants flourished in the well-planned port city. The Quakers believed in equality and provided good hospitals and charity for the poor, setting an example followed later by the United States. Because of his religious convictions, Penn set very liberal laws for the colony, and a group of elected officials helped the proprietor run the colony. Thus it was the attitudes of the settlers and of Penn himself, more than the geographic conditions, which determined the colonial way of life in Pennsylvania.

The colonial way of life differed in the three areas of settlement. The types of people who settled and their reasons for colonizing—religious or economic—played a key role in determining these differences. Of course geography—climate, ports, soil, and available crops—affected what people could do, but it was the people themselves who made the difference. The settlers not the geography determined the colonial way of life as we do ours.

Comments on Sample Essays

It is clear that each writer followed the easy yet effective method of organizing material by geographic areas. It should also be clear that after that, the writer of Essay 1 simply presented factual information as it occurred to him with little attempt to relate the facts to each other and with no attempt to relate these facts to the topic. The writer of Essay 2, however, has organized material within each paragraph to follow the same pattern; motivation for settlement, effect of motivation on lifestyle, an acknowledgment of the role of geography. He or she also continually relates the ideas to the thesis and to the overall topic.

To illustrate this point, prepare an outline of the second answer, following traditional outline form. The form is as follows:

I.   Major Topic 1
　　A. Primary evidence A
　　　　1. Secondary evidence to support A
　　　　　a. Tertiary evidence to support A-1
　　B. Primary evidence B
　　　　1. Secondary evidence to support B
　　　　　a. Tertiary evidence to support B-1

  II.   Major Topic 2
       A. Primary evidence A
          1. Secondary evidence to support A
             a. Tertiary evidence to support A-1
. . . and so forth.

   Basically, outlines simply provide an organizational format or structure. A
formal outline of the body of Essay 2 would look like this:

   I.   New England
       A. Why settlement?—Religion
          1. Cotton Mather
          2. Salem witches
          3. read
             a. public school
             b. Harvard
       B. Lifestyle: Success for God
          1. work
             a. resources
             b. sea
             c. merchants
          2. triangular trade
       C. Struggle with England: Mercantilism
       D. Geography
          1. harbors
          2. lumber
  II.   Virginia (the South)
       A. Why settlement?—Profit
          1. London Co.
          2. tobacco
       B. Lifestyle
          1. slaves
          2. English education
          3. plantations
       C. Geography
 III.   Pennsylvania
       A. Why settlement?—Penn's idealism
          1. economic prosperity
          2. religious toleration
       B. Lifestyle
          1. Philadelphia
             a. port
             b. equality
             c. hospitals
          2. religion
             a. liberal laws
             b. legislature
       C. Geography
  IV.   Conclusion
       A. Different lifestyles

      1. types of people
      2. reasons for settling
    B. Geography
      1. climate
      2. ports
      3. soil
      4. crops
    C. Settlers made lifestyle; so do we

As the outline illustrates, Essay 2 has a very clear structure and organization. If you outlined the answer for Essay 1, it would be hard to see the structure. Making outlines, either formal or informal (see Step Two of the Seven Steps in Essay Writing) is an important skill to have and a great help in creating good essay answers. For every question there are different ways to organize an answer. For this question you could organize by geographic region, by lifestyle, or by climate.

Summary of Comments on Essay Answers 1 and 2

The writers of answers 1 and 2 are both knowledgeable students. They both include the type of effective factual information required for Advanced Placement work. They are aware of details, and their sentence structure is sound. The writer of Essay 2, however, has demonstrated two additional skills that clearly mark him or her as an above-average student. These skills are that of organization and analysis. The writer of Essay 1 clearly demonstrates a lack of analytical work, and the reader is left wondering if the student understood the question. Because of this, the student would receive an average grade on the Advanced Placement examination, while the writer of Essay 2 would receive a very good one.

Summary

We have now looked at two sample answers for our first essay question, and, in doing so, we have presented several definitions and rules for the writing of essay answers. As you study for the AP exam, you will want to practice writing essays. The technique summarized as Seven Steps in Essay Writing, presented here, will provide an effective method for answering all types of essay questions both on tests and in your classes.

SEVEN STEPS IN ESSAY WRITING
Step One—Analyzing the Question

Understanding the Question Is Essential

In writing an essay, the first step is always to analyze the question. Without a clear understanding of what the question is, you cannot possibly write an adequate answer. Let us now look at the question again.

> "The geographic conditions of the three major areas of English settlement in America—New England, the mid-Atlantic region, and the South—were the primary factors in determining the differences in the colonial way of life in these three areas." Evaluate this statement.

The Meaning of Evaluate

The question presents a statement and then asks the student to evaluate the statement. The key word here is, obviously, *evaluate*. What does it mean? According to the dictionary, it means to determine the value of or to appraise carefully. In other words, the question is asking the student to determine the value measured in terms of historical accuracy of the statement. Does it express what you believe happened in the past or is there some truth that must be qualified?

The *Evaluate This Statement* format is a popular type of essay question. It presents a statement or idea and forces the student or writer to judge the suitability of the statement as a thesis. In many ways, it is one of the easiest forms of questions for the student. The statement can be accepted or rejected as the thesis of the essay. The writer is not required to express a personal opinion or thesis in his or her own words. As you will see later, the formulation of one's own thesis is often the most difficult aspect of producing good, effective essay answers.

The Importance of Geography

This particular question presents a thesis involving geographic influences on the development of patterns of living. The word geographic in this question may be understood to mean environmental geography. The general topic of geography or environmental influences on human activity is an important one historically. Most historians have strong opinions on the topic, and every student of history has confronted the question directly or indirectly at some point. Therefore, it is a good topic for the Advanced Placement examination and a good topic with which to begin a study or review of American history. The quotation suggests that the extreme environmentalist interpretation of history—that the colonial way of life was *determined* by geographic influences—is the correct view.

The quotation assumes there were three different geographic regions in the English colonies and a different way of life in each. It uses general terms for these three regions—South, mid-Atlantic, New England—so the writer is forced either to supply specific names for colonies in these regions or to deal in generalizations. It is always better to be specific, so you should immediately focus on one or two colonies in each region. Most histories of colonial America emphasize Virginia in the South, Pennsylvania in the mid-Atlantic region, and Massachusetts Bay Colony in New England as typical of the three regions. You would then use these colonies to illustrate the geography of the region.

The Colonial Way of Life

Thus, having decided on specific illustrations for the three regions mentioned in the question, the next step in the analysis would be to focus on the phrase *colonial way of life*. This phrase suggests social conditions and relations as opposed to political structures. It is very much in line with the direction taken by the AP Development Committee, which announced in 1996 that 35 percent of the questions on the examination would relate to social history.

What was the colonial way of life in each of these three colonies? That is, how did the people live and make a living? A few ideas should come quickly to mind. Then you must decide if geography was the primary factor in *determining* that way of life or if other factors helped determine it. If you have a strong opinion about geography's importance or lack of importance and some evidence of both the geography and the way of life, then you may decide that this is a question you wish to answer.

You have now completed the analysis of the question. You have taken the question apart, considered the definition of words and decided what is being asked. You have identified some evidence. You are ready to proceed.

This process may have seemed simple or obvious but it is often overlooked in the rush of an exam. It is crucial that you develop the habit of analyzing every question in detail to be certain that you understand

the words used,

the evidence needed, and

the question asked.

Step Two—Collecting and Sorting Information

Determine What You Know

Once you know what the question asks, you should move on to the next step: *collecting and sorting your information*. The best way to do this is to create an informal outline. For this question, write down on a piece of paper the name of each colony you have decided to use as an illustration. Under each colony write a few simple phrases illustrating the way of life in the colony and a few brief phrases illustrating the geographic conditions. The notes might look something like the box shown here but you may have a different style, such as mapping, for informal note taking. (The columns and letters are referred to later in the text; they would not be part of your actual note taking.)

Notes for Answering Question

Column M	Column O
(Way of Life)	(Geography)

Virginia
- e. plantations — warm mild
- r. Church of England — river transport
- London Co. for Eco. Reasons — tobacco
- e. slaves — good soil
- p. House of Burgesses

Penn.
- e. merchants — mix of S. and N.E.
- r. Quakers/Germans — little river transport
- p. Wm. Penn, proprietor — grains and vegetables
- melting pot

Mass. Bay
- e. merchants/sailors — cold
- r. Puritans — rocky soil
- p. town meetings — lumber
- harbors

You have collected your information in this informal outline. You now need to sort it to find a way of using it most effectively in your answer. Your goal is to relate the way of life to the geography and the obvious approach suggested is to write about each colony separately. But how to organize the information in the paragraphs? As you look at the brief notes in **Column M**, you will see that **r** under each region refers to religion, **p** to political developments or organization, and **e** to economic activities. Within each paragraph you can present evidence from these three areas in the same order, thus giving fine structure to the paragraphs. How would you organize the information in **Column O**?

Other Ways to Organize the Answer

There are other ways of organizing the answer to this question. You might organize your answer with a section on religion in all three regions, followed by sections on political developments and economic activities. This organization would appear more complicated and less effective, but it illustrates the variety of ways in which one can organize answers.

The idea of including religion, politics, and economics in your answer should jump at you from the notes. This is one reason why collecting and sorting information in an informal outline is so important in preparing essay answers—it focuses attention on possible ways of presenting material. For this answer the best organization is by colony or region as done in Sample Essay 2. As you collect information and sort through the facts, be sure that you

write an informal outline,

group ideas by letters to provide structure, and

consider different organizational patterns.

After you have analyzed the question and collected and sorted information, you are ready for the third step in essay writing—developing your thesis.

Step Three—Developing Your Thesis

A Thesis Is Necessary for Every Essay

As mentioned previously, every essay *must* have a thesis. Your thesis is your personal opinion on the given topic and should be included in the opening paragraph. When you look over the information you have gathered, a thesis will usually, but not always, become clear. You must take the time to think through just what you believe on the topic and how you will prove it with the information you have. On an exam you do not have the luxury of doing further research to gather more information, so you must rely on what you have written down to prove whatever opinion you state as your thesis. What is your opinion on this sample question?

The writer of Sample Essay 1 agreed with the statement but never clearly stated that in the essay. Do you see that? Does this criticism make sense to you? That is the great weakness of Essay 1.

The writer of Sample Essay 2 did not believe that the statement made complete sense and saw an alternative explanation or cause for the differences in the way of life of the three colonial regions. In the last sentence of the introductory paragraph, the writer presents a personal opinion or thesis on the issue only partly agreeing with the statement. It is very important to realize that **you**

may disagree with any given statement. The grade on an essay depends on how well you prove your opinion and not on the opinion. What would your thesis be for this question? Would you accept the view expressed in the quotation after analyzing the question, or would you qualify it, as the author of Essay 2 has done, or would you reject it totally? As you develop your thesis, remember that you should

present your opinion in every essay and

put your opinion in the opening paragraph.

Step Four—Writing the Introduction

**Introductions
Answer Two
Questions**

In many ways the introductory or opening paragraph is the most important one of any essay. It is here that the reader gets the first idea of you, the writer. As in friendships, the first impression remains with one. As stated above, an effective opening paragraph must answer two questions: What is the topic? and What is the author's opinion on the topic? When these two questions are not answered, the reader is confused. Usually, the statement of the topic comes in the first part of the paragraph, and the writer's opinion or thesis is the last sentence of a paragraph.

In Sample Introduction 2, the question is quoted and the author's opinion, without stating it as "my opinion" or "I believe," is clearly stated in the word *exaggerated.* The thesis then follows in the last sentence and is clear to the reader.

This introductory paragraph also illustrates another very important aspect of a good essay introduction. It begins with a broad, general comment on the topic, which is meant to catch the reader's attention, slowly narrows the focus of the topic to the specific question, and then narrows it more to the thesis. The good opening paragraph is like a lighthouse or a flashlight beam.

The beam catches the viewer in its broad beam or sweep and then brings his or her attention to the source of the light. Your introduction should always work like a lighthouse beam, starting broad enough in scope to get the reader's interest, and then pulling attention to a specific point—your thesis.

An effective introductory or opening paragraph is one in which the writer

identifies the topic,

states a personal opinion, and

catches the reader's attention in a broad beam similar to a lighthouse.

Step Five—Writing the Body of the Essay

Paragraphs Must Connect

Once the crucial introduction is completed, you are ready for the fifth step: *the writing of the body of the essay*. It is in this section that the factual information to prove your thesis should be presented. The facts should be organized in a logical sequence. Each major set of facts should be presented in a separate paragraph. These paragraphs might be considered as the separate batteries that power a flashlight. Each must work separately, yet they must be connected if the light is to work. If the essay is to work, each paragraph must connect with the thesis and all the paragraphs must connect.

There are many ways to achieve such connections—similar ideas, linking words (such as *however, therefore, but*), or repetition of an aspect of the question. Look again at Essay 2. Paragraphs 1 and 2 are linked by the idea of trade; 2 and 3 by repeating the word *lifestyle*; 3 and 4 by economic conditions; and 4 and 5 by repeating a phrase. All the paragraphs present information related to the thesis. The essay works. As in a flashlight, the connections are made, the beam shines and catches your attention.

Often, in defending a position, you will come across several strong arguments that can be used against your view. If you are able to refute any of these arguments, you should introduce them and refute them immediately. Otherwise, admit that they exist in the first paragraph of the body of your essay. Then present your strong facts in the succeeding paragraphs, ending with your strongest point. This is a good lawyer's or debater's technique, and in your essay you are like a lawyer arguing a case. You want the reader to believe your position—your case.

Brief Notes Provide a Structure

When you jotted down your brief notes as part of Step Two, you were collecting information to prove your thesis. Look at these brief notes and arrange them in the most effective sequence for proving your thesis by numbering the items 1, 2, 3, etc. These numbered items will provide both your outline and the basis for a separate paragraph or for several sentences within paragraphs as you expand on the concept represented by each. For example, in the brief notes presented on page 27, the single word *Puritans* could easily be expanded into several sentences within a paragraph. This is the way you will use your brief notes to help write the body of your essay.

In the case of this sample, the notes jotted down on the colony of Virginia might logically be presented in the order numbered 1–6. You might leave out the House of Burgesses and the Church of England, as they seem to have little relation to geography. You could include river transportation as number 7 as a link to Pennsylvania's lack of rivers.

Column M	Column O
(Way of Life)	*(Geography)*
Virginia	
5. *plantations*	2. *warm mild*
Church of England	7. *river transport*
4. *London Co. for Eco. Reasons*	3. *tobacco*
6. *Slaves*	1. *good soil*
House of Burgesses	

Remember in writing the body of the essay that you must use paragraphs that stand like the batteries in a flashlight—each linked together at the contact point (your paragraph links), but each a separate unit giving power to the beam of light. The batteries are held together by the casing, which provides the structure for the flashlight, just as the brief items you numbered provide your essay with an outline—a structure.

The body of an essay consists of

separate paragraphs that are connected and

information that proves the thesis.

Step Six—Writing the Conclusion

The Conclusion Holds the Essay Together

When you have completed the body of the paper, you are ready for the sixth step: *writing the conclusion*. The conclusion of the essay is the second most important paragraph. The conclusion holds the essay together and might be compared to the cap on the end of a flashlight, which holds the batteries in and forces them into contact to make the beam. Without a good cap, the flashlight does not work; without a good conclusion, the essay also does not work.

The conclusion should bring the reader back to the question and back to the thesis. An excellent preparation for writing the conclusion is to read through your introduction and the body of your essay before writing the conclusion. Then, keeping in mind what you have said and what your thesis is, write a paragraph that reintroduces the thesis and the topic without merely repeating the introduction. If possible, you should end your conclusion with an indication of the applicability of your thesis to other situations, thus leaving the reader with the idea that you have proven something of general significance or with reference to the broad general idea in the first sentence of your introduction.

A Conclusion Is Not Just a Summary

There are two things one should avoid doing in the conclusion. The first thing to avoid is presenting a summary of all you've included. There is nothing worse than the conclusion that begins, "Now I have shown that . . .," yet many students end an essay this way. It is simplistic, boring, does nothing to help your case, and antagonizes the reader. If you have "shown that," then it should be obvious to the reader and you do not have to tell it again. Secondly, do not introduce new evidence in the conclusion—evidence that will help prove your thesis. Get all the evidence into the body of the paper. The conclusion is simply your flashlight cap, and it is not one of the batteries.

With these two negative warnings in mind, you might wonder how you can possibly write a conclusion. The conclusion to Essay 2 provides a good example to look at and follow. The writer rephrases the question, clearly indicates his or her differences with it, and ends emphasizing the significance of people as was done in the opening. The conclusion to Essay 1 is a poor one because the writer begins by saying what he or she had done, introduces new materials, does not reintroduce the topic or the thesis, and makes no attempt to relate his or her ideas to other situations. Other good conclusions will be presented in later chapters.

In summary, when writing a conclusion

restate the ideas in the introductory paragraph,

put a tight "cap" on the essay,

do not introduce new facts, and

do not merely list what has been said.

Step Seven—Reading Over Your Essay

The Conclusion and Introduction Must Agree

When you have completed writing your essay, there is one step left—reading it over to check the spelling, style, and consistency. It is very helpful if you start reading with your conclusion and then read the introduction, checking to see that they agree. Often, students who have not analyzed the question well and who have not developed an effective thesis will contradict themselves in these two paragraphs. Make sure you have not done that. Then read the body of the paper and the conclusion again. Correct any spelling or punctuation errors. Finally, check to see if the paragraphs link together smoothly.

The final step in writing a good essay is to read over the essay to check for

agreement between opinion expressed in the opening and conclusion,

clarity of expression,

spelling and grammar, and

links between paragraphs.

One Final Point...

There is one last item to consider about the essay style. Most essayists avoid the use of the personal pronoun *I*. The reader assumes that everything in the essay is what the writer believes, so "I think" or "I believe" is redundant. The usual pronouns used are those of the third-person editorial *we* or the impersonal *one*. Although there are times when an author uses the *I* with great effect, it is rare. Stylistically it is better for the beginner to avoid using *I* in essay writing.

**Conclusion
Use the Seven Steps**

As you work through this book, studying and reviewing for the Advanced Placement examination, use these seven steps to make essay writing easy. They should become habit for you so that you do not have to think about them. This technique will help you to write effective, well-organized, and factually sound essays. Follow these seven steps as you prepare essay answers for questions in this book. Make formal outlines of your answers until you are satisfied that your answers are well organized.

Summary of the Seven Steps

To recapitulate, the seven steps to make essay writing easy are

1. ANALYZE THE QUESTION
2. COLLECT AND SORT INFORMATION
3. DEVELOP YOUR THESIS
4. WRITE THE INTRODUCTION
5. WRITE THE BODY OF THE ESSAY
6. WRITE THE CONCLUSION
7. READ OVER THE ESSAY

As you use these seven steps, keep in mind the image of the flashlight. It should prove a valuable image for you as you construct your essays.

Developing Your Own DBQ

**Developing a DBQ
Tests Research
and Analytical Skills**

One purpose of the DBQ is to test your analytical skills, and one way to study for the Advanced Placement examination is to play the role of historian—researching, analyzing, and interpreting various sources. Developing your own DBQ is an excellent study tool combining those skills. With the availability of many original documents on the Internet, students have a greater opportunity to do this now than in the past. However, there are many other sources of documents such as published collections; papers held in archives at historical societies, libraries, and universities; old newspapers and magazines; and government records. The following is one way to develop a DBQ. (See page 118 for more information on the DBQ.)

**Time Period and
Topic**

First, you need to decide on a time period. For this DBQ we'll use the period 1765–1815. Next, you need to decide on a general topic. Will you focus on political, economic, social or cultural history, or a combination? What specific ideas interest you? Since this time period covers the American Revolution, you might decide to focus on ideas of freedom and rights as seen in a variety of documents and that cover a combination of historical perspectives. At this point we do not need a specific question; that can come later. Although some individuals might wish to start with a specific question and then look for documents to illustrate differing views on it, it is often easier to let the documents lead you to the question.

The third step is to begin to look for documents. To do this you need to think of what you know of the period—of the mainstream events and ideas—and how they relate to freedom and rights. The first thing that might come to mind are ideas that are part of the Declaration of Independence. This is an important document that everyone should have studied. The year 1776 fits the time period. The document might be too obvious, too mainstream, but it is a good starting place. Here is the passage you might use:

Document A

> *Source:* **The Declaration of Independence of the United States, 1776.**
> We hold these truths to be self-evident, that all men are created equal, that they are endowed by their Creator with certain unalienable rights, that among these are Life, Liberty and the pursuit of Happiness. That to secure these rights, Governments are instituted among Men, deriving their just Powers from the consent of the governed. That whenever any Form of Government becomes destructive of these ends, it is the Right of the People to alter or to abolish it, and to institute new Government, laying its foundation on such principles and organizing its Powers in such form, as to them shall seem most likely to effect their Safety and Happiness.

You need to analyze the terms and see what other ideas you can develop: "Where did these ideas come from?" "Were they Jefferson's own?" A little research will lead you to John Locke whose ideas greatly influenced colonial

America. Some research will lead you to Locke's *Second Treatise on Government* and the following paragraphs.

Document B

Source: John Locke, *Second Treatise on Government*, 1688.

4. To understand Political Power right, and derive it from its Original, we must consider what State all Men are naturally in, and that is, a *State of perfect Freedom* to order their Actions, and dispose of their Possessions, and Persons as they think fit, within the bounds of the Law of Nature, without asking leave, or depending upon the will of any other Man.

A *State* also *of Equality,* wherein all the Power and Jurisdiction is reciprocal, no one having more than another: there being nothing more evident, than that Creatures of the same species and rank promiscuously born to all the same advantages of Nature, and the use of the same faculties, should also be equal one amongst another without Subordination or Subjection, unless the Lord and Master of them all, should by any manifest Declaration of his Will set one above another, and confer on him by an evident and clear appointment an undoubted Right to Dominion and Sovereignty. . . .

6. But though this be a *State of Liberty,* yet it is *not a State of Licence,* though Man in that State have an uncontrolable Liberty, to dispose of his Person or Possessions, yet he has not Liberty to destroy himself, or so much as any Creature in his Possession, but where some nobler use, than its bare Preservation calls for it. The *State of Nature* has a Law of Nature to govern it, which obliges every one: And Reason, which is that Law, teaches all Mankind, who will but consult it, that being all equal and independent, no one ought to harm another in his Life, Health, Liberty, or Possessions. For Men being all the Workmanship of one Omnipotent, and infinitely wise Maker; All the Servants of one Sovereign Master, sent into the World by his order and about his business, they are his Property, whose Workmanship they are, made to last during his, not one anothers Pleasure. And being furnished with like Faculties, sharing all in one Community of Nature, there cannot be supposed any such *Subordination* among us, that may Authorize us to destroy one another, as if we were made for one anothers uses, as the inferior ranks of Creatures are for ours.

These rather long paragraphs set forth the main points of Locke's philosophy on the origin of government. How closely do they relate to ideas in the Declaration? The vocabulary is complex. On the exam it might well be simplified. Also, the passage would be shortened with just a few sentences presenting one or two important points used on the exam. In preparing your own DBQ you should return to this passage, after identifying other documents you would use and focusing on a question, and edit it to three or four sentences at the most. You would do the same for other long documents.

Finding Documents

You are now at the point where your own ideas, the resources available to you, and the amount of time you have become crucial. As a New Hampshire resident with the New Hampshire State Records and Archives and Historical Society nearby, my research took me in the following directions:

Wondering if any of Locke's ideas affected early New Hampshire, I found the following passage from an early New Hampshire history.

Document C

> *Source:* Jeremy Belknap, *History of New Hampshire,* 2nd edition, 1812.
>
> Their next care [in 1680 in restructuring the government of the colony] was to frame a code of laws, of which the first, conceived in a style becoming freemen, was "that no act, imposition, law or ordinance should be made or imposed upon them, but such as should be made by the assembly and approved by the president and council." Idolatry, blasphemy, treason, rebellion, wilful murder, manslaughter, poisoning, witchcraft, sodomy, bestiality, perjury, man-stealing, cursing and rebelling against parents, rape and arson were made capital crimes. The other penal laws were in their main principles the same that are now in force.

The quote seems to support the idea of the settlers believing themselves "freemen" (all equal?) and that no law should be "imposed" on them. Pursuing this idea, the following passage from a work of Roger Williams, founder of Rhode Island and strong believer in religious freedom, was located. The date, 1644, is out of the time period but it might be possible to start the DBQ with this quote to set the framework of the question. It certainly suggests that colonists long before Locke believed that civil power (government) belonged to "the people." You may wish to pursue who they considered to be the "people."

Document D

> *Source:* Roger Williams, *The Bloody Tenent of Persecution for Cause of Conscience, discussed in a Conference between Truth and Peace.* 1644.
>
> "... the Sovereign, original, and foundation of civil power lies in the people ... and if so, that a People may erect and establish what form of government seems to them most meet for their civil condition ..."

Documents about Equality

Documents C and D relate to the idea of creation of government. What documents might reveal colonial attitudes toward equality stated so clearly in the Declaration and in Locke's *Second Treatise?* It is clear there were slaves in 1776. Were they considered equal?

Fortunately for dealing with this particular topic, in the New Hampshire State Records and Archives there is a document written in 1779 by 20 slaves in Portsmouth, New Hampshire, and sent to the state legislature. It is a petition expressing their reasons for asking to be freed.

Document E

Source: Petition from 20 Slaves of Portsmouth, New Hampshire, to the Council and House of Representatives of Said State, November 1779.

State of New Hampshire

To The Hon[ble] the Council and House of Representatives of said State now sitting at Exeter in and for Said State—

The Petition of Nero Brewster [the names of 18 other slaves are listed], & Prince Whipple, Natives of Africa, now forcably detained in Slavery in said State most humbly Sheweth, That the God of Nature, gave them, Life, and Freedom, upon the Terms of the most perfect Equality with other men; That Freedom is an inherent Right of the human Species, not to be surrendered, but by Consent, for the Sake of social Life; . . .

That all men hold themselves in Duty bound, strenously to exert every Faculty of their Minds, to obtain that Blessing of Freedom, which they are justly intitled to from the Donation of the beneficient Creator . . .

Tho' Fortune hath dealt out our Portions with ruged hand, Yet hath She smiled in the Disposal of our Persons to those, who claim us, as their Property; of them, as Masters, we do not complain: But from what Authority, they assume the Power to dispose of our Lives, Freedom and Property, we would wish to know; Is it to be found! . . .

Therefore your humble Slaves most devoutly Pray, for the Sake of injured Liberty, for the Sake of Justice, Humanity, and the Rights of Mankind; for the Honour of Religion, and by all that is dear, that your Honours would graciously interpose in our Behalf, and enact such Laws and Regulations, as you in your Wisdom think proper, whereby we may regain our Liberty & Be rank'd in the Class of free Agents, and that the Name of Slave may not more be heard in a Land gloriously contending for the Sweets of Freedom; And your humble Slaves as in Duty bound will ever Pray

The whole document is very revealing. These excerpts illustrate the thrust of the ideas presented. The document was written three years after the Declaration of Independence while the Revolutionary War was still being waged. It is clear the writers are intelligent, well educated, aware of the political issues of the day, and aware of those ideas expressed in the Declaration.

Reading Document E, several questions immediately come to mind: "What was the legislature's reaction?" "Were there other events going on that led the slaves of Portsmouth to write in 1779?" "Were any slaves freed?" Fortunately, with a little research and help from state archivists—in developing a DBQ be sure to use all resources available, especially librarians and archivists—information relating to all three questions was quickly located. The New Hampshire House of Representatives *Journal* included the following entry.

Document F

Source: New Hampshire House of Representatives *Journal*, June 9, 1780.

According to the order of the day, the Petition of Nero Brewster and other Negro Slaves praying to be set free from Slavery, being read, considered and argued by Counsel on behalf of the Petitioners before this House, It appears to this house, That at this time the House is not ripe for a Determination in this matter; Therefore ordered that the further consideration & determination of the matter be postponed till a more convenient opportunity.

Obviously, the members of the House were not ready to deal with the important issue of freedom for slaves; in fact, New Hampshire never passed a law freeing slaves.

On the second question, it turned out that in 1779 the New Hampshire legislature was struggling to gain the people's approval of a new state Constitution. Following the concept expressed in Belknap's 1812 *History of New Hampshire* (Document C), the Constitution was submitted to the people for a vote and was rejected. However, the slaves of Portsmouth must have been aware of the ideas being suggested for inclusion in the state Constitution. The most relevant passages from the two-page Constitution are the following.

Document G

Source: A Plan of Government for the State of New Hampshire, Proposed June 5, 1779.

A Declaration of the Rights of the People of the State of New Hampshire

First, We declare, that we the people of the State of New Hampshire, are free and Independent of the Crown of Great Britain.

Secondly, We the People of this State, are entitled of Life, Liberty, and Property: and all other Immunities (protection, safety) and Privileges which we heretofore enjoyed.

. . .

Fourthly, the whole and entire Power of Government of this State is vested (placed) in and must be derived from (based upon) the People thereof, and from no other source whatsoever.

Finally, the following document from 1777 recording the freeing of a slave in Durham, New Hampshire (near Portsmouth) was located. The concept of freeing slaves was clearly known in New Hampshire at the time of the Revolution and this meant there would be freed slaves living in the state as examples to the slaves of Portsmouth.

Document H

Source: Slave Liberation Document, Durham, New Hampshire, 1777.

Know all men by these presents that I, John Woodman, of Durham in the county of Strafford and State of New Hampshire, yeoman, for and in consideration of the sum of sixty pounds lawful money to me in hand paid before the delivery hereof by my negro man Dan, a servant for life, about twenty-eight years of age, the receipt whereof I do hereby acknowledge, have given, granted, bargained & sold & by these presents do give, grant, bargain and sell unto the aforesaid Dan his time for life, liberating & making him a free man to all intents as tho' he had been born free, hereby engaging for myself, my heirs, exec[rs] & admin[rs] that no person or persons claiming from, by or under me or them shall have any right to demand any service of him in future as a slave.

In witness whereof I have hereunto set my hand & seal this 23d day of June Anno Domini 1777.

Signed Sealed & delivered   JOHN WOODMAN.
in presence of
JOHN SMITH
JON. CHESLEY.

Thinking about the 20 slaves of Portsmouth, the question quickly arose: "What was their life like?" While little is known in detail now, research is going on in Portsmouth to find more information on this topic. However, some things are known about one of the signers of the petition, Prince Whipple. He served his owner, General Whipple, in the Revolution, for which, according to the story, he was promised freedom. It was finally granted some years later. Prince Whipple was a fiddler and played at dances and worked in the Moffatt-Ladd house in Portsmouth. He and his wife lived in a small house at the back of the large, Federal-style house after they were freed. It is believed his wife ran a school. The photograph of the Great Hall of the house illustrates the surroundings in which Prince Whipple worked. He, and the other Portsmouth slaves were obviously not field laborers. Knowing this, it becomes clear how they would be aware of political, economic, and cultural events.

Document I

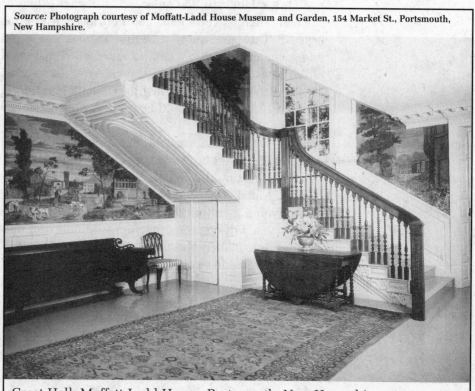

Source: **Photograph courtesy of Moffatt-Ladd House Museum and Garden, 154 Market St., Portsmouth, New Hampshire.**

Great Hall, Moffatt-Ladd House, Portsmouth, New Hampshire, 1763.

Creating a Question

Now that we have nine documents, let us look at them and decide if a question could be formed using them. Since we began with the idea of freedom and rights and went to the Declaration that states that "all men are created equal," we might form a question on what equality meant to those colonists fighting for independence. Document B (Locke's *Second Treatise*), although from an earlier time period, certainly affected the thinking of the colonists. It speaks of equality and Section 4 would certainly be relevant to a question on equality in colonial America. (Documents may be from a time outside the designated time period *if* the ideas are relevant to the announced time period.) Documents E (slave petition), F (response from New Hampshire House), and H (freed slave) all also speak directly to equality. A Declaration of the Rights of the People of New Hampshire (Document G) implies equality when it says, "We the people of this state are entitled to life, liberty and property. . . ." By reading these five documents carefully you can learn a great deal about the colonists' views of equality. Then you can draw on your knowledge of the mainstream history of the period including the writing of the Constitution and its ratification, the Bill of Rights, and the Northwest Ordinance, which abolished slavery, to provide a context for the material in the documents.

If you wished to include the other documents, you might expand the question to include the idea in the Declaration that "governments are instituted among men, deriving their just powers from the consent of the governed." This idea has a long history in the colonies as seen in Documents D (Roger Williams, 1644), C (Jeremy Belknap, 1688), and B (John Locke, 1688). The new question might focus on how the colonists could state their belief in the right of the governed to approve of government when their view of equality allowed for slavery. Or it might raise the question, "To what extent did the colonists adhere to the belief that 'governments get their just powers from the consent of the governed'?" This latter question, while it appears to be political, also raises cultural and social issues. Who were the governed? What were the rights of women and children as well as those of slaves? Were they considered part of those governed? How did equality manifest itself? For this last question, Document I (Moffatt-Ladd House) could be used as it illustrates social history.

Summary

While it is important for you, the student, to develop a specific question, this exercise illustrates how one goes about constructing a DBQ. You should realize that by collecting documents that relate to a general topic or theme, you will expand your knowledge of United States history. By reading the documents carefully and then thinking how they relate to the mainstream of United States history, you will be preparing yourself to do well on both the DBQ and analytical multiple-choice questions, so going through this exercise of developing a DBQ will provide excellent review. There are many documents—charts, cartoons, maps, photographs, and paintings, as well as the written ones—that you can use. Thousands are now available on the Internet. The language used in older documents, as illustrated by Documents B, D, and E, may be difficult to understand but it is important that you take time to study some of them.

1 Colonial America Before 1763

Important Facets of This Period

It is generally acknowledged by historians that the foundations for the American nation were laid during the colonial period. If this is accepted, then in studying the colonial period an important focus would be to identify these foundations. The more one can identify links among periods and begin to develop meaningful cause-and-effect relationships, the more effective a study of the past will be. The identification of these relationships should provide the basic pattern for the study of the colonial period before 1763 and for all the study done for the Advanced Placement examination in American history.

Today many courses in American history begin with the Treaty of Paris in 1763, which ended the French and Indian War. In the years that followed, the differences between the colonists and the British, which had evolved over the preceding 150 years of settlement, reached a climax with the Declaration of Independence. These differences in social, political, military, economic, and cultural attitudes should form the basis of a study of colonial history. It should include information on the Native American cultures and the clash between them and the European cultures, especially the English, Spanish, and French. In courses starting in 1763 a quick look should be taken at the origin of the differences in the early colonial period. The Advanced Placement examination acknowledges this trend in teaching American history, and therefore on the examination less emphasis is placed on the history of America before 1763 than on other periods. However, some information on events before 1763, on pre-Columbian, and on Hispanic culture of the Southwest is expected.

In studying this period, the connections between the colonial period and later periods of American history should be emphasized. For instance, the concept of a written constitution is rooted in colonial history as illustrated by such items as the Mayflower Compact, colonial charters, and the Albany Plan. There is therefore an important connection between the U.S. Constitution and colonial history and it is this type of information that you should explore.

There will be multiple-choice questions on the colonial period before 1763, and there may be an essay question for which information from this period will be necessary. Although the sample essay questions presented below are restricted to the colonial period before 1763, the information required for effective answers is related to many later developments in American history.

Among the important developments of the colonial period that have a bearing on later history are

1. Pre-Columbian Native American social and cultural developments
2. The reasons for European exploration, the areas explored, and the conflicts that ensued
3. The relations between the Native Americans and the colonists in all regions of settlement

4. The geographic differences among the regions of settlement and the motivation for the settlement of the different European colonies, including Spanish and French
5. The economic development of each colony and the English mercantilist system
6. The development of social and cultural attitudes within each colony and the resulting differences among the colonies and the Native Americans
7. The attempts at unity among various colonies
8. The establishment of local political institutions in each colony
9. The westward expansion of each colony
10. The military conflicts between the English settlers and both the Native Americans and other European settlers

Sample Essay Question—Assess the Validity/Evaluate This Statement

In each chapter we will present and analyze different types of essay questions. We will also present in each chapter a sample answer to at least one essay question. The essay questions presented in this chapter are examples of the *Evaluate This Statement* form discussed in Part Two and a very popular variation of that type, the *Assess the Validity* form.

In Part Two we presented two sample answers to a question dealing with the colonial period. The following question deals with that era, but it goes beyond the colonial period and calls for information from the period of the American Revolution. As stated above, essay questions on the exam may require knowledge of the colonial period.

Sample Question

> In the 1600s the major issues of U.S. colonial history revolved around theological issues. In the 1700s the major issues revolved around political issues.
> Assess the validity of this statement.

Comments on Sample Question

Recalling our Seven Steps in Essay Writing, we must first analyze the statement. For some students the understanding of centuries is difficult, and this would be the first matter to clear up. In the Christian dating method, those dates since the birth of Christ are designated as A.D. Because we must designate the years 1–99 as the first century A.D. or the first 100 years, the second century begins with the year 100 and goes to 199 even though the dates begin with one. All A.D. centuries are one number higher than the first or first two digits of the number of the year. Therefore, dates in the 17th century are those years starting with 16, so that 1607, 1620, 1688 are all 17th-century dates, and 1701 and 1756 are 18th-century dates. Until that matter is clear, the question cannot be analyzed.

The next concern in analyzing this question is to determine the meaning of the words *theological* and *political*. As you study American history, be certain you understand the specialized vocabulary used. Work at building your vocabulary. To help you, a glossary of important terms is included in the appendix of this book.

Theological comes from the Greek words *theos,* meaning God, and *logos,* meaning word or speak. *Theology,* therefore, means speaking about God and *theological* is the adjective form of the word. Theological issues are issues dealing with God or religion. *Political* is an adjective. It means pertaining to the conduct of government. It too has a Greek origin, coming from the word *politikos,* meaning of the citizens. Students often find it helpful to learn the origins of words; it is an excellent way to build vocabulary.

Once you are certain of the meaning of the words and time period, it should be clear the statement suggests that the great concerns of one century revolved about religious issues while the concerns of the next were "largely political." You are asked to assess the validity of the statement. Assess means to determine the value of something as a tax collector assesses the value of property to determine how much tax a person should pay. You must determine what value or truth there is to this statement. Is it true or only partly true or is it false? What do you think? Following the Seven Steps in Essay Writing, you will next want to jot down information about the theological and political issues in two columns labeled 17th century and 18th century. Once you have done that you'll be ready to write your thesis, since you will have determined your opinion on this topic. Then you will go on to write your essay following Steps Four through Six. You may wish to write your own answer before proceeding to read the following sample answer.

Sample Answer

Religion and politics always seem to be important issues in people's lives. Beginning with the first colonists in America during the 17th century, theology was an important issue. Indeed, the greatest reason that many of the colonists had for moving to America was the desire to find freedom of religion in a new land. Many of the fundamental concepts that emerged in the first colonies founded for religious reasons were later, in the 18th century, the ideals for which colonists fought political battles.

At first, the North American continent did not reward individuals who migrated to win a fortune. Several attempts—such as that of Sir Walter Raleigh in the Carolinas—of businesspeople, trying to get rich searching for gold or hoping for big farming profits, failed. Therefore, people generally went to America in search of freedom from the political, economic, social, and especially religious binds of European society.

The Puritans were a prime example of religious development in America. They had become social outcasts in England, where they had little voice in matters, and so they migrated to America. There they set up the Massachusetts Bay Colony, which flourished. With religious motivation to fulfill a "covenant" with God to establish the "New Jerusalem," a successful model colony in America, they laid many of the foundations that would later be of great political importance. They established a two-part representative body or legislature elected by the people and had a single leader, or executive, who for many years was John Winthrop. Winthrop might easily have preserved all legislative power to himself, but he did not, perhaps inspired by a theological view that believers within the community are all equal.

The Massachusetts Bay Colony had many conflicts that revolved about the meaning of the word *believer.* With the Puritans, if you did not agree with them, you were damned and could not live in their "perfect society." People such as Roger Williams became involved in these conflicts and were forced to leave the colony. He founded Rhode Island. The poor witches of Salem show how theological issues dominated the century.

Other colonies also were involved in theological conflicts; the Quaker William Penn founded Pennsylvania for religious freedom, and the Catholic Lord Baltimore supported religious toleration in Maryland when it was not the popular stand. Even Virginia had religious Blue Laws and the colony grew rapidly as Church of Englanders fled England during the rule of the Puritan Cromwell. The century was full of religious conflict, both in England and the colonies.

Under the influence of Puritan ideas as well as the philosophies of many other men, such as John Locke and Montesquieu and leaders of the European Enlightenment, legislatures were formed in each of the colonies, and charters, though requiring approval by the king, were written. Objections began to arise when the lack of power of these representative legislatures was felt.

After 1763, when England had ended its Seven Years' War with France, it turned its attention to America to try to find a way of paying the expense of war. Internal taxes, such as the excise tax on paper (Stamp Act) to which there was strong objection, and external taxes on trade were enacted by Parliament without the consent of the colonial legislatures. Puritan tradition was one force that warned America that "taxation without representation" was wrong. The theological issues of the 17th century—who was a believer and could live in a colony? —gave way to the political issues of the 18th century—who would control the life of the colonies? When the Acts of Trade and Navigation were enforced and other acts were enacted, especially the Declaratory Act, emphasizing the power of Parliament to tax and legislate without the consent of the colonists, the colonists felt that their political rights had been infringed upon, and they revolted.

The period of the Articles of Confederation was a testing period in American history. There was trust in the workability of a true democracy, and though an attempt at this was made, the federal government, unable to tax or enforce any laws, was too weak and could not tie the nation together. The political issue had become one of how to set up a new government.

The Constitution brought all the political ideas of Americans together in compromise. Puritan ideals were certainly present here, but the issues were not theological but political. The political conflicts between financial and agrarian influences would persist for many years, but a new government was formed that allowed the way for political issues to be compromised. This had not been done with 17th-century theological issues.

In the 17th century, theological issues were not compromised, but in the struggle over these issues ideas of identity and self-government were developed that became the great political issues Americans fought for in the 18th century. Religion and politics were important colonial issues.

What is your evaluation of the above essay? What are its strong points and its weak points? You should make a formal outline of the answer in order to identify the structure of the essay. Once you have made your own evaluation of the essay, you should compare your notes with the following teacher comments.

Teacher Comments on Sample Answer

"The student answering this question on theological and political issues has written an adequate but not an outstanding paper. The paper includes enough factual information to provide a very good answer, but the student fails to use this information to respond to the question asked. The student does not understand the difference between reciting information and using information to support a thesis.

"The student has written an introductory paragraph and has presented a thesis in the last sentence of the introduction. The thesis is interesting and could be developed, but as worded, the thesis does not relate to the 'great issues' of the 17th and 18th centuries. What is suggested is that the 'great' theological issues of the 17th century became the 'great' political issues of the 18th. Unfortunately, in the body of the paper this relationship is not clearly explored. Instead, the student describes important theological incidents in the 17th century, such as the Salem witch trials, and only briefly focuses on issues. Still, the 17th-century material is better presented than the 18th-century information.

"In the 18th century, the student too often loses sight of the relationship he or she is trying to establish between the issues in the two centuries. Although the student refers to Puritan ideas in the section, he or she falls into the all-too-open trap of listing information without using it to advance the argument. When discussing the Articles of Confederation and the Constitution, it seems the student is most interested in presenting his or her knowledge of the struggle over the development of the U.S. government, and that he or she has forgotten the theological issues of the 17th century, which, according to the original thesis, had become the major political issues of the 18th.

"The student has an adequate conclusion in which the thesis is restated. He or she avoids repeating arguments and also makes an attempt both in the conclusion and introduction to relate the question to a broader time period. The organization follows a clear pattern established by the quotation—chronology. Apparently the student did not consider the possibility of organizing the paper around those issues that were theological in the 17th century and political in the 18th century. Such an organization would appear to have a closer connection to the thesis than the organization used, and it might have helped the paper.

"In the future the student needs to be more careful in analyzing the question and relating information to the question. The student had fully adequate information, and the body of his or her paper has an obvious organization. The student should receive an above average but not a top grade."

Did your analysis develop the same points as the teacher's? If you did not agree, then reread the sample answer and see where you and the teacher diverged.

Summary

The *Assess the Validity* question has appeared on many recent Advanced Placement examinations. It allows the student great freedom of choice in designing the answer, as the statement may be accepted or rejected and the specific information to be used is determined by the writer.

There are many variations of this basic type of question. The directions may ask you to *evaluate* or *discuss* a statement or generalization, and again the writer has many choices as to what position to take and what evidence to use. The important point is to stay on the subject and evaluate or judge the statement if the direction says to evaluate. If you are asked to discuss, be certain to write about the statement in the essay discussing it using historical evidence. Sometimes more directions will be given, as in the following examples of this type of question.

Variations on the
Assess the Validity
Type of Question

1. Evaluate this statement as it relates to the years 1763–1776 and indicate to what extent you agree or disagree with it.
2. Assess the validity of this generalization for the period 1763–1776.
3. Discuss the validity of this quotation as it applies to the presidencies of George Washington, John Adams, and Thomas Jefferson.
4. Judging from evidence drawn from the years 1763–1776 and 1850–1861, assess the validity of this viewpoint.
5. Evaluate the applicability of this quotation to two of the following incidents.

You will want to practice your own writing ability and develop your knowledge of the colonial period by writing essay answers to several of the following questions. These questions, as with all of those presented in this book, are not inclusive of all the issues that might arise on the Advanced Placement examination. These questions are representative examination questions, and they will help you organize your knowledge of American history. These five questions will give you practice with the popular *Assess the Validity* and *Evaluate This Statement* type of essay questions. Remember, this type of question can be used to test material from any period of American history.

Practice Essay Questions

1. "The English founded colonies to escape oppression in England." Evaluate this statement.
2. "Economic issues not religion determined the development of the English colonies in North America." Assess the validity of this quotation as it applies to THREE of the following colonies before 1763:
   Virginia
   Maryland
   Pennsylvania
   Massachusetts Bay
   Rhode Island
3. "Before 1763 British mercantilist policy, while restricting colonial economic development, allowed colonial political life to develop unhampered by the Mother Country." Evaluate this statement.
4. "The colonial wars fought between the British and the French for domination of the North American continent created a sense of national spirit among the British colonies and created the basis for later unity." Assess the validity of this statement.
5. "As long as the French controlled parts of North America, they accepted the Native American population as equal, whereas the British colonists viewed them as hostile." Evaluate this statement as it relates to the years 1608–1763.

**Comments on
Question 1**

Note that question 1 focuses on the reasons for colonization. The quotation suggests that there was one cause for colonization. This would appear an over-simplification. In your answer you should explore other reasons for colonization and compare several different British colonies.

**Comments on
Question 2**

The second question raises the issue of economic determinism, often called the Marxist view of history because it was first articulated by Karl Marx. One does not have to be a Communist to support this concept. Therefore, you should analyze the question as you would any other and decide for your thesis whether religion or economics was more important in colonial development or if there are other factors to consider. You are given five colonies from which you must pick three to write about. Virginia, Pennsylvania, and Massachusetts Bay are discussed at some length in all textbooks; Maryland and Rhode Island are often less well covered but religion was important in each. Pick the three that will best support your thesis.

**Comments on
Question 3**

A definite time period is set in the third question, which is also a more complex and perhaps more interesting question. It requires an understanding of specific historic terms—Mother Country—and of a particular historical policy, mercantilism. The question involves a double relationship, and therefore it resembles the sample essay in this chapter. Develop your thesis and decide on an organizing method to avoid being overwhelmed with detailed information.

**Comments on
Question 4**

Question 4 introduces the topic of colonial wars and their impact on the colonists. Military events provide an important element in American history, but one should not merely study battles. Here the question forces you to deal with the impact of war on the life of the colonies. It requires you to know the wars, but you must also include causes and results, peace terms, frontier developments, and, most important, the psychological impact upon the people. Since there is no time period, you will need to consider the aftermath of the French and Indian War, which ended in 1763.

**Comments on
Question 5**

The last question raises an interesting and timely topic, that of British and French racial attitudes as expressed in colonial history. The question assumes a difference in the attitudes of two European colonizing powers, and you need to test this difference. The French were essentially forced out of North America in 1763. The question requires information from different sources to properly evaluate the quotation, so do not be trapped by the word *hostile* into discussing wars and massacres only. Hostility can manifest itself in a variety of ways. The answer should include social and cultural history as well as military. The question, then, becomes a complex one and may be more challenging since it does not deal directly with the topics considered in the usual history book.

These brief analyses should start you on your way to writing effective and well-prepared essays on the five sample topics. Be sure and use the Seven Steps in Essay Writing. The questions will force you to study and review key information from colonial American history and thus be aware of the information you need to know for the Advanced Placement exam.

Multiple-Choice Questions—The Chronology Question

As indicated in the introduction, the Advanced Placement examination includes 80 multiple-choice questions. In each chapter of this book, sample questions dealing with information from the different periods will be presented. Different types of multiple-choice questions will be analyzed in each chapter and the correct answer for each question will be discussed. This is done to stimulate your thinking about different periods and to illustrate the many types of multiple-choice questions. Although many topics will be introduced, these questions alone cannot provide a full review of American history.

In this chapter we will look at the most obvious type of multiple-choice question—the type that requires a factual recall of chronological information. Many people find historic dates boring and difficult. Some dates are important, however, and in the Western concept of historical cause and effect, a knowledge of the chronological order of events is essential. You should know important dates, but you must also know the order in which events occurred. As suggested in Part One, the making of time lines dealing with related events can be a very valuable device in studying history.

Advice on Skipping Questions

One thing to remember is you may make marks on the test booklet. As you eliminate possible answers on a difficult multiple-choice question, you may find putting an ✗ beside the choice or crossing it out to be helpful. You should also skip questions you are uncertain of and return to them. A check (✔) by the number will alert you to which questions you skipped. However, after skipping a question, be sure and check that you are placing a black pencil mark in the correct oval for the next question.

Sample Question 1

> Which of the following British colonies was founded last?
> (A)   Plymouth
> (B)   Pennsylvania
> (C)   Georgia
> (D)   Massachusetts Bay Colony
> (E)   Virginia

Comments

The correct answer is (C) Georgia. The same question could be phrased, "Which colony was founded first?" In any case, you must know the chronological order and preferably the dates of the founding of the colonies. This is why a time line is helpful. There is very little you can do with a question of chronology unless you know the chronology. However, if you recognized some of the events but not all, you may be able to arrive at an answer. Sample Question 2 is an example of such a question.

Sample Question 2

Which of the following English acts or documents was issued first?
(A)   Iron Act
(B)   Proprietary Grant to William Penn
(C)   The Charter of the Dominion of New England
(D)   Molasses Act
(E)   Massachusetts Bay Company Charter

Comments

The correct answer is (E) Massachusetts Bay Company Charter. You are probably familiar with the Molasses Act and the Iron Act. They both deal with the regulation of trade, which was not a major issue until after 1660, by which time the majority of the colonies had been founded. Logically, since several of the choices deal with colonial charters, you would suspect that these two trade acts did not come first. You are then left with three acts, one of which, the Charter of the Dominion of New England, is probably unfamiliar. It dealt with the union of New England and New York under one royal governor, as an idea for efficiency in colonial rule developed by James II about 1685. The last two, choices B and E, are probably vaguely familiar. The wording of each choice should give you the subject dealt with.

The founding of colonies is a major part of colonial history. If you know when colonies were founded, then you would know that Massachusetts came before Penn's Pennsylvania. You should also be able to deduce that one colony in New England would be granted a charter before one would be granted for the entire area. This type of analysis of the choices offered as answers to multiple-choice questions dealing with chronology will often help you to locate the correct answer. Usually, however, it is essential that you know the chronology or dates of the events offered as possible answers.

Study the following multiple-choice questions. How well can you do on them? The various types presented will be analyzed in later chapters. Following the 16 questions are brief analyses of each correct answer.

Practice Multiple-Choice Questions

1. All of the following important colonial cities are correctly paired with the colony EXCEPT
   (A) Williamsburg—Virginia
   (B) Annapolis—Maryland
   (C) Salem—Rhode Island
   (D) Charleston—South Carolina
   (E) New London—Connecticut

2. Which of the following events occurred first?
   (A) Bacon's Rebellion
   (B) Glorious Revolution in England
   (C) War of Spanish Succession
   (D) Formation of the New England Confederation
   (E) French and Indian War

3. The chief significance of the Great Awakening was that it
   (A) led to the foundation of colleges
   (B) provided Jonathan Edwards with an opportunity to preach
   (C) was the first genuine unified movement of the American colonists
   (D) revived intolerance
   (E) created new interest in the churches

4. In which region is Fort Duquesne located?
   (A) 1
   (B) 2
   (C) 3
   (D) 4
   (E) 5

5. The first permanent English settlement on the mainland of North America
    was at
    (A) St. Augustine   (D) Jamestown
    (B) Plymouth   (E) Raleigh
    (C) Quebec

6. The Treaty of Tordesillas
    (A) divided the New World between the Spanish and the Portuguese
    (B) established Spanish as the official language of South America
    (C) resolved the French and English claims to Martinique
    (D) determined the border between Florida and Georgia
    (E) proclaimed the Papacy's desire to prevent warfare between colonies
        and Native Americans

7. The Native Americans did all of the following EXCEPT
    (A) aid the Pilgrims in Plymouth
    (B) split in their support of the French and English in the 18th-century
        colonial wars
    (C) felt their way of life was threatened by the territorial expansion of
        the colonists
    (D) converted to Christianity in very limited numbers
    (E) organized effectively to block English expansion west of the
        Appalachians

8. Which of the following men explored in North America for the French?
    (A) Magellan   (D) Frobisher
    (B) Coronado   (E) Champlain
    (C) Hudson

9. The trial of Peter Zenger in New York has often been considered an impor-
    tant step in the development of
    (A) religious toleration   (D) the right to bear arms
    (B) freedom of the press   (E) concepts of privacy
    (C) trial by jury

10. Which of the following was NOT an important cause of the French and
    Indian War?
    (A) Formation of the Ohio Company
    (B) Desire of Massachusetts colonists to clear the French out of Canada
    (C) Washington and Braddock's attack on Fort Duquesne
    (D) trade limitations imposed by the Acts of Trade
    (E) French exploration in the Great Lakes region and westward

11. Which of the following had the LEAST significance in providing experi-
    ence and concepts that were used by the colonists in their arguments and
    fight for independence?
    (A) French and Indian War
    (B) New England town meetings
    (C) Use of the Power of the Purse by the Virginia House of Burgesses
    (D) The Albany Plan
    (E) Development by the colonists of crops for export

12. "The hatchet is a hard stone, eight or ten inches in length and three or four in breadth, of an oval form, flatted and rubbed to an edge at one end; near the other end is a groove in which the handle was fastened; and their process to do it was this: When the stone was prepared, they chose a very young sapling, and splitting it near the ground, they forced the hatchet into it, as far as the groove, and left nature to complete the work by the growth of the wood, so as to fill the groove and adhere firmly to the stone. They then cut the sapling off above and below, and the hatchet was fit for use."

The above passage indicates the following about the people who used the process described:
   (A) They made tomahawks for military purposes
   (B) They had very few tools
   (C) They made all their tools from stone
   (D) They made intelligent use of their natural surroundings
   (E) They were Native Americans

Answers and Answer Explanations

1.	C	2.	D	3.	C	4.	C
5.	D	6.	A	7.	E	8.	E
9.	B	10.	D	11.	E	12.	D

1. (C) Salem in Massachusetts is famous as the location of the colonial witch trials. The other cities are correctly matched.

2. (D) The formation of the New England Confederation was the first attempt at colonial union. This was formed to combat the Native American threat to frontier settlements. The other events involving violent actions occurred later in colonial history.

3. (C) The Great Awakening was the first movement of religious revival experienced in all the colonies. Although each choice offered is true, the chief significance of the Great Awakening would be its unifying nature, and therefore C would be the best answer.

4. (C) Fort Duquesne was founded by the French in western Pennsylvania (area 3). The British changed the name to Fort Pitt when they captured the fort, and it later became the city of Pittsburgh.

5. (D) The first permanent English settlement on the mainland of North America was at Jamestown.

6. (A) The Treaty of Tordesillas in 1494 redefined the demarcation line by which one year earlier the Pope had assigned the Americas to Spain and Africa and India to Portugal. With the new demarcation line Portugal was given a claim to Brazil.

7. (E) The Native Americans did all of the items listed except organize effectively to block English expansion westward. Many tribes supported the French in the French and Indian War. They later tried to block the westward movement of the colonists, but they were not successful.

8. (E) Each of these men were early explorers of the New World, but only Champlain, for whom Lake Champlain in New York State is named, explored under the French flag.

9. (B) The trial of Peter Zenger is often cited as the true beginning of the free press in America. The trial was one of the most important in the colonies although some historians now believe its significance has been exaggerated.

10. (D) There were many causes of the French and Indian War, but the limitation on trade under the British Acts of Trade and Navigation was not one of them. The acts were a major cause of the American Revolution.

11. (E) The first four events listed provided the colonists with the experience and/or concepts to be used in the fight for independence. Fighting methods were developed in the war. Town meetings and the Power of the Purse (appropriation of money) gave good arguments for the rights of English subjects (see Number 14 above for the Albany Plan). While the development of export crops and subsequent trade was essential in creating viable colonies, the process supplied little experience useful in the fight for independence.

12. (D) The passage, from Jeremy Belknap's *History of New Hampshire, 1812*, is a description of the process used by Native Americans in the Northeast to make a hatchet, but there is no indication it is a tomahawk or that the people described are Native Americans. While only one tool is mentioned, there is no indication whether they had many tools or not. Be careful in your reading and do not jump to conclusions that are not clearly stated in quotations. As we know, the Native Americans of the Northeast had a large variety of specialized tools. They were made from many natural materials—bone, stone, wood, shells—but no metal until after contact with Europeans. As the passage clearly indicates, they made intelligent use of their natural surroundings waiting for a sapling to grow around a stone hatchet head to provide a handle.

Bibliography

As every student of American history is aware, there are innumerable books and pamphlets one may read on the topic. Many adults are history buffs and do all their recreational reading in American history; some even focus on one aspect of American history, such as the Civil War or colonial history. With this mass of material available, it is very difficult for the young student or the experienced teacher to pick and choose the most recent significant publications or the most interesting material from each period to supplement the standard textbooks mentioned in the bibliography in Part One. To provide some direction at the end of each chapter, a few works will be suggested that may stimulate your study. As stated above, you do not need to read all of these books for the Advanced Placement exam. You should, however, read beyond the standard textbooks in areas that interest you. Texts include suggested bibliographies, and you may find listed there books that relate more to your interests than any of those books listed at the end of chapters.

It is important that you supplement your textbook reading, but it is unimportant whether it be with books of the age, such as Benjamin Franklin's *Autobiography*; with collections of documents, such as H. S. Commager's *Documents of American History*; with secondary historical accounts, such as Wright's *The Atlantic Frontier: Colonial American Civilization, 1607–1763*; or with good fictional accounts that supply the feel of a period, such as Arthur Miller's play *The Crucible*.

The Internet

Today there are many web sites on the Internet that contain material helpful in the study of United States history. These sites vary greatly in value and credibility and they often change. While students are encouraged to seek specific information on the Internet, unless you know the sites, know their reliability, and know how to efficiently use the Internet, you can spend hours seeking information, time that could better be used for study and review from established texts.

One of the valuable uses of the Internet is to access documents that are often hard to locate. These original documents from United States history can be used in the design of DBQ's. They can also be used to improve your skills of reading and analysis. However, because of the continuing changes in web sites, it was decided not to include web sites in any of the bibliographies.

Brandon, William. *Indians.* New York: American Heritage, 1985.

Leach, D. E. *Roots of Conflict 1677–1763*. Chapel Hill: University of North Carolina Press, 1989.

Morgan, E. S. *The Puritan Dilemma: The Story of John Winthrop*. Boston: Addison-Wesley, 1999.

Wright, L. B. *The Atlantic Frontier; Colonial American Civilization: 1607–1763*. New York: Greenwood Publishing Group, 1980.

Documents

There are many collections of documents relating to American history that can be used to supplement textbook readings and to provide experience in analyzing important writings.

Commager, H. C. *Documents of American History.* Englewood Cliffs, NJ: Prentice-Hall, 1988.

Corbett, P. S. et al. *Life, Liberty and the Pursuit of Happiness: Documents in U.S. History.* 2 volumes. New York: McGraw Hill Humanities, 2003.

Biographies

For those students particularly interested in studying history as reflected in the lives of important individuals, there are many excellent works to choose from. Check your library to find biographies of people who interest you.

Franklin, Benjamin. *The Autobiography of Benjamin Franklin*. New York: Dover Pub., 1996.

Fiction

Many works of fiction supply the feel for an era. These six works listed are particularly good in this aspect, although they will not help broaden your factual knowledge. Similar works can be found for each period of United States history.

Cannon, L. G. *Look to the Mountain*. Woodstock, VT: Countryman, 1991.

Cather, Willa. *Shadows on the Rock* (Quebec). New York: Vintage Books, 1995.

Edmonds, W. D. *Drums along the Mohawk*. New York: Bantam Books, 1992.

Hawthorne, Nathaniel. *House of Seven Gables* (Salem). New York: Oxford University Press, 1991.

Miller, Arthur. *The Crucible* (Salem Witch Trials). New York: Penguin, 1976.

Roberts, Kenneth. *Northwest Passage* (French & Indian War). Maine: Downeast Books, 2001.

2 The Era of the American Revolution 1763–1789

Important Facets of This Period

The issues and conflicts that led to the independence of the British colonies, the winning of that independence, and the establishment of the new nation— the United States of America—are the major themes of this period. It is a crucial period for understanding American history and one that should be studied in all American history survey courses. One can expect questions dealing with various aspects of this era on any American history examination.

As stated in Chapter 1, today many courses in American history begin with the Treaty of Paris in 1763. However, many issues and ideas from the colonial period before 1763 had an impact on developments after 1763 and on our independent history. They include Puritanism; attitudes toward slaves, Native Americans, and free blacks; religious toleration; economic independence, especially in trade and manufacturing; self-government; the legal status of the individual and the right to vote; access to free land and the settlement of the West and conflicts between the European powers. These issues and ideas were important immediately after 1763 and should form part of one's study of this period, but their roots can be found in the colonial era.

As implied above, the years 1763–1789 logically divide into three separate but related time periods. These are: the steps to independence, 1763–1776; the War of the American Revolution, also called the War for American Independence, 1775–1783; the establishment of an independent government, 1783–1789. This latter period is sometimes referred to as "the critical period," a phrase coined by the American historian John Fiske in the 19th century and used ever since.

In studying these three periods, there are many points that need to be understood. There are also several important questions that run through all three periods. Among these are
1. Who will control the frontier lands across the Appalachian Mountains?
2. Who has the power of taxation of citizens?
3. Who will control the legislative power?
4. What are the "inalienable rights" of human beings?
5. Should government be democratic, republican, oligarchical, or monarchical?
6. When are protest, civil disobedience, and revolution legitimate instruments of political action?
7. How should slaves and Native Americans be treated?
8. What are the social and cultural differences between the colonists and Europeans?

Sample Essay Question—Describe . . . Explain

The following question is a very good question for covering the history of 1763–1789, since it ties two of the three time periods together in a comparison. The question is of the *Describe . . . explain* type, which often gives the writer a wide choice for the content or focus of an answer.

Sample Question

> Between 1763 and 1776, the colonies confronted many issues in their relations with England. Under the Articles of Confederation (1780–1789), the same major issues were behind the tensions in state/federal relations. Describe three of these issues and explain how the central government under the Articles of Confederation tried to solve them.

**Comments on
Sample Question**

Following our first step in essay writing, we now need to analyze the question. For your benefit, before you proceed, read the question carefully and decide what is being asked. You may even wish to make a few notes on your ideas so you can compare them with the following analysis and see how well you are doing.

The directions in the *Describe . . . explain* type of essay are clearly stated. The writer is asked to describe one or more particular situations, relationships, or, as in this example, issues and then to explain something about the issue, situation, relationship, or problem described. The question allows the writer to pick the issues. This becomes an important decision, since you must pick issues or situations about which you not only know the facts, but one for which you can describe the relationship. The choice is yours, but the success of your answer will be determined by how wise a choice you make.

There should be no difficulty in understanding the words *describe* and *explain*. The difficulty in this type of essay comes in how well you describe the situation and how valid an explanation you present. Also, sometimes it is not easy to interpret what explanation is desired. In this question it is clear that you must discuss how the central government under the Articles of Confederation tried to solve the issues you have described. Fortunately, Advanced Placement questions are usually very clear because they have been developed and carefully analyzed by a committee over a period of at least a year.

The above general comments on the *Describe . . . explain* type of question apply to all of them. Now let's look closely at this particular question. What are you asked to describe? Obviously it is issues, but what "issues?" The question states "Between 1763 and 1776, the colonies confronted many issues in their relations with England." This should not be too difficult to understand. The colonies are the British colonies in North America. The history of the period 1763–1776 in America is full of issues that created tension and difficulties between these two. This part of the question appears, therefore, to be asking for a rewriting of the history of the 13 years, but be careful! Note the rest of the question, "Under the Articles of Confederation (1780–1789) the same major issues were behind the tension in state/federal relations." The question is tighter than the first part would lead you to suspect. *Issues*—and note, *major issues*—is the key to the question. You must not simply rewrite the history of 1763–1776; you must identify the issues of that era that recur in the years

1780–1789 *and* recur in state/federal relations as the issues had occurred in relations between colonies and England earlier. You can now begin to determine what issues you will deal with in your answer. You must at the time you pick the issues remember to "explain how the central government under the Articles of Confederation tried to solve them." Therefore, you must pick issues (1) that you can describe; (2) that recurred; (3) that you can explain how they were dealt with under the Confederation. This should not be difficult, but it illustrates how carefully you should analyze even the simplest-appearing question. Finally, you are to discuss only three major issues.

You are now ready for the second step—collecting and sorting your information. You should do that now, following the points mentioned above. You should first make brief notes on as many issues as you can and then, pick the three issues faced between 1763 and 1776 that you wish to write on. Add more specific information about each and, finally, jot down information on how the issues were dealt with between 1780 and 1789. After this, move on to the third step—developing your thesis. In this type of question, some people would say no thesis is required. If that is the case, you would not be writing an essay, but merely a historic composition. This question *does* require you to determine personal viewpoint. You must pick the issues, explain what the Confederation did about them, and, looking at the word *tried*, decide if the Confederation solved the problems or not. Your thesis or personal opinion might well revolve around the word *tried*. Unlike the *Evaluate This Statement* type of essay question, the *Describe . . . explain* type forces you to write your thesis in your own words. You should do that now. Then follow the remaining four steps in essay writing and write an answer to this question.

After you have written your own essay on this question, read the following student answer. You will then want to outline the student answer and your own to compare the outlines. You will also want to compare the teacher's comments on this student essay with your own comments on it.

Sample Answer

Taxation, currency, and defense are three problems every government and people must deal with. In the period between 1763 and 1776 they were issues of colonial/English relations. Later, in 1780–1789, these three issues involved relations between the Confederation and the states. All four groups—colonists, England, states, Confederation—had ideas on how the problems should be resolved and attempted to do so, but no real solution was found until the Constitution was written in 1789.

The main problem from 1763 to 1776 was that of taxation. The colonists insisted that as members of the British Empire they were entitled to the same rights that Englishmen living in England enjoyed. They propounded that taxation without representation was unfair and that taxation for the sole purpose of raising revenue was equally unjust. Actually, what they were demanding was Dominion status, something not granted to Canada until 1839.

In 1764 the Grenville Ministry passed the Sugar Act. Shortly thereafter, the Stamp Act appeared. These taxes the colonists considered far too heavy. They felt that they had been made law without colonial consent. The colonists became very agitated. When, in 1773, changes in the law and tea tax gave the Dutch East India Company a virtual monopoly on all tea imported to America, the colonists were furious. In December they staged the Boston Tea Party, an act that resulted in the "Coercive" or "Punitive" acts.

Another cause for grievance between the colonies and the Mother Country was the currency situation. In 1764 the Grenville Ministry passed the Currency Act, which was, in effect, a prohibition against the coining of money. The colonists, except in certain specific cases, were forbidden to coin their own currency or to issue paper money through their own banks. This, though not as controversial as the taxation situation, did arouse a considerable amount of protest, especially on the frontier and in North Carolina. The colonists felt that they deserved a certain amount of self-government and that they understood the need for currency better than Parliament. After all, they were a group of different colonies, with different backgrounds, different modes of living, and each with its own debtor-creditor problems as well as a need for cash.

A third issue of disagreement between the colonies and the Crown concerned the raising and housing of troops. Parliament, naturally, assumed that since America was a colony, it needed to be protected. Consequently, British regulars would have to be sent over and housed in the colonies. This situation first arose in the Quartering Act. This act stated that Americans must house British Regulars and help pay for their maintenance. This seemed absurd to the colonists, who felt that they themselves could, with less expense and more efficiency, raise the requisite troops for protection as they had been doing since 1607. One provision of these "Coercive" Acts stated that the colonists must within 24 hours comply with any troop quartering regulation that might be enacted.

Taxation under the Articles of Confederation was just as important as it was during the colonial period. The Congress's main weakness was that it did not have the power to tax the states. As one can see, the problem was entirely different in substance. Instead of the central government forcing the taxes upon the people, it could only tax with the people's (states') acquiescence. However, the situation is in one respect similar. The states and the people protested against any taxation. When Robert Morris was Secretary of the Treasury, he tried three times to impose taxes but met with failure every time. When he tried to resign from the thankless job, his resignation was not accepted. Under the Articles of Confederation the government could only remedy the taxing problem of 1763–1776 by asking for taxes rather than demanding them. They found, however, that the states were equally as unresponsive as the colonies had been.

The Congress under the Articles of Confederation met currency problems by saying that the states could coin their own money. However, this engendered new complications. People found that there were so many currencies that it was difficult to distinguish the worth of each one. When one state refused to issue huge amounts of currency, and farmers demanded that it do so, the result was Shays' Rebellion of 1786. There was so much currency and so many different currencies that inflation soon resulted. Farmers were unable to pay their debts and merchants were unable to purchase the raw materials necessary to increase their business and prosperity.

Finally, the Articles of Confederation attempted to solve the troop question by leaving it up to the states themselves. Congress was not permitted to raise an army; instead, each state would have its own army or militia that could be called upon by Congress when needed. This, however, created new difficulties. It made it impossible for the country to have a central army, centrally trained and operated. And what was to happen if one state army refused to cooperate with another?

Although these three issues of taxation, currency, and army were apparently solved in the new Constitution in 1789, the solutions have been questioned at other times in history. These issues seem to reflect continual concerns of the American people.

Teacher Comments on Sample Answer

"This essay is an excellent answer to the question. It is very effectively and clearly organized with both introductory and concluding paragraphs. The student's personal view on the question is stated in the last sentence of the introduction and again in the conclusion. Although the body of the paper does not deal specifically with the thesis, it is obvious in the presentation of the information and in the discussion of it that the student believes no solutions to the issues were discovered in either period.

"The factual information presented to describe the three issues is excellent. The student illustrates a clear understanding of the steps leading to the revolution and mentions many of them, but not in a mere recitation of events. Instead, the student carefully chooses particular events to illustrate the three issues under discussion. Use of the currency situation in the colonies and under the Confederation is particularly interesting, as it is often not covered or understood by students. Taxation and the army are good choices to illustrate issues.

"Considering the student's thesis, it was wise not to include the problem of western lands or the frontier as an illustration. The issue in this area *was* settled effectively by the Confederation government with the Northwest Ordinance."

Summary

Do you agree with these teacher comments? Overall, this essay is excellent. Students should study its organization and the choice of vocabulary and information as both a review of this time period and an example of an answer that would have received a high grade on the Advanced Placement United States History exam.

Practice Essay Questions

1. Between 1763 and 1789, the use and control of the frontier regions presented problems to both the British and the Americans. Describe the problems involved in the use and control of the frontier and explain how both the British and the Americans attempted to solve them.

2. After 1763, in the face of recurring crises, the colonists slowly developed a theory of political independence and government. Describe these recurring crises and explain how they led the colonists to develop their theory of political independence and government.

3. The government under the Articles of Confederation has been considered a failure. Describe four of the following events that occurred under the Confederation government and explain how these actions may or may not be considered failures of that government.

    Treaty of Paris 1783
    Land Ordinance 1785
    Shays' Rebellion 1786
    Annapolis Convention 1786
    Northwest Ordinance 1787

4. "The Declaration of Independence issued a call for a democratic govern-ment of equal citizens that was rejected by the writers of the Constitution, who created an aristocratic government that benefited only the wealthy few." Assess the validity of this statement.

5. The American people experienced periods of revolutionary change brought about by political action in the years 1783–1789 and 1828–1836. Describe two political changes in each time period and show how these changes were revolutionary.

Before you read the brief comments on the above questions, you may wish to make your own analysis of the questions and write out answers to several of them.

Comments on Question 1

Question 1 is very similar to the question analyzed above. It narrows the choice of problems to those involved with the frontier, but other than that the format is the same.

Comments on Question 2

Question 2 uses the same format of *Describe . . . explain* but changes issues or problems to crises. The time period is narrower than for the other questions, thus requiring a more detailed knowledge of the period 1763–1776 than is needed for the other questions. As you describe crises, be clear in your mind how the situation furthered the colonists' development of a theory of political independence and government. Do not just describe all the steps leading to independence, but carefully pick those that can help you illustrate the devel-oping theory of political independence and government.

Comments on Question 3

The third question is a slight variation of the *Describe . . . explain* type. It has a similarity to the *Evaluate This Statement* type, since the first sentence is a state-ment that you are then expected to evaluate as you "explain how these actions may or may not be considered failures of that government." In this form you are given the events you are to use in the answer, thus narrowing your options but providing a clear focus to the question. You are to pick FOUR of the five events given. Be sure in such questions to pick the number stated. Writing on more events than the directions say will not increase your grade. You are expected to describe the events and then evaluate them as you explain them. The question does not use the word *evaluate*, but "may or may not" requires an evaluation. Did you spot this slight variation in the type of question? The five events listed should be familiar so the key is to pick the four you know the most about and that you can relate to your thesis on the success or failure of the government.

Comments on Question 4

The fourth question is typical of the *Assess the Validity* type. The issue raised by the statement is one of major interest to historians and one on which you should have ideas. The question basically asks, "Did the Constitution reject the principles set forth in the Declaration of Independence?" You need to under-stand several key words—*democratic, equal, aristocratic*—in order to answer the question. This illustrates the importance of building your vocabulary.

Comments on Question 5

The last question uses the *Describe . . . explain* form but deals with two widely different time periods. It also uses the word *show* in place of *explain* but this type of variation should not upset your analysis. You should expect different words to be used from time to time. You may not be prepared to answer this question now because you may lack knowledge of the 1828–1836 period. It was included here to illustrate how differing time periods can be used. There will be more in later chapters. The wording of this question may seem to force you to accept the political changes as revolutionary. Actually, in spite of such wording, you always have the option of arguing the other side of a statement and, in this question, you could argue against the political changes being revolutionary. Do not be trapped into taking positions you do not believe in by the wording of a question, but at the same time, do not lose sight of the point of the question as you defend an unusual position. You should feel free to state and defend your personal opinion or thesis on every question.

Multiple-Choice Questions—The Quotation Question

On the Advanced Placement examination there are a number of multiple-choice questions that are not strictly recall questions. These questions are often referred to as "stimulus" questions because they provide you with information that should stimulate your thinking. The information provided can take many forms—quotations, charts, maps, graphs, cartoons—and we will present information and analysis of various ways such stimulus questions may be presented. In this chapter we present the quotation-based question, which is a very important type of multiple-choice question.

A variety of questions can be developed based upon quotations. The most obvious type is the one in which the student must identify the author or the source of the quotation. Such quotations will either be obvious and well known or the content of the quotation will be easily identifiable with the position or viewpoint of the author or with the content of an important document. The documents might include letters, speeches, laws, party platforms, or anything else that could be read to reveal the history of a period. Other multiple-choice questions based on quotations or historical documents will require you to understand the content of the passage in view of the history of the time, to identify the philosophical viewpoint expressed, or to analyze the passage to reveal your own analytical and interpretive skills.

The quotation-based multiple-choice question has many forms. Samples will be included in each chapter, but we will analyze several of the possible variations in this chapter. Although we are discussing documents from the era of the American Revolution, you must realize that you may have documents from any period of American history on the examination. We have chosen to present this type of stimulus question here for several reasons. First, there are many documents that are discussed in all American history texts dealing with the era of the American Revolution and you should be familiar with them. Using these documents will illustrate how quotations from any period might be used.

The second reason is that quotations are often connected with individuals. In this unit and throughout the remainder of your study, you will read about many important people and as you do, you should relate particular ideas and positions to them. The type of specific information needed to answer many of the quotation-based multiple-choice questions can be acquired as you study your history, if you know what to look for. Names and authors of documents and important laws, the changing concept and interpretation of the laws as they apply to economic and social activity, major speeches and who delivered them, the changing attitudes of people living in various parts of the country—all of this information can be absorbed as you study the past.

Another reason is that on the DBQ you will have to read, analyze, and interpret information taken from various documents. If you begin now to practice reading documents to find key ideas and relate these to the "mainstream" of our history, you will be preparing all through your study or review for the DBQ. Read the quotations looking for the key ideas and connect these to individuals and the history of the time.

As the following examples of quotation-based multiple-choice questions are studied, it should become clear how various types of information will help you respond to such questions.

Sample Questions 1–2

"So soon as there shall be 5,000 free male inhabitants of full age in the district upon giving proof thereof to the Governor, they shall receive authority, with time and place, to elect representatives from their counties or townships to represent them in the General Assembly: *Provided.* That, for every 500 free male inhabitants, there shall be one representative, and so on progressively with the number of free male inhabitants shall the right of representation increase, until the number of representatives shall amount to 25; after which, the number and proportion of representatives shall be regulated by the Legislature . . . "

1. The above quotation is most likely from
   (A) the U.S. Constitution
   (B) Galloway's Plan of Union
   (C) Quebec Act
   (D) Northwest Ordinance
   (E) Stamp Act

2. The previous quotation (from the Northwest Ordinance) established the basic American political concept of the
   (A) equality of men
   (B) right of governors to set election dates
   (C) size of legislature
   (D) right of 5,000 free men to have elections
   (E) right of free men to govern themselves through their own legislatures

Comments on Question 1

Question 1 is a most common form of question. It requires you to be familiar with five acts and be able to understand the passage. The passage states how and when a legislative body will first be set up. You might remember the line "5,000 free male inhabitants," as many books point out that this clause has set the pattern for the government of territories and the admission of states into the union throughout our history. Chances are, however, that you will not recognize the quotation but that you will be able to understand its content and purpose.

You must then look at the choices offered in this question to determine which one most likely contained the quotation. As is often the case, several choices will be very familiar. All students should know the U.S. Constitution well enough to realize that it does not establish the pattern for creating legislatures. State legislatures were in existence and the Constitution establishes the two branches of the U.S. Congress only. The U.S. Constitution can obviously be eliminated.

You should be aware of the Stamp Act. It would then be obvious that the Stamp Act did not deal with legislatures; therefore, it can be quickly eliminated. You are now left with three choices, each of which is a possibility. You should recall the Quebec Act, Galloway's Plan of Union, and the Northwest Ordinance, all of which deal with the establishment of government. The Quebec Act of 1774 extended the Province of Quebec to include all the land north of the Ohio River under the authority of the Provincial government. It also continued the French method of government. There was no place in such an act for the establishment of new legislatures.

The same holds true of Galloway's Plan of Union of 1774. It is probably the least familiar of your choices, but the title alone should identify it as an attempt to unite the already established colonies. The goal of the plan was the union of existing colonies, not the creation of new ones.

By elimination, we come to the Northwest Ordinance, which was designed in 1787 to provide organized government for the land between the Ohio River and the Great Lakes west to the Mississippi gained in the 1783 Treaty of Paris— the area known as the Northwest Territory. Various states claimed the land but ceded their claims to the federal government under the Articles of Confederation at the insistence of Maryland and New Jersey. The territory lacked a governmental system, and this ordinance established it. The concept of new and equal legislatures formed by free men when the population of a territory reaches a certain point is one of the great contributions of the American people to the concept of colonial government. You may have been familiar with the document and the idea and have been able to identify the Northwest Ordinance immediately. However, if you find that with such questions you cannot immediately spot the answer, think through the choices and see if you can come to the correct answer.

Comments on Question 2

Question 2 has been phrased to see if you understand the significance of the content of the question. In this version you need not identify the document as it is given to you in the statement. Even if the name of the document were eliminated (note the parentheses), you could still identify the political concept stated in the passage. The multiple-choice question now becomes one of checking your analytical and reading abilities—those two skills essential for every historian.

You may know that the Northwest Ordinance dealt with the establishment of governments in the territories that were to be free and equal to the governments of the original 13 colonies. In this case you would probably consider choices A and E and eliminate the others. Since A is very general and equality is not mentioned in the passage, you would quickly decide on choice E, which is a summary of the main idea in the quotation.

Simply reading the passage you would realize that choices B, C, and D are all included in the quotation. However, none of these should qualify as a "basic American political concept." It is true that the Northwest Ordinance allowed the governor to set the election date, but governors do not do that today. Again the passage allows 5,000 free men to have an election, but that has no relation to basic American political concepts. The passage does state a rule concerning legislative size, but that also is not a basic American political concept. This leaves you with choice E, which is very basic to American political life. It is the correct answer since choice A, although a basic American political concept, is not mentioned in the passage.

Sample Question 3

3. The previous quotation (from the Northwest Ordinance) establishes
    I.   The right of free males to vote for members of a legislature
    II. The authority of the legislature to set its own size once there are 25 members
    III. The control of the governor over the legislative body
    IV. The power of the governor to set the time and place for the first voting of the legislature
    (A) I and II
    (B) I and III
    (C) I, II, and IV
    (D) I, III, and IV
    (E) I, II, III, and IV

Comments on Question 3

The format of this question is somewhat different from that used previously. Instead of having five choices lettered A–E you have four statements lettered I–IV and five combinations of those four Roman numerals lettered A–E. Your task is to determine which statements with Roman numerals are correct. Then find the letter that lists those correct statements. To make your analysis easier, you should mark with a check (√) the correct or appropriate items that have Roman numerals. If you read the quotation carefully you will find that statements I, II, and IV are correct. The correct answer is thus C and so the oval lettered C on your answer sheet would be filled in. The quotation established the right of free males to vote for a legislative body when there are 5,000 free males in the district. The governor is the one to set the time and place for the first voting. Finally, once the General Assembly (legislature) reaches 25 members, they may decide the future size of the legislative body. The quotation does not set the governor's control over the legislative body.

This format can be used in a variety of questions and not only with quotations. You will find examples of this format in the following chapters. It is an interesting format. As you analyze the four choices offered and determine their accuracy, it is often more difficult to eliminate choices, because these questions rely less on recall and more on analysis. However, if you read the questions carefully, analyze the statements, and think of the history of the stated or implied time period, you will easily master this format.

On the Advanced Placement examination sometimes more than one question will be asked about the same quotation, map, chart, or cartoon. We have presented three questions here based on the same quotation and will often present two questions about one item in these sample stimulus questions. This is done deliberately to illustrate various types of questions that could be asked although it is rarely done on the exam itself. As in the case of the essay section, in the multiple-choice section of the Advanced Placement examination the first crucial step toward achieving success on multiple-choice questions is to analyze the question.

Let us look at several other quotation-based multiple-choice questions. Read them carefully, analyze the question, and decide on your answer. Then read the brief descriptions of the questions that follow.

Sample Questions 4–5

"All communities divide themselves into the few and the many. The first are the rich and well born, the other the mass of the people. The voice of the people has been said to be the voice of God; and however generally this maxim has been quoted and believed, it is not true in fact. The people are turbulent and changing; they seldom judge or determine right. Give therefore to the first class a distinct, permanent share in the government. They will check the unsteadiness of the second, and as they cannot receive any advantage by a change they therefore will ever maintain good government. Can a democratic assembly, who annually revolve in the mass of the people, be supposed steadily to pursue the public good? Nothing but a permanent body can check the imprudence of democracy. Their turbulent and uncontrolling disposition requires checks."

---

4. The writer believed all of the following EXCEPT
   (A) the people are quick to change ideas
   (B) there should be stability in government
   (C) the rich and well born deserve a permanent share in the government
   (D) government should be headed by a king
   (E) government should be designed with checks and balances

5. The above statement is most likely to be found in
   (A) the *Virginia Resolves*
   (B) *Notes on the Debates in the Federal Convention in Philadelphia*
   (C) *The Letters of a Pennsylvania Farmer*
   (D) an account of the Boston Tea Party
   (E) the Peace of Paris 1783

Comments on Questions 4–5

The quotation is from a speech by Alexander Hamilton at the debates on the Constitution in 1787 and is found in the *Notes on the Debates of the Constitutional Convention*. It briefly summarizes the position held by Hamilton until his death. He believed in government by the few who are rich. Unlike Jefferson, who believed that the people, especially the small farmers, should be the deciding power in government, Hamilton distrusted the people who had no economic stake in society.

Question 4 requires that you understand the paragraph. There is no mention of rule by a king, although it may be implied. The hasty reader might miss this point.

A statement of this type would not be suitable for a treaty or for a description of an action-packed event, such as the Tea Party. The remaining three choices for question 5 must be recognized if you are to analyze them properly. *The Virginia Resolves* and the *Letters* will then be understood to present a pro-people position. The Debates remains the correct answer and you might have suspected this type of statement would be in a debate where a particular opinion is being expressed.

Sample Questions 6–7

"That government is, or ought to be instituted for the common benefit, protection, and security of the people, nation, or community; of all the various modes and forms of government, that is best which is capable of producing the greatest degree of happiness and safety, and is most effectually secured against the danger of maladministration; and that when any government shall be found inadequate or contrary to these purposes, a majority of the community hath an indubitable, unalienable and indefeasible right to reform, alter or abolish it, in such manner as shall be judged most conducive to the public weal."

6. The philosophy expressed in the above quotation most closely resembles that held by
    (A) Jean-Jacques Rousseau
    (B) Montesquieu
    (C) John Locke
    (D) Voltaire
    (E) Hobbes

7. The philosophy expressed in the above quotation finds its most famous expression in American history in the
    (A) Declaration of Independence
    (B) Constitution
    (C) Articles of Confederation
    (D) Northwest Ordinance
    (E) Declaration and Resolves of the Continental Congress

Comments on Questions 6–7

The quotation forms part of the Virginia Bill of Rights, a document adopted in 1776. It is an excellent statement of John Locke's philosophy as stated in his *Two Treatises on Government.* Locke's philosophy was well known to the colonial leaders and provided the philosophical basis of the Declaration of Independence. In the Declaration Jefferson adopted Locke's ideas about inalienable rights and the "right of revolution." The latter is the main idea in this passage. The other men listed in question 6 were important philosophers of the 17th and 18th centuries and their ideas were important to many of the colonial leaders, but Locke's ideas were crucial in the Declaration.

In question 7 the other choices are all important documents, but all students should recognize the similarity between this passage from the Virginia Bill of Rights and the Declaration of Independence, which is the most famous American document to express Locke's idea of the right of revolution.

Sample Questions 8–10

Quotation A

"Resolved. That the first adventurers and settlers of this His Majesty's Colony and Dominion of Virginia brought with them, and transmitted to their posterity . . . all liberties, privileges, franchises, and immunities, that have at any time been held, enjoyed, and possessed, by the people of Great Britain . . .

"Resolved therefore, That the General Assembly of this Colony have the only and sole exclusive right and power to lay taxes and impositions upon the inhabitants of this Colony . . .

"Resolved, That His Majesty's liege people, the inhabitants of this Colony, are not bound to yield obedience to any law or ordinance whatever, designed to impose any taxation whatsoever upon them other than the laws or ordinances of the General Assembly aforesaid."

Quotation B

"The inhabitants of this country in all probability in a few years will be more numerous than those of Great Britain and Ireland together; yet it is absurdly expected by the promoters of the present measures, that (the colonists') property shall be disposed of (taxed) by a House of Commons at three thousand miles distant from them; and who cannot be supposed to have the least care or concern for their real interest: who have not only no natural care for their interest, but . . . every burden they lay on the colonists is so much saved or gained to themselves. The colonists have been branded with the odious names of traitors and rebels, only for complaining of their grievances; how long such treatment will, or ought to be borne, is submitted (offered for debate)."

8. The writer of Quotation A bases his argument upon the idea that
   (A) colonists brought with them their rights as English subjects
   (B) colonists do not have to obey English laws
   (C) English people are better than people of other nationalities
   (D) England is a small country and the colonies are large
   (E) the Virginia General Assembly has the exclusive right to tax

9. The writer of Quotation B bases his argument upon the idea that
   (A) the king of England has no power to tax his subjects
   (B) the rights of colonists are the same as those of English subjects
   (C) the colonists should not be called traitors
   (D) England will have fewer people than the colonies
   (E) members of the House of Commons have no real interest in the colonists

10. Although the writers of Quotations A and B differ as to the bases of their arguments, according to the quotations, they agree on all the following EXCEPT
   (A) the House of Commons does not have the right to tax the colonies
   (B) the colonists have the right to complain about their grievances
   (C) the number of inhabitants in a territory should affect the legal power of the territory
   (D) the English actions are curtailing American rights
   (E) the right of taxation is at the heart of the disagreement

Comments on Questions 8–10

Quotation A is from the *Virginia Resolves,* introduced into the Virginia House of Burgesses by Patrick Henry, and Quotation B is from a letter by Sam Adams. It is unusual to include two quotations in one multiple-choice question, but this format allows for a comparison of ideas and can test the student's reading and analytical abilities. The reasoning used in the *Resolves* appears much more sound than that used by Adams, but both agree on many points.

The *Virginia Resolves* assumed that the colonists brought with them to America their rights as English subjects, and this is the answer to question 8. The passage states that the Virginia Assembly has the right to tax and that the colonists do not have to obey English laws, but these two points are the *result* of the argument, not its *basis.*

In question 9 the answer would be the House of Commons' lack of interest in the colonies. The passage talks about traitors and about comparative population, but the basis of the rather flimsy argument seems to be the interest of the House of Commons in the colonies.

In spite of the differences in the basis of their arguments, the two documents agree on four points given as possible answers to question 10—they agree about taxation, the right to complain, and the curtailment of American rights, but the *Virginia Resolves* makes no reference to population.

Sample Questions 11–12

"But with the greatest submittion we beg leave to informe your Honours that unles something takes place more favourable to the people, in a little time att least, one half of our inhabitants in our oppinion will become banckerupt—how can itt be otherwise—the constables are dayly (selling at auction) our property both real and personal, our land after itt is appraised by the best judges under oath is sold for about one third of the value of itt, our cattle about one half the value . . . , and other things att the same rate. And we beg leave further to informe your honours that sutes att law are very numerous and the atturneys in our oppinion very extravigent and oppressive in their demands . . . What can your honours ask of us unles a paper curancy or some other medium be provided so that we may pay your taxes and debts."

11. The quotation most nearly reflects the views held by a(n)
    (A) English gentleman in London in 1783
    (B) Virginia planter of tobacco in 1787
    (C) Boston merchant in 1788
    (D) settler in eastern Kentucky in 1784
    (E) frontier farmer of western Massachusetts in 1786

12. The quotation discusses a recurrent issue in American history, the concern of the
    (A) merchant for a fair income from investment
    (B) farmer for easy credit
    (C) attorney for a living wage
    (D) judge for equal justice
    (E) legislator for fair laws

Comments on Questions 11–12

The spelling and grammar have not been changed in this quotation. The meaning should be perfectly clear, but the language of the quotation may slow down your reading. The spelling and style will often provide a clue as to the date of the writing.

The quotation is from the Petition of the Town of Greenwich, Massachusetts, in January 1786. It is a post-revolutionary war document and focuses on a new aspect of the taxation/money issue. Here the small farmers of the western part of the state are protesting high prices, tight (or limited amounts of) money, and what seemed to be unfair bankruptcy laws and judges. These farmers were soon to participate in Shays' Rebellion.

The answer to question 11 is, therefore, a frontier farmer of western Massachusetts in 1786. The other choices are not suitable, as these complaints were not issues to an English gentleman, a Virginia planter, or a Boston merchant, and Kentucky was not yet organized enough in 1784 to have farmers' complaints formalized.

The quotation is an early example of a recurrent issue in American history, the farmer's desire for easy credit, and this is the answer to question 12.

Summary   The Sample Questions illustrate the variety of questions that can be asked about documents. There will be further examples in each review chapter. As you study American history, look for important quotation and document selections that might be used in multiple-choice questions. Practice analyzing the content or meaning of these various selections so you can answer questions such as 1, 5, 6, 7, 8, and 12. Practice identifying the philosophy or attitudes of American leaders and groups so you can answer questions such as 3, 4, 9, 10, and 11. Questions 2 and 5 illustrate the need for knowing certain documents, and, therefore, as you learn the factual information, include such documents among your facts.

Practice Multiple-Choice Questions

Questions 1–3 refer to the following map

1. The First Continental Congress met in the region numbered
    (A) 1   (D) 4
    (B) 2   (E) 5
    (C) 3

2. The British surrender at Yorktown took place in the region numbered
    (A) 1   (D) 4
    (B) 2   (E) 5
    (C) 3

3. The region numbered three on the map is remembered as including the site of:
   I. the Battles of Lexington and Concord
   II. the settlement of Plymouth
   III. the meetings of the House of Burgesses
   IV. the Battle of Saratoga
   (A) I
   (B) I and II
   (C) I, II and III
   (D) I and IV
   (E) I, II and IV

4. All of the following played a role at the Constitutional Convention of 1787 EXCEPT
   (A) George Washington
   (B) Alexander Hamilton
   (C) Thomas Jefferson
   (D) Benjamin Franklin
   (E) James Madison

5. The *Federalist Papers* were written by
   (A) Hamilton, Jefferson, Jay
   (B) Hamilton, Madison, Washington
   (C) Hamilton, Madison, Jay
   (D) Hamilton. Jefferson, Adams
   (E) Madison, Jefferson, Adams

6. Which of the following was NOT a reaction of the American colonists to the Stamp Act?
   (A) The Stamp Act Congress
   (B) Virginia Stamp Act Resolutions
   (C) Instructions of the town of Braintree on the Stamp Act
   (D) Nonimportation measures
   (E) Declaratory Act

7. Which of the following was NOT a reason for the calling of the federal Constitutional Convention?
   (A) Northwest Ordinance
   (B) Shays' Rebellion
   (C) Annapolis Convention
   (D) Near-bankruptcy of the Confederation government
   (E) Lack of executive leadership in the confederation

8. Thomas Jefferson's philosophical position during the period prior to 1789 could best be described as
   (A) aristocratic and internationalist
   (B) monarchical and agrarian
   (C) democratic and mercantilist
   (D) democratic and agrarian
   (E) socialistic and internationalist

9. The Bill of Rights was added to the Constitution primarily to
   (A) curtail state power
   (B) protect the states from the power of the federal government
   (C) protect individual liberties from the power of the federal government
   (D) protect individual liberties from the power of state and local government
   (E) protect the states from the power of the church

Questions 10–11 refer to the following quotation

"... The power of Parliament is uncontrolable, but by themselves, and we must obey. They only can repeal their own Acts. There would be an end of all government, if one or a number of subjects or subordinate provinces should take upon them so far to judge of the justice of an Act of Parliament, as to refuse obedience to it. If there was nothing else to restrain such a step, prudence ought to do it ... Reasons may be given, why an Act ought to be repeal'd, and yet obedience must be yielded to it till that repeal takes place."

10. The argument presented in the above quotation is based on the assumption that
   (A) government is a blessing for mankind
   (B) the state of nature is one of conflict and war
   (C) Parliament derives its power from the consent of the governed
   (D) the people are at the complete mercy of the ruling authority
   (E) laws should be obeyed until they are changed or modified by legal means

11. The above statement is most likely to have been made by a(n)
   (A) English gentleman in 1775
   (B) frontier settler in 1763
   (C) Boston merchant in 1773
   (D) moderate colonist in 1765
   (E) Virginia planter in 1776

12. "You are to be diligent in the execution of the powers and authorities given you by several Acts of Parliament for visiting and searching of ships, and for seizing, securing and bringing on shore any goods prohibited to be imported into, or exported out of said plantations; or for which any duties are payable, or ought to have been paid, by any Act of Parliament."

The above quotation sets forth the British theory that Parliament had the right to
   (A) dominate the seas
   (B) regulate production in the colonies
   (C) seize missing seamen
   (D) control colonial trade
   (E) issue Bills of Attainder

Answers and Answer Explanations

1.	B	2.	D	3.	B	4.	C
5.	C	6.	E	7.	A	8.	D
9.	C	10.	E	11.	D	12.	D

1. (B) The first Continental Congress met at Philadelphia in the colony of Pennsylvania in 1774. Region 2 includes Pennsylvania, New York, and New Jersey.

2. (D) Yorktown, Virginia, is in Region 4.

3. (B) The Battles of Lexington and Concord and the settlement of Plymouth by the Pilgrims took place in New England, which is region 3 on the map. The House of Burgesses was the Virginia assembly and met in Williamsburg, Virginia (region 4), and the Battle of Saratoga took place in New York (region 2). This is a good example of the question format that uses four statements, any combination of which may be correct.

4. (C) Thomas Jefferson did not attend the Constitutional Convention. He was in Europe. The other men all played crucial roles at the Convention.

5. (C) The *Federalist Papers* were written by Hamilton, Madison, and Jay to support the Constitution. The papers helped win votes for the Constitution in New York and elsewhere. They are considered one of the finest analyses of the new federal system of government and they provide excellent examples of 18th-century essay style.

6. (E) The Declaratory Act of 1766 was passed by Parliament at the same time the Stamp Act was repealed. The act declared that Parliament had the right to tax the colonies even though the Stamp Act was being repealed as a response to the violent reactions of the colonies.

7. (A) The Northwest Ordinance was one of the successes of the Confederation government and was not a cause for calling the Constitutional Convention.

8. (D) Thomas Jefferson was a strong believer in the yeoman farmer—the agrarian—as contrasted with the mercantilist interest in society. He also supported the people, which would suggest his support for democracy—not yet a commonly used term. His support of the people is illustrated in his writing of the *Declaration of Independence*. Selection D best summarizes Jefferson's philosophical position.

9. (C) The Bill of Rights was added to the Constitution to protect the liberties of the individual from the power of the new federal government. The Constitution written without these protections almost failed ratification. Massachusetts ratified the Constitution with the provision that the Bill of Rights be added, and several other states followed that lead by ratifying the document with this qualification.

10. (E) James Otis, in this selection from his *Rights of the British Colonies*, 1764, bases his argument on the assumption that laws should be obeyed until they are changed or modified by legal means. He believes Parliament has the wisdom to understand when its laws are oppressive and that Parliament will change these laws.

11. (D) The argument presented in this document would most likely be held by a moderate colonist as was James Otis before the development of major controversies between colonies and the Mother Country. Choice D is the best answer.

12. (D) This quotation, from a summary of the British Acts of Trade made in 1769, clearly assumes the right of the British Parliament to control colonial trade.

Bibliography

The following books will allow you to explore different issues of the Era of the American Revolution 1763–1789.

Andrews, L. M. *Colonial Background of the American Revolution.* New Haven: Yale University Press, 1961.

Bailyn Bernard. *The Ideological Origins of the American Revolution.* Cambridge, MA: Belknap Press, 1992.

Becker, Carl. *The Declaration of Independence.* Magnolia, MA: Peter Smith.

Farrand, Max. *The Framing of the Constitution of the United States.* New Haven: Yale University Press, 1962.

Middlekauff, Robert. *The Glorious Cause: The American Revolution 1763–1789.* New York: Oxford University Press, 1985.

Morgan, E. S. *The Birth of the Republic.* Chicago: University of Chicago Press, 1993.

Wood, G. S. *The American Revolution: A History.* New York: Modern Library, 2003.

———. *The Creation of the American Republic, 1776–1787.* New York: W. W. Norton & Co., 1993.

PART THREE 3 The New Nation 1789–1824

Important Facets of This Period

The adoption of the Constitution by the United States in 1789 ushered in a new phase of our history. The Constitution is a remarkable document and should be studied carefully by all students. It will be clear that the Constitution established the simplest framework for the new government, a framework that had to be fleshed out with laws, policies, and programs and by the development of customs. This filling out of the framework of the Constitution occurred in the generation after 1789 against a background of international tension and war.

The period from 1789 to 1824 often seems confusing as the manipulations on foreign policy are followed. The intrigues of the British, French, Spanish, and Americans brought the nation close to war several times and finally resulted in the War of 1812. The problems of control of the western frontier were as complicated, and throughout this period there were dramatic developments internally, as seen in the Hamilton-Jefferson, Hamilton-Burr, Federalist-Republican conflicts. All of these issues are of importance, but probably the most important development in the era was the establishment of those laws and the setting of those policies that established the United States as a viable nation.

These laws and policies have affected all later United States history and should therefore be understood by every student. The developments of the years 1789–1824 should be studied from this perspective. Among the more important developments of the years 1789–1824 are the following:

1. The creation of political parties or factions
2. The establishment of the judicial system and its functioning, especially under Chief Justice John Marshall
3. The imprint George Washington put on the new government
4. The development of conflicting interpretations of the Constitution as exemplified by Alexander Hamilton and Thomas Jefferson
5. The continuing conflict with the British over both the 1783 Treaty of Paris and the idea of freedom of the seas and the political, economic, and social consequences
6. United States relations with the revolutionary government of France and the political, economic, and social consequences
7. The growing sense of nationalism in the country, especially after 1814
8. The physical and economic growth of the United States
9. The beginnings of a cultural identity established through the work of writers and artists.

If you have a factual knowledge of these major developments and are able to see their interrelations and to develop parallels to other periods of our history, you should have an excellent understanding of this era.

Sample Essay Questions—*Who? What? When? Where? Why? How?*

A common type of essay question is the type based on one of those crucial six words the historian continually uses—*Who? What? When? Where? Why? How?* Every historic event and development can be studied by applying these words. All six words do not always apply to each event, but if you know the *Who?* or *What?,* the *When?* and *Where?* you will be able to identify the event, and when you understand the *How?* and/or *Why?* you will have mastered the causal relationship of events that is at the heart of Western civilization's understanding of the process of history. These six little words are decisive in one's study of history.

Definitions

The meaning of these words and what they ask you to do should be familiar to you. For instance, *When?* requires an indication of time—either a date or a period such as "the presidency of John Adams." *Where?* requires an indication of place—either a city, state, region, or country. *Who?* requires an indication of the participants, while *What?* requires specific information not involving people—either laws, actions, or details of actions. The words *Why?* and *How?* are the more important and complicated ones. They require an analysis of the information collected in answering the other four words. The analysis must seek the reasons for the actions and an explanation of the relationships between all the information or data collected.

A first reaction to questions based on these six words—especially *What? How?* and *Who?*—may be that they ask for a recitation of events in a logical cause-and-effect sequence. You might think that there is no place for a personal opinion or thesis and thus questions using these words would not qualify as essay questions. Of course, as in the case of the *Describe . . . explain* type of essay noted in Chapter 2, this is not true. In such questions you need to determine your personal opinion on the question (Step Three in essay writing) before you can organize the factual material into a meaningful and effective answer. *Why? What? How?* and *Who?* questions all require a personal opinion stated as a thesis.

In this chapter we will look at several essays built around these six words. Our analysis of multiple-choice questions will focus on the cause-and-effect relationship suggested by the two words *Why?* and *How?* This chapter, therefore, should leave you prepared to approach historic material as a historian trained in Western civilization, to think in terms of cause-and-effect relationships, and to identify events by using the four W's—*Who? What? When? Where?*

Sample Question

> How was war with England and France avoided in the years 1793–1810?

Before you read the analysis of the student answer to this question, you should follow the first three steps in writing an essay answer—analyze the question, collect and sort information, develop a thesis. Then you will want to compare your notes with the analysis, sample answer, and teacher comment.

Analysis

This is a typical *How?* or *Why?* question format. The *How?* question asks the writer to explain the way or manner in which a certain event or events took place, that is, to explore the cause-and-effect relationship among events. The danger for the student is to avoid a simple listing of events. Both interpretation of the events and a personal opinion need to be included. In this time period the nation almost went to war against England and then against France. Individuals felt strongly and many steps were taken to avoid the war. You need to pick from the many possible pieces of evidence and put them together to show how you believe war was avoided. The words used should present no problems. The time period given suggests a chronological organization for the question. This sample answer was written just after the Persian Gulf Crisis of 1990–1991.

Sample Answer

War is a concern to all people, and avoiding war has been a major desire of the United States throughout our history. We were more successful avoiding war in the early years of the country than we have been since 1914. The newly independent country avoided war with England in 1794, with France in the years 1797–1800, and with both countries in the early 1800s. The way or reason we were able to avoid war then was that the presidents, unlike recent ones, refused to lead the nation into war. They—Washington, Adams, Jefferson—put domestic concerns ahead of schemes to prove our strength or to right "wrongs," and they were willing to *compromise** on issues of "honor."

For instance, Washington was willing to *compromise* our 1778 alliance with France. The French had allied with us in our Revolution, and the alliance stated it was to be "forever." The Jeffersonians were thrilled by the outbreak of the French Revolution and wanted to support them, but Washington felt that the struggle was not ours. When England and France went to war in 1793, Washington proclaimed our neutrality in spite of the alliance, thus compromising our "honor" in the eyes of the world, to borrow a modern term. The Jeffersonians were angry but could do nothing except receive the French envoy, Citizen Genet, with open arms. He misread the American mood, ordered warships built for French use, and praised the Republicans. These actions infuriated the Federalists, and Washington asked the French to recall him, which was done. Washington did not want the nation provoked into war. He knew we were not prepared and faced many *economic* and other *problems* at home, which took priority over "honor."

One *economic problem* involved our expanding merchant fleet. As a result of the English-French war, the British needed more sailors for their ships. They practiced impressment—the seizing of British or suspected British citizens off American ships and seized American ships that were trading with the French. Impressment was wrong in the eyes of Americans, and a cry rose up to have our government force an end to it, to defend our rights on the sea, and to protect our ships.

There were other *problems* with the British. They had ignored the clause in the 1783 peace treaty and had never evacuated the frontier forts, such as Detroit. These issues seemed to justify war in the eyes of many Americans, especially the Jeffersonians, but instead of asking for a declaration, Washington sent John Jay to negotiate a treaty with the British. The terms were not very good; the British agreed to evacuate the forts, which they had already promised to do in their 1783 treaty, and they agreed to pay for ships already seized, but

---

*See Teacher Comments on Sample Answer.

they made no mention of future impressments, and the Americans agreed to pay all pre-1776 debts to the British. Washington was not pleased with the treaty, but he strongly supported it in the Senate, knowing the terms were the best the United States could get and that to reject them meant war. Again he compromised on an issue and may have sacrificed our "honor" in the process, but war was avoided and the nation gained time to *expand* and grow.

Our westward *expansion* was affected by frontier wars against the Indians and Washington negotiated the Treaty of Greenville with them, which granted to the United States certain Indian lands north of the Ohio River. It was another attempt on his part to avoid war, as were the 1795 negotiations with Spain. Pinckney's Treaty provided free shipping on the Mississippi, which helped the West by expanding markets. It gained this "right" for the frontier farmers by a step short of war and without establishing *alliances*, which Washington warned against in his Farewell Address.

John Adams's four-year term was full of international intrigue and turmoil, but he too avoided *alliances* and kept the peace. The French had been furious over Jay's Treaty and began seizing American ships to retaliate. Adams sent men to Paris to negotiate, but when the French asked for bribes, the men came home and a great cry about war, rights, and "honor" broke out. "Millions for defense but not one cent for tribute" became a slogan as the Federalists pushed for war with France. The Navy department was expanded, Congress agreed to expand the Army, and Washington said he would take command, but preferred a younger man to lead the forces. The Federalists in Congress passed the Alien and Sedition Acts to keep out foreign (read French) ideas and to suppress opposition to government policy. War looked inevitable, but then the president reversed the movement by announcing he would send a new ambassador to France. An agreement was negotiated, the Convention of 1800, which again compromised the issues. The Alliance of 1778 was ended, but the Americans had to agree to pay for seized shipping. Adams had followed in Washington's footsteps in compromising to avoid war. He infuriated Alexander Hamilton and other Federalists, and historians believe his courage in going against the popular opinion for war cost him the *election* of 1800.

Jefferson won that *election*. During his first term relations with England and France were calm. However, after 1805 it was clear that neither England nor France was winning the Napoleonic War, so they turned to indirect attacks. The British began impressing American sailors again, the French and English battled via economic boycotts, and both seized American ships. Again the time seemed ripe for war. Jefferson, by his actions against the Barbary pirates, had shown that he was not a total pacifist, as some had suspected, but he, as had Washington and Adams, moved to avoid proving our strength and trying to right wrongs. Instead of a war declaration, he asked for an embargo on all U.S. trade. The French "helped" enforce the embargo by seizing U.S ships, but even that did not provoke Jefferson to war. The embargo was replaced with a Non-Intercourse Act (no trade with England and France) in 1809. The embargo was not popular; it compromised American "honor" and it seemed to say we would not defend what was right. It did have some beneficial results, as American manufacturing increased, but no one saw that at the time. People were angry at the embargo, but again war was avoided by the strength of presidential action in the field of *foreign policy*.

Practice Writing a Good Conclusion

In Step Six of essay writing we discussed the importance of a conclusion and what should be included. Before you read on, write your own conclusion for this essay. Then read the three conclusions presented below. How do they compare? Which one is most like yours? The teacher comments include reactions to all three conclusions. Do you agree with the teacher? You may find it helpful to write your own conclusion to other sample essays in this book. Conclusions are difficult to write, but a good conclusion is an important part of every essay.

Conclusion A

Clearly, there is a consistency in the *foreign policy* actions of Washington, Adams, and Jefferson. The three were not to be provoked into war by either the English or the French and were willing to compromise on important issues. By avoiding war they may have sacrificed American "honor," but we owe them a great debt because their astute policies and farsightedness permitted the nation to grow strong. Modern American presidents could learn a great deal on how to handle foreign policy by studying the actions of our first three presidents.

Conclusion B

As you can see, Washington, Adams, and Jefferson all followed the same type of *foreign policy* actions. I have shown how they compromised and went against popular opinion: Washington with the Neutrality Proclamation and in Jay's Treaty; Adams by arranging the Convention of 1800; Jefferson by pursuing the embargo. These men were great presidents, and we could learn a great deal from them. I hope our president will learn.

Conclusion C

Washington's, Adams's and Jefferson's *foreign policy* actions were taken to avoid war, and they were ready to compromise and to go against popular opinion. By their actions they gained time for the nation to grow and develop. In 1812 the war hawks from the frontier areas gained control of Congress and forced a declaration of war against England. Later presidents also led us into war. This ended the "avoid war" policies of our first three presidents. These were wise presidents following a wise foreign policy, and presidents today could learn a great deal from them.

Teacher Comments on Sample Answer

"This is an excellent essay answer. In this answer the writer has presented a clear thesis to explain the way or manner in which war was avoided—by strong presidential action. Sound evidence is presented from the presidential terms of Washington, Adams, and Jefferson to support the thesis. The evidence is factually correct and in enough detail for the reader to understand what is being proven. The writer's chronological organization is clear and an obvious organizational device to use for the answer.

"The writer uses paragraphs well and links them effectively. The reader moves easily from one paragraph to the next as the writer has repeated a word from the last sentence of one paragraph in the first sentence of the next (see italicized words). There are other ways to link paragraphs in the body of a paper, which make the contact between the batteries using our flashlight image of the essay. This repetition of words is one way, and it is a very effective technique as seen in this essay."

Teacher Comments on the Three Conclusions

"Of the three conclusions offered, Conclusion A is the most effective. The writer's thesis and the question are restated but in slightly different ways than in the introduction. The information in the body of the essay is pulled together by the word *consistency,* and the writer's interest in honor, which he makes a major point of the essay, is commented upon again. No new information is introduced. The writer's thesis is expanded to a broader context because he suggests modern presidents can learn from the first three. All of these elements are part of a good conclusion.

"Conclusion B is the poorest. The writer links it to the previous paragraph, but her use of the phrases *as you can see* and *I have shown* belittle the reader, who does not need to be told about what has been read. The writer summarizes what is said in the essay, yet fails to restate either her thesis or the question. Although the writer applies the question to a larger area than early America, she does not clearly state what we might learn from these 'great presidents.'

"Conclusion C also links the conclusion to the previous paragraph and applies the topic to a broader context. This writer indicates his thesis and the topic, but introduces new material about the War Hawks and the War of 1812. The question ended with 1810. If this information were to be introduced, and it is not called for by the question, it should have been presented in the body of the essay. This is a common error in conclusions, and yet it is one the student can easily learn to avoid.

"Basing the judgment on the use of Conclusion A, the writer of this answer would receive an excellent grade. Using Conclusion A, this is a fine paper and one that students could well use as a model, although it may be a little more detailed and a little longer than essays usually written for the Advanced Placement examination. You should refer to these three sample conclusions as you practice writing essays.

An effective conclusion is different from a simple summary in which you repeat what you have already stated in the body of the paper. The best AP papers will have a conclusion that restates the thesis and suggests the larger implications of the thesis. You may wish to refer to Step Six—Writing the Conclusion—in Part Two. In summary,

a good conclusion *must* include
  • a restatement of the thesis
  • an indication of what the question was
a good conclusion *should* include in addition to the above
  • a reference to how the thesis affects other broad issues
a good conclusion should NOT include
  • new evidence or facts not included in the body of the essay
  • the pronoun *I*
  • a statement saying "It is now proven" or similar wording
  • a simple listing of the evidence included in the essay

Practice Essay Questions

The following essay questions have as their roots one of the six little words. Read the questions over and analyze them as in Step One of our essay-writing technique. You should write down some notes on these questions before reading the analyses given below. You will want to prepare answers for several of the questions either by collecting notes, making an outline, or writing out answers. Any of those approaches will help your review by giving you practice with essays and forcing you to recall events in American history. You should do this for each chapter.

1. Why were political parties formed in the new nation and what were the major differences among political parties in the years 1791–1820?

2. What events on the frontier had a major impact on national history in the years 1789–1829?

3. Each of the following individuals expressed strong opinions concerning the policies of the new nation. What opinions were expressed by TWO of the following? Of the two, whose opinions had the greatest impact on the new nation?
   (A) George Washington
   (B) Alexander Hamilton
   (C) Thomas Jefferson
   (D) John Marshall

4. How did the Jeffersonian Republicans' policy of economic boycott in the years 1807–1812 affect the new nation?

5. Why did the United States not go to war against England in 1794 and against France in 1798–99?

Comments on Question 1

Question 1 is a typical *Why?* question. It asks for an explanation of a major development in United States history. Therefore, you may use a familiar or already stated thesis if your personal opinion agrees with it. However, you should not study history by simply learning others' opinions or theses. You will retain information better and enjoy the study more if you become personally involved in each topic. That is why you are asked to develop theses and answers to the essay questions presented in the book.

The *Why?* Part of Question 1

Question 1 has two parts, each introduced by one of the six little *words—Why?* and *What?* The issue being considered in each part has to do with political parties. First, you must explain the origin of parties and, second, you must clarify the differences between parties in the early years of the republic—1791–1820. As a study of these years reveals, there was no provision for parties, or factions as they were then called, in the Constitution. In fact, one of the major concerns of George Washington was the growth of these factions during his administration. Responses to such questions as, "Why was he concerned?" "Why did he oppose factions?" "Are factions bad?" could provide one aspect of your answer to the first part of the question. These three subquestions illustrate how you should analyze questions. They provide a place for you to start and from which to develop a personal opinion or thesis.

In the dictionary, *why* is defined as, "For what cause, reason, or purpose; on what account . . ." *Why?* demands the establishment of a cause-and-effect relationship among events, ideas, and attitudes. For instance, how do you explain

George Washington's fear of political parties when, to most Americans and for almost 200 years of our history, the political life of our nation has revolved around such parties? When you determine what you consider the cause of George Washington's attitude, then you are answering a *Why?* question historically.

The issue usually cited as decisive in separating groups in Washington's first administration into what would become parties was Hamilton's economic program, and specifically his plan for a Bank of the United States. This is by no means the only issue that divided citizens into two opposing camps, but it is a major issue and one usually cited in all books. There are many subquestions you can ask about the bank and about economic policies. What has emerged in our analysis of the first half of question 1, the *Why?* half, is that there are many subquestions to ask yourself. The raising of these subquestions is an excellent illustration of what you do in Step One of essay writing—analyzing the question.

The *What?* Part of Question 1

The second half of question 1 asks a *What?* question—"What were the major differences among the political parties?" This provides a great deal of room for personal opinion or a thesis, since it asks for major differences, and who is to decide this but you? The question covers a long period of time (29 years), and you cannot possibly list all the differences, so you must make choices as to the differences you will discuss. Major differences occurred over attitudes toward England and France, the interpretation of the Constitution, western settlement, and economic growth. What will you include?

What? is an interrogative and refers to the nature or identity of an object or matter. In a *What?* question, therefore, you must explain or identify the nature or identity of the object or matter. Specifically, in question 1 you must explain or identify the nature of the major differences in political parties. An understanding of the meaning of the words used, and an understanding of what is needed in an answer are *essential* if you wish to do well in Advanced Placement work.

Question 1 presents a challenge organizationally. The two questions within the question suggest dealing with each separately. This is one possibility. Another would be to pick two or three differences that manifested themselves during the years 1791–1820 and show how each difference helped to bring about political parties. This approach is complex, but would make an interesting and effective answer. Of course, there are many other ways you might organize the material. As a general rule, one interrelated answer to double questions makes the best and most sophisticated answer, but it is the most difficult approach.

Comments on Question 2

Essay question 2 is another *What?* question. You need to identify those "events on the frontier" that "had a major impact on national unity." In choosing the events to be discussed you will be able to indicate your personal opinion or thesis. You might even decide that no frontier event had a major impact and thereby produce a rather unexpected answer. The answer should be rather easy to write once you have analyzed the question and determined your thesis. The inclusion of the phrase *years 1789–1829* presents an easy method—chronological—for organizing your answer, although your brief notes may provide other organizational ideas.

Comments on Question 3

The third question combines several types of essay questions. It begins with a statement of fact similar to the *Evaluate This Statement* form, but you are not asked to evaluate the statement, which is very simple and almost noncontroversial. The question then presents a *What?* and a *Who?* (*Whose?*) question. Four individuals are then listed from which you must pick two. As you realize, many types of essay questions can be written to include a choice from which you must pick one or more items to discuss in your answer. This format is quite popular on the AP exam. It is of utmost importance in this type of question that you choose those items about which you know the most *as they relate to the question asked*. All four men mentioned in question 3 had strong opinions, some of which had a great impact throughout our history, such as Marshall's Supreme Court decisions and Washington's attitude toward "entangling alliances." But what impact did these opinions have "on the new nation?" You must decide *that* before answering the question.

To analyze this particularly complex question you must
1. pick two individuals to write about
2. present the nature of and identify the opinions of the two men in regard to "policies of the new nation"
3. indicate "whose opinions had the greatest impact on the new nation."

There is plenty of room for the development and presentation of a thesis as you follow these three steps.

Perhaps the most difficult point in answering question 3 will be in organizing your material. Chronology is not important. As you follow Step Two in essay writing and make brief notes, several organizational frameworks may emerge. One would be to present the opinions of one man followed by the second and then present in a paragraph which opinions had the greatest impact. Another way would be to present the opinions of the two men on specific policies, such as the development of parties, the chartering of a Bank of the United States, U.S. relations with England and France, the interpretation of the Constitution (loose or strict construction), the Louisiana Purchase, or other policies that had to be determined by the federal government. As each policy is discussed, you could indicate which man's opinion had the greatest impact, then you could present your estimation of which individual's impact was greatest (that is your thesis) in your conclusion. Although the organization of this essay may be complicated, there are several organizational schemes that could be very effective.

Comments on Question 4

Question 4 is a *How?* question. In the dictionary *how is* defined in several ways, all of which provide help in understanding what is expected in the answer. *How* means, "in what manner or way; to what degree or extent; in what state or condition; for what reason; why . . .; what?" In answering question 4, you must deal with the manner, degree, and state or condition in which "the Republican party's policy of economic boycott" affected the nation. The question also requires specific knowledge of the Republican party's policy, and this entails an understanding of another frequently used historic term—*boycott*. If you do not have this information, do not answer the question. If you have the facts, then you can develop a thesis presenting your views on the "manner" and "degree" of impact of the economic boycott on the new nation. The most obvious organizational scheme is to pick different examples of the impact of the boycott, such as its impact on New England merchants, on the Federalist party, and on a frontier settler and to explain in separate paragraphs the manner in which the impact was felt by each.

Comments on Question 5

Question 5 is similar to the sample essay question for this chapter; the questions involve essentially the same information. They both require knowledge of U.S. foreign policy in the years 1791 to 1812. Yet the questions are different in terms of the expected answer. Question 5 asks *Why?*—"The reason or purpose; on what account"—and the sample asks *How?*—"The manner, degree, state"—by which we avoided war in the first 23 years of our nation's history. These two questions were included to show the similarity of *Why? and How?* questions, but also to show what a difference there can be. They also illustrate how carefully questions are constructed in order to extract the expected answer and how carefully they must be analyzed. They seem so much alike, but each question seeks a different answer.

Multiple-Choice Questions— How? Why? Cause-and-Effect

The majority of multiple-choice questions are based on those very important six little words—*Who? What? When? Where? Why? How?* How often have you been asked questions such as, "Who won the Battle of Tippecanoe?" or "When was the Battle of New Orleans fought?" or "Where was the Cumberland Road?" These questions lend themselves naturally to short, factual answers easily incorporated into multiple-choice questions.

The *When?* multiple-choice type of question was analyzed in Chapter 1. *When?* multiple-choice questions are those requiring a knowledge of dates or chronology. *Where?* multiple-choice questions require geographic information. Sometimes these questions involve maps, as in the sample multiple-choice questions in Chapters 1 and 2, and sometimes they simply require factual recall of places. We will consider *Where?* questions and particularly multiple-choice map questions in Chapter 4. *Who?* and *What?* are behind the majority of the remainder of multiple-choice questions. They are usually quite direct and rather easy *if* you know the facts. However, some multiple-choice questions, particularly the more complex ones, require *How?* or *Why?* knowledge. These *How?* or *Why?* multiple-choice questions are really designed to test the student's ability to analyze the cause-and-effect relationships that underlie, as has been stated several times, the whole interpretation of history in Western civilization. Questions will appear on the multiple-choice section of the AP exam in many forms. For example, a cause-and-effect relationship is often sought without using *Why?* or *How?* In such questions you can easily tell a causal relationship is asked for by switching the wording of the question to use *How?* or *Why?* Sample question 2 illustrates this and will be discussed below.

The chronological-type question discussed in Chapter 1 can be a way of asking a *Why?* or *How?* question. Very often the student will be asked to learn chronology, such as the British acts that led to the Revolution, because the teacher wants the student to understand how one event has caused another. As you develop chronologies and time charts, use them as keys to cause-and-effect relationships. This will help you a great deal in answering some multiple-choice questions. Do not use them simply as lists of dates to be learned.

Many times a seventh little word, *Which?*, will be used to introduce a *Why?* or *How?* question. *Which?* is an undeclinable, both singular and plural pronoun used to refer to objects, while *Who?* is used to refer to persons or animate objects. Therefore, everything that has been said about *Who?* also refers to *Which?* The word *which* can also be used as an adjective; it then seeks the one or ones out of a group that are most relevant to the question asked. Sample question 1 provides a good example of a *Which?* question.

Sample Question 1

Which of the following was NOT a cause of John Adams's defeat in the presidential election of 1800?
  (A) The Alien and Sedition Acts
  (B) The XYZ Affair
  (C) Alexander Hamilton's disagreement with John Adams
  (D) The British impressment of American sailors
  (E) The failure of Adams to support war with France

Comments on Question 1

It should be obvious that the question is asking a *Why?* question and could be worded, "Why did John Adams lose the presidential election of 1800?" It is an excellent example of a *Which?* question when *Which?* is used as an adjective asking which one. To answer this question the student must not only know the facts, such as the XYZ Affair and the meaning of impressment, which are presented as possible answers to the question; he or she must also understand a cause-and-effect relationship. In simplest terms, we are acknowledging that Adams was defeated for many reasons, and the student is expected to know the reasons. Since the word *cause* is used in the question, it should be obvious that a cause-and-effect relationship is being sought.

The correct answer would be D, "The British impressment of American sailors." Although the British were still following this practice, it was of minor significance in 1800 compared with our relations with France. Hamilton and the war faction of the Federalist party wanted to fight France, so Hamilton attacked Adams when he refused to support the war. The XYZ Affair in Adams' presidency illustrated the tension in our relations with France, and the Alien and Sedition Acts were part of our preparation for war. The XYZ Affair and the Alien and Sedition Acts antagonized many citizens who therefore voted for Jefferson and the Republicans.

Not all multiple-choice questions asking a *How?* or *Why?* question are as obvious. For instance, another question might ask the following.

Sample Question 2

> The declaration of war against the British in 1812 illustrates the importance of the
>   (A) establishment of a regular army
>   (B) Native Americans in the frontier area
>   (C) Congressional representatives from the newly admitted western states
>   (D) growth of manufacture in New England
>   (E) Department of the Navy

Comments on Question 2

Again the question does not use a little word, but the question is asking, "How did the declaration of war in 1812 get passed?" or "Why did we go to war in 1812?" The question does not mention the words *cause* or *effect,* but essentially a cause-and-effect relationship is being sought. The student must know what issues led to the War of 1812, and from that knowledge he or she must analyze the choices offered. It is a complex process, but it illustrates how many forms of multiple-choice questions seek cause-and-effect relationships and are really asking *How?* or *Why?* questions in shorthand form. The same analytical process and the same type of information is required to deal with the multiple-choice question, which seeks a cause-and-effect relationship, as is needed to write an essay on such questions. To repeat, the six little words are crucial in developing an understanding of history and should be continually used as you study.

The correct answer is C. The major force in pushing for war were the so-called War Hawks, the young Congressional representatives from the new western states. Our army and navy were unimportant at the time. The Native Americans were a concern, but their activities did not cause this war—in fact, General William H. Harrison had defeated the Indians at the Battle of Tippecanoe in 1811. New Englanders generally opposed the war and voted against it in Congress. If it had not been for the representatives of the new states, we would not have fought the War of 1812.

Other Ways to Phrase Cause-and-Effect Questions

The following forms of multiple-choice questions all seek a cause-and-effect relationship. They are asking *How?* or *Why?* It is important to understand in how many different ways questions can be asked.

1. The chief reason for the formation of the party known as the Jeffersonian Republicans was . . .
2. Because of the attitude of the frontier settlers toward whiskey, the first major domestic crisis under the Constitution of 1789 involved . . .
3. The impressment of American sailors by the British led the United States to . . .
4. The Hartford Convention of 1815 was a result of . . .
5. The Jeffersonian Republicans supported the French in the years immediately after the start of the French Revolution because . . .
6. Which of the following was most directly responsible for Napoleon's offer to sell Louisiana to the United States . . .?
7. The XYZ Affair affected relations between the United States and France by . . .
8. How did members of the Federalist party respond to Washington's Proclamation of Neutrality in 1793 . . .?

9. The chief reaction to Jay's Treaty in 1794 was . . .?
10. Why do the terms of the Treaty of Ghent suggest that the War of 1812 was a useless undertaking . . .?

As you analyze these, you will realize that there are many ways to phrase such questions. Practice making up such questions as you study American history. Involve yourself in the material as a teacher would. Look for relationships, make up questions about the relationships, and see how many different ways you can phrase questions to obtain the information sought using the six little words. These words can be your greatest friends when studying history, so never forget to ask as you study American history—*Who? What? When? Where? Why? How?*

Practice Multiple-Choice Questions

1. The Rush Bagot Agreement called for
   (A) the expulsion of the British from Canada
   (B) a new boundary in Florida
   (C) the expulsion of aliens
   (D) mutual disarmament of the Great Lakes
   (E) commemoration of Perry's victory

2. Which of the following is NOT true concerning the Treaty of Ghent?
   (A) It was signed before Jackson's victory at New Orleans.
   (B) It stated the British would rebuild the burned city of Washington.
   (C) It referred boundary disputes to arbitration committees.
   (D) It called for no exchange of territory.
   (E) It made no reference to impressment.

3. Who of the following did NOT hold Federalist ideas?
   (A) Alexander Hamilton   (D) John Marshall
   (B) George Washington   (E) Albert Gallatin
   (C) John Adams

4. Which of the following treaties granted the right of navigation on the Mississippi to the United States?
   (A) Pinckney's Treaty   (D) Treaty of Utrecht
   (B) Jay's Treaty   (E) Treaty of Ghent
   (C) Treaty of Greenville

Questions 5–6 refer to the following map:

5. Which state's southern boundary of 36°30′ was the basis of the Compromise of 1820?
   (A) 1   (D) 4
   (B) 2   (E) 5
   (C) 3

6. What state did Henry Clay represent in the U.S. House of Representatives?
   (A) 1   (D) 4
   (B) 2   (E) 5
   (C) 3

7. How would one best explain the location of Washington, D.C.?
   (A) It was at a natural ford in the Potomac River.
   (B) The rapids in the river provided power for water mills.
   (C) It was convenient to George Washington's home at Mount Vernon.
   (D) It was selected as a compromise between the claims of New York, Boston, Princeton, and Philadelphia.
   (E) The land was granted by the state of Maryland to the federal government as the site of the capital city.

8. Why would the average frontier settler in Illinois most likely support the United States' acquisition of New Orleans?
   (A) It would provide a good market for midwestern corn.
   (B) It would prove the nation supported expansion.
   (C) It would provide convenient access to a large slave market.
   (D) It controlled the Mississippi River trade route.
   (E) It was an urban center with a cosmopolitan lifestyle.

Questions 9–10 refer to the following quotation:

"Now it appears . . . that this general principle is inherent in the very definition of government, and essential to every step of the progress to be made by that United States, namely: that every power vested in a government is in its nature sovereign, and includes, . . . , a right to employ all the means requisite and fairly applicable to the attainment of the ends of such power . . . which are not precluded (denied) by restrictions . . . in the Constitution, or not immoral, or not contrary to the essential ends of political society . . . "

9. The above quotation expressed the position on the Constitution advocated by a
   (A) states-righter
   (B) loose constructionist
   (C) Federalist
   (D) Jeffersonian
   (E) strict constructionist

10. The above quotation is most likely from
    (A) Washington's Farewell Address
    (B) The "Kentucky Resolutions"
    (C) Jefferson's "Letter on the Constitutionality of a National Bank"
    (D) Hamilton's "Letter on the Constitutionality of a National Bank"
    (E) Marshall's decision in *McCulloch v. Maryland*

11. " . . . How unfortunate, and how much is it to be regretted then, that whilst we are encompassed on all sides with avowed enemies and insidious friends, that internal dissensions should be harrowing and tearing our vitals. The last, to me, is the most serious, the most alarming, and the most afflicting of the two. And without more charity for the opinions and acts of one another in governmental matters, . . . , I believe it will be difficult, if not impracticable, to manage the reins of government or to keep the parts of it together . . .

    The author of the above quotation is concerned with the
    (A) threat of foreign enemies
    (B) problem of spies within the government
    (C) best way to organize dissension
    (D) problem of states' rights
    (E) issue of faction or party in government

12. Which one of the following events did NOT have a direct connection to the international conflict between England and France in the years after 1789?
    (A) Alien and Sedition Acts
    (B) Louisiana Purchase
    (C) Embargo Act of 1807
    (D) Macon's Bill Number Two
    (E) Ban on the importation of slaves

Answers and Answer
Explanations

1.	D	2.	B	3.	E	4.	A
5.	A	6.	E	7.	E	8.	D
9.	B	10.	D	11.	E	12.	E

1. (D) The Rush Bagot Agreement between the United States and Great Britain in 1817 established the principle of the undefended border between Britain's Canadian colony and the United States. It called for the disarming of the Great Lakes. It was a result of an arbitration committee established under the terms of the Treaty of Ghent in 1814 and illustrates the growing cooperation between the United States and Great Britain.

2. (B) The Treaty of Ghent in 1814 essentially reestablished the situation as it existed before the war. Those issues that had led to war were not mentioned, and the British made no offer to repair damages inflicted during the war, such as their burning of the nation's capital.

3. (E) A. Gallatin was Jefferson's very successful secretary of the treasury and a Jeffersonian Republican. The other four men all supported Federalist ideas.

4. (A) Pinckney's Treaty with Spain was signed in 1795. It permitted navigation on the Mississippi. At the time Spain owned the Louisiana Territory and controlled the city of New Orleans, so Spain controlled navigation by owning one side of the river and the port at the mouth. France later acquired Louisiana from Spain and we bought the territory from France in 1803. The other treaties dealt with various international issues in the years 1713–1814.

5. (A) The southern boundary of Missouri is the parallel 36°30′, which, with the exception of Missouri, became the boundary between slave and free states in the area of the Louisiana Purchase, according to the terms of the Missouri Compromise of 1820.

6. (E) Henry Clay, a War Hawk elected to Congress first in 1812, represented Kentucky.

7. (E) The state of Maryland granted the site of Washington, D.C., to the federal government as the site of the federal capital. It was a compromise location between the North and the South but not between the cities listed. It did not grow up as so many cities did because of fords or water power. Being close to Washington's home in Mount Vernon had no bearing on the situation, as New York City served as the capital throughout Washington's presidency.

8. (D) A frontier settler in Illinois would most likely support the acquisition of New Orleans because it controlled the Mississippi River trade route to the ocean and thus to the East Coast, Europe, and the Caribbean. Illinois was a non-slave state, so there would be no interest in the slave market. New Orleans would provide only a small market for corn. The other two are true of New Orleans but would have little importance to a frontier settler as far away as Illinois.

9. (B) The quotation expresses the idea of loose construction of the Constitution, also referred to as the doctrine of implied powers. It says that if a power is *not* specifically *denied* in the Constitution, is not immoral or opposed to the ends of political unity, and is needed to carry out one of the powers expressly mentioned in the Constitution, then the federal government should have that power. Loose construction has been advocated by different parties at different times. Usually the party in power supports the concept. The Federalists did in the 1790s, but opposed loose construction at the time of the Louisiana Purchase and after 1812. The Jeffersonians opposed it during John Adams' administration.

10. (D) The quotation is from Alexander Hamilton's "Letter on the Constitutionality of a National Bank," a strong statement on loose construction, which was written in opposition to Jefferson's statement on the Bank, a statement that opposed a bank since the power to establish one was not specifically mentioned in the Constitution. At that time, 1790, Jefferson was a strict constructionist. Marshall supported the concept of implied powers in *Marbury v. Madison*.

11. (E) The author of this quotation, George Washington, was greatly concerned about factions (division or disagreements that led to the formation of political parties) in the government. He believed, as indicated here, that unity against the foreign foe was essential and that all groups within the nation should work together for the benefit of the new country.

12. (E) The ban on the importation of slaves after 1808 was part of Article I, Section 9 of the Constitution written in 1787 and adopted in 1789 before the outbreak of conflict between England and France after the start of the French Revolution. The other choices all had a direct connection to the conflict. The Alien and Sedition Acts were passed by the Federalists in 1798 to control the impact of French revolutionary ideas and actions on the United States. The Louisiana Purchase of 1803 was possible because Napoleon, ruler of France, needed funds to prepare his planned invasion of England, believed he could not defend the area from possible English attack, and had lost interest in his plan for an empire in the new world. The Embargo of 1807 was Jefferson's attempt to avoid U.S. involvement in the conflict and Macon's Bill Number Two was President Madison's effort to do the same.

Bibliography

The following books focus on different important issues of the years 1789–1824. To supplement your textbook, you may wish to read sections in different books about matters of particular interest to you.

Cunliffe, Marcus. *The Nation Takes Shape 1789–1837*. Chicago: University of Chicago Press, 1960.

Dayton. Duncan. *Lewis and Clark: An Illustrated History*. New York: A. A. Knopf, 1997.

Ellis, J. J. *Founding Brothers: The Revolutionary Generation*. New York: Vintage Books, 2002.

Goodman, Paul (*ed.*). *Federalists vs. the Jeffersonian Republicans* (Am. Problem Series). Melbourne, FL: Krieger, 1977.

Perkins, Dexter. *The Monroe Doctrine 1826–1867*. Magnolia, FL: Peter Smith, 1975.

Documents

Madison, James et al. *The Federalist Papers*. New York: Viking Penguin, 1987.

Grafton, John. *The Declaration of Independence and Other Great Documents of American History: 1775–1865*. Mineola, NY: Dover Publications, 2000.

Hamilton, Alexander et al. *The Federalist Papers*. New York: Mentor Books, 1999.

Biography

Flexner, T. J. *Washington: The Indispensable Man*. Boston: Little, Brown & Co., 1994.

McCullough, David. *John Adams*. New York: Touchstone Books, 2002.

Randall, W. S. *Thomas Jefferson: A Life*. New York: Perennial, 1994.

———. *Alexander Hamilton: A Life*. New York: HarperCollins, 2003.

Thayer, James B. et al. *John Marshall*. Chicago: University of Chicago Press, 1967.

PART THREE 4 Jackson and the West 1824–1850

Important Facets of This Period

Jacksonian Democracy and Manifest Destiny are the two chief issues of these years. Andrew Jackson, the dominant figure, is in the eyes of one historian, J. W. Ward, the symbol of an age. Other historians, while acknowledging the significance of the era, question the contributions Jackson made and the amount of democracy present. However, Jackson's name has been given to the period 1824–1837, the Age of Jackson, which is considered by some historians as the adolescence of the nation. In preparation for the Advanced Placement examination, every student should have a thorough understanding of Jackson's career and of the meaning of Jacksonian Democracy. Also, the concept of Manifest Destiny must be understood and the way Americans followed it to expand the nation.

The Age of Jackson was a period marked by many social and economic changes. The age is recognized as the start of the operation of the political system as we know it today. It was a time of contrasts—of great intolerance and of great concern for the underprivileged. Jackson's presidency was followed by economic depression and then by a decade of expansion for which the slogan became Manifest Destiny.

Manifest Destiny culminated in the acquisition of Oregon and the Mexican War. These events in turn opened up the issue of the spread of slavery, which was temporarily settled at the end of this time period with the Compromise of 1850.

Among the topics one would want to consider in studying these years would be the following:

1. The reasons for the breakup of the Era of Good Feelings, which culminated in the election of 1828
2. Jackson's "War on the Bank of the United States"
3. The tariff issue and Calhoun's ideas on nullification
4. The growth of sectionalism and the distinguishing features of the three sections—Northeast, South, and West
5. Emerging social concerns and attitudes as exemplified by educational, institutional, and literary developments
6. The Panic of 1837 and its impact upon the nation
7. Manifest Destiny and the presidency of James K. Polk
8. The Mexican War and its aftermath
9. The spread of slavery to new territories.

Sample Essay Question—In What Ways...?

The question that begins *In what ways* . . . is a common type of essay question and one that has many variations, such as *In what manner . . . ?* or *In what respects . . . ?* or *To what extent . . . ?* Basically, this form is a version of the simple *What?* type, but with the addition of the other words, the writer is given more specific direction as to what must be done. Therefore, in the *In what ways?* type, the important word becomes the one after *what.*

How do you approach answering an *In what ways?* question? The key word in this type of question is *ways.* The word *ways* implies a progression or movement from one point to another and suggests a chronological organization by which the writer can illustrate how an event or idea led to other events or ideas.

What do you do when you are asked to focus on the *manner* in which something occurred? The word *manner* means a mode of procedure or customary way of acting. The focus of the answer to this type of essay would be less on the sequence of events and more on what lay behind them. Why did they occur, or what made people act the way they did, would be the important part of the answer.

If you are asked *In what respects?* you are being asked about relationships again. *Respect* is defined as relation or relationship, regarding an act of noticing with attention. This version of the basic type is very similar to the *In what way?* version and would require a cause-and-effect approach with events carefully related together. You would want to dwell on the reasons, paying strict attention to all the *whys* and *wherefores* you can consider. There are other variations of the *In what ways?* type of question such as *to what extent?* The key is always to look at and analyze the word after *what.*

"Do You Agree or Disagree" Means You Must Argue Your Position

Sometimes the *To what extent?* variation will have added the phrase *Do you agree or disagree?* This phrase can be attached to many essay questions and simply reinforces the invitation to argument. **Remember, in every essay answer you are arguing a case as a lawyer or debater does**. You may take any personal view you wish on any issue, and the quality of your paper will be judged on how well you argue and prove your personal opinion or thesis. The *Do you agree or disagree?* phrase simply makes it clearer that your personal opinion is being sought. The phrase is another way of asking the writer to evaluate the statement, and much of what was said about that type of essay question in Part Two applies to any essay question in which you are asked to agree or disagree.

A typical *In what ways?* essay question is the following:

Sample Question

> In what ways did the emerging sectional conflicts within the United States manifest themselves in the election of Andrew Jackson and in the domestic policies of the nation in the years 1828–1837?

Comments on Sample Question

The question asks you to consider the "ways"—that is, the progression or movement from one point to another in which "the emerging sectional conflicts within the United States manifested themselves" in two areas. In order to answer the question you must know that the word *manifest* means to reveal or else you would be in trouble with the question. You must deal with the two areas also—the election of Andrew Jackson in 1828 and his domestic policies. It is important that both areas be treated thoroughly.

You will want to begin your analysis by deciding what the sectional conflicts were. If you cannot remember them, then this is not a question for you. If you do know them, then list the issues of the election of 1828 and Jackson's domestic policies. If you have knowledge of them, then you are ready to answer the question. After you have worked up notes or written your answer to this question following the Seven Steps in Essay Writing, you will want to read and judge the following student answer to the question.

Sample Answer

Andrew Jackson was elected president in 1828, having run and been defeated in 1824 by J. Q. Adams, whom he beat in 1828. The campaign was a dirty one, the first really dirty campaign. In fact, Jackson later felt that the accusations against his wife and her divorce from her first husband were the cause of her death, which took place early in his first administration.

J. Q. Adams was a very intelligent man, but he was not a very good president. This helped defeat him, as some members of his own party, including the later president, Van Buren, left Adams to support Jackson. Jackson, on the other hand, had proven himself a fine general by winning the Battle of New Orleans He was called Old Hickory and his supporters claimed he was born in a log cabin. Actually, Jackson was wealthy and had a beautiful plantation home, the Hermitage, but the log cabin idea caught on and many men running for office during our history have capitalized on their log cabin backgrounds.

When Jackson became president, he used the Spoils System to put his friends in office. He did not start the system, as was once believed, but he used it extensively. Jackson believed any American could operate the government, and since the government was the people's, he appointed ordinary citizens to fill important posts. Jackson also believed, since he was the only official in the federal government elected by all the people, that he represented the people. This encouraged him to act as a strong president. An example of this position is when Chief Justice Marshall declared in a case that Georgia had no claim to Indian territory in the state. Rather than enforce the ruling, which he disapproved of, Jackson said, "Marshall made the decision; let him enforce it." Along with the Spoils System, Jackson was known for the Kitchen Cabinet, which was made up of a group of his friends who gave him advice on various domestic and foreign issues. They did not hold government positions, yet they were more important than the regular cabinet.

During Jackson's administration, the sale of western lands was important. There was a lot of speculation in the land sales and this led to inflation, which Jackson didn't like. He therefore issued the "specie circular," which forced people to pay for lands with gold or silver. This was a cause of the Panic of 1837.

The name Jackson is connected with the word *democracy*. Many historians believe the nation really became democratic during the 1830s. To support this idea they report the spread of universal male suffrage. Also, behind this coming of age of democracy are many other important developments, such as the spread of free public schools, the growing rate of immigration, the growth of industry, and the rise of labor unions, which supported the common man. Industry grew the most in the North, and the South remained agricultural. The West wanted roads and transportation. The idea emerged to have a high tariff on imports to help the North's industry and to use the money to build roads. The South didn't like the high tariff since they imported many goods. The tariff was a major issue during Jackson's presidency. Another issue of Jackson's time was the bank issue, which involved a long fight with Nicholas Biddle and a refusal to recharter the Second Bank. Then there were problems with Indians, England, and picking Jackson's successor. These all affected different people and sections.

Questions about the Sample Answer

As in the case of the other sample essays, reflect on this one before you read the teacher comments. The making of a formal outline of this answer will help you better understand what the writer has done. What are its good features? What are its bad features? Do you think the writer followed the Seven Steps in Essay Writing? What grade would you give to it? What advice do you have for this student? Have you ever written an essay similar to this one? What did the teacher tell you?

Teacher Comments on Sample Answer

"The writer of this essay has plenty of important and accurate factual information at his or her command, but he or she has simply spewed it out with no reference to the question at all. It is an unfortunate case of rushing into answering a question. The writer has focused on a few words in the question, in this case *election* and *Andrew Jackson,* and written what he knew about them with no reference to how the words are used in the question. The student's references to Van Buren's desertion of Adams, to the "specie circular," to the purchase of western lands, to the North, South, West split over internal improvements, and to the tariff reveal that he or she has valuable information to develop a viewpoint on "emerging sectional conflicts." Unfortunately, in no place does the student present a personal viewpoint or thesis on the topic under consideration, nor is the topic of the question mentioned. A thesis is badly needed. The writer has left out the two essentials of a good opening and has clearly not analyzed the question.

"The writer presents detailed information on the Spoils System, the Kitchen Cabinet, and Jacksonian Democracy. All of these items could have been used to illustrate sectional differences, although the Kitchen Cabinet may be a little far-fetched as an illustration. Still, the idea of the use of friends and the common people to run the government could be used to illustrate the change in government brought about when the West took the presidency from the educated, aristocratic East.

"The writer of the essay uses several paragraphs, but the last one includes several ideas—democracy, industry, tariff, and Bank—which should be presented in separate paragraphs. There is no clear linkage of the paragraphs and the organization—a mixture of topic and chronology—is confusing and seems to follow a free association of ideas rather than any formal structure. Finally, the essay just stops; there is no conclusion. Therefore, in spite of the fine information this writer has, the failure to answer the question and the poor essay style earned a low grade. It is an all too common failure among students. It is particularly unfortunate in this case since the student obviously is bright and knowledgeable. If the student had thought before writing and used the Seven Steps, with the information presented, he or she should have been able to write a fine essay and to earn a very good or outstanding grade."

Practice Essay Questions

The above student essay clearly demonstrates the importance of the Seven Steps in Essay Writing. Before you read and prepare the answer to the following essay questions, you may want to check back to Part Two and review these Seven Steps in Essay Writing. Also, as you prepare to deal with these five essays, do not forget our image of the flashlight. Your essay needs a beam to catch the reader, connected batteries to make the beam shine, and a cap to hold the batteries in contact and to make the whole flashlight work.

1. In what ways did the concept of Manifest Destiny affect the foreign and domestic policies of the United States in the years 1840–1850?

2. To what extent did Jacksonian Democracy reflect social and economic developments in the nation?

3. In what respects did TWO of the following represent in their expressed opinions and actions the viewpoint of the section of the nation from which he came?
   Calhoun—The South
   Clay—The West
   Webster—New England

4. "Both the Jacksonian Democrats between 1828 and 1836 and the Populists between 1890 and 1896 wanted to eliminate special privilege in American society. The Jacksonian Democrats succeeded; the Populists failed." Assess the validity of this view.

5. In what manner did the Jacksonian Revolution mark the establishment of democracy in America, whereas the Jeffersonian Revolution merely marked the arrival of a new party in political power?

Comments on Question 1

Question 1 is typical of the *In what ways?* type of question. It is seeking a cause-and-effect relationship as in a *What?* question, and it asks you to present the manner in which this relationship came about. This particular question is dependent upon your understanding the concept of Manifest Destiny.* This is one of those phrases students should know; it summarizes a whole series of attitudes and beliefs held by the Americans at a particular point in history. Once you have the meaning of the phrase clear in your mind, then you should list

---

* Manifest Destiny summarizes the idea that it was the destiny of the United States to control the continent. The idea guided most American attitudes on foreign policy in the late 1830s and '40s. Americans then believed their destiny should be manifest or obvious and clear to everyone, especially all foreigners.

some of the foreign and domestic issues of the years 1840 to 1850. Once you have done that, you will want to ask yourself the question, "How did Manifest Destiny relate to the issues listed?" Your answer to that question will be your thesis; your list of issues should provide organizational clues, and so you should be ready to write.

Comments on Question 2

The second question is one variation on the *In what ways?* type discussed above. The *To what extent?* form is a *What?* question seeking cause-and-effect relations, but it clearly asks for your personal opinion about the question and in that sense it is asking you to agree or disagree with the material. This particular question seeks your judgment on the relationship between Jacksonian Democracy and social and economic development. It is a good example of a question dealing with social history. It asks you to focus on social and economic developments and determine whether they are causes of or simply reflections of political changes and developments. This is an interesting question and one of the first sample questions in this book to require a thorough knowledge of social developments. It is a difficult question, which may be hard to organize, but if you struggle with it, the personal satisfaction gained from writing a good answer will be great.

Comments on Question 3

The third question, an *In what respects?* form, is another variation on the *In what ways?* type. It is another one of those questions in which a personal opinion may appear not to be needed, but as always, you must make and express a judgment. In this case you must know the opinions and actions of at least two of three important leaders of the period before 1850 and you must know the viewpoints of the major sections of the nation in those years. Finally, you must decide if two men's opinions and actions reflect the ideas of their section of the country. If you are in command of details involving all of these points, then you can develop your thesis and prepare to answer the question. In this question the obvious organizational format would be to discuss each man in turn and write introductory and concluding paragraphs that tie the three men together with the general topic.

Comments on Question 4

This is a typical *Assess the Validity* (*Evaluate This Statement*) type of question discussed in Chapter 1. The quotation asks you to deal with two specific movements in American history in two different periods. They are major movements that all students should be familiar with, but the focus of the question is on eliminating "special privilege" in American life—an aspect of these movements that may not be as familiar. The question illustrates how an AP examination question may focus on an unusual aspect of the period. If you are not in control of such information, it would be wise not to attempt the question, but if you are, it is not a difficult question. In this case, once you have analyzed what you know about eliminating special privilege in these two eras, you must decide if you agree that the Jacksonians were successful and the Populists were not. Obviously, your decision on this issue will provide you with the thesis statement. There are several ways to organize the answer. You can write about the Jacksonians and then the Populists separately or you might find issues, such as the monopoly of transportation, that appeared in both time periods and discuss how each group handled it.

**Comments on
Question 5**

The last question presents the *In what manner?* variation of the *In what ways?* form. The question asks for a comparison of time periods, and in this case you are comparing two periods with which you should be familiar by now if you are studying American history chronologically as you read this book. The issue raised—when did the United States become a democracy?—is one investigated in most U.S. history courses. The Jackson and Jefferson revolutions are often compared. The question takes an extreme position, and you should be able to react strongly with a personal opinion. The facts should then follow, and they should supply you with an organizational framework. Finding such a framework may be the most difficult task with this question.

Multiple-Choice Questions—Maps

As indicated when discussing the sample essay in Part Two, many historians believe that geography or environmental factors are at the heart of history. They believe these factors determine and control the choices people can make about their lives. This is perhaps an extreme interpretation, but it does illustrate how central geography is for understanding history. For you, as a student of American history, geography must be learned and understood. A knowledge of the location of states and of geographic features, such as rivers and mountains, and of their importance in the development of the nation and of the movement of people must be understood. Your knowledge of this information may be needed in essay answers (see question 3 on page 99), or it may be tested in multiple-choice questions. Map questions are a good example of a stimulus question. They also provide an excellent way to gain fundamental information about American history and to help the student review basic information. Map questions have already been included in the sample multiple-choice questions in Chapters 1, 2, and 3, and will be included in the remaining chapters. The following examples of multiple-choice questions involving maps will illustrate the wide range of questions that can be asked based directly on maps and on the analysis of maps. Many other questions might be asked in addition to these. These questions should make you realize the importance of geography, of studying the maps in the textbooks, and of locating places where events took place as you read about those events.

Sample Questions 1–3

TERRITORIAL ACQUISITIONS
1783–1853

Oregon Country,
British Claims
Extinguished
1846

Louisiana Purchase
from France
1803

United States
1783

Mexican Cession
1848

Gadsden Purchase
from Mexico
1853

Texas Annexed
1845

Florida Purchase
from Spain
1821

1. The map indicates our largest single territorial acquisition after
   independence was the
   (A) Oregon Country
   (B) Mexican Cession
   (C) Gadsden Purchase
   (D) Louisiana Purchase
   (E) Florida Purchase

2. The Gadsden Purchase was particularly important because it
   (A) gave us a more defensible border with Mexico
   (B) included a new source of gold
   (C) included the best southern route for a railroad to the West
       Coast
   (D) provided land for an Indian reservation
   (E) smoothed our relations with Mexico after the strain of the
       Mexican War

3. The map indicates the period of greatest territorial growth of the
   United States was in the decade
   (A) 1790–1800
   (B) 1800–1810
   (C) 1820–1830
   (D) 1840–1850
   (E) 1850–1860

**Comments on
Questions 1–3**

Question 1 assumes that you can read a very familiar map. There should be no question that the Louisiana Purchase was the largest single territorial acquisition shown on the map. You may want to say Alaska, but it is *not* on the map and *not* offered as a choice. Sometimes your recall knowledge will *not* be offered as a choice for an answer, and then you must analyze the data given to pick the best answer from the choices.

Question 2 tests learned knowledge. There is no way from looking at the map that you will know that the Gadsden Purchase included the best southern route for a railroad to the West Coast. That is something you should have learned, although you might have figured it out by eliminating the other choices or by realizing railroads were of growing significance in the 1850s and the purchase is on the extreme southern border. Some map questions will simply test your factual recall.

Question 3 requires that you combine territories acquired in the same decade to determine in which decade the nation grew the most. Although the largest single territory acquired before 1853 was Louisiana in 1803, we acquired more territory in three different sections in the decade of the 1840s. The question is an easy test of map-reading skill.

Sample Questions 4–5

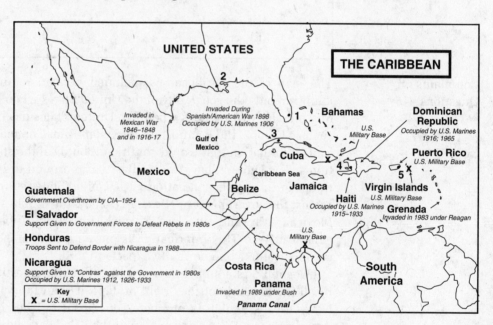

4. Information presented on the above map of the Caribbean would support all of the following EXCEPT
   (A) The United States has military bases ringing the Caribbean
   (B) The United States has not always supported the government of Caribbean nations
   (C) The United States has sent occupation troops to several Caribbean nations
   (D) President Roosevelt recognized the independence of Panama immediately after Panama separated from Colombia
   (E) The United States has fought wars in Caribbean nations

5. United States Trade expanded when the United States acquired the "right of deposit" at the location identified on the map as
   (A) 1
   (B) 2
   (C) 3
   (D) 4
   (E) 5

Comments on Questions 4–5

The map of the Caribbean is included here to remind you that you must know not only the geography of the United States when studying American history but also that of areas where the United States has been involved overseas, such as Europe, the Pacific, and the Asian Rim. The map of the Caribbean presents information that would confirm all but D of the statements given in question 4. The United States has military bases around the Caribbean and has sent troops to occupy several nations. The United States supported the Contra rebels against the government of Nicaragua. The United States invaded Mexico in the Mexican War and attacked Spanish forces in Cuba during the Spanish-American War. This information is placed on the map in addition to the geographic features one normally expects to find.

Question 5 is a straightforward identification question that requires you to recall the meaning of the "right of deposit" and to connect it with the city of New Orleans, which is number 2 on the map. The right of deposit allowed Americans to unload the goods from their flatboats, which had come down the Mississippi River onto oceangoing vessels without paying import duties on the goods. This allowed trade to expand. The other locations are all important ones for United States–Caribbean relations but do not relate to the right of deposit. Miami is number 1; 3 is Havana, Cuba; 4 is Port-au-Prince, Haiti; 5 is San Juan, Puerto Rico.

Sample Question 6

NATIVE AMERICAN LAND CESSIONS

6. From studying this map, one could conclude that
    (A) Native Americans ceded large tracts of land along the Atlantic coast to white settlers prior to the writing of the Constitution.
    (B) Native Americans and white settlers believed in treaties
    (C) white settlers were greedy for land
    (D) the Native Americans made money from the sale of lands
    (E) the Supreme Court under Marshall protected the Cherokee lands in Georgia

Comments on Question 6

Question 6 offers several choices that are true statements but for which there is no evidence on the map. It is important to realize there are limits as to what can be proven by a map. The Supreme Court under Marshall did protect Cherokee lands and white settlers were greedy, but the map doesn't prove it—it may suggest it, but there may have been other motivations for the Native American cession of lands. Belief in treaties and money is not mentioned on the map. You can, however, prove that Native Americans ceded land to the colonists along the mid-Atlantic seacoast prior to the writing of the Constitution. Statement A does appear true based on evidence from the map.

Sample Question 7

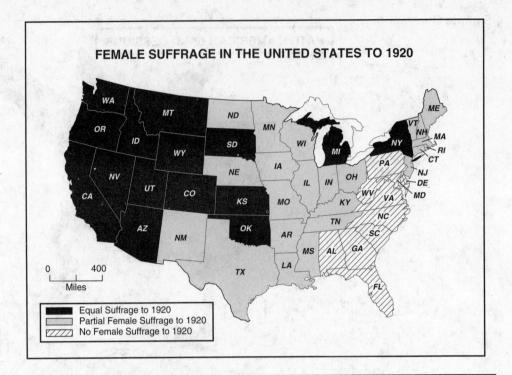

FEMALE SUFFRAGE IN THE UNITED STATES TO 1920

Equal Suffrage to 1920
Partial Female Suffrage to 1920
No Female Suffrage to 1920

7. Which of the following generalizations could NOT be supported by information presented in the map?
   (A) The western half of the nation was more responsive to the issue of women's suffrage than the eastern half.
   (B) States created from the Louisiana Purchase and Mexican Cession all had at least partial female suffrage by 1919.
   (C) It would be impossible in 1919 to get a constitutional amendment passed giving the vote to women.
   (D) States along the eastern seaboard would be most likely to reject a constitutional amendment giving the vote to women before 1919.
   (E) New York was the most liberal state of the original 13 on the issue of votes for women.

Comments on Question 7

Question 7 again asks you to confirm generalizations or speculations based on evidence from a map. It is a good test of map-reading ability. The map on female suffrage would support all the generalizations given, except that it would be impossible to get a constitutional amendment passed in 1919 giving the women the right to vote. You might assume this, but there is no way of knowing how the states with partial female suffrage would vote. You would *suspect* the states with equal suffrage would support the amendment and those states with no female suffrage would vote against the amendment, but there is no way to be sure from the map how they would vote or how that crucial group of 24 states with partial suffrage would vote. One must be careful not to assume too much from the map. The other four assumptions would appear quite safe. The states created from the Louisiana Purchase and the Mexican Cession, all west of the Mississippi River, had either granted equal or partial suffrage by 1920. Only states in the East had granted no suffrage by then. Of the original 13, only New York allowed women to vote equally with men. The western states all had granted female suffrage. If liberal means to grant suffrage, then the West and New York are liberal. It might be argued that there is no certainty the eastern seaboard would vote against a constitutional amendment. However, since they don't allow women to vote, it would seem likely they would vote against an amendment, which is all the question suggests. The generalization does not suggest certainty on this matter, as does option C with the word *impossible*.

Sample Questions 8–9

ADMISSION OF
NEW STATES
INTO THE
UNITED STATES
TO 1837

8. According to the map, AFTER the original 13 states, the first three states admitted to the Union were admitted in the following order
    (A) Ohio, Indiana, Illinois
    (B) Kentucky, Tennessee, Ohio
    (C) Kentucky, Ohio, Louisiana
    (D) Vermont, Kentucky, Ohio
    (E) Vermont, Kentucky, Tennessee

9. What was the first state admitted to the Union from the Louisiana Purchase territory?
    (A) Mississippi
    (B) Louisiana
    (C) Missouri
    (D) Ohio
    (E) Kentucky

Comments on Questions 8–9

Questions 8 and 9 are even less complicated tests of map-reading ability. Simply by reading the dates of admissions you can establish that the first states admitted to the Union in order after the original 13 were Vermont, Kentucky, Tennessee; of course, you must know which states were the original 13. A fast reading of the map might lead you to miss Vermont and then you would have picked the wrong answer—Kentucky, Tennessee, Ohio. Question 9 requires you to know the area of the Louisiana Purchase, and then you can easily see that Louisiana is the first state admitted to the Union from that territory.

Sample Questions 10–11

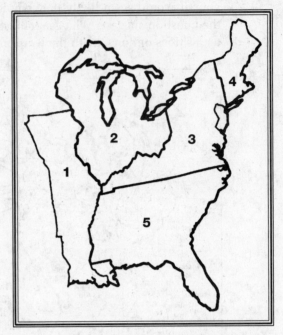

REGIONS OF THE UNITED STATES

10. The Northwest Ordinance applied to the region on the map numbered

(A) 1
(B) 2
(C) 3
(D) 4
(E) 5

11. On the map the region numbered 4 is considered the

(A) birthplace of all great presidents
(B) place of the first permanent European settlement in North America
(C) area of strongest support for the Mexican War
(D) center of American Transcendentalism
(E) region of outstanding development of new forms of land transportation

Comments on Questions 10–11

The map for questions 10 and 11 is a type commonly used in multiple-choice questions. The type requires that you know the geography of the United States so that you can identify regions, states, major cities, and territories. In question 10 you must know that the Northwest Ordinance applied to the Northwest Territory and be able to recognize this region on the map. It is 2—the area east of the Mississippi River, north of the Ohio River, south of the Great Lakes, and west of Pennsylvania. The question tests recall and factual geographic knowledge. Question 11 does the same but it is a little more sophisticated, requiring you to identify a region with an activity. It also tests literary knowledge—an example that map questions can be used to bring about a recall of all types of information. In this question, area 4 is New England, the center of Transcendentalism—the American version of a European philosophical movement. Its leaders were Emerson and Thoreau, but many other intellectual leaders of New England, such as Hawthorne and Parkman, were connected with Transcendentalism. Some people may believe that all great presidents are New Englanders, but that is ridiculous. The first permanent European settlement was the Spanish settlement at St. Augustine, Florida. New Englanders opposed the Mexican War, and new land transportation was developed in the West while New Englanders concentrated on clipper ships and the sea. Question 11 is a good use of the simple map question where you need to know the geography of the country and to recall factual information about it.

Sample Questions 12–13

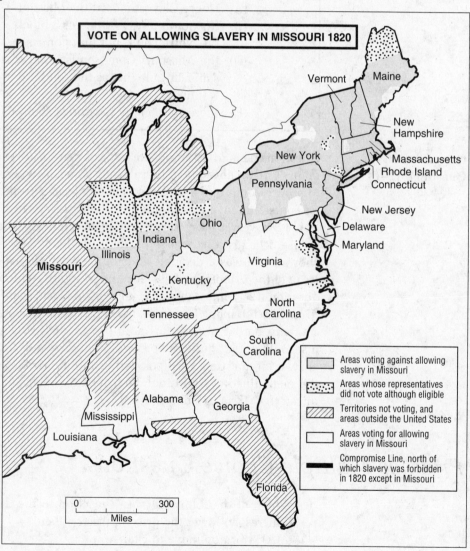

VOTE ON ALLOWING SLAVERY IN MISSOURI 1820

Legend:
- Areas voting against allowing slavery in Missouri
- Areas whose representatives did not vote although eligible
- Territories not voting, and areas outside the United States
- Areas voting for allowing slavery in Missouri
- Compromise Line, north of which slavery was forbidden in 1820 except in Missouri

0   300
Miles

12. According to the previous map, which one of the following statements is true?
    (A) There were no southern states in favor of the extension of slavery into Missouri.
    (B) Of those eligible, only delegates from slaveholding states failed to vote.
    (C) No New Englanders favored extending slavery into Missouri.
    (D) Florida was a non-slaveholding territory.
    (E) There was a decided division between the North and the South on the issue of the extension of slavery to Missouri.

13. The map illustrates that
    (A) Henry Clay proposed the Missouri Compromise
    (B) the South always voted as a block
    (C) the North could not unite on issues
    (D) the Missouri Compromise line was approximately the same latitude line as the southern border of Virginia and Kentucky
    (E) there were many territories about to be states

Comments on Questions 12–13

Questions 12 and 13 are good tests of map-reading skill. For number 12 the map clearly shows that there were some New Englanders in favor of the Missouri Compromise and that some delegates from all regions failed to vote. Of course the map shows nothing about slavery in Florida. Choice A of question 12 is very tricky. You might read it quickly and say it was true, but, of course, it is just the reverse of the truth. Be careful in your reading. The map shows there was a decided division between the North and the South on the issue of the extension of slavery into Missouri, which is the correct answer for question 12. You might have known this, but again your knowledge is confirmed by the map. The map also shows that the compromise line follows the southern border of Missouri and, if extended east, would run parallel to and just south of the southern border of Kentucky and Virginia, which is the correct answer for question 13. Block voting and unity cannot be shown by a map and the map illustrates nothing about territories becoming states nor who introduced the Missouri Compromise.

Practice Multiple-Choice Questions

1. Which of the following was a reaction to the desire of some members of Congress to lower the price of western land?
   (A) Mormon move to Utah
   (B) Hayne-Webster Debate
   (C) Seneca Falls Convention
   (D) American Colonization Society
   (E) Manifest Destiny

2. Jackson had the "specie circular" issued in 1836 because he
    (A) disliked the Bank of the United States
    (B) thought it would win his party the presidency
    (C) feared the high rate of debt and the speculation brought about by the sale of western land.
    (D) hoped it would force England to open West Indian ports
    (E) felt there was enough gold and silver in the country

3. All of the following men are connected with the development and admission of California to the union EXCEPT
    (A) Thomas Larkin   (D) Washington Irving
    (B) John Sutter   (E) John Slidell
    (C) John C. Fremont

4. Of the 19th-century inventions listed below, each is correctly paired with its inventor EXCEPT
    (A) Reaper—McCormack
    (B) Vulcanization of rubber—Goodyear
    (C) Sewing machine—Howe
    (D) Steamboat—Fulton
    (E) Telegraph—Bell

Questions 5–6 refer to the following quotation:

"The modifications of the existing (bank) charter proposed by this act are not such, in my view, as make it consistent with the rights of the States or the liberties of the people. . . . All the objectionable principles of the existing corporation, and most of its odious features, are retained . . .

"If we must have a bank with private stockholders, every consideration of sound policy and every impulse of American feeling admonishes that it should be *purely American.* Its stockholders should be composed exclusively of our own citizens, who at least ought to be friendly to our Government and willing to support it in times of difficulty and danger . . . To a bank exclusively of American stockholders, possessing the powers and privileges granted by this act, subscriptions for $200,000,000 could be readily obtained . . .

"It is maintained by the advocates of the bank that its constitutionality in all its features ought to be considered as settled by precedent and by the decision of the Supreme Court. To this conclusion I can not assent."

5. The author of the above quotation appears to believe all of the following EXCEPT
    (A) the Bank is not constitutional
    (B) it is dangerous to have foreign stockholders
    (C) stockholders should be friendly to the government
    (D) $200,000,000 cannot be raised by Americans
    (E) the Bank is not consistent with personal liberty

6. The opinion expressed in this quotation proved to be that held by the American people as indicated by
   (A) the victory of Andrew Jackson in the 1832 election
   (B) Nicholas Biddle's support of New England manufacture
   (C) the Webster Ashburton Treaty
   (D) Calhoun's doctrine of nullification
   (E) the essays of Ralph Waldo Emerson

7. The important foreign policy known as the Monroe Doctrine
   I. was first proposed by the British government to the United States
   II. was presented by President Monroe in a State of the Union message
   III. was designed to protect United States business interests in the Americas
   IV. suggested the United States would not become involved in European affairs
   (A) I and II
   (B) I, II, and III
   (C) I, II, and IV
   (D) II, III, and IV
   (E) I, II, III, and IV

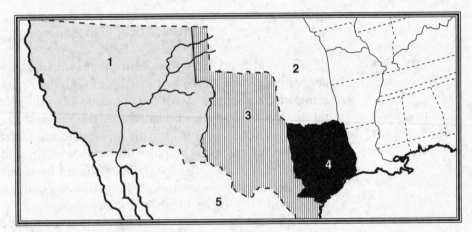

SOURCE: U.S. Bureau of the Census *Historical Statistics of the U.S., Colonial Times to 1957*.

8. On the map above the area numbered 4 was the
   (A) area where the U.S. Army was defeated by the Mexican Army in the Mexican War
   (B) Republic of Texas
   (C) southern area of the Louisiana Purchase
   (D) birthplace of Andrew Jackson
   (E) great cattle-grazing region of Texas

Questions 9–10 refer to the following chart

IMMIGRATION TO THE UNITED STATES

Year	Total	Gr. Britain	Ireland	Scandinavia	Germany	Poland
1820	8,385	2,410	3,614	23	968	5
1830	23,322	1,153	2,721	19	1,906	2
1840	84,066	2,613	39,340	207	29,704	5
1850	369,980	51,085	164,004	1,589	78,896	5

9. According to the chart on immigration, all of the following are true EXCEPT
   (A) more immigrants came from eastern Europe than from the British Isles
   (B) the total number of immigrants more than doubled each decade
   (C) Polish immigration remained rather constant
   (D) there was a very significant increase in immigration in 1850
   (E) the smallest number of immigrants from Great Britain arrived in the 1830s

10. The figures in the previous chart on immigration in the period 1820–1850 reveal that
    (A) the total immigration remained constant
    (B) Polish immigration increased in 1830
    (C) in each year shown, the Irish formed the largest single group of immigrants
    (D) British immigration declined over these years
    (E) Scandinavian immigrants formed a high percentage of the total immigration

11. Which of the following events occurred last?
    (A) Purchase of the Louisiana Territory
    (B) Lewis and Clark Expedition
    (C) Settlement of Independence, Missouri
    (D) Extensive use of the Oregon Trail
    (E) British sending of Vancouver to explore Puget Sound area

Fort Laramie, Wyoming, lithograph from *Fremont's First and Second Expeditions 1841–2–3*. Washington, D.C., Blair and Rives, 1845.

12. All of the following are indicated by the picture EXCEPT
   (A) U.S. civilians are using or staying near a Native American-type tepee
   (B) The large square structure left of the center of the picture is a fort
   (C) A number of people may be living in tepees outside the large square structure
   (D) Carts and horses are available for transportation for U.S. civilians
   (E) Traditional farming is not an important occupation for those living in the area

Answers and Answer Explanations

1.	B	**2.**	C	**3.**	D	**4.**	E
5.	D	**6.**	A	**7.**	C	**8.**	B
9.	A	**10.**	C	**11.**	D	**12.**	B

1. (B) The Hayne-Webster Debate had as its start a proposal to reduce the price of western land. It was one of the most important congressional debates of the 19th century. Its focus became the role of the federal government as opposed to that of state government.

2. (C) Although Jackson disliked the Bank of the United States, he also disliked paper currency, speculation, and the increase in the level of private debt. The "specie circular" required payment for western lands in gold or silver and was meant to cut down speculation and inflation.

3. (D) Washington Irving is an early American author and member of the Knickerbocker School. The other four men all played key roles in the acquisition of California.

4. (E) Inventions were important in stimulating the economic and industrial growth of the nation, especially of the Northeast. Except for the telegraph, which was invented by Morse and not Bell, these inventions were made before 1850 by the men indicated. Bell invented the telephone later in the century.

5. (D) An analysis of this quotation from Jackson's veto message of the bill renewing the charter of the Second Bank of the United States reveals that he believed $200,000,000 *could* be raised in the United States without foreign support. He also believed the other four points presented as possible choices.

6. (A) The American people apparently supported Jackson's position on the Bank since they overwhelmingly voted for him in 1832, and the Bank was a major issue of the campaign.

7. (C) The Monroe Doctrine was presented in a State of the Union message by President Monroe, developing a concept suggested by the British government. President Monroe indicated that the United States would stay out of the affairs of Europe just as he expected the European nations to stay out of the affairs of the Americas. United States business interests developed in the Americas but it was not part of the design of the Monroe Doctrine.

8. (B) Region 4 was the pre-Mexican War independent Republic of Texas.

9. (A) An understanding of immigration from different sections of Europe is an important aspect of the analysis of immigration to America and of this question. The question requires an understanding of European geography as does any analysis of European immigration. If you do not have this information, you would have difficulty with this question. It is therefore important to study maps of Europe and other parts of the world as you study American history relating to those regions. Before the 1890s the majority of immigrants came from western and northern Europe, England, Ireland, Scandinavia, and Germany, as this table clearly shows. Therefore, A is incorrect. Poland is the only eastern European country listed, and the number of immigrants is insignificant.

10. (C) The chart reveals that in each year reported, the Irish were the largest single group of immigrants. Scandinavian and Polish immigration was less than that from the British Isles, which makes choice A incorrect. Later in the century, immigration from eastern Europe did increase. Total immigration greatly increased. British immigration, except for one small drop reported in 1830, did also. Irish immigration remained large through these years. This is a good example of a stimulus question that requires good reading of charts.

11. (D) The Oregon Trail became important after the other events. Vancouver explored the Puget Sound area first. After Jefferson's purchase of the Louisiana Territory, he sent Lewis and Clark to explore it. Trails west were opened later. Independence, Missouri, was the starting point for the Oregon Trail and was settled before the Trail was used extensively.

12. (B) The picture is of a lithograph of Fort Laramie, Wyoming, found in *Fremont's First and Second Expeditions 1841–2–3*, Washington, D.C., Blair and Rives, 1845. J. C. Fremont, a captain in the army, led exploratory expeditions through the West in the early 1840s. He later ran for president. In the picture there is no clear indication that the large square structure is a fort; there are no soldiers, no guns, not even any flags flying on it. There are some men dressed in civilian clothes near a tepee, a type of North American Native American dwelling found in the Great Plains area. Next to the tepee are some carts and a horse. The U.S. flag is flying from a flagpole identifying the individuals and carts and horse as being from the United States. There are a number of tepees near the large square structure indicating a number of people may be living outside the structure. There is no indication whether those living in the tepees are Native Americans, although the three figures in the foreground suggest they might be. Nowhere in the picture is there any indication of farming of any kind, which suggests it was not important for those living in the area at the time of the picture. Chapter 6 includes a discussion of the use of photographs in multiple-choice questions.

Bibliography

Brooks, Van Wyck. *The Flowering of New England.* New York: AMS Press, 2003.

de Tocqueville, Alexis. *Democracy in America.* Richard D. Heffner (*ed.*). New York: Signet Classic, 2001.

Fish, C. E. *The Rise of the Common Man: 1830–1850.* Westport, CT: Greenwood, 1983.

Franklin, J. H. *From Slavery to Freedom.* New York: Alfred A. Knopf, Inc., 2000.

Hammond, Bray. *Banks and Politics in America, from Revolution to Civil War.* Princeton: Princeton University Press, 1991.

Mabee, Carlton, and Susan Newhouse. *Sojourner Truth: Slave, Prophet, Legend.* New York: New York University Press, 1995.

Merk, Frederick. *Manifest Destiny and Mission in American History.* New York: Cambridge: Harvard University Press, 1995.

Remini, R. V. *The Life of Andrew Jackson.* New York: Perennial, 2001.

Schlesinger, A. M. Jr. *The Age of Jackson.* Boston: Little, Brown & Co., 1988.

Stampp, K. M. *The Peculiar Institution.* New York: Vintage Books, 1989.

Ward, J. W. *Andrew Jackson—Symbol for An Age.* New York: Oxford University Press, 1962.

PART THREE **5** Coming of the Civil War,
Civil War, and Reconstruction
1850–1877

Important Facets of This Period

The Civil War has often been considered the great transitional point in American history. In this view the prewar period was one of territorial growth and the establishment of the framework of the nation. The Civil War intensified all the previous developments and precipitated rapid growth of the nation, which made it an industrial giant and a world power by 1900. Whether this view is valid you need to decide. It certainly is a thesis worth testing in your study of the history of this period.

This thesis permits a focus on the Civil War era and as is the case with the era of the American Revolution, the years 1850–1877 logically fall into three time units. The first, 1850–1860, covers those years when the union appeared to be moving inexorably toward war. The second unit encompasses the war years 1860–1865, and the third unit includes the postwar or Reconstruction era, 1865–1877. Factual information from all three periods will certainly be needed on any American history exam. Questions on these years may cover the entire time span, may require intensive knowledge of one period, or may ask for comparison among the three periods. In your study you may wish to break the time into the three units mentioned above, but be certain you understand the relationship between events in one period and the next.

Although historians place events in time units or periods as they attempt to make sense of the past, you must remember that the events occurred with no division between them. History occurs as a flowing stream. The image of pouring concrete to form a wall comes to mind. The historian sees the solid wall and draws lines on the concrete wall to make the wall appear to be a brick one. In history books we write as though the wall were made of separate bricks, but in reality the wall is one solid mass of material. The bricks help us to analyze, compartmentalize, and master details, but they are not the real history. If you keep this image in mind as you study the periods to which historians have assigned the events of history, you will never lose sight of the Western concept of the chronological interrelatedness of all historical developments.

Among the developments you will want to study in detail from the years 1850–1877 are the following:

1. Events leading to war, 1850–1860—political, economic, social, intellectual
2. Secession and the outbreak of war
3. Military and naval war strategy
4. The strengths and weaknesses of the Confederacy and the Union
5. International relations in the war and post-Civil War period
6. Reconstruction plans and policies

7. The presidency of Ulysses S. Grant
8. The social and intellectual changes that took place in both the South and North during the war and Reconstruction
9. The growth and development of the West
10. The election and compromise of 1876

Sample Essay Question—The DBQ

The DBQ or document-based question became a required part of the essay or free response section of the Advanced Placement examination in 1973. The DBQ is a unique type of question and a very important part of the examination. The DBQ essay answer receives 45 percent of the score given for the free response section of the exam. The remaining 55 percent is divided between the two required standard essays, which thus count 27.5 percent each. Your total score on the free response section counts for 50 percent of the exam score.

The DBQ is a special type of essay question. In the essay-type questions we have discussed so far you must recall all the data or factual material to use in your answer. In the DBQ some of the information you need is presented in documents. These documents may include maps, graphs, cartoons, photographs, and art as well as the printed word from many different sources—speeches, newspapers, diaries, novels, laws, legal decisions. **For the DBQ in its present format, you are expected to analyze and interpret the documents and *at the same time* relate the information in the documents and your analysis of it to the "mainstream," that is, the main chronological development, of American history. You must include in your answer information from this chronology that is not found in the documents.**

The question asked concerning these documents may be of any essay type. The fact that the form or wording of the DBQ may be the same as any essay type illustrates how important and widely applicable are the methods of question analysis presented in previous chapters and in the next three chapters. In answering the DBQ, you must begin by analyzing the question, the familiar first step in essay writing. After that step, the second step becomes slightly different. You will still need to make an outline or brief notes, but for the DBQ these notes must be *both* on your reading and analysis of the documents *and* on your recall of information that is relevant to the documents presented and to the question asked.

The DBQ Tests Analytical Skills

The reading and understanding of documents lies at the heart of the DBQ, but the real test of your ability is in how well you, the student, relate these documents to your understanding of the mainstream of United States history. The DBQ was added to the Advanced Placement examination as a means of testing your understanding of the role of the historian and to test your analytical and interpretive skills rather than merely to test your memory or recall skills. Many multiple-choice questions have been designed to test analytical skills, but they can test skills in a very limited way. The DBQ provides a much greater, in-depth test, since you are allowed 15 minutes to read, analyze the documents, and make notes, and 45 minutes in which to write your answer. For multiple-choice questions you have less than 1 minute to read, analyze, and decide on your answer for each question.

The goal of the DBQ is to present a question that will force students to combine their historical research and analytical techniques with their recall of historical data in order to answer the question. There is no way a student can memorize or become familiar with all the documents that might appear on the DBQ. The only way to prepare for it is to practice being a historian as you study. In answering questions in this book or writing for class, practice analyzing documents of all types, questioning statements made by the authors, seeking cause-and-effect relationships to illustrate your personal opinion on issues, and continually relating the information in documents you read to the "mainstream" issues in American history. The student who approaches all of the material in this way will do well on the DBQ.

Summary

In summary, the DBQ tests your ability to work with historical documents and your knowledge of the mainstream of American history. You are asked to do two related things in a unified essay: to formulate an answer derived from the evidence contained in the documents, as it relates to and has bearing on events in United States history that you must recall from your study; and where relevant to your answer, to assess the value of the documents as historical sources. Reference to historical facts and developments not mentioned in the documents must be included in your answer and, where information is taken from the documents, you should make reference to the documents. It is better not to quote the documents verbatim but rather to paraphrase them or refer to information in them.

Document-Based Question

The election of Lincoln and its relation to the abolition of slavery is the topic of the following sample DBQ. All courses in American history will include information on the abolitionist movement, the election of Abraham Lincoln, and the secession of the Confederate states and Lincoln's attitude toward slavery. This is "mainstream" information. The sample question requires that you have this information, but the documents also present other information that you might not have had at your command. In this question there are ten documents. Under the present DBQ format the number and length of documents and the type of documents will vary but there would rarely be more than ten.

Read the directions, the question, and the documents carefully.

Section II
Part A
Suggested Writing Time—45 minutes*

Directions: The following question requires you to construct a coherent essay that integrates your interpretation of documents A–J *and* your knowledge of the period referred to in the question. High scores will be earned only if you cite important evidence from the documents and include information from your knowledge of the period.

---

*In the general directions for Section II you will be given 15 minutes to read and analyze the documents and prepare your answer. Then you will have 45 minutes to write your DBQ answer.

1.   To what extent was the election of Abraham Lincoln a mandate for the abolition of slavery in the United States?

Document A

Source: Dan Stone and Abraham Lincoln, representatives from the county of Sangamon. Entry in the Journal of the House of Representatives of Illinois on March 3, 1837

The following protest was presented to the House, which was read and ordered to be spread on the journals, to-wit:

"Resolutions upon the subject of domestic slavery having passed both branches of the General Assembly at its present session, the undersigned hereby protest against the passage of the same.

"They believe that the institution of slavery is founded on both injustice and bad policy; but that the promulgation of abolition doctrines tends rather to increase than abate its evils.

"They believe that the Congress of the United States has no power, under the Constitution, to interfere with the institution of slavery in the different States.

"They believe that the Congress of the United States has the power, under the Constitution, to abolish slavery in the District of Columbia; but that the power ought not to be exercised unless at the request of the people of said District.

"The difference between these opinions and those contained in the said resolutions, is their reasoning for entering this protest."

Document B

Source: Letter from Abraham Lincoln to George Robertson in Lexington, Kentucky—August 15, 1855

My dear Sir, . . . You are not a friend of slavery in the abstract . . . you spoke of "the peaceful extinction of slavery" and used other expressions indicating your belief that the thing was, at some time, to have an end. Since then we have had thirty-six years of experience; and this experience has demonstrated, I think, that there is no peaceful extinction of slavery in prospect for us. The signal failure of Henry Clay and other good and great men, in 1849, to effect anything in favour of gradual emancipation in Kentucky, together with a thousand other signs, extinguishes that hope utterly. . . . When we were the political slaves of King George, and wanted to be free, we called the maxim that "all men are created equal" a self-evident truth; but now when we have grown fat, and have lost all dread of being slaves ourselves, we have become so greedy to be masters that we call the same maxim "a self-evident lie." The Fourth of July has not quite dwindled away; it is still a great day for burning fire-crackers!!

Our political problem now is, "Can we as a nation continue together permanently—forever—half slave, and half free?" The problem is too mighty for me. May God in his mercy superintend the solution.

Your much obliged friend, and humble servant,

Document C

Source: Abraham Lincoln in the Lincoln-Douglas Debate at Freeport, Illinois, September of 1858

In relation to that, I have my mind very distinctly made up. I should be exceedingly glad to see Slavery abolished in the District of Columbia. I believe that Congress possesses the constitutional power to abolish it. Yet as a member of Congress, I should not, with my present views, be in favor of endeavoring to abolish Slavery in the District of Columbia, unless it would be upon these conditions: First that the abolition should be gradual; second, that it should be on a vote of the majority of qualified voters in the District; and third, that compensation should be made to unwilling owners. With these three conditions, I confess I would be exceedingly glad to see Congress abolish Slavery in the District of Columbia, and in the language of Henry Clay, "sweep from our Capitol that foul blot upon our 'nation.'"

Document D

Source: Comments on the Lincoln-Douglas Freeport Debate from the *Louisville* [Kentucky] *Journal*, as quoted in the *Chicago Tribune*—September 4, 1858

According to Senator Douglas, the Territorial Legislatures, though prohibited by the Constitution from abolishing slavery within their respective jurisdictions, may lawfully abstain from enforcing the rights of slaveholders and so extinguish the institution by voluntary neglect . . . In the name of common sense and common fairness, if slavery is to be prohibited or abolished in the Territories by any legislative tribunal, let it be done by one in which the whole nation is represented, . . . let it be done by the people of the United States. . . . not squatter sovereignty. Senator Douglas, as we have seen, gives us the latter—Mr. Lincoln the former. Between the two, no intelligent, discerning patriot can hesitate a moment. Mr. Lincoln's position . . . is infinitely less unfriendly to the constitutional rights and just interests of the South. When, furthermore, we reflect that the Supreme Court has pronounced this identical position unconstitutional, and would nullify any Congressional legislation in pursuance of it, the practical consequence of Mr. Lincoln's error vanishes into a political dream.

Document E

Source: **Editorial from the Springfield, Illinois, *Register*—November 7, 1860**

THE QUESTION OF DISUNION

At the hour we write these lines, the American people, in all parts of the United States, are exercising their constitutional privilege of electing a president and vice-president of the United States for the next four years . . .

But, much as we may deplore the election of Lincoln, because of its calamitous consequences, we choose to put on record now, before the result of the election is declared, that under no circumstances, can disunion be the remedy or redress for the unfortunate choice. Mr. Lincoln may obtain a majority of the election college, and yet receive less than one-third of the popular vote, yet he will nevertheless be constitutionally elected.

. . . It has been proposed by those who seek a disruption of the Union, that in case Mr. Lincoln shall be elected president the southern states shall withdraw from the Union; . . . We wish to place on record now, that . . . such secession . . . will become rebellion and treason . . .

There is another class who propose to "submit" to the election of Lincoln, but who propose to secede when he shall attempt to do, or shall do, any unconstitutional act. We do not see that this proposed secession has any higher or more commendatory sanction in law or morals than that which is contingent upon Lincoln's election . . .

If Mr. Lincoln shall in any manner . . . violate the constitution . . . the constitution provides: "The president . . . shall be removed from office, on impeachment for, and conviction of treason, bribery, or other high crimes and misdemeanors." . . . We believe . . . the Senate would, upon a constitutional form of trial convict Abraham Lincoln and dismiss him from office . . .

Should Mr. Lincoln be elected, great as the calamity will prove to be, still we think it is the duty of every democrat to give to his administration (not his party) every aid and support that the government can constitutionally demand of citizens.

Document F

Source: Barron's Educational Series, Inc.

ELECTION OF 1860

Legend:
- Lincoln
- Douglas
- Breckinridge
- Bell
- Vote Divided

NEW JERSEY
Lincoln 4
Douglas 3

	Electoral Vote	Popular Vote	Percent of Popular vote
Lincoln	180	1,866,452	40
Douglas	12	1,375,157	29
Breckinridge	72	847,953	18
Bell	39	590,631	13
Total	303	4,680,193	

Document G

Source: Editorial from the Reading, Pennsylvania, *Berks and Schuylkill Journal*—December 15, 1860

"It is much to be regretted that in the present crisis of our national affairs, the disposition of events will be, to a great extent, in the hands of mere politicians; and that the sentiments of the masses will be scarcely known. The present unfortunate state of public feelings has, to a great extent, been created by ultra men on both sides, while we believe that the great body of the people, North and South, love the Union, and would deplore its dissolution as the greatest of earthly calamities, and a death blow to the cause of freedom throughout the world. . . . In so large a party as the Republican, it cannot but be supposed that a great variety of sentiment exists. There are, no doubt, many who voted for Lincoln, who are entirely indifferent to the subject of Slavery, who have never given it any consideration, and have no particular views in regard to it, while, on the other hand, many genuine abolitionists may have voted the ticket, though not the more rabid ones, for these refused to vote at all, and denounced Lincoln more bitterly than did any other of his opponents.

"The great mass of the Republican party hold the conservative views so often expressed by Lincoln himself."

Document H

Source: **South Carolina** *Declaration of Causes of Secession*—**December 24, 1860**

. . . A geographical line has been drawn across the Union, and all the States north of that line have united in the election of a man to the high office of President of the United States whose opinions and purposes are hostile to Slavery. He is to be intrusted with the administration of the common Government, because he has declared that "Government cannot endure permanently half slave, half free," and that the public mind must rest in the belief that Slavery is in the course of ultimate extinction.

We, therefore, the people of South Carolina . . . have solemnly declared that the Union heretofore existing between this State and the other States of North America is dissolved . . .

Document I

Source: **Abraham Lincoln's First Inaugural Address—March 4, 1861**

Apprehension seems to exist among the people of the Southern States that by the accession of a Republican administration their property and their peace and personal security are to be endangered. There has never been any reasonable cause for such apprehension. Indeed, the most ample evidence to the contrary has all the while existed and been open to their inspection. It is found in nearly all the published speeches of him who now addresses you. I do but quote from one of those speeches when I declare that "I have no purpose, directly or indirectly, to interfere with the institution of slavery in the States where it exists. I believe I have no lawful right to do so, and I have no inclination to do so." Those who nominated and elected me did so with full knowledge that I had made this and many similar declarations, and had never recanted them. And, more than this, they placed in the [party] platform [adopted at Chicago] for my acceptance, and as a law to themselves and to me, the clear and emphatic resolution which I now read:

> Resolved, That the maintenance inviolate of the rights of the States, and especially the right of each State to order and control its own domestic institutions according to its own judgment exclusively, is essential to that balance of power on which the perfection and endurance of our political fabric depend, and we denounce the lawless invasion by armed force of the soil of any State or Territory, no matter under what pretext, as among the gravest of crimes.

I now reiterate these sentiments; and, in doing so, I only press upon the public attention the most conclusive evidence of which the case is susceptible, that the property, peace, and security of no section are to be in any wise endangered by the now incoming administration . . .

Document J

Source: New Jersey Peace Resolutions—March 18, 1863

1. *Be it Resolved by the Senate and General Assembly of the State of New Jersey,* That this State, in promptly answering the calls made by the President of the United States, at and since the inauguration of the war, for troops and means to assist in maintaining the power and dignity of the Federal Government, believed and confided in the professions and declarations of the President of the United States, in his inaugural address . . .

. . . . (now we) make unto the Federal Government this our solemn

PROTEST

Against the power assumed in the proclamation (Emancipation Proclamation) of the President made January first, 1863, by which all the slaves in certain States and part of States are for ever set free; and against the expenditures of the public moneys for the emancipation of slaves or their support at any time, under any pretence whatever; . . .

Comments on the DBQ

All DBQs are divided into three parts. First are the general directions, second is the question itself, and third are the documents, which in this question include a map. Let us consider each of these three parts in turn.

The Directions Must Be Read Carefully

First, the directions specify the time allotted, which is 45 minutes for writing. The directions on the examination will indicate that you are to take 15 minutes to read the documents and to make notes. At the examination you will not be allowed to start writing your answer during these 15 minutes. If you finish reading and organizing your answer before the 15 minutes end, you may start preparing your other essay answers but do not rush your DBQ preparation. The examination papers you will be given include space for you to take notes, another indication that the Advanced Placement examination writers strongly support Step Two in Essay Writing. Incidentally, the directions also tell you where you are to write your answer—keep alert to such details in the directions for any exam. **Read all directions carefully; do not rush over them to get to the question**. This is a fundamental rule of all test taking. After taking notes and organizing your information, you have 45 minutes in which to write the answer.

The directions also indicate the purpose of the DBQ—when they state, ". . . a coherent essay that integrates your interpretation of documents A–J *and* your knowledge of the period referred to in the question." This idea is then repeated in the second sentence and links it to obtaining a "high score." These directions should leave no doubt as to what is wanted. **The DBQ is designed to test your ability to analyze the documents presented, to relate the material to the "mainstream" American history, and to write a unified essay expressing your personal opinion on the question raised**. The DBQ does *not* ask you to simply describe what each document includes; it requires information from the "mainstream" of American history not included in the documents; it requires a *unified* essay. Writing the essay should present no difficulty once you have analyzed the question and the documents.

The Question

The second part of the DBQ is the question itself. The question is a *To what extent?* type and, as indicated in Chapter 4, the key word here is *extent.* You are to determine, on the basis of the evidence presented and of your recall of American history, whether Lincoln's election as president of the United States was a mandate for the abolition of slavery in the United States. The word *mandate* may provide some difficulty for you. A mandate is an order. It may not be voiced directly, but rather it is implied by the circumstances. With this interpretation of the word, you can see that the question is asking you to determine if the people of the United States were ordering the abolition of slavery when they voted for Abraham Lincoln. As you will recall from your study, and as the documents imply, there were many different views as to what Lincoln stood for and what the election of 1860 meant. You must determine what your opinion is, and from this decide on a thesis for the essay. You will have the limited evidence from the documents and the information you can recall to help you to determine your thesis. As you read the documents and take notes on them, as in Steps One and Two in Essay Writing, a thesis should emerge that will determine your approach to the question.

The Documents

The third part of the DBQ is made up of the documents. As you look at them, remember that you are to write a unified essay and **not** a mere summary of what is in each document. What would you look for in making your brief notes? One important piece of information is the source of the document. How biased would it be? Next, note the date of the document if given. How will that affect its accuracy? Finally, you must read the document carefully and determine exactly the point being made. Sometimes the language can be confusing. The following comments on the documents are more extensive than you need to make. However, are there points you would add?

DOCUMENT A

The first document is an entry dated March 3, 1837 in the Journal of the Illinois House of Representatives in which Lincoln and his fellow representative from his home county protest the legislature's support for the idea of the U.S. government abolishing slavery. Lincoln clearly states that he believes the federal government has no power to abolish slavery in the nation. Is this view a surprise to you? Did Lincoln believe this in 1860? How does this affect your response to the question? Would the journal of a legislative body be biased? Why might Lincoln have supported this view in 1837? What was happening in the country?

DOCUMENTS B AND C

Document B (you may identify documents this way in your answer, but a better way is to identify documents by the author or source) gives a view on slavery expressed privately by Abraham Lincoln in a personal letter. Letters are not meant for publication and writers can be expected to express their true thoughts when writing them. Lincoln clearly indicates that he is torn by the question and yet is not prepared to come up with a clear solution. This document is dated 1855. What events have taken place in the 18 years since 1837 that might have affected Lincoln?

The quotation (Document C) from Lincoln's address at Freeport, Illinois, in 1858 as part of the Lincoln-Douglas Debate in their race for the U.S. Senate gives another view from Lincoln. Has Lincoln changed his mind since 1837? What events occurred in the 1850s that would have an impact on one's view of slavery? On the basis of this speech, how do you think he will act as president? How honest a statement of his beliefs would this be? Remember that Lincoln is running for a political office—United States senator. The speech would be reported widely. These are the type of questions you should address as you read the documents, relating them both to the question and to the "mainstream" of American history.

DOCUMENT D

The comments (Document D) from a southern newspaper on the Lincoln-Douglas Debate were quoted in a northern newspaper, the *Chicago Tribune* from Chicago, Illinois, and this suggests that some people in both the North and the South might be in agreement on this particular interpretation of the famous Freeport Debate. This editorial comment should spark your recall of this major event in the 1850s. The editor opposes "squatter sovereignty" as a way to determine the future of slavery in the territories. He prefers Lincoln's idea of congressional action because the Supreme Court has already declared such action unconstitutional. Do you remember the case? The Dred Scott Decision declared the Missouri Compromise, passed by Congress, unconstitutional. The editor is supporting the Southern view even though he is writing in Chicago—a northern city. Did you see that? It is believed that Lincoln's position lost him the Senate race but endeared him to the Republicans and thus won for him the presidential nomination. How would you use this information in your answer?

DOCUMENT E

The editorial presented in Document E is from another Illinois newspaper—one that opposed the election of Lincoln. This editorial clearly supports the Constitution and opposes secession as a way to deal with Lincoln's election. Does this support or reject the idea of Lincoln's election as a mandate for the abolition of slavery? This 1860 editorial can be a most important document in developing your case.

DOCUMENT F

The map (Document F) can easily be understood. You may have this information in your head, but if not, this could be of benefit to you in developing your argument. Is the document biased? The map shows Lincoln won overwhelmingly in the Electoral College yet received only 40 percent of the vote. What does that mean? What states did he carry?

DOCUMENT G

The editorial (Document G) suggests that there was not unified support for Abraham Lincoln even in the Republican Party. The date is after Lincoln's election. It suggests that Lincoln did not have the full support of his party. Does this help explain his actions during his first months in office? How does this information relate to the idea of a "mandate"?

DOCUMENT H

Part of the actual secession document from South Carolina is presented in Document H. It is a document that you may never have read before, but the issue presented should be familiar to you. How does the document suggest the people of South Carolina viewed the election of Lincoln? Do the authors interpret the election of Lincoln as a mandate to abolish slavery in South Carolina? What is the bias of the authors?

DOCUMENT I

In his first Inaugural Address in 1861 (Document I), Lincoln revealed how he viewed his election. Included in the document is an important quote from the Republican Party platform. Does it suggest that Lincoln or the Republicans viewed the election as a mandate for the abolition of slavery? This is the issue that you must resolve in your reading and analysis of the documents.

DOCUMENT J

The final document (Document J), from a series of resolutions passed by the legislature of New Jersey long after the war had begun, clearly suggests New Jersey was not in full support of the war effort. How does this document fit into the overall question? The date is important. As you should know from your study of American history, the Emancipation Proclamation that is alluded to in the Peace Resolutions of New Jersey went into effect on January 1, 1863. Was New Jersey in favor of the abolition of slavery?

Summary

These brief comments on the documents raise many issues. What are your answers to the questions suggested? What other questions do these documents raise in your mind? During the 15 minutes allotted for reading and analyzing the documents and taking notes, you will want to go over documents in this manner. From your notes you should then develop your thesis. You need not refer to all the documents in your answer. You should pick *only* those that help you to present your case and to prove your thesis. However, if you have time, you should refute a document that does not support your thesis. If you can do this with evidence from outside sources, it would be to your credit. In answering the DBQ the greatest danger is in merely describing or listing what is in each document and not writing an essay answering the question. Too many students write only a summary of each document. You can clearly see that this does not answer the question and is an ineffective answer.

Writing the Introduction

At this time you should write your own answer for this DBQ. Use the documents by grouping common ideas found in them. Do not quote what is said verbatim. Identify the source of the document. Remember to include information from the "mainstream" of American history during the years 1837–1863.

For this question we have not included a sample answer. There is a sample answer for a DBQ included with Model Examination A in Part Four. Here we have focused on the introductory paragraph. After writing your own answer to this question, read the sample introductions provided here and make your judgment of them. Recall what was said in Part Two about a good introduction. If you have forgotten, go back and read that section again. A good introduction is crucial for a good essay.

Sample Introduction A

Lincoln's election as President of the United States was a mandate to abolish slavery in the United States. It took Lincoln a long time to get around to this act, but in the Emancipation Proclamation, he finally freed the slaves. Although the New Jersey Peace Proposals were opposed to this move, they were certainly not in agreement with the majority of the American people.

Sample Introduction B

Abraham Lincoln was known as the Great Emancipator, and he deserves the title since he freed the slaves.

Sample Introduction C

The political process in America is often confusing. To determine clearly what the results of an election mean is a difficult task. Although slavery appears to be the major issue in the election of Abraham Lincoln, there were others including transportation to the West and the tariff issue. Considering these factors and Lincoln's personal comments on the issue of slavery, it is clear that the election of Lincoln was not a mandate for the abolition of slavery in the United States.

Sample Introduction D

Slavery was a divisive issue at the Constitutional Convention and had been throughout the years of our history to 1860. Compromise after compromise was tried, but as Lincoln asked, "Can a nation continue together permanently half slave and half free?" The answer was certainly no, and the election of Lincoln in 1860 was a mandate for the abolition of slavery in the United States.

Sample Introduction E

These documents have a lot of conflicting viewpoints. It is very hard to see that anybody agreed on anything. Although Lincoln was consistently opposed to slavery in the District of Columbia, he was not prepared to abolish it. The election in 1860 was viewed in different ways by South Carolina and by the Reading, Pennsylvania, newspaper. Since Lincoln had said that the nation could not be half slave and half free, he must have thought he should abolish slavery. When he did this in the Emancipation Proclamation, which was in agreement with what he had said at Freeport, the country could truly say it was free and all men were created equal.

Teacher Comments on Sample Introductions

As should be very clear, the writers have interpreted the question in a variety of ways. Each position could be defended based on the evidence of the documents and outside information.

Sample B

"Considering the merits of these five introductions, Sample B is the poorest. The writer fails to set a broad context and fails to introduce the question. This viewpoint on Lincoln does not really relate to the question except indirectly. Sample B confirms the point that a one-sentence introduction is usually not sufficient to set the broad context of the question and to state your thesis.

Sample E

"Sample E is also poorly written. The author has included a good deal of information, much of it from the documents, but there is no clear organization. Instead, a shotgun-spatter approach has been used, and the topic of the question is not included. A thesis is implied in the fifth sentence, but it is not clearly stated, nor is it related to the election of 1860.

Sample A

"In Sample A a thesis is clearly stated in the first sentence, and the question is introduced. Unfortunately, since there is no broad context set, the reader is somewhat taken aback by the opening. The author then elaborates on the thesis in the second sentence. Unfortunately, the last sentence introduces information that somewhat contradicts the thesis—information that could be better used in the body of the paper. It almost appears as if the author of Sample A, just like the author of Sample E, did not take time to organize the material before starting to write. In Sample A one can understand the way the writer's thoughts are moving, but the three sentences do not make as effective an introduction as we find in Samples C and D.

Samples C and D

"These two introductions are both good. Each begins with a broad topic related to the question, moves from this topic to the specific topic of the question (Lincoln, his election, slavery), and ends with a clearly stated thesis. The two writers disagree completely about their interpretation of the meaning of the election of Lincoln. It would be interesting to read their essays and to trace their arguments, as either thesis could be defended. Both Samples C and D conform most closely to what has been set in this book as the pattern for good introductory paragraphs."

Do you agree with the above analysis? Do you see why Samples C and D are considered the best of the five? Do you now have this pattern of an introductory paragraph established in your mind?

Sample Introduction and Conclusion

Introduction

Slavery was an issue in American history starting in 1619. The leaders of the country in the first half of the 19th century shared many different opinions on the topic. Beginning in the 1830s, the Abolitionist sentiment was fanned by many events. These events culminated in the election of Abraham Lincoln. Based on his personal views and those of the North, Lincoln's election was a mandate for the abolition of slavery.

Conclusion

Slavery was abolished as a result of the Civil War. The election of Lincoln determined that this would be so, since it was understood by the Republican Party and its leader, Abraham Lincoln, that slavery must not spread to the territories and that ultimately it should be abolished. The election of 1860 ended years of attempted compromise and eliminated slavery as an issue for the American nation.

Were you able to write comparable paragraphs? You see how well they relate together: The introduction sets a broad issue (i.e., slavery), presents the question (i.e., to what extent was the election of Lincoln a mandate for the abolition of slavery?), and concludes with a thesis. The conclusion returns to the question and presents the writer's thesis in the second sentence. It then goes on to bring the question back to the broad issue of slavery paralleling the first sentence in the introduction. This neatly frames the entire essay.

Summary of How to Write a DBQ Answer

The following five points summarize the key concepts to remember when writing the answer to the DBQ.

1. Remember that you are writing a **unified essay** answer involving the documents and events in the "mainstream" of American history.
2. Some documents will be more valuable or reliable than others. Pick and choose the documents you use and rearrange the order. Group documents with similar ideas together and dismiss the less valuable. Be imaginative! **Do not merely summarize the content of each document.**
3. **Identify the documents** by source or letter.
4. Summarize the key idea(s) found in the document, but **do not quote the full document**.
5. Refer to other events of the age, and **clearly indicate how these documents relate to these events and help you gain a better understanding of events in the "mainstream" of American history.**

If you keep these five points in mind and remember the Seven Steps in Essay Writing, you should have little difficulty in writing a good answer for any DBQ.

Practice Essay Questions

1. Describe two problems that were important causes of the Civil War and explain how the Civil War and Reconstruction provided solutions to the problems.

2. To what extent do you agree or disagree with the idea that the North had won the Civil War before it began?

3. How did THREE of the following lead to the secession of South Carolina in 1860?
   a. Nullification Crisis of 1832–1833
   b. Kansas-Nebraska Act of 1854 and its aftermath
   c. Dred Scott Decision 1857
   d. Lincoln-Douglas Debates 1858
   e. Election of Lincoln 1860

4. In what ways are the issues that led to the Civil War similar to those that led to the American War for Independence?

5. "The Civil Rights legislation of the 1960s recaptured for African Americans the social and political status they held briefly under Reconstruction." Assess the validity of this generalization.

Comments on Question 1

Question 1 is a typical *Describe . . . explain* essay question. There should be no difficulty in analyzing what the question requires after your practice in Chapter 2. Whether you have the factual information to deal with this question is another matter, since it is rare that the period 1850–1876 is studied in terms of how the Reconstruction era solved the problems that caused the war. If you are able to organize information in this way, you could write an exciting essay. Among the usual causes of the war cited are slavery and economic differences between the North and the South. How were these affected by Reconstruction and the war? Can you think of other ways of stating these causes or of other causes that were "solved" during the war and Reconstruction? The fact that Congress passed the first railroad construction bill for a transcontinental railroad after the South seceded is one example of economic action impossible before secession. It and other similar examples could be used to illustrate many problems that could not be resolved as long as the union remained united. The question is easy in format, could be easy to organize, but might prove difficult factually.

Comments on Question 2

The second question illustrates the *To what extent?* type of question used in the DBQ example in this chapter. It adds those familiar words *agree or disagree,* which invite a strong statement of personal opinion. The idea presented is an intriguing one—the idea that the South had lost the war before it began. Considering the length of the war and the difficulty Lincoln had in finding a general to win the war, you might wonder how this could be true, but some historians have suggested that the railroad network of the North plus its industry made it undefeatable. What do you think? This question requires good factual knowledge and good insights into how facts from different sources can be put together to defend a position. The question is completely open as to organizational format and the organization would depend entirely on what you put down in your brief notes. This question illustrates the importance of organizing your essay from the brief notes you make.

Comments on Question 3

Question 3 is a *How?* question that needs a personal opinion or thesis that bridges a long time span in which many changes in attitudes, people, and problems occurred. The five choices all relate to states' rights issues and that is one key to their connection to the secession of South Carolina. The last four relate to slavery and are always given as steps leading to the Civil War but that is not the question. If you are to discuss slavery or the coming of the war, you must connect your ideas to secession. When you have your thesis, an organizational scheme should emerge. This is a difficult question.

Comments on Question 4

The fourth question is a very broad question directly in the mainstream of American history. You are asked to relate two of the most important periods of American history. The question asks you to find the similarities, but, of course, you could disagree with the premise of the question and state that there is no similarity. Among the issues you might describe are economic issues, majority-minority political issues, and social issues involving differences in lifestyles. These three issues should give you some ideas of how these two periods could be compared in terms of similarities. The essay might be best organized around similarities—relating first the Revolutionary War situation and then the Civil War situation before moving on to the next similarity to be treated. Remember that it is an *In what ways?* question so you must concentrate on how the issues are similar or different and not merely retell events.

Comments on Question 5

The last question is the broadest question we have had so far in the book. It takes one situation—the treatment of the African American—and asks you to compare the status of African Americans in two periods. You must know something about the way African Americans were treated in the South socially and politically during Reconstruction. You also must know some of the details of the civil rights legislation of the 1960s. If you know both, then you may wish to answer this question. You will need to define status and this will help you develop a thesis. The question combines social and political history and you must include examples from each to have a top answer. The question also illustrates how you may be asked to compare different time periods.

Multiple-Choice Questions— Charts and Graphs

A popular type of multiple-choice question used to test analytical skills is one based on charts and graphs. It is an excellent type of stimulus question. Many textbooks today present large amounts of information in this manner. Summaries of election results, votes on various issues in Congress, the pattern of immigration,

manufacturing growth or other economic data, even the numbers of enlistees compared to draftees in World War I can be presented in this way. There are a variety
of types of charts and graphs—ranging from simple statistical tables presenting
raw numbers to complex bar and line graphs where several items are presented for
comparison. Today in texts, as well as in magazines and newspapers, we are presented with a great variety of statistical data that we need to understand. As you
study, be certain you look at the charts and graphs in your books and learn how to
interpret them and get information from them. Do not skip over such items
because they form an important method of presenting historical information, and
your ability to understand and interpret information in this way will be tested on
the Advanced Placement exam. Also, learning to read and interpret charts and
graphs and applying this information to the mainstream history you are studying
will help you prepare for analyzing documents presented on the DBQ.

Study the following examples of multiple-choice questions based on charts
and graphs. There will be other examples in the sample multiple-choice questions at the end of succeeding chapters. The charts and graphs present information from later than 1870 but you should be able to understand the context
even if you have not yet studied the time period.

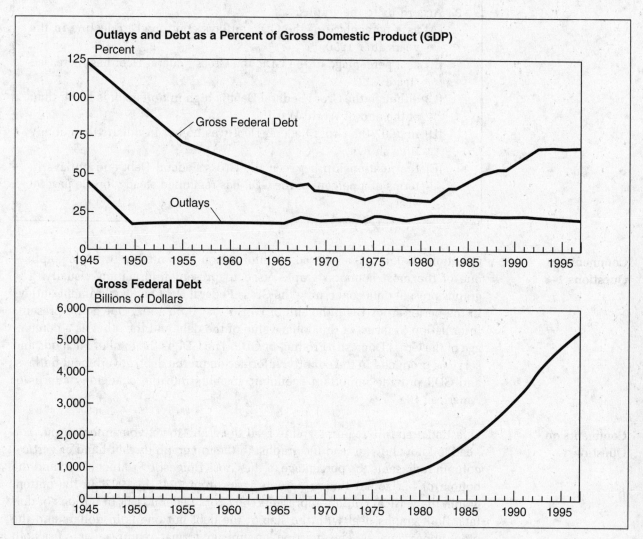

Source: U.S. Bureau of the Census, *Statistical Abstract of the United States: 1997* (117th edition) Washington, D.C., 1997.

Sample Questions 1–3

1. According to the graph, which one of the following statements is NOT correct?
   (A) The Gross Federal Debt in dollars was largest in 1945.
   (B) The Gross Federal Debt in dollars began to increase in the 1970s.
   (C) The Gross Federal debt as a percentage of the Gross Domestic Product (GDP) declined until 1967.
   (D) The outlays of the government as a percentage of the Gross Domestic Product has essentially been steady since 1950.
   (E) The Gross Federal Debt as a percentage of the Gross Domestic Product has been approximately steady from 1992 to 1997.

2. The rise in the Gross Federal Debt both in dollars and as a percentage of Gross Domestic Product after 1981 was most likely a result of the
   (A) aftermath of the Vietnam War
   (B) intensification of the Cold War
   (C) dramatic rise in poverty in the United States
   (D) supply-side economic policy of Reaganomics
   (E) decline in immigration

3. According to the graphs,
   (A) as a percentage of the GDP, outlays continued to decline in the years after 1950
   (B) as a percentage of the GDP, the Gross Federal Debt has increased steadily
   (C) although the Gross Federal Debt is high in dollars, it is lower than at the end of World War II
   (D) in 1997 the Gross Federal Debt was higher in dollars than at any time shown
   (E) the relationship between the Gross Federal Debt and outlays in terms of a percent of the GDP has remained steady for the past 50 years

Comments on Questions 1–3

Questions 1, 2, and 3 are based on information presented in two line graphs—one of the most common graphs used to present information visually. The graphs present data concerning the Gross Federal Debt and government outlays in the period from 1945, the end of World War II, to 1997. One graph presents information in terms of the dollar value of the debt and the other as a percentage of the Gross Domestic Product or GDP. The GDP is the total of all goods and services produced in the country. Information on the debt, government outlays, and GDP provide important economic insights into the changing patterns of American life.

Comments on Question 1

Question 1 simply requires you to read the graph to get your information. You need to know how to read the graphs. In the top graph the left-hand or vertical column represents the percentage of the Gross Domestic Product (GDP) and the bottom or horizontal line represents years from 1945 to 1997. In the bottom graph, the vertical column represents the Gross Federal Debt in billions of dollars. Both graphs deal with the size of the debt but one is in dollars and the other in percentages. The question, an unusual format, requires you to use both graphs. A quick reading of A might lead you to believe it is correct but, although the debt was low in dollars in 1945 compared to 1997, it was very high as a percentage of the GDP. The other answers are all correct. This question requires simple graph reading skills—skills you can practice as you study the graphs found in most textbooks, but, in case your text does not have graphs, you can find graphs in newspapers and news magazines. Graph reading is a simple skill yet an important one.

Comments on Question 2

Most questions based on charts and graphs are testing skills similar to those tested in the DBQ—skills of analysis and interpretation—and most of them are not testing recall, although you may need to know the mainstream conditions surrounding the question. For example, in question 2, you need to know the dates of the Vietnam War and the Cold War as well as something about the issues of poverty, Reaganomics, and immigration. Using your knowledge of these topics from the mainstream of U.S. history, you would conclude that the supply-side economic policies known as Reaganomics adopted during Reagan's first term in 1981 had the greatest impact on increasing the debt after 1981. Also, choice D is the only choice that is clearly related to economic policy. Question 2 illustrates how a multiple-choice question based on a graph can test not only a skill but also factual knowledge.

Comments on Question 3

Question 3 simply requires that you read the line graph. This time only one statement is correct and it is D—"in 1997 the Gross Federal Debt was higher in dollars than at any time shown." The other statements are false. For instance, choice B could be misread. It refers to the top chart where the GDP is the basis of comparison, but if you looked at the lower chart, which shows the debt in dollars increasing steadily, particularly since 1970, you might think that choice B is correct. If you have trouble seeing that, use the edge of a piece of paper placed parallel to the horizontal or bottom line to help you read across. It is always important to be careful and to take time in reading charts.

Sample Questions 4–6

LIFE EXPECTANCY AT BIRTH

Year	Total			White			Nonwhite		
	Both Sexes	Male	Female	Both Sexes	Male	Female	Both Sexes	Male	Female
1995	75.8	72.6	78.9	76.5	73.4	79.6	NA	NA	NA
1986	74.7	71.2	78.2	75.4	71.9	78.8	70.9	66.8	74.9
1976	72.9	69.1	76.8	73.6	69.9	77.5	68.4	63.7	72.4
1966	70.1	66.7	73.8	71.0	67.6	74.7	64.0	60.7	67.4
1956	69.6	66.7	73.0	70.2	67.3	73.7	63.2	61.1	65.9
1946	66.7	64.6	69.4	67.5	65.1	70.3	59.1	57.5	61.0
1936	58.5	56.6	60.6	59.8	58.0	61.9	49.0	47.0	51.4
1926	56.7	55.5	58.0	58.2	57.0	59.6	44.6	43.7	45.6
1916	51.7	49.6	54.3	52.5	50.2	55.2	41.3	39.6	43.1
1906	48.7	46.9	50.8	49.3	47.3	51.4	32.9	31.8	33.9

Source: U.S. Bureau of the Census, *Historical Statistics of the U.S., Colonial Times to 1970*
U.S. Bureau of the Census, *Statistical Abstract of the United States 1981*, 2nd 1997, Washington, D.C.

4. According to the statistics presented in the table, the individual with the shortest life expectancy at birth was a
   (A) white male in 1995
   (B) nonwhite female in 1936
   (C) white female in 1926
   (D) nonwhite male in 1906
   (E) white male in 1906

5. The statistics indicate all of the following to be true EXCEPT
   (A) The greatest increase in life expectancy for all people occurred between 1936 and 1946.
   (B) Male life expectancy for white and nonwhite males has always been shorter than for females in the same year.
   (C) Life exptectancy for both sexes of the white population has always been longer than the life expectancy for both sexes of the nonwhite population.
   (D) White female life expectancy in 1986 was over twice that of nonwhite females in 1906.
   (E) For all whites the smallest increase in life expectancy occurred between 1966 and 1976.

6. The statistics in the chart could most effectively be used to support the idea that
   (A) more females are born than males
   (B) life is harder for males who have to work more years
   (C) it is better to be born nonwhite than white
   (D) life expectancy reflects the social and economic condition of nonwhites
   (E) whites are always older than nonwhites

Comments on Questions 4–6

Questions 4, 5, and 6 are based on a statistical table, another very common method of presenting a large amount of information. The table deals with life expectancy at birth for the total population, the white population, and the nonwhite population. These three divisions or headings appear at the top of the table identifying three wide columns, each of which in turn is divided into three parts representing life expectancy for both sexes, for males and for females. The careful reading of column headings will save you from many silly errors. The years to be compared are presented in the left-hand column. For 1995 NA appears in the boxes under Nonwhite. This means this information was not available at the time of writing. The Bureau of the Census has made changes in the way information is collected and reported. The information is presented by decades except for 1986–1995. Again, information for 1995 was not yet available at the time of writing. While a great deal of information is presented in the table, this is a rather simple lineal table. There is no accumulative data to be presented in peripheral boxes as you sometimes find in statistical tables.

Comments on Question 4

Question 4 offers five choices for the individual with the shortest life expectancy at birth. Looking at the appropriate column for each choice, you see that the life expectancy of a white male in 1995 was 73.4 years, of a nonwhite female in 1936 was 51.4 years, of a white female in 1926 was 59.6 years, of a nonwhite male in 1906 was 31.8 years, and of a white male in 1906 was 47.3 years. If you have located these same numbers, then you can read the table. The answer is clearly the nonwhite male in 1906, choice D.

Comments on Question 5

Question 5 involves a comparison of data in the table and you are asked to locate the one untrue statement. It is that for all whites, the smallest increase in life expectancy occurred between 1966 and 1976, which is choice E. While the increase between 1966 and 1976 for all whites (use column for both sexes) was small—2.6 years—the increase between 1956 and 1966 was smaller—.8 years, and between 1926 and 1936 it was 1.6. In analyzing the question you must read the suggested answers, look up that information in the table, and determine its truth. Look at the total column for both sexes and you will see that life expectancy increased 8.2 years for all people between 1936 and 1946. The increase in all other decades is smaller, ranging from .5 to 5 years, so A is true. Comparing all the male statistics with female statistics will show that male life expectancy has always been shorter than female. So B is true. Again comparing white and nonwhite statistics, you will find choice C is true. If you look in the box for nonwhite females in 1906 you will see their life expectancy was 33.9 years; for white females in 1986 it was 78.8 years—well over twice 33.9 years. Thus you see that choices A through D are all true. Another type of question based on these statistics might ask you to explain or account for the timing of this large jump.

Comments on Question 6

Question 6 moves beyond the statistics in the table and asks you to figure out how they might be used. Five possible theses or ideas are presented, and you are asked to decide which would be most effectively supported by these statistics. The best choice would appear to be D—life expectancy reflects the social and economic condition of nonwhites. The statistics do not prove more females are born—only that they live longer. In fact, more males are born. Life may be harder for males, but the statistics do not prove it. Unless you find life unattractive and wish to die young, it is certainly not better to be born nonwhite and, of course, whites are not always older than nonwhites—a ridiculous statement, but one you might accept if you read too quickly! You should know from your study of the mainstream of American history that the living conditions, socially and economically, of a higher percentage of nonwhites has always been below that of the percentage of whites in our nation and that living conditions affect life expectancy. The two ideas—living conditions and life expectancy—are related, and these statistics could be used effectively to support this idea. This question thus tests your ability to understand the statistics, to apply them to historic situations, and to make judgments as to the best use of given data. It is a good type of multiple-choice question based on charts.

Sample Questions 7–8

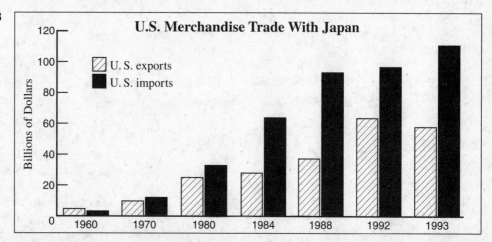

7. In reading the bar graph all of the following are accurate statements EXCEPT:
   (A) U.S. imports from Japan have increased throughout the years shown.
   (B) The graph presents information on U.S.-Japan trade relations.
   (C) At no time have U.S. exports to Japan exceeded U.S. imports from Japan.
   (D) The number of years between bars are not always the same.
   (E) The greatest increase in U.S. exports came between 1988 and 1992.

8. According to information presented in the graph, you can conclude that
   (A) the U.S. trade deficit was a problem from 1960–1984
   (B) the Vietnam War forced the United States to buy from Japan
   (C) the wages paid to Japanese workers are lower than those paid to Americans
   (D) the Reagan tax cut program hurt our trade balance with Japan
   (E) the exports of the United States grew more rapidly from 1975 to 1980 than in any other period

Comments on Question 7

Question 7 simply asks you to read the graph. It is a test of your ability to read and understand the information in the key. The numbers at the bottom on the horizontal represent years, and billions of dollars are presented on the vertical. U.S. imports, beginning very small in 1960, have increased throughout the years shown. The title tells you that the graph is about *U.S. Merchandise Trade with Japan*. The number of years between bars vary. The greatest increase in U.S. exports, represented by the hatch marks, came between 1988 and 1992. You may need to measure this using the edge of a piece of paper. This leaves choice C as the wrong statement—U.S. exports to Japan exceeded imports in 1960. This is a good test of your ability to read all parts of a graph.

**Comments on
Question 8**

Question 8 asks you to interpret the graph and relate information in it to some ideas in recent mainstream history. The only point you can clearly conclude from the graph and not from outside sources is choice E, "the exports of the United States grew more rapidly from 1975 to 1984 than in any other period." The U.S. trade deficit was not a problem in 1960, as we exported more than we imported, so choice A is inaccurate. Choices B, C, and D cannot be proven from the graph. We did not have to buy from Japan as a result of the Vietnam War and you can learn nothing about Japanese wages or Reagan's tax cut from the graph, although both have been suggested as reasons for the imbalance of trade. They are ideas from mainstream history that are important but cannot be proven from the graph.

These sample multiple-choice questions based on charts and graphs should illustrate the range of questions that might be asked. The analysis should provide you assistance in reading the charts and graphs you find as you study. Several of these charts contain more complex information than may be found on the exam. However, they provide good practice in analysis. Charts can provide helpful information on the United States. Do not skip over such information, but look at it with care to learn more about the factual content of American history and to gain an understanding of how to read and use charts and graphs.

Practice Multiple-Choice Questions

1. Which is the correct chronological order to illustrate a cause-and-effect relationship among the following events leading to the Civil War?
   (A) South Carolina secedes, Election of Lincoln, Lincoln-Douglas Debates, Dred Scott Decision, Kansas-Nebraska Act
   (B) Kansas-Nebraska Act, Dred Scott Decision, South Carolina secedes, Lincoln-Douglas Debates, Election of Lincoln
   (C) Dred Scott Decision, Kansas-Nebraska Act, Lincoln-Douglas Debates, Election of Lincoln, South Carolina secedes
   (D) Kansas-Nebraska Act, Dred Scott Decision, Lincoln-Douglas Debates, Election of Lincoln, South Carolina secedes
   (E) Dred Scott Decision, Lincoln-Douglas Debates, Election of Lincoln, South Carolina secedes, Kansas-Nebraska Act

2. After the South seceded, the Congress was able to pass special legislation to benefit the North and the West, such as the
   (A) Kansas-Nebraska Act   (D) Sherman Anti-Trust Act
   (B) Pacific Railroad Bill   (E) Chinese Exclusion Act
   (C) Underwood Tariff

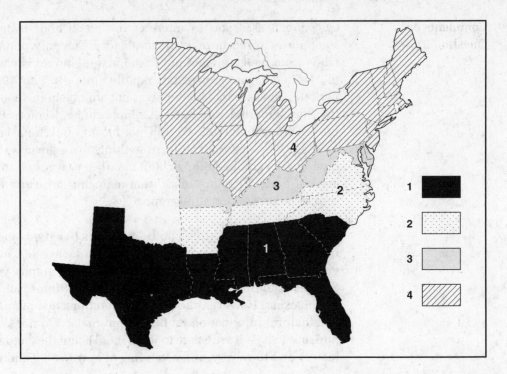

3. On the map, the Confederate States of America are those included in the
   area numbered
   (A) 1 and 4
   (B) 1 and 3
   (C) 1, 2, 3
   (D) 2 and 3
   (E) None of the above

4. The so-called border states at the time of the outbreak of the Civil War
   were those states
   (A) bordering the Atlantic
   (B) that bordered but did not join the Confederacy
   (C) bordering the Mississippi River south of Missouri
   (D) bordering Canada that Confederate sympathizers could raid from
       Canada
   (E) that bordered Mexico

5. The following were important Civil War battles:
   I.   Saratoga
   II. Gettysburg
   III. Bull Run
   IV. Atlanta
   (A) I and II
   (B) I, II, and III
   (C) I, II, and IV
   (D) I, III, and IV
   (E) II, III, and IV

6. All of the following comments would apply to *Uncle Tom's Cabin* EXCEPT
   (A) It was written by a talented woman.
   (B) It originated a common phrase used in race relations—*Uncle Tom.*
   (C) It is a story of living conditions under slavery.
   (D) It was an important element in creating antislavery feeling in the North.
   (E) It was not widely read until ten years after publication.

7. The purpose of the Freedman's Bureau was to
   (A) gain the vote for the freed slave
   (B) provide 40 acres and a mule for each slave
   (C) get Radical Republicans in positions of power in the South
   (D) feed, adjust, and educate the former slaves, thus aiding their adjustment to freedom
   (E) work against the Black Codes

8. With malice toward none, with charity for all, with firmness in the right as God gives us to see the right, let us strive on to finish the work we are in, to bind up the nation's wounds, to care for him who shall have borne the battle and for his widow and orphan, to do all which may achieve and cherish a just and lasting peace among ourselves and all nations.

   The above quotation from a speech expresses the view of the post-Civil War period held and initiated by
   (A) Thaddeus Stevens   (D) Stonewall Jackson
   (B) Abraham Lincoln   (E) Horace Greeley
   (C) Jefferson Davis

9. "All persons born or naturalized in the United States, and subject to the jurisdiction thereof, are citizens of the United States and of the states wherein they reside. No state shall make or enforce any law which shall abridge the privileges or immunities of citizens of the United States; nor shall any state deprive any person of life, liberty, or property, without due process of law; nor deny to any person within its jurisdiction the equal protection of the laws."

   The above quotation is a key clause in the
   (A) Black Code of South Carolina
   (B) Gettysburg Address
   (C) Thirteenth Amendment to the Constitution
   (D) Fourteenth Amendment to the Constitution
   (E) Fifteenth Amendment to the Constitution

10.   VALUE OF SELECTED EXPORTS FROM THE UNITED STATES

Year	Total Value* Millions of Dollars	Cotton Millions of Dollars	Leaf Tobacco Millions of Dollars	Wheat Millions of Dollars
1850	101	72	10	1
1853	124	109	11	4
1855	151	88	15	1
1858	157	131	17	9
1860	270	192	16	4
1863	74	7	20	47
1865	154	7	23	30
1868	206	153	23	30
1870	359	227	21	47

*Selected Exports

Source: U.S. Bureau of the Census, *Historical Statistics of the U.S., Colonial Times to 1957.*

According to information presented in the above table, all of the following would appear true concerning United States exports EXCEPT

(A) Export of leaf tobacco was not affected by the Civil War the way the export of cotton was.

(B) The export of wheat grew rapidly during and after the Civil War.

(C) The total value of U.S. exports rapidly recovered from the setback and disruption of the Civil War.

(D) Except for the period of the Civil War, cotton accounted for 50 percent of total U.S. exports.

(E) The total value of selected exports from the U.S. increased at a steady rate from 1850 to 1870.

11.   Which one of the following individuals is incorrectly paired with his area of contribution to the arts?

(A) Herman Melville—novelist

(B) Walt Whitman—orator

(C) Ralph Waldo Emerson—essayist

(D) William Sydney Mount—artist

(E) Henry Hobson Richardson—architect

Source: Harper's Weekly, May 17, 1862

12. The above sketch done by the artist Winslow Homer clearly indicates
    I. U.S. cavalry on the move
    II. a tent encampment possibly of Native Americans
    III. the troops had no guns or gunpowder
    IV. a time period after the invention of the telegraph

    (A) I, III,
    (B) I, III, IV
    (C) I, II, III
    (D) I, II, IV
    (E) II, III, IV

Answers and	**1.**	D	**2.**	B	**3.**	E	**4.**	B	**5.**	E
Answer Explanations	**6.**	E	**7.**	D	**8.**	B	**9.**	D	**10.**	E
	11.	B	**12.**	D						

1. (D) Question 1 presents five steps leading to the Civil War in varying chronological listings. The correct answer is D, which is a direct reversal of A. A starts with the most recent event and moves backward and, therefore, cannot reflect cause and effect. D starts in 1854 with the Kansas-Nebraska Act, which had an impact on the Dred Scott Decision in 1857, which affected the Lincoln-Douglas Debates in 1858, which prepared the way for the election of Lincoln in 1860, which was a major cause of the secession of South Carolina in 1860.

2. (B) The Pacific Railroad Bill, providing federal financial aid and land grants for a railroad from St. Louis west, was passed after the South seceded. Until then no bill could be passed because of controversy concerning whether a northern or southern route should be followed. The other four choices are important congressional acts from other times.

3. (E) The Confederate States are 1 and 2 on the map, a choice not given specifically, so the correct answer is none of the above.

4. (B) The border states at the time of the Civil War were those states that might have seceded but did not. They are identified as 3 on the map in question 3.

5. (E) Saratoga was an important Revolutionary War battle, the other three choices were Civil War battles. Therefore E, which includes II, III, and IV for Gettysburg, Bull Run, and Atlanta respectively, is the correct answer to this question.

6. (E) *Uncle Tom's Cabin,* written by Harriet Beecher Stowe, was published in 1854 and immediately became popular. Its tale of slavery was a major factor in stirring up Northern anger at the South's "peculiar institution."

7. (D) The Freedman's Bureau was formed to help the newly freed slaves adjust to their new condition. It was especially important in supplying food and education until it fell under the control of the Radical Reconstructionists, who used it for political purposes.

8. (B) The quotation is from Lincoln's Second Inaugural Address and is often considered a summary of his view for Reconstruction. Certainly the plans for Reconstruction initiated by Lincoln reflect this view. None of the other men, except possibly the *New York Tribune* editor Horace Greeley, expressed such conciliatory sentiments, and Greeley was in no position to initiate action.

9. (D) The question asks you to identify a section of the Fourteenth Amendment. It is a clause you should know. The Thirteenth Amendment abolished slavery and the Fifteenth granted the vote without regard to color or previous condition of servitude. "Black Codes" restricted rather than granted liberty, and the famous Gettysburg Address was delivered at the dedication of a cemetery and would not include such language or ideas. The Republicans felt they needed to incorporate their ideas in the Constitution and made ratification of this amendment a condition for re-entry of the seceded states into the union.

10. (E) Question 10 asks you to read a simple statistical table dealing with U.S. exports in the years 1850–1870. In studying the table you will see that all the statements except the last, "The total value of selected exports from the United States increased at a steady rate from 1850 to 1870," are true. U.S. exports dropped during the Civil War. You must know that the Civil War years were 1861–1865 in order to interpret the other four choices.

11. (B) Walt Whitman was a noted poet whose reputation was guaranteed by the publication of his work *Leaves of Grass* in 1855. Herman Melville was a novelist and his most famous novel, *Moby Dick,* was published in 1851. Ralph Waldo Emerson of Concord, Massachusetts, and a Transcendentalist was noted as an essayist and orator. His Phi Beta Kappa lecture at Harvard in 1837 titled *An American Scholar* is considered a wake-up call for cultural independence for the United States free from the restraints of European culture. William Sydney Mount was an important genre painter noted for his scenes of daily life in the period 1836–1867. His scenes of farm life, country dances, and horse trading are especially noteworthy. He was the first artist of note to include African Americans in his paintings of daily life. Henry Hobson Richardson, born in Louisiana and educated at Harvard and the Ecole des Beaux Arts in Paris, was an architect noted for his revival of Romanesque designs. Trinity Church in Boston (1872–1877) was an early work in what became known as Richardson Romanesque.

12. (D) Winslow Homer, later famous for his seascapes and scenes of late 19th-century life, was sent as a young artist to portray events of the Civil War when cameras were relatively new. Homer's sketches appeared in *Harper's Weekly*. This one is from May 17, 1862, and shows "The Union Cavalry and Artillery Starting in Pursuit of the Rebels up the Yorktown Turnpike." Homer portrays Northern cavalry; see the large "US" on the rump of the horse in the foreground. There is a collection of tents in the background that may be Indian tepees. The wires, whether telegraph (1844) or telephone (1876), indicate it was *after* the telegraph was invented. This demonstrates a need for careful reading of information. While the weapons portrayed on the cavalry are swords, there is no indication the troops did not have guns. In fact, a careful study of the sketch will show a cannon in the center left.

Bibliography

Blassingame, John. *The Slave Community: Plantation Life in the Ante-Bellum South.* New York: Oxford University Press, 1979.

Cash, W. J. *Mind of the South.* New York: Vintage Books, 1960.

Donald, David. *Lincoln Reconsidered: Essays on the Civil War Era.* New York: Vintage Books, 2001.

Elkins, Stanley. *Slavery, A Problem in American Institutional and Intellectual Life.* Chicago: University of Chicago Press, 1976.

Fogel, R. W., and S. L. Engerman. *Time on the Cross: The Economics of American Negro Slavery.* New York: W. W. Norton Co., 1995.

Franklin, J. H. *Reconstruction: After the Civil War.* Chicago: University of Chicago Press, 1961.

Morrison, M. A. *Slavery and the American West: The Eclipse of Manifest Destiny and the Coming of the Civil War.* Chapel Hill, NC: University of North Carolina Press, 1997.

Perman, Michael. *The 'Causes of the American Civil War.* (Problems in American Civilization.) Lexington, Massachusetts: D. C. Heath and Company, 1993.

Stampp, K. M. *Era of Reconstruction 1865–1877.* New York: Random House Inc., 1967.

Ward, Geoffrey C. *The Civil War: An Illustrated History.* New York: Knopf, 1992.

Woodward, C. Vann. *The Strange Career of Jim Crow.* New York: Oxford University Press, 2001.

Fiction

Benet, S. V. *John Brown's Body.* New York: I. R. Dee, 1990.

PART THREE **6** Growth of Industrial America, Populists, and Progressives 1877–1916

Important Facets of This Period

The two related yet separate reform movements—the Populist and Progressive movements—that bridged the turn of the century should be studied in any survey course either in their own right as significant developments in our history or as part of a general study of reform movements in America. These would include, in addition to these two movements, the Jacksonian period, the New Deal, and Lyndon Johnson's War on Poverty. Changes continually occur in human affairs, but at certain periods these changes seem to occur more rapidly and are, in some cases, the result of deliberate decision. The periods in American history when changes came rapidly have been of particular interest to historians.

The years 1877 to 1916 include many important developments. Some were causes, some results, and some had no real connection to the reform movements. Such issues include literary and artistic developments, growth of manufacturing methods, our changing relations with England and other European nations, the establishment of the American empire in the Pacific, immigration concerns, and changing lifestyles as a result of economic and social developments. These years saw the nation grow to be the world power it was in the 20th century.

Among those items you should consider in studying this period are

1. The meaning of Populism
2. The effect of the closing of the frontier on American life
3. The impact of the growth of manufacturing and the railroads on the farmer
4. The economic or business cycles
5. The causes and results of the Spanish-American War
6. American expansion in the Pacific and U.S. relations with the European powers
7. The growth of cities
8. The changing status of African Americans, both in the South and throughout the country
9. The changing patterns of immigration and Americans' response to it
10. The meaning of the Progressive movement, especially through a comparison of Theodore Roosevelt and Woodrow Wilson
11. Developments in American literary and artistic expression

Sample Essay Question—Compare

One type of essay question often found on Advanced Placement examinations asks you to compare several items, which can be people, events, or ideas. The word *compare* means to represent as similar, to examine the character or qualities of two or more items for the purpose of discovering their resemblances or differences. Usually you will be asked to compare two items but at times, more items may be included. In the definition, it is suggested that *compare* implies similarity, but note that the word *differences* is used as well as *resemblances*. In a question asking you to compare, you may stress either differences or similarities, but you should consider both.

Often in such questions another word is included. You will often find the word *contrast* used, so the question reads *Compare and contrast*. . . . In this situation you must discuss both the differences and similarities between the items since contrast means to show the differences between objects. However, compare does require you to consider both similarities and differences and this should not be forgotten. Another word that might be added to a *Compare* question to clarify what you are to do is *explain*, which we discussed in Chapter 2 with the *Describe . . . explain* question. You may find *Compare* questions that include *discuss, defend*, or *analyze*. It should be clear by this point that many essay questions are combinations of several other type questions, and that within every type there are many variations possible.

Sample Question

Compare the contributions of TWO of the following to the economic well-being of the United States in the period 1881 to 1915:
 Ida Tarbell
 John D. Rockefeller
 Theodore Roosevelt
 Henry Ford

Comments on Sample Question

The question is quite straightforward. It is a *Compare* question without any additional words, so you are to find the similarities and differences in the contributions of the two individuals you pick to the economic well-being of the United States in the years 1881 to 1915. Before you pick the two individuals you will write about, it is important that you understand the question. It is somewhat loosely worded as to just what is meant by well-being. The idea behind the phrase is that which makes a situation healthy. The question focuses on economic history and events related to it and not the more usual political history, but you will need to include some political history especially if you pick Ida Tarbell and Theodore Roosevelt. The dates given are interesting. In 1881 John D. Rockefeller established the Standard Oil Trust. By 1915 war had broken out in Europe and Henry Ford was making an attempt to stop the war. He had already introduced the Model T car and the eight-hour work day. The time span thus covers the period of rapid industrial growth in the United States and you will need to be aware of those events.

Once you have analyzed the question, the next step is to pick the two individuals about whom you will write. Assuming that you know something about all four choices, you should make brief notes about what you know and then decide which two to pick. As you make the notes, you will want to begin thinking of the approach you will take to the question.

In a *Compare* question you can either weave together information about the items being compared showing how they are similar or different on various points, or you may present information on the items separately and then write an analysis of the ways they are similar and different. In the former approach you would want to decide on the points for comparison first and organize material around them. In the latter approach, you need first to decide what you know of the individuals. Then, draw conclusions from the notes what you will include in the paragraphs where you present your analysis. Whatever approach you take, you will want to have notes on the items to be compared.

The four choices in this question are interesting individuals. Two, Rockefeller and Ford, are clearly related to economics. Each made major contributions to the development of business in the United States. Theodore Roosevelt is remembered as a political leader of the Progressive Era. A link to economic well-being may seem tenuous but he had views on trusts, supported legislation regulating food and drugs in the United States, and intervened in the Coal Strike of 1902. These events are related to both politics and economics and are the type of information to include in your answer. Ida Tarbell made her reputation as a muckraker, exposing the Standard Oil Trust and other evils as she saw them in the U.S. society at the turn of the century. If you pick her, you need to connect her social concerns with their economic impact on the United States. Write an answer to the question, doing additional research if needed. When you have written your essay, read the following student essay. Again, if you make a formal outline of the answer before you read the teacher comments on the essay, you will be able to see how the student organized the answer, and it will help you review the history of this time period.

Sample Answer

Economic well-being, which would include not only business prosperity but also the quality of that prosperity for all the people, is an important aspect of life in any society. Many individuals contributed to the economic well-being of the United States between 1881 and 1915. Their contributions were of different types from presidential to business leadership. Ida Tarbell and Henry Ford represent two very different contributions to that well-being, but they both had the best interests of the nation as their guiding principle.

During the early part of the 20th century, a group of journalists, called *Muckrakers,* prompted the reform of government and big business. Particularly important among these journalists was Ida Tarbell, whose work was significant in opening the eyes of America to problems facing the country and led to the reform of business and government. What she is most famous for is the writing she did on Standard Oil and its president, the business genius, John D. Rockefeller. Her series in *McClure's Magazine* revealed that the surreptitious Standard Oil Company was selling its oil at lower prices than other oil producers, yet it was still making a larger profit. Tarbell showed that the company had established a horizontal integration of the oil industry. In her articles, Tarbell revealed that Standard Oil had conspired to monopolize trade by getting rebates and preferences from railroads and by controlling pipelines, and had used local price cutting and espionage to eliminate competition.

Tarbell's work was revolutionary; she had exposed the most powerful corporation in America, and she was a *woman* no less! It was easy for the oil workers to see the evil in what Rockefeller had done, but for the average American who knew of Rockefeller only as the man who gave enormous sums of money to universities and who employed thousands of people, this evil was difficult to believe and comprehend.

There was no denying that the information that Tarbell had uncovered was valid; thus, Rockefeller was forced to reform. State government passed bills to control railroad and pipeline rates. The federal government became involved, and in response to the company's monopolization, Congress passed a bill creating a Bureau of Corporations, which had the authority to oversee the accounts and activities of corporations. In 1907 the government charged Standard Oil with violating the Sherman Anti-Trust Act of 1890 (which declared trusts illegal and gave the government the right to dissolve them) as the company and its related associates had conspired to monopolize interstate commerce in oil. Other charges brought against the company were ones that Tarbell had revealed. In May of 1911 the Standard Oil Company was dissolved by the Supreme Court. The hard work of Ida Tarbell had been rewarded, and the economic well-being of the country improved as people benefited.

After years of tinkering and experimentation, by 1903 Henry Ford had raised enough capital to incorporate the Ford Motor Company. Attempting to construct a car for the "great multitude," Ford introduced the Model T in October 1908 and fulfilled his vision of an affordable automobile. Although there were roughly 20 established automakers at the time, Ford was successful because of his low price. Once seen as a luxury perk, the automobile soon came within the grasp of the common man and revolution was underway.

From an economic standpoint, the development of the Model T and the rise of the automotive industry provided the nation with a uniquely "American" product. In the years of Model T production, millions of cars were sold in the United States and abroad, thus, the Model T began to symbolize globally the quality of American industry. With this rapid production came the need for various raw materials and products. The automobile became the main stimulant of the American economy. Industrially, coal, steel, and rubber companies benefited greatly from Ford. Agriculturally speaking, the abundant use of the automobile rendered the horse obsolete and the rapid shift from hay production to other crops caused a major farming change. The car made long trips short and tied the country into one community, so highways became essential and America responded with the best road system in the world. With every industry now cross-related, big business and industry boomed between 1896 and 1915.

Through his work with the Model T, Henry Ford revolutionized manufacturing. He used a constantly moving assembly line, which increased car production. He paid his workers $5, twice the industry average. Ford kept his workers happy and thus more productive. To finance these absurd salaries, Ford slashed prices and increased production.

Socially, the birth of the automobile changed America drastically in a few short years. Readily available to the working man, automobiles led to the rise of the middle class. Suburbs sprouted, as commuting was made easy. The country gained a stronger sense of unity, as it became easier to travel. Americans became quite proud of their automobiles and their success overseas. The auto became a symbol of quality and Henry Ford became a folk hero. A true American success story that inspired others throughout the nation. Certainly he changed the economic well-being of the United States.

Ida Tarbell and Henry Ford made dramatic but very different contributions to the economic well-being of the United States at the start of the 20th century. Just think what this country and the world would be like if monopolies ran all businesses and we did not have the automobile. These two individuals changed the economic lives of all Americans for the better.

Teacher Comments on Sample Answer

"The organization of the essay around Tarbell and Ford is fine, but the writer fails to make an effective comparison between the two. The writer merely presents information, all of which is very good, about the two individuals and makes no attempt to relate it to the thesis or to find common or contrasting points for comparison, which is what is expected in a *Compare* question. For instance, the writer might have compared how both Ford and Tarbell wished to change industry or how the work of both benefited the nation by reducing prices. The writer might have preferred to concentrate on the dissimilarities, which might range from the contrast of Tarbell's working through the press and Ford working in factories to the fact that Tarbell was destroying a large company and Ford was creating one.

"In conclusion, this essay is very satisfactory in terms of information. There is an obvious organization, but it does not focus on a comparison and, although it has a thesis, the body of the essay does not support it. It is an example of an essay with many possibilities that are not fulfilled."

Do you agree with these comments? The introductory paragraph of the sample student essay is a good one and could be used as a model in your writing.

Practice Essay Questions

The following essay questions will test your knowledge of this period, and in addition, question 5 forces you to relate this period of time to an earlier one you have studied. Types of essay questions we have discussed in previous chapters are used in these five sample questions to provide practice with different type questions.

1. "In understanding the nature of a reform movement it is as important to know what it seeks to preserve as to know what it seeks to change." Compare the Populist and Progressive Reform movements of the late 19th and early 20th centuries in light of this statement.

2. "The nation (United States) whose Constitution is so perfect that no man suggests change and whose fundamental laws as they stand are satisfactory to all . . . The nation in which the right of the minority, the right of property and . . . of free labor are most secure."

    In what ways is this statement an accurate summary of the situation in the United States at the end of the 19th century? To what extent do you agree or disagree with the statement?

3. "The closing of the frontier in 1890 had a profound effect on the social and economic development of the United States in the succeeding 20 years." Evaluate this statement.

4. In what ways did THREE of the following affect the development of the West?
    Introduction of barbed wire
    Building of the railroads
    Introduction of the McCormack reaper
    End of the Indian Wars

5. "In the period 1793–1812 the United States was a small nation pushed around by the big powers; in the period 1895–1911 the United States was a big power that pushed around small nations."

    Compare the foreign policy of the United States in these two time periods to test the validity of this generalization.

Comments on Question 1

Question 1 is a straightforward *Compare* question. The quotation is an interesting one that could be applied to any reform movement. In this case you are asked to compare two movements that sometimes appear rather similar, but that are quite different. These differences should be clarified in an essay based on this quotation. Your thesis would have to state what you believe each movement sought to preserve, assuming, of course, you don't take the extreme position that the movements tried to preserve nothing. An organization based on similarities and differences in the two movements would seem more satisfactory than a chronological organization. If you have studied these two important reform movements, the question should be rather easy, since there are no unusual words or twists to the question.

Comments on Question 2

Question 2, on the other hand, is long and complicated. It is a typical combination essay-type question involving an *In what ways? To what extent?* and an *Agree or disagree* section. Once you figure out what each part is asking you to do, then you need to analyze the quote. The author of the quote is very optimistic about the United States. He believes everything is fine for everybody. He mentions particularly the security of the rights of the minority, of property, and of free labor. These three form an interesting combination. Who are the minority in the speaker's eyes? What is property? What is free labor? These three terms are crucial in understanding the meaning of the quotation and in determining whether you agree or disagree with what the author describes as the situation of the United States at the end of the 19th century. What is your opinion? Once you decide on your thesis, then factual information can be organized in different ways to answer the question. The question suggests an interesting approach to the period of time at the end of the century.*

Comments on Question 3

Question 3 is a straightforward *Evaluate This Statement* type. The quotation uses a familiar idea from the Bureau of the Census report for 1890. The *closed frontier* is the phrase that Frederick Jackson Turner used to develop his important thesis on the significance of the frontier in America. If the thesis is not familiar, you can still develop an interesting essay on the issue of the impact of the frontier on social and economic developments. This essay would best be organized around the various social and economic effects and *not* by chronology.

Comments on Question 4

This is a straightforward *In what ways?* question in which you are asked to discuss three of four items. As in all questions with a choice of this type, you must pick the three items carefully. For instance, you may know a lot about the fighting of the Indian Wars but if you cannot connect this information to the development of the West, do not pick that item. The four choices all changed the way life in the West was lived. Barbed wire allowed cattle to be controlled, the McCormack reaper made it possible to harvest large fields of wheat, and railroads opened markets. You may know all these facts, but the key to the question is to connect them to the development of the West and not simply describe the three items you pick. An organization focusing on how the items interconnect would be better than a chronology or a description of each item separately. As always, you must express your opinion on the topic.

Comments on Question 5

The fifth essay question again combines several types of essay questions. There is a statement about U.S. foreign policy, but then, instead of being asked to evaluate the statement, you are asked to compare the two time periods mentioned in the statement with the goal of testing the validity of the generalization. What the writer of this question is seeking in the way of an answer is very close to an evaluation of the statement, but the writer has given directions as to how this is to be achieved—by a comparison. Your thesis will reflect how true you believe the statement to be. Examples of the United States being pushed around in the years 1793–1812 contrasted with the examples of the United States pushing small nations or not pushing them, depending on your personal thesis, in the years 1895–1911, would provide an effective organization.

In analyzing the statement, you will no doubt recall many examples of U.S. foreign policy activity from which you may choose. In the years 1793–1812 the United States had innumerable dealings with France and England, to say nothing of Spain and the Barbary Pirates, while in the later period we were involved in the annexation of Hawaii, the Spanish-American War, incidents in Panama and Venezuela, and several incidents involving European powers, such as the Algeciras Conference, the Russo-Japanese War, and the Second Hague Disarmament Conference. Again, you will have many examples of foreign policy activity to choose from, so the major difficulty in this question will be in picking information to support your thesis and being certain to refute any major piece of evidence that does not agree with your thesis. For instance, if you do not believe the United States pushed small nations around in the 1895–1911 period, you must not ignore Theodore Roosevelt's use of the "big stick," but

---

*The author of the quote is not given in the question. When you have organized your thoughts, you may be interested to know that the author was Andrew Carnegie, writing in 1873.

either explain that this was an exception to your thesis or that T. R. had certain larger goals in mind. As mentioned in Part Two, when defending a thesis, you are being a lawyer or debater; they often concede points before going on to make their main argument. This technique is important if you wish to win readers to your side.

Multiple-Choice Questions— Cartoons and Photographs

In Chapter 5 we discussed multiple-choice questions based on charts and graphs and indicated that the primary purpose of such questions was to test your analytical skills. Another popular type of multiple-choice question designed to test analytical skill more than recall of information is the multiple-choice question based upon a cartoon or a photograph. The cartoon is often a politically oriented one. Although they are not as common, questions are sometimes based on paintings or sketches. As is true in the case of multiple-choice questions based on charts and graphs, when dealing with questions based on cartoons and pictures, you will often be expected to know about the history of the period in which the cartoon or picture was produced. Therefore, although the main purpose of such multiple-choice questions is to test analytical skills needed by the student of history, there is also often an element of factual recall involved. As in the case of the DBQ, in these questions you will often be expected to relate the cartoon or photograph to the mainstream of American history.

The following multiple-choice questions are examples of what you might find on an examination. The cartoons are all from *Harper's Weekly*. There are many other sources for cartoons and sketches, but those that appeared in *Harper's Weekly* are typical of 19th-century cartoons. Many textbooks today use such cartoons to illustrate points, and it would be wise to take time to look carefully at the cartoons and other illustrations as you study. The old expression, "A picture can convey a thousand words," is often true, so look at the illustrations in your books and see what you can learn. These cartoons and pictures and the comments and questions based on them will supply some practice in developing your skill in *reading* illustrations. If your text or the books you are using to study American history lack cartoons and pictures, you can practice by analyzing the cartoons and photographs in the daily papers, in newsmagazines, or in special books of cartoons such as *The Art and Politics of Thomas Nast,* edited by Morton Keller, or *A Century of Political Cartoons,* edited by Allan Weins and Frank Weitenkampf, or special illustrated histories, such as *The Illustrated History of World War I* by A. J. P. Taylor.

**Sample Questions
1 and 2**

DON'T SWAP HORSES

JOHN BULL. "Why don't you ride the other Horse a bit? He's the best Animal."
BROTHER JONATHAN. "Well that may be; but the fact is, OLD ABE is just where I can put my finger on him; and as for the other—though they say he's somewhere out in the scrub yonder—I never know where to find him."

Source: Harper's Weekly

---

1. In which of the following years was this cartoon published?
    (A) 1844   (D) 1940
    (B) 1860   (E) 1968
    (C) 1864

2. In the cartoon the words in the bushes refer to
    (A) John Bull's economic policies
    (B) the horse trader's promises
    (C) the charter of the city of Chicago
    (D) the main planks in the Democratic Party's Chicago Platform
    (E) the goals of the Republican Party of "Old Abe"

**Comments on
Question 1**

The first cartoon is from *Harper's Weekly* of November 1864. The artist is not identified. The subject is Abraham Lincoln's campaign for reelection to the presidency. To answer the question you must be able to recall several items that are suggested by points in the cartoon. The biggest point for identification is the reference to "Old Abe." The face on the horse then should be identifiable as Lincoln's. If you recall the years of Lincoln's elections and presidency—1860–1865—you have narrowed the choices down to 1860 and 1864. You then need to decide what the title of the cartoon means. *Don't swap horses* is a western expression meaning "don't change." When was Lincoln or the country, represented here by Brother Jonathan, involved in changing? There were times Lincoln changed generals, but this was not a decision made by the country (Brother Jonathan) or of interest to other nations (John Bull representing England). Another change, and one involving the years given as possible answers, was that offered to the country in the election of 1864. Old Abe was president—note the horse being ridden—and the other possible horse was off in the bushes, an "unknown" quantity as Brother Jonathan says. This is further confirmed, if you recognize the face in the bushes as McClellan, Lincoln's Democratic opponent, or if you know the Democrats held their convention at Chicago and their platform called for peace and compromise. Perhaps you were able to identify the years without such a detailed analysis, but this analysis illustrates how you can read cartoons using your knowledge of history to understand what is being presented. Incidentally, the *Don't swap horses* slogan was also used by the Democrats in 1940 to support the third-term election of Franklin D. Roosevelt, with the idea being that we should not change presidents at a period of such international crisis. The year 1844 has no connection to the cartoon; 1968 was the year of turmoil at the Democratic Party Convention in Chicago, where peace and compromise in Vietnam were major issues, but this is irrelevant to the cartoon.

Comments on Question 2

In answering the second question about the 1864 cartoon, you would have to know what the Democrats stood for in 1864. It is a question based more on recall than on analysis, but you might be able to arrive at the correct answer by eliminating the other choices. John Bull's economic policies have nothing to do with the topic of the cartoon, and the cartoon is *not* about horse trading, so you should be able to eliminate those two choices. Although Lincoln was from Illinois and Chicago is in that state, choice C about the charter of the city has no obvious connection to the conversation between Brother Jonathan and John Bull, so it should be eliminated. Finally, you are left with two choices involving political parties. If you have identified "Old Abe" as Lincoln, then you could probably eliminate the words in the bushes as the goals of the Republican party. The Republicans were ready to fight the Civil War and not compromise for peace. Thus, even with a limited amount of knowledge of the period, by careful elimination, you could probably arrive at the correct answer. Remember that on the Advanced Placement examination statistically the odds are in your favor to guess at answers, provided you can eliminate one or more of the five selections. In preparation for the exam, practice this type of analysis and elimination as you look at cartoons, and as you practice doing multiple-choice questions, see how often you guess correctly.

**Sample Questions
3 and 4**

THE BATTLE OF THE BULLS AND BEARS.
"HUMPTY DUMPTY on a wall,
HUMPTY DUMPTY got a fall!"

Source: Harper's Weekly, September 10, 1872.

3. The cartoonist is chiefly concerned with making a point about
   (A) wild animal attacks on domestic cattle
   (B) earthquakes knocking down walls
   (C) the high cost of pork and flour
   (D) the high price of stocks on Wall Street
   (E) a fall in the price of gold on the Wall Street stock exchange

4. All of the following used by the cartoonist are common symbols
   EXCEPT
   (A) bulls and bears to represent attitudes toward stock pur-
        chases
   (B) Humpty Dumpty to represent gold
   (C) a wall to represent Wall Street
   (D) a bale to represent cotton
   (E) a barrel to represent pork

**Comments on
Question 3**

The cartoon for questions 3 and 4 is from *Harper's Weekly* of September
10, 1872. The cartoonist is no doubt concerned with the high cost of pork and
flour and the high prices of stocks and their fluctuations, but the real point of
the cartoon has to do with a fall in the price of gold. Of course, earthquakes and
animal attacks have nothing to do with the chief concern of the artist.

Comments on Question 4

The artist has used common symbols to represent various items in his cartoon, and the animals and the wall are examples. Question 4 requires that you be familiar with such symbols from your study. The use of a wall for Wall Street and of a bale for cotton are obvious. Most people today have heard of a *bull* or *bear* market in regard to stock purchases, as these are very common symbols. The *pork barrel* is also a very commonly used expression in American history. Salted pork was stored in a barrel, and when a person on the frontier had plenty of pork stored, he was considered fortunate and wealthy. Therefore, the political term evolved of dipping into the pork barrel, which meant helping yourself to the wealth or valuable items available for political patronage. This term does not apply to this cartoon, but it illustrates how common terms or symbols develop and become part of common usage. Finally, we come to Humpty Dumpty, as a representation of gold, and this is *not* a common symbol. It is unique to the artist and helps to make his point about the fragility of gold prices and what will happen as they fall, as the artist assumes everyone knows what happened to Humpty Dumpty when he fell off the wall.

Sample Questions 5 and 6

Source: Library of Congress

5. The photograph most likely portrays
   (A) workers on an automobile assembly line
   (B) child laborers in a factory
   (C) Civil War recruits waiting for uniforms
   (D) two boys preparing hot dogs at a baseball game
   (E) Vietnamese boat people

6. The conditions presented in the previous photograph were largely eliminated by
   (A) new industrial methods
   (B) the Child Labor Amendment to the Constitution
   (C) Supreme Court decisions before World War I
   (D) legislation under the New Deal
   (E) the Great Depression

Comments on Question 5

The photograph used for questions 5 and 6 is of two young boys working in a glass factory in 1908. It is an example of child labor and reflects factory conditions at a time when the ideas of the Social Darwinists and trust builders dominated American business. Photographs have been used less often for multiple-choice questions than cartoons, but questions can be designed around photographs that do not merely require recognition and recall of facts. By studying this photograph it would be clear that it is not an assembly line or a hot dog stand. The caps may make you think of Civil War recruits, but the chimney tongs and work table make it appear more a factory than a recruiting station. The boys are obviously not Vietnamese. The photograph is a good thought provoker and is typical of what might be found on an exam.

Comments on Question 6

Question 6 illustrates how a photograph may lead to a multiple-choice question requiring both analysis and factual recall. For question 6 you must recognize the conditions as being those of child labor in a factory, and then you must know how the conditions of child labor were changed in this country. New industrial methods changed working conditions, but many industrialists continued to employ children. The Child Labor Amendment to the Constitution was never ratified by the states, and though it may have had some impact on child labor, it did not eliminate it. Before World War I the Supreme Court was conservative and would not interfere in private business matters, and depressions generally create worse situations for workers; they do not eliminate bad conditions. It was not until the New Deal labor legislation that child labor was eliminated and factory working conditions improved.

Sample Questions 7–8

Source: *Harper's Weekly*, August, 1888

7. In this cartoon the cartoonist, W. A. Rogers, is protesting all of the following EXCEPT
   (A) free immigration
   (B) high taxes on manufactured items
   (C) the power of trusts and monopolies
   (D) James G. Blaine's comment that the immigration issue is "first to last . . . a question of labor."
   (E) the poor-quality work of American labor

8. The T. M. & Co. tag on the immigrant's arm stands for Trust, Monopoly and Company, which is
   (A) John D. Rockefeller's company
   (B) a fictitious organization representing the power of trusts
   (C) a company created by the U.S. Congress
   (D) a worldwide conglomerate
   (E) a government corporation formed to aid immigrants to the United States

Comments on Question 7

W. A. Rogers' cartoon titled "A Question of Labor" provides the basis for questions 7 and 8. It is from the August 1888 issue of *Harper's Weekly*. Question 7 asks what Mr. Rogers is protesting about in the cartoon, and the question is phrased in that very common way that seeks the one point that is incorrect. This phrasing, "all of the following EXCEPT," has been used in many multiple-choice questions in this book. It provides a positive approach to the information because four out of the five choices are correct, rather than the reverse where four choices are wrong. In this cartoon you can tell Mr. Rogers is unhappy about free immigration since the sign indicates that the immigrant is imported "duty free . . . to compete with American labor." *Compete* is the key word here. He also opposes high taxes he believes only help the trusts. Implied in both these points is Rogers's dislike of the power of the trusts and monopolies, as such phrases as *compete* and *sole benefit* indicate. He is also protesting James G. Blaine's comment, although that is not as easy to see. The title of the cartoon, "A Question of Labor," picked up Blaine's comment, and the impact of the entire cartoon is to indicate that the question is *not* merely a question of labor, it is also a question of labor competition, monopoly control, and high taxes. Rogers is thus protesting the points indicated in the first four choices and he is not protesting "the poor-quality work of American labor," which then is the correct answer for this all-but-one type of multiple-choice question. The answer was arrived at simply by analyzing the cartoon, and there was no need to understand the historical circumstances in which it was placed. These circumstances were a presidential campaign in which Benjamin Harrison, the Republican, was running against Grover Cleveland, the Democrat, whom he defeated. Blaine had been defeated by Cleveland in 1884. Blaine was considered the leading Republican. He was appointed Secretary of State by Harrison, he was a supporter of trusts and big business, and was a U.S. Senator from Maine.

Comments on Question 8

In question 8 the T. M. & Co. tag stands for Trust, Monopoly, and Company, which is mentioned in the sign under the immigrant's feet. It is a fictitious organization created by Rogers to represent the power of the trusts. The other choices given are all possibilities, and you might pick one of them unless you know a little of the history of the period. The cartoon gives you the date so you do not have to figure that out. Rockefeller's company was Standard Oil; the U.S. Congress was not creating companies at this time—it was done by private enterprise; worldwide conglomerates are a later historic development (in the pre-1900 period national trusts were being created); the United States did very little to aid immigrants in this or any period.

These illustrations of multiple-choice questions based on cartoons and a photograph should help you in your study and analysis of such items in your texts. As you can see, many types of questions can be based on cartoons and pictures, some of which will require a simple analysis of the illustrations, some of which require pure recall, and some of which require both. There will be examples of such multiple-choice questions in the following chapters.

Practice Multiple-Choice Questions

1.

OUR PRESIDENT PUTS HIS FOOT DOWN, AND THE BRITISH LION WILL HAVE TO WRIGGLE OUT.

Source: *Harper's Weekly*, July, 1872

The cartoonist is making a point concerning the *Alabama* claims, claims that
- (A) resulted from the attack of the *Alabama* on Northern shipping
- (B) were presented against British shipping in the West Indies
- (C) were British complaints against the quality of *Alabama's* cotton
- (D) involved *Alabama* businessmen and the British government
- (E) resulted from Union attack on the South during the Civil War

2. VOTE OF THE STATE OF CONNECTICUT 1872–1886

Date	Office	Parties					
		Dem.	Rep.	Gr.	Pro.	Plurality	
1872	President...............	45,880	50,638	...	...	*4758	R.
1874	Governor...............	46,755	39,973	...	4942	6782	D.
1876	President...............	61,071	59,034	774	378	2900	D.
1878	Governor...............	46,385	48,867	8314	1079	2482	R.
1880	President...............	64,415	67,169	863	448	2656	R.
1882	Governor...............	59,014	54,853	697	1034	4161	R.
1884	President...............	67,167	65,893	1684	2489	1284	D.
1884	Governor...............	67,910	66,275	1379	1636	1636	D.
1886	Governor...............	58,817	56,920	4687	2792	1897	D.

*Majority.

Source: Harper's Weekly, 1888

For the years presented in the table, all of the following are true about political parties OTHER than the Republican (Rep.) and Democrats (Dem.) EXCEPT:
  (A) Votes for only two third parties are recorded.
  (B) The Prohibition Party (Pro.) obtained its largest number of votes when it was the only third party.
  (C) The two small parties listed polled the largest combined number of votes in the gubernatorial election of 1878.
  (D) The votes of the two small parties added to the Democratic votes for president in 1880 would have given the state's electoral college votes to the Democrats.
  (E) No votes for third parties were recorded in the presidential election of 1872.

3. "The millionaires are a product of natural selection acting on the whole body of men to pick out those qualified few who can meet the requirements of certain work to be done…"

The author of the above quotation is most likely
  (A) Woodrow Wilson
  (B) William Graham Sumner
  (C) William Jennings Bryan
  (D) Eugene V. Debs
  (E) Theodore Roosevelt

4. The ideas of natural selection and survival of the fittest, when applied to business and economic activity, are referred to as
  (A) Communism
  (B) Trust-busting
  (C) Anarchism
  (D) Dollar Diplomacy
  (E) Social Darwinism

5. In 1895 President Cleveland turned to J. P. Morgan and a Wall Street syndicate to borrow gold for the U.S. Treasury because
   (A) the U.S. gold reserves were so low the government could not otherwise redeem its outstanding paper money
   (B) Cleveland had Morgan's support in the election and wished to help him
   (C) he could not get Congress to repeal the Sherman Silver Purchase Act
   (D) the government needed the money to pay salaries
   (E) it was the only way Wall Street could recover from the Panic of 1893

6. The major point of difference between Booker T. Washington and W. E. B. Du Bois was over their view of
   (A) the need for education
   (B) the importance of better race relations
   (C) the need for immediate equality for African Americans
   (D) the significance of independence for Africa
   (E) using white institutions to help the African Americans

7. The Populist Party platform in 1892 called for
   I. a graduated income tax
   II. government ownership of railroads and the return to the government of land grants held by railroads but not used in their construction
   III. a gold-based currency
   IV. support for initiative and referendum legislation
   (A) I and III
   (B) I, III, and IV
   (C) I, II, and IV
   (D) I and IV
   (E) I, II, III, and IV

8. Among the major political issues on which Congress passed legislation during the years 1877–1892 were all of the following EXCEPT
   (A) civil service reform
   (B) civil rights
   (C) control of the trusts
   (D) the coinage of silver
   (E) tariffs

THE FINISHING TOUCH
Drawn by E. W. Kemble

Source: *Harper's Weekly*, November, 1912

9. E. W. Kemble in the above cartoon is particularly commenting upon and making the point that
   (A) Woodrow Wilson was a skilled bullfighter
   (B) campaigns are like bullfights
   (C) there were few issues in the campaign
   (D) lectures delivered by Woodrow Wilson always had a point
   (E) the "Professor" Woodrow Wilson defeated Theodore Roosevelt's Bull Moose Party

10. The U.S. Supreme Court in the case of *Lochner v. New York* declared a law limiting the hours of labor in a bakery unconstitutional because it
   (A) discriminated against women workers
   (B) increased the cost of bread
   (C) interfered in the worker's right of free contract
   (D) gave an advantage to the owners
   (E) compromised the health of the workers

11. Important legislation that impacted the health and economic life of Americans passed during the presidencies of Progressive presidents Theodore Roosevelt and Woodrow Wilson included
    (A) Pure Food and Drug Act, Federal Reserve Act, Medicare Act
    (B) Meat Inspection Act, Newlands Act, Federal Deposit Insurance Corporation
    (C) Pure Food and Drug Act, Meat Inspection Act, Clean Air Act
    (D) Pure Food and Drug Act, Meat Inspection Act, Federal Reserve Act
    (E) Meat Inspection Act, Federal Reserve Act, Clean Air Act

12. All of the following increased in importance in the years 1890 to 1916 EXCEPT
    (A) the Yellow Journalism press
    (B) the Civil Rights Movement
    (C) Women's Suffrage Movement
    (D) Temperance Movement
    (E) an Urban Reform Movement

Answers and Answer Explanations

1.	A	2.	D	3.	B	4.	E	5.	A
6.	C	7.	C	8.	B	9.	E	10.	C
11.	D	12.	B						

1. (A) Question 1 refers to a cartoon about the *Alabama* claims. It appeared in *Harper's Weekly* on June 6, 1872. One piece of paper in the foreground, titled the "Alabama Claims," suggests the topic of the cartoon and requires that you know what the claims were. The *Alabama* was a warship built in Great Britain for the Confederacy during the Civil War. It raided Northern shipping. The immediate situation almost led to the North declaring war on Great Britain. The Northern financial losses resulting from ships sunk by the *Alabama* were blamed on the British who had built the ship. The situation after the war was referred to international arbitration during Grant's presidency when he "put his foot down." The lion has been a common symbol for Great Britain. Note how, in the cartoon, Grant has his foot on the British Lion's tail. This is a good example of a multiple-choice cartoon-based question requiring recall rather than analytical skill.

2. (D) Question 2 requires that you read the columns other than those marked *Rep.* and *Dem.* on the Table. You will see when you do that all the choices are correct except that the votes in these columns added to the Democratic votes for president in 1880 would not have given the state's electoral college votes to the Democrats. To eliminate this choice you must understand the operation of the electoral college at that time. In 1880 the party with the largest number of votes won *all* the electoral college votes from that state.

3. (B) The quotation in question 3 is from William Graham Sumner, a Yale sociologist who became the chief spokesperson for the philosophy of Social Darwinism. The other men were not active supporters of Social Darwinism.

4. (E) Social Darwinism is briefly described by the two terms used in question 4. Social Darwinists believe that Darwin's laws of evolution—natural selection and the survival of the fittest—also apply to social and economic activity. They

hold that government should not interfere in such activity but should allow business and social activities to progress naturally.

5. (A) Question 5 touches on the monetary problems of the government. A major political issue in 19th-century history involved a freer and more flexible currency. One solution to the problem called for coinage of silver in a ratio with gold and the issuance of paper money redeemable in either gold or silver. When the Panic of 1893 hit, the gold reserves dropped to what Cleveland considered was a dangerous level. The only way he could see to keep the U.S. credit good was to go to J. P. Morgan and his associates on Wall Street to get a loan of gold to redeem outstanding paper money. It created an enraged outcry from the Democrats and Populists, but it maintained America's credit.

6. (C) Booker T. Washington and W. E. B. Du Bois were two outstanding African American leaders at the beginning of the 20th century. They agreed on many issues, but they disagreed strongly on the need for immediate equality. Washington, the president of Tuskegee Institute, was more popular with whites and was entertained at the White House. He held that first African Americans should prove their economic importance and then equality would follow. Du Bois, a graduate of Harvard and an outstanding scholar, wanted immediate equality, and to gain this equality, he helped found the N.A.A.C.P. Both men saw a need for education, but of different types; both men would use white institutions to help African Americans and saw the importance of good race relations; African independence was not an issue in Washington's lifetime, so the other choices can be eliminated.

7. (C) The Populist Party platform in 1892 seemed to many a very radical document, but most of its provisions were adopted by 1935. Since the Populists desired a more flexible currency, they did *not* want a gold standard. Instead, they wanted silver and gold as the basis of the currency. They supported a graduated income tax, which would tax the millionaires more heavily than the poor; the return to the government of unused land grants and government ownership of railroads; the initiative and referendum, which they felt would put more political power in the hands of the people. The platform of 1892 provides an excellent statement of the goals of the Populists.

8. (B) Question 8 lists four areas in regard to which Congress passed legislation in the years 1877–1892. All the issues except civil rights were major political issues of these years. Congress passed civil rights legislation immediately after the Civil War, but not again until after World War II.

9. (E) The cartoon in question 9 was drawn by E. W. Kimble in November 1912, as a comment on Theodore Roosevelt and his Bull Moose Party's defeat in the presidential election by Woodrow Wilson, then the governor of New Jersey and a former college professor and president. Wilson is portrayed in the cap and gown of the college professor while Theodore Roosevelt is portrayed as a Bull Moose stuck in the sand and stopped by the bullfighter Wilson. The cartoon makes use of such symbols as the Bull Moose representing Roosevelt's Progressive Party and the college cap and gown. If you recognize these symbols from your study, interpreting the cartoon would be easier, but if you did not, you still might be able to eliminate several choices.

10. (C) In the case of *Lochner v. New York* in 1905 the U.S. Supreme Court declared a law regulating the number of hours a worker could work in a bakery unconstitutional because it interfered in the worker's right of free contract. This decision reflects the support of the Court for the concept of laissez-faire and support of business, which, in general, opposed government regulation and guidelines. The law's intent was to protect workers' health. It might have increased the cost of bread but the Court did not consider that. The law more likely would have given an advantage to the workers in that they could demand fewer hours of work. Later, in *Muller v. Oregon* in 1910, the Supreme Court accepted a law regulating hours of work for women.

11. (D) The Meat Inspection Act and Pure Food and Drug Act were passed under President Theodore Roosevelt. Both greatly affected the health of Americans by assuring safer food and drugs. The Federal Reserve Act passed under President Wilson reformed the banking system greatly affecting the economic life of everyone. The Newlands Act (1902) was a conservation measure. The Federal Deposit Insurance Act (1933) protected individuals' bank deposits. Medicare (1965) and the Clean Air Act (1977) affected health. These last three were not passed in the administrations of Presidents Roosevelt and Wilson.

12. (B) The Civil Rights Movement gained momentum in the 1950s after the Supreme Court in *Brown v. Board of Education* reversed the concept of "separate but equal" established in *Plessy v. Ferguson* in 1893. The Yellow Press flourished in the 1890s and helped push the nation into the Spanish-American War. Women's Suffrage, temperance, and urban reform were all important movements of the period 1890 to 1916.

Bibliography

Handlin, Oscar. *The Uprooted.* Boston: Little, Brown & Co., 1990.

Hofstadter, Richard. *The Age of Reform: From Bryan to F. D. R.* New York: Random House, 1966.

——. *American Political Tradition and the Men Who Made It.* New York: Vintage Books, 1989.

——. *Social Darwinism in American Thought.* Boston: Beacon Press, 1992.

Link, Arthur, S., & R. L. McCormick. *Progressivism.* Arlington Heights, IL: Harlan Davidson, 1983.

McGrath, R. C. Jr. *American Populism: A Social History, 1877–1898.* New York: Noonday Press, 1992.

Meier, August. *Negro Thought in America: 1880–1915.* Ann Arbor: The University of Michigan Press, 1963.

Riley, Glenda. *Women and Indians on the Frontier, 1825–1915.* Albuquerque, NM: University of New Mexico Press, 1984.

Woodward, C. Vann. *Origins of the New South, 1877–1913.* Baton Rouge: Louisiana State University Press, 1972.

Zimmerman, Warren. *First Great Triumph: How Five Americans Made Their Country a World Power.* New York: Farrar, Straus & Giroux, 2002.

Biography
The following biographies and autobiographies will provide insights into the personalities of the leaders of this period, but will also supply interesting and important background information as to what the age was like.

Adams, Jane. *Twenty-Five Years at Hull House.* Champaign, IL: University of Illinois Press, 1990.

Blum, J. M. *The Progressive Presidents.* New York: W. W. Norton & Co., 1982.

——. *The Republican Roosevelt*. Cambridge: Harvard University Press, 1977.

——. *Woodrow Wilson and the Politics of Morality*. New York: Addison-Wesley, 1998.

Holbrook, S. H. *The Age of the Moguls*. Salem, NH: Ayer Publishing Co., 1981.

Morris, Edmund. *Theodore Rex*. New York: Random House, 2001.

Steffens, Lincoln. *Autobiography*. New York: Harcourt Brace Jovanovich, 1968.

Strouse, Jen. *J. Pierpont Morgan: A Biography*. New York: Random House, 1999.

Washington, Booker T. *Up From Slavery*. New York: Oxford University Press, 2000.

Fiction

Churchill, Winston. *Coniston*. Philadelphia: Folcroft Library Editions, 1906.

Dreiser, Theodore. *An American Tragedy*, New York: H. Liverwright, 1929

Sinclair, Upton. *The Jungle*. New York: Viking Penguin, 1985.

Stegner, Wallace. *Angle of Repose*. New York: Penguin Books, 1992.

PART THREE **7** World War I, the Interwar Period, and World War II 1916–1945

Important Facets of This Period

The years 1916–1945 include several major events of American history with which every student should be familiar. These are World War I, the stock market crash of 1929 and the Great Depression that followed, the New Deal, and World War II. Every American history exam would include multiple-choice questions involving these events and often the Advanced Placement examination will have essay questions about them. The Great Depression and the New Deal responses to it are two of the major historic developments of the 20th century. These events had tremendous social impact on America as well as political, economic, and international impact. They should be considered from each of these viewpoints. Other events that occurred in these years are also very important but did not have the impact the above-listed events had.

The *Roaring Twenties* is a phrase describing the 1920s used to cover a variety of events from the political policy of Normalcy, advocated by President Harding, to the Florida land boom. The phrase *New Deal* incorporates many events in the 1930s, largely economic, social, and political. Phrases such as these are important and help to summarize periods but there are other developments of the twenties and thirties that you should be aware of. The division of the country between isolationists and internationalists and the growth of the urban population are two such developments that should be understood, but that are not strictly part of the Roaring Twenties or the New Deal.

The two world wars and the international relations connected with them involve many issues. The specific events of each war—general strategy and major battles—are important, but of even greater significance are the events surrounding the wars—the causes, the economic and social consequences, and the efforts at peacekeeping. Information on some of these aspects of the two wars appears in Chapters 6 and 8. This illustrates how difficult it is to compartmentalize history into units and chapters.

As we move closer to the present, there seem to be more and more details that are included in the history texts. If you look in the average text you will usually discover that the chapters devoted to recent history (such as the last half of the 20th century) are more detailed and cover shorter periods of time than the earlier chapters. The closer we are to events, the more information we have. For instance, eyewitness accounts are still available, and it is more difficult to see the important and crucial patterns that later historians develop. Therefore, do not be overwhelmed by the factual details of the history of these years, but use your skills to organize the details into your interpretation of the events. In other words, practice being a historian as you work through the history of recent years, establishing your theses and organizing material to support them as you have been doing in writing essays throughout your study. Studying these recent years should be an enjoyable culmination to your study of American history and to your development of skills of historical research. Be your own historian as you pursue information on the following issues:

1. The reasons for the United States' entrance into World War I, the war strategy, and the Treaty of Versailles
2. The Red Scare of the early 1920s
3. The scandals of the Harding administration
4. The effect of the automobile on the economy of the United States and the social habits of its citizens
5. The causes of the Great Crash of 1929 and the Great Depression
6. The New Deal legislation and its impact
7. The New Deal as an economic, social, and political revolution
8. The social changes in America between World Wars I and II
9. The isolationist policies of the United States after World War I and our relations with Europe and the League of Nations
10. The most significant contributions to American social, intellectual, and cultural history in the years between World War I and World War II including the Lost Generation and the Harlem Renaissance
11. The coming of World War II in Europe and Asia
12. The strategy of fighting World War II, including wartime conferences, domestic organization, and the founding of the United Nations

Sample Essay Question—Defending a Position

Occasionally you will be asked to *Defend a position* or to *Define* and/or *Identify* a particular viewpoint. Sometimes the question is to *Discuss* the viewpoint. The meaning of the word *defend* suggests that you are to argue in favor of the position stated and usually you will want to do that when answering this type of question. However, remember that an essay by definition calls for a thesis and you can present a thesis that the position you are asked to defend is indefensible. Normally, in such essay questions the position presented is the one accepted by most historians. However, with the many revisionist schools of American historians who present new and different interpretations of old positions, you may find that you have studied views other than the one presented in the question. Do not be afraid to argue for the revisionist view.

Define and *identify* type questions have the same difficulties. However, you do have more leeway to express your views in a *define* question. For example, the question, "Defend the actions of the United States government toward business in the years 1881 to 1914"* appears to provide you with little choice but to argue in favor of them, whereas the question, "Define the actions of the United States government toward business in the years 1881 to 1914"* or "Identify the actions of the United States government toward business in the years 1881 to 1914"* appears to allow you to make some choice. In all these cases you may formulate a thesis and argue for it in spite of this apparent difference.

---

*1881 is the date of the founding of the Standard Oil Trust. The Clayton Antitrust Act was passed in 1914 under President Wilson.

A final type of question in this category is the *Discuss* question. "Discuss the relations of the U.S. government between 1919 and 1941 with Germany and Japan." This seems to ask for a recall of these relations and yet it should be clear by now that you can make a statement of judgment on the relations and then argue it by presenting the evidence. If you include the selective facts concerning U.S. relations to prove a point, you are discussing these relations.

In all these cases it is important to remember the definition of the word. That is, you must understand how *define* differs from *defend*, how *defend* differs from *discuss*, etc. You must keep in mind what the question is asking in the word used. Both facts and thesis are important in this type question as in all essay questions.

In this chapter, two student answers are given to the question. Read Sample A *before* you read the question. After reading Sample A, write down what you think the question is that the student was answering. This is a very good test of how well the student has understood the question and how well he or she has responded to it in the essay. When you have written down your ideas about what the question was, read the Sample Answer B.

Sample Answer A

Franklin D. Roosevelt was both autocratic and democratic. Roosevelt had to stop a severe depression and had no precedents with which to work. Many of the measures he took provided both relief and long-range reform, which have proven important for the democratization of American life. His first action was to pass the Emergency Banking Act, closing the banks, and thus stop the serious runs on the banks. He allowed them to reopen only after passing tests of stability and gave them loans if needed to prevent the run from occurring again. He provided for insurance of up to $5,000 on future bank deposits.

To help business recover and to provide jobs, Congress passed the NIRA (National Industrial Recovery Act), which gave management wide powers of operation, including the suspension of antitrust cases, as well as assuring labor's rights to collective bargaining. For the farmers, Roosevelt developed two agricultural acts (A.A.A.) that paid farmers to reduce and store crops.

To help Americans get jobs several acts were passed. The CCC (Civilian Conservation Corps) employed 500,000 workers, especially young men from urban areas, on conservation projects. The FWA (Federal Works Administration) provided work for thousands making parks and sidewalks. The WPA (Works Projects Administration) was established to coordinate the various programs. He also set up the TVA (Tennessee Valley Authority) to provide cheap electric power. When the Supreme Court nullified some of what he thought was his greatest legislation, he tried to get Congress to pass a law allowing him to pack the Supreme Court.

Roosevelt also cleverly supported the British while keeping the nation out of war until the Japanese bombed Pearl Harbor. He then provided strong leadership to the nation and the alliance. Although he died before the final victory, his wartime conferences with Churchill and Stalin paved the way for the unconditional surrender of the Nazis and Japan and for the United Nations.

Obviously, Roosevelt was a great autocratic and democratic president.

Before you read on, write down what you think the question was for this essay.

Sample Answer B

The power of government has two appearances, one during calm and another during crises. Because the president is the head of state and the top official within our system, his power also takes on different appearances. In time of crisis the president seems to be all-powerful. Franklin D. Roosevelt faced two crises successfully and by the way he handled them, has earned the title of our greatest president.

Of course, other presidents have faced crises and handled them well to preserve our freedom and our nation. For instance, George Washington, while establishing the office of president, had to avoid war with England, and Woodrow Wilson kept us out of World War I for three years before finally entering and winning a victory for democracy. Other presidents faced domestic crises. Andrew Jackson faced the nullification issue and Abraham Lincoln had to fight the Civil War, but only Roosevelt successfully confronted major domestic and international crises and thus deserves his title of greatest president.

Roosevelt ruled the country with an iron hand because he realized his New Deal program had to be instigated if America was to recover economically from the Great Depression. His programs, such as the CCC and the WPA, gave Americans an opportunity to work while improvements in the country were also being completed. Roosevelt set up a program to rebuild the banks, including emergency banking legislation and the FDIC to insure private deposits in banks. He also started reforms of agriculture with the AAA and of business with the NRA. The Supreme Court declared much of the legislation unconstitutional and Roosevelt threatened to pack the Court. The Court soon accepted his measures to combat domestic crises. The United States was in need of a strong man who could understand the circumstances and take definite steps toward improving the nation's conditions. FDR was such a man.

Hitler had come to power at the same time as FDR and by the time the New Deal legislation was enacted, Hitler had transformed Germany into a world power. FDR saw the threat but the American people were devoted to neutrality. FDR aided the British secretly after the war began in 1939 and some say that he set the stage for the Japanese attack on Pearl Harbor. In any case, once America was attacked, he led the Allies to victory. His foresight laid the foundations for the United Nations, which was set up in San Francisco in 1945 just after his death.

There have been many types of men who have sat in the White House—intellects, lawyers, professional soldiers—some of whom have been strong and some weak. But during certain times, years of war or depression, the man who heads the government must be strong. Franklin D. Roosevelt was such a man. He faced both a major war and a major depression and found solutions to both. He definitely deserves the title of our greatest president.

The above essays were written as answers to the following question:

Sample Question

> "Defend the position that Franklin D. Roosevelt was the greatest president in the history of the United States."

Comments on Sample Question

How close to this question did you come in formulating a question for Sample Answer A? Where did you differ? Did the answer in Sample A seem to relate to this question? If you have not thought of this topic before, you should write your own answer to the question. A formal outline of each student answer will help you compare the two in detail. You will want to read the teacher comments to see how they relate to your own analysis of the two student answers. Before that, however, there is one important point to make concerning this question.

This question seems to ask for information on Franklin D. Roosevelt only, but in Sample Answer B, the writer has referred to other presidents to prove the case in favor of Franklin Roosevelt. This is a very good thing to do. You may wish to reject the statement, in which case it would be essential to introduce information concerning other presidents to prove that Franklin D. Roosevelt was not the greatest. You must think about the broadest implications of a question before starting an answer.

Teacher Comments on Sample Answers

Answer A: "The writer has no introduction and it is not clear just what he or she is discussing until the final paragraph of the essay, when he or she presents a statement indicating that Franklin D. Roosevelt was our greatest president. In the body of the essay there is a lengthy discussion of the actions of FDR and the information is accurate. On the basis of the answer, it is hard to know what the question was, yet the answer has sound information that does relate to the question. The writer is factually knowledgeable about Franklin Roosevelt but he or she overlooks the fact that in defending FDR, some comment about other presidents who might be considered great would be helpful. From a strictly factual viewpoint, this is a more than adequate answer, but it is a listing of information rather than an interpretation of a question. From that point of view it is a poor answer. It is hard not to reward the student who knows facts but this essay lacks a clear thesis and re-statement of the question and should receive a grade in the mid range."

Answer B: "The writer of this essay is more of a generalist than the writer of Answer A. He or she has an interesting introduction with a broad opening and a clearly stated thesis. The writer then goes on to consider other presidents who might be considered the greatest but rejects their claims while focusing on Franklin D. Roosevelt. He or she presents accurate specific information on the New Deal and summarizes the war. The writer thus covers the two crises, one domestic and one foreign, which he or she mentions in the opening. He or she might produce more detailed information but it is clear that the writer has understood the question and knows the presidency of Franklin D. Roosevelt. The conclusion returns to the general philosophical statement at the opening and restates the thesis. The essay clearly was written by a knowledgeable young writer and deserves a score in the top range on the AP rating scale."

Do you agree with these comments? Do you see how the writer in Answer A missed the question yet had very good information? Essay A is an excellent example of what *not* to do and of the importance of analyzing the question as suggested in the First Step of Essay Writing. Both writers organized the material well but there is more to writing an essay than that, as you are aware. Writer B clearly demonstrates that he or she analyzed the question and is using information to prove his or her thesis. Writer A is simply spilling out information which he or she has learned about Franklin Roosevelt and has made no effort to analyze the question. Such presentations of information without thought are often referred to by Advanced Placement readers as "laundry lists." They are reflections of good memorization but not of great thinking.

Practice Essay Questions

The following essay questions require information from the years 1916–1945 and one other period in American history. They provide a good review of materials studied earlier as well as of the years covered in this chapter. The first three questions are not typical of those that will appear on the Advanced Placement examination. On the examination you may be asked to analyze ideas from different time periods, but the common practice is to have the time periods closer together. These questions, however, provide you an excellent review of three very important issues of United States history.

1. Defend the position that European culture fascinated Americans in the period 1789–1801 and in the period between World Wars I and II.

2. "War has united Americans more closely than any other activity."

   Discuss this statement and test its validity by references to American history during the years 1812–1824 and 1912–1924.

3. "The social changes of the Jacksonian Period were greater and more profound than the social changes of the post-World War I period."

   Assess the validity of this statement.

4. "Republicans have been the party of Big Business and depression; the Democrats have been the party of the Common Man and of war."

   State whether you agree or disagree with this statement and defend your position with reference to TWO of the following events:

   Panic of 1893 and Spanish American War
   Panic of 1907 and World War I
   Great Depression and World War II

5. Defend the proposition that "the proposals of the Populists as to how to handle the economic conditions of the early 1890s were not enacted but these proposals provided the framework for the New Deal's response to the economic conditions of the early 1930s."

Comments on Question 1

Question 1 is a typical *Defend a position*-type essay question. You are asked to *defend* a particular statement, which may be difficult to do. You are given specific directions as to the two periods you are to discuss. There should be no difficulty understanding what is expected. There may be, however, difficulty in finding factual information to defend this position. When you find yourself in that situation you have two options: first, not to write on the question and, second, to take the opposite view than that expected and argue that the position is not defensible. This is always an option that you have in writing an essay even though the author has clearly stated what you are supposed to do. In an essay you are always, as you learned at the beginning of this book, expected to express your own opinion.

The word *culture* is one of those commonly used words that is rarely defined. It is important to have a concept about what culture is before answering this question. Culture is defined in *Webster's Eleventh New Collegiate Dictionary* as "a particular state of advancement in civilization and the characteristic feature(s) of such a stage or state." Usually we think of culture as the "arts," as those aspects of society that are not related to economic or political life. However, the definition says it includes "characteristic feature(s) of" and these often have to do with economic and social developments. In history we often use the expression *economic, political, and social* in describing events or developments. Many people consider social in this phrase as equivalent to culture, but it is not, since culture is the inclusive term under which economic, political, social, and intellectual all fit as the following diagram illustrates:

Therefore, you should include political and economic ideas in your answer, although the usual approach to this question would be to discuss those ideas we usually consider as social and intellectual—matters concerning manners, attitudes, lifestyles, literary and artistic development, religious attitudes and the like. Certainly these latter matters should be discussed in your answer to this question but you would not want to narrow your answer to these matters only.

Finally, the question states that European ideas were attractive to Americans in the early years of the nation and in the 1920s and 1930s. What is your viewpoint on that question? That is, what is your thesis?

Comments on Question 2

Question 2 is a typical *Discuss* question. There should be no confusion about what is wanted in an answer. Again, the time periods may be difficult, but as mentioned above, the questions in this chapter cover different time periods and are thus excellent review questions for American history since 1789. You have studied all these periods since you began work on this book. How well you can respond to these questions without doing research will provide a good indication of how well prepared you are for the Advanced Placement exam. The generalization in question 2 is an interesting one requiring a new look at or special theses on periods of American history. You should be able to analyze what is needed and prepare a thesis and outline without much difficulty.

Comments on Question 3

Question 3 is a typical *Assess the validity* question. The question focuses on social change and, therefore, unlike the question on culture, you should *not* include economic and political changes except as they might cause social changes. The two periods—the Jacksonian and the interwar period, especially the 1920s—were times of great change in the American way of life. Which period do you feel had the more profound and greater changes? In a way this becomes a comparison question without using that word. Certainly a comparison of the changes provides the obvious organization for this question. Questions asking for your opinion based on a comparative value such as "more profound" are always difficult. The key is to define your understanding of the phrase.

**Comments on
Question 4**

Question 4 is another *Generalization* question where the directions are given in detail. You are to state whether you agree or disagree, which, of course, is what a thesis is, and then it tells you to defend your position, which, of course, is what you have been doing in every essay you have written. The directions should be easy and obvious. The events are those you have studied most recently, so you should have the facts about the six items. However, with six items in three combinations, it may be difficult to decide which two to use. **Pick the two based on how well the information you have about them relates to your thesis and not on how much you know about them.** This is often a hard choice for students to make. The major problem in question 4 is the baldness and simplicity of the generalization. It is the type of statement we often hear, but it is so blatantly broad and unthinking that it is hard to deal with. Is there truth in it? Your introduction will probably include general comments on the generalization; that is, such matters as its simplicity and the meaning of "Common Man" and "Big Business." Your thesis will then present your interpretation of the generalization. How to organize this question is a challenge. When you make your brief notes on the information, a pattern should emerge that will supply the organization. The question itself supplies no simple, obvious pattern. This is a difficult question in many ways, but the information should be readily at hand.

**Comments on
Question 5**

Question 5 is another variation of the *Defend* question. The question states what you are to discuss in your answer. The generalization is quite straightforward, and the question should not be difficult to understand. There should be no difficulty developing a thesis for question 5. An obvious organization is suggested in the question when it states "both the Populist proposals and the New Deal's use of them." Following this statement you could in each paragraph in the body of the paper make a statement of a Populist proposal followed by a discussion of how the New Deal used or failed to use the proposal. This format would give an excellent structure to the essay.

The major problem in this question centers on how specific your knowledge is of the Populist proposals. The chances are you will have detailed knowledge of the New Deal response to the economic conditions of the 1930s. How well can you relate these to the Populist proposals? This again is an excellent review question.

On the Advanced Placement exam essays, most detailed information that is required will come from the mainstream of American history and should be familiar to you if you have studied the periods of U.S. history emphasized in this book. Several essay questions may require information from social or literary history or the history of minorities but they will relate to mainstream U.S. history.

Multiple-Choice Questions—The Value of Sources

The six multiple-choice questions in this section test your knowledge of different historical sources, of historical bias and interpretation, and of historical research technique. You should be prepared for these questions as a result of your general study and particularly as a result of any research papers you have done. What sources to turn to first, how you recognize bias, where data are stored are all important matters for the historian. Many of the answers are supplied merely by common sense, but many will have been learned or absorbed from your study.

Also, as a result of your study you should be aware of the best sources to use in writing history. Read and answer the questions before reading the comments.

Sample Questions 1–2

1. In doing research for a history project, to which one of the resources listed below should you turn first if you were seeking information on the text of Franklin D. Roosevelt's First Inaugural Address?
   (A) *Encyclopaedia Britannica*
   (B) Collection of documents of U.S. history
   (C) A biography of Franklin Roosevelt
   (D) *Books in Print*
   (E) *Dictionary of American Biography*

2. In doing research for a history project, which one of the resources listed below would give you the quickest access to information on the current population of New York City?
   (A) *Encyclopaedia Britannica*
   (B) *Guinness Book of World Records*
   (C) A historical atlas
   (D) A world almanac
   (E) *Facts on File*

Comments on Question 1

Questions 1 and 2 test your knowledge of sources used in historical research. The sources listed in question 1 should be familiar to every history student. An encyclopedia includes informative, summarizing articles on many items and is often a good source as an introduction to a topic. Articles would not include the full texts of speeches. In doing effective research, it would *never* be your only source. There are many collections of documents related to U.S. history. They usually include famous speeches, important congressional legislation, treaties, Supreme Court decisions, and letters. The contents vary according to the point of view of the editor. A biography of Franklin Roosevelt might include excerpts from his speeches but it is unlikely a complete address would be included; again, what is included would depend upon the writer. *Books in Print* is an important source of information on books currently available. They are listed by author and subject. There you could find if any works by FDR are in print but his speech would not be in *Books in Print*. The *Dictionary of American Biography* is an invaluable source of information on famous Americans. It includes brief but thorough accounts of the lives of famous Americans. With this description of the sources that were probably familiar to you, the answer to the question should be rather obvious: choice B. The text of Franklin D. Roosevelt's First Inaugural Address would most likely be included in a book of documents, which would be the place to look first. The Internet would be another source, but it is not offered as an option.

Comments on Question 2

In the choices for question 2 the *Guinness Book of World Records* is an interesting listing of records but most of them have little historical significance. An historical atlas contains maps and charts relating to geography. *Facts on File* is a compilation of many facts using a chronological presentation. It is helpful in checking on recent events but the best place to find the population of New York City would be in a world almanac, choice D.

These two questions test your knowledge of sources and your research ability by finding where you would go first for information. It is one method of testing your knowledge of the value of sources.

Sample Question 3

3. If you were involved in a research project on the Teapot Dome oil scandal during President Harding's administration, which one of the following would provide you with the most complete unbiased report on the scandal?
   (A) A personal friend of the president
   (B) A newspaper article written when the scandal first was publicized
   (C) The records of the oil companies involved
   (D) The complete transcript of the court trial of the men involved
   (E) A biography of President Harding

Comments on Question 3

Question 3 is a test of your perception or understanding of the reliability of sources. It does not require that you know the details of the Teapot Dome scandal, but that you can determine how biased sources would be. Obviously, a friend of the president would have a particular case to state, as would the writer of a biography. The report of these individuals might be biased either for or against the case. The records of the oil companies would present only one side of the case. The newspaper account, although claiming to be unbiased, is often biased, and one written when the case was just starting would obviously not have a complete record. The complete transcript of the trial would include information on both sides of the scandal and should include all the information available at the time. It would be a good place to begin your research (choice D).

Sample Question 4

4. Which of the following would most likely include information on the wealth of the individuals listed on a voting register for a colonial New England town?
   (A) The Bible in the local church
   (B) The tombstones in the churchyard
   (C) The military roster for the town
   (D) The original charter for the town
   (E) The local town rolls

Comments on Question 4

Question 4 tests your understanding of where information can be found. Bias is not involved as there is only one place listed where a person's wealth would be recorded. The question is more a test of your knowledge of types of sources than in research. Local town rolls in colonial New England listed the wealth of the citizens for purposes of taxation (choice E). The church Bible and tombstones would be a good source of names of citizens and birth and death dates, but they would not reveal wealth. The military roster would supply the names of males and perhaps ages. The original charter of the town would be of no help in learning about the wealth or anything else about the citizens.

Sample Question 5

5. In the 1970s revisionist historians of the Cold War reinterpreted events to suggest that all of the following are true EXCEPT
    (A) Truman overreacted to the postwar developments in Greece.
    (B) The Yalta Agreement was a fair document based on historic circumstances.
    (C) The Communists carefully followed a master plan to bring on the Cold War.
    (D) Blame for the Cold War should be split between the Soviet Union and the Western allies.
    (E) Churchill's goal was more the preservation of British power than world peace.

Comments on Question 5

Question 5 tests your understanding of historiography. It is the only question in the book so far that does so. In recent years the Advanced Placement exam has placed less emphasis on historiography. In this question you must know what the Cold War is and you must know what that group of historians who are revising the interpretation of the Cold War is saying. The question tests factual knowledge of a very particular and very important kind. It tests your knowledge of historical interpretation, which in turn reveals the types of sources you have used in your study. As your study of American history has progressed, you should have learned of various interpretations of the facts by the leading historians of the different periods, and not just the facts. There are standard and accepted interpretations of the major events of American history, and some of these interpretations have been challenged from time to time. Thus, there are recent revisionist schools on causes of the American Revolution and the Civil War, on the character and politics of Abraham Lincoln, on the Turner thesis concerning the significance of the frontier in American history, on Beard's economic interpretation of the Constitution, on the origins of the Cold War, and on many other events. Also, different publishers over the years have published works that include conflicting opinions on important topics. One of the earliest, designed for college freshmen, was the "Amherst Series" on *Problems in American Civilization,* published by D. C. Heath & Co. Works of this type can be very helpful in discovering how historians differ in their interpretations of the past. The Cold War historians reinterpreting the Cold War suggest that, except for C, the choices given are correct.

Sample Question 6

6. If you read the statement "Violence was a way of life in pre-Civil War Southern society," you would be more inclined to accept it as valid if you learned
    (A) the author was a leading Southern historian of the pre-Civil War era
    (B) there were more lynchings in the South than in the North
    (C) that on a per capita basis there have been more volunteers for the army from the South than from the North
    (D) the writer was a trained psychologist and a leading historian of the South
    (E) the statement was quoted in two textbooks and used in a speech by a historian

Comments on Question 6

The last question in this group of examples, question 6, asks you to make a judgment on the reliability of a statement when you know its source. If you read the statement on violence, you might question it and hopefully reject it if it were based solely on the number of lynchings in the South or Southern volunteers in the U.S. Army. Also, simply because textbooks quote ideas does not make them true. *Who* said them is crucial! In this case, if "the writer was both a trained psychologist and a leading historian of the South," you *should* be more inclined to accept the statement than if it were simply made by a "leading Southern historian." This is an excellent example of the multiple-choice question designed to test the value of sources. As you review the last years of American history, test your ability to judge sources. The closer we are to events, the more possibility there is for rashness of judgment and bias. Read the material you study carefully to check on such rashness. This is particularly important when using the Internet.

Practice Multiple-Choice Questions

1. "The world is so deeply divided into opposing classes that social wrongs can be corrected only by revolution" summarizes a position held by many supporters of
   (A) Socialism
   (B) Nazism
   (C) Isolationism
   (D) McCarthyism
   (E) Communism

2. The best and most reliable way to locate the latest research on or discussion of a particular topic of current national concern is to consult the
   (A) index of *Books in Print*
   (B) editor of your local newspaper
   (C) *Periodical Guide to Literature*
   (D) *New York Times Index*
   (E) local television station

3. Which of the following programs did NOT provide jobs, work opportunities, or direct aid to unemployed or disabled individuals?
   (A) Civilian Conservation Corps
   (B) Federal Emergency Relief Administration
   (C) Works Progress Administration
   (D) National Recovery Administration
   (E) Social Security Program

4. Which of the following developments did NOT occur in the 1920s?
   (A) The first "talking" motion picture
   (B) The development of commercial radio
   (C) The Monkey Trial of John Scopes in Dayton, Tennessee
   (D) The end of Prohibition
   (E) The rebirth of the Ku Klux Klan

5. If you were seeking information on Franklin D. Roosevelt's personal opinions concerning U.S. foreign policy toward Great Britain from 1933–1939, in which one of the following would you be more likely to find the information?

    (A) The Franklin D. Roosevelt Library in Hyde Park, New York
    (B) The National Archives in Washington, D.C.
    (C) The State Department Library
    (D) The Library of Congress
    (E) The British Museum

6. Which of the following were events that led directly to the United States involvement in World War I?

    I.   Zimmermann Note
    II. Russian Revolution of March 1917
    III. Sinking of the *Lusitania*
    IV. Unrestricted submarine warfare

    (A) I, II, and III   (D) II, III, and IV
    (B) I, II, and IV   (E) I, II, III, and IV
    (C) I, III, and IV

7. The United States in the 1920s refused to cancel the war debts of its European allies because the United States

    (A) wanted to force Germany to pay the wartime reparations
    (B) needed the money to help pay for economic development at home
    (C) believed the money paid was needed for loans to Germany
    (D) considered that all honestly incurred debts should be paid
    (E) thought debt payment would reduce the arms race in Europe

8. The United States issued a Declaration of Neutrality in 1937 as a result of the

    I.   outbreak of the Spanish Civil War
    II. growing strength of Hitler in Germany
    III. Nye Committee's Report on War Profiteering in World War I
    IV. invasion of Ethiopia by Mussolini's Italy

    (A) I and II
    (B) I, III, and IV
    (C) I and IV
    (D) II, III, and IV
    (E) I, II, III, and IV

9. All of the following involved American military forces EXCEPT the

    (A) Battle of Stalingrad   (D) defense of Bataan
    (B) invasion of Iwo Jima   (E) Battle of the Bulge
    (C) Battle of Midway

10.

According to his presentation in the above cartoon, you could assume the artist, Barclay, would support

(A)   the Republicans' not providing direct aid to the unemployed
(B)   the need for slum clearance in Washington
(C)   the Republican interpretation that the depression would be quickly over
(D)   specific action to aid the unemployed
(E)   the Democratic Party's program of reform of business

11.   Which of the following was not a leader of a nation allied with the United States in World War II?

(A) Winston Churchill
(B) Charles de Gaulle
(C) Joseph Stalin
(D) Benito Mussolini
(E) Chiang Kai-shek

12.

That's Why It's Not Time for a Change

Source: *Richmond Times Dispatch*, November 12, 1944

In the cartoon, the cartoonist, Fred O. Seibel, is suggesting that
 (A) the colonel has an old-fashioned record player
 (B) Dewey is a poor record salesman
 (C) Virginia will not vote for the Republican candidate for the White House
 (D) Virginia has its own record and is not interested in changing it
 (E) the White House is a loudspeaker for ideas of Virginians

Answers and	**1.**	E	**2.**	C	**3.**	D	**4.**	D
Answer Explanations	**5.**	A	**6.**	C	**7.**	D	**8.**	E
	9.	A	**10.**	D	**11.**	D	**12.**	C

1. (E) The statement in question 1 summarizes a view held by Communists in the tradition of Marx and Lenin. There has been some shift away from this "classical view" in recent years in China and the Soviet Union before its disintegration in 1991.

2. (C) Of the choices given the best source of information on a current national topic is the *Periodical Guide to Literature.* This contains information on all of the latest articles written on a particular matter. It would be more up to date than books, which take longer to appear in print. Therefore, you would consult the *Periodical Guide* before consulting the Index of *Books in Print.* The editor of your local newspaper or your local television station just might have information on your topic but it would be difficult to be certain that they know all of the latest research unless they are experts in the field. The *New York Times Index* would list only articles carried in that newspaper and would not suggest other sources for such information. With the arrival of Internet and developments in library use of computers, there are new ways to find the latest research but such new sources were not mentioned in the question.

3. (D) One aspect of the New Deal was to provide immediate relief for the unemployed, and each of these acts, except the National Recovery Administration which dealt with business recovery and conditions of labor, provided either direct relief in the form of unemployment benefits or jobs for the unemployed.

4. (D) Prohibition was ended in 1933; it was in effect during the 1920s. The other developments listed all occurred in the 1920s and reflect different aspects of that very interesting period, the Roaring Twenties.

5. (A) The five choices in this question are all important depositories of letters and papers dealing with history. The British Museum would be the one least likely to contain Franklin D. Roosevelt's personal opinions on foreign policy, but it might have some of the Churchill-Roosevelt correspondence. In seeking knowledge of U.S. history you must not confine yourself to American sources only. The Library of Congress, National Archives, and State Department would all have some of the official documents of the Roosevelt years, but the personal correspondence and other personal statements of F. D. R. would most likely be found in the Roosevelt Library at Hyde Park, which houses his personal papers. Although you might not have been familiar with these five items, you should be able to figure out the best source for information on personal opinions from this list; personal opinions are least likely to be found in official places.

6. (C) The Russian Revolution of March 1917 (number II) is not usually considered as an event that led to the U.S. involvement in World War I although the establishment of a democratic government in St. Petersburg made Russia a more appealing ally than Tsarist Russia was. Therefore C, which includes I, III, and IV, is correct as those three events are all considered events that led to our entry into World War I. The Zimmermann Note was a secret message sent by the German

Foreign Minister to the German Ambassador in Mexico on March 1, 1917, suggesting an alliance between Mexico and Germany in case the United States entered World War I on the side of the Allies. The message was decoded by the British and turned American sentiment against Germany. When a German submarine sank the British passenger liner, *Lusitania,* 128 Americans lost their lives. After an exchange of messages, German submarine warfare was decreased but its resumption in February 1917 led directly to the Declaration of War on April 7, 1917.

7. (D) The United States under the Republican leadership of Harding, Coolidge, and Hoover insisted that honestly incurred debts should be paid. With the stock market crash in 1929, Hoover allowed a one-year moratorium on debt payment, but by then it was too late to renegotiate the debts and they were never paid except by Finland.

8. (E) Question 14 seeks reasons for the U.S. Declaration of Neutrality in 1937 and all four choices offered in I-IV were used as reasons to justify the declaration.

9. (A) The Battle of Stalingrad was a turning point in World War II. The Russians at Stalingrad stopped the German advance into the Soviet Union without U.S. forces, but with the aid of U.S. supplies. The other four choices involved U.S. troops and are among the most important battles fought. Iwo Jima was a major step on MacArthur's path back to the Philippines and Japan. The naval Battle of Midway stopped a Japanese advance across the Pacific and is considered the turning point of World War II in the Pacific. Bataan, a peninsula in the Bay of Manila, fell to the Japanese after a significant defensive action that allowed the United States to recover from Pearl Harbor and prepare to wage war in the Pacific during World War II. The Battle of the Bulge was the final attempt by the Germans to prevent the Allied invasion of Germany.

10. (D) The artist, Barclay, is making a comment on the apparent blindness of the Republicans to the fact that there are 15 million unemployed and that living conditions, as depicted in Hooverville, are terrible. He portrays the Republican elephant as blind and insensitive to these conditions. If this is Barclay's idea, then it would seem logical that he would support specific action to aid the unemployed. The other choices do not appear to reflect the viewpoint expressed in the cartoon.

11. (D) Benito Mussolini was the Fascist dictator of Italy during World War II. The others ruled Allied nations: Churchill—Great Britain; de Gaulle—Free France; Stalin—USSR; Chiang Kai-shek (Jiang Jie-shi)—China.

12. (C) The cartoon, drawn by Fred Seibel in October 1944, refers to the Dewey-Roosevelt presidential campaign of that year, when Franklin Roosevelt defeated Dewey winning an unprecedented fourth term. Seibel suggests that the state of Virginia will not vote for Dewey, the Republican (G.O.P.).

Bibliography

Allen, F. L. *Only Yesterday*. New York: Perennial, 2000.

——. *Since Yesterday*. New York: Harper & Row, 1986.

Dalleck, Robert. *Franklin D. Roosevelt and American Foreign Policy, 1932–1945*. New York: Oxford University Press, 1995.

Eisenhower, D. D. *Crusade in Europe*. Baltimore: Johns Hopkins University Press, 1997.

Freidel, Frank. *FDR: Rendezvous with Destiny*. Boston: Little Brown, 1991.

Galbraith, J. K. *The Great Crash of 1929*. New York: Mariner Books, 1997.

Goodwin, Doris Kearns. *No Ordinary Time: Franklin and Eleanor Roosevelt*. New York: Touchstone, 1995.

Lynd, R. S., and H. M. *Middletown*. New York: Harcourt Brace Jovanovich, Inc., 1959.

Strachan, Hew (*ed.*) *The Oxford Illustrated History of the First World War*. New York: Oxford University Press, 2001.

Time Life (*ed.*) *World War II: Time Life History of the Second World War*. New York: Prentice Hall, 1989.

Widenor, William C. *Henry Cabot Lodge and the Search for an American Foreign Policy*. Berkeley: University of California Press, 1983.

Wintz, C. D. *Black Culture and the Harlem Renaissance*. Kingsville, TX: Texas A&M University Press, 1997.

Fiction

Fitzgerald, F. S. *The Great Gatsby*. New York: Macmillan, 1988.

Lewis, Sinclair. *Babbitt*. New York: Harcourt Brace Jovanovich, Inc., 1989.

Steinbeck, John. *The Grapes of Wrath*. New York: Viking Penguin, 1977.

Wright, Richard. *Native Son*. Reading, MA: Addison-Wesley Educational, 1989.

PART THREE # 8 The Postwar Period, the Cold War, and After 1945–2003

Important Facets of This Period

Coverage of the Years 1945–2003 on the AP Exam

The period after World War II presents many problems for the student of history and for the creators of the Advanced Placement examination. As indicated in the Introduction, since the exam is given in May, those schools that present a chronological history and that continue in session until mid-June will most likely not have studied much of this time period before the May examination. Responding to the problem created by this situation, the Advanced Placement test creators have indicated that, although one-third of the multiple-choice questions will be on the time after 1914, very few questions will be on the period after 1980. Likewise, the test creators have indicated that no essay question will focus exclusively on the time after 1980, although in some cases an essay will ask for knowledge of that era as it relates to earlier U.S. history. The 1980 date was set recently. It means that such major events as the Reagan presidency, the end of the Cold War, the Persian Gulf War, the economic boom of the Clinton years, and the war on terrorism, including the wars in Afghanistan and Iraq, will not be the *exclusive* subject of an essay. However, as the years pass, this date may be changed. Presently there are multiple-choice questions on post-1980 history. The sample essay questions in this chapter indicate how history after 1980 may be included in essay questions.

Interpreting Recent History

Another problem these years present to the student of history is that mentioned in the previous chapter concerning the interpretation of recent events and historic perspective. Until a generation or two has passed it is difficult to be certain what events are important and particularly how these events have truly affected the course of history. For instance, everyone believes the Vietnam War has had a profound impact on American life, but what the impact will prove to be by 2025, when today's high school students are in their 40s is hard to determine. In the meantime, we have a great deal of data about the war to absorb. You need to know the details of war activities, of domestic protest, of presidential politics, of social changes, and all the rest, yet by 2025 the social changes, for example, may have been totally reversed, and we will consider them of little historic significance. Thus, as events recede into the past, we simplify and interpret them to make them more manageable and, we think, more understandable.

Since we lack historic perspective on the developments of recent years we must consider all events with equal care. This means there is much more factual information to absorb. One can easily become overwhelmed with the details of the recent past and lose sight of any interpretation or themes that are emerging. This is particularly true of the years since World War II, during which time the methods of recording information have multiplied so rapidly. Recording devices, copying machines, television, and computers provide us with quantities of factual data we have not had available before. Watergate is an excellent example of how this phenomenon can affect politics and history. Nixon's own tape recordings proved the downfall of his presidency. Sorting out the data to write the focused and definitive history of Watergate or any event of the past 50 years will require extensive and dedicated research as hours of TV coverage, taped interviews, and computerized records as well as the more traditional sources of books and diaries of those involved, Congressional Records, news stories, and personal interviews must be read and analyzed. You may be involved in this process as a future historian. However, until historic perspective is gained and focused interpretations are presented, the student has a quantity of information to learn and interpret.

U.S. History Since 1941 Is World History

Another matter that makes recent U.S. history more difficult to study is that from 1941 on, U.S. history has really become world history, and economic globalization and the Internet have intensified this trend. No longer can we study developments such as those on the frontier and feel we are learning American history. Since 1941 the student must not only know domestic developments, but must also be aware of what has happened to the former Soviet Union, what the map of Vietnam looks like, where and when the United States has come under terrorist attacks, why the Arab-Israeli conflict seems unresolvable, how the independence of African nations has affected African Americans in the United States, and many other points involving nations throughout the world. Until 1941 many Americans and many American decisions ignored these areas. It was probably wrong to do so, but it certainly made American history up to 1941 much easier to study and to understand.

Although the problems stated above make U.S. history more complex, they also offer the student a chance to be an active historian analyzing primary sources and seeking new information and interpretations. As World War II recedes in time, more definitive interpretations of its aftermath are becoming available, and with the end of the Cold War, many historians are offering new interpretations of it.

Many of the trends and concerns of recent years began in the immediate post-World War II era or in the time between the two world wars. Since you are expected to know these time periods on the examination, one helpful way to study the post-World War II period is to analyze it by comparing events and trends with those following World War I. Then you should focus your study on the direction the trends took in the more recent past. The trends listed below are some of those that have been identified as significant ones in the post-World War II era. Note how many of the trends are contradictory, reflecting the dynamic tension that has existed in the post-World War II world.

Major Trends in U.S. History Since the End of World War II

1. Move toward internationalism—the United Nations—and multilateralism, as shown in treaty commitments and concern for undeveloped nations
2. Emergence of the United States as the sole superpower, of unilateralism, and of the United States as policeman of the world
3. The emergence of the Cold War and fear of communism
4. The desire for détente
5. Greater government control of the business cycle, including the role of the Federal Reserve Bank

6. Desire for deregulation of business and industry
7. Development and growth of service industries, advertising, computers, and e-commerce
8. The continuation of poverty within a generally affluent society
9. A general distrust of, and disillusionment with, the political process
10. Expanding globalization, growing awareness of environmental issues and spaceship Earth, concerns about international terrorism and use of weapons of mass destruction
11. Increasing frankness in human relations, sexual freedom, and intellectual and artistic expression, as well as government support for the arts
12. Desire to restore "family" values, to control education and stamp out drug use
13. Struggle for the civil rights of all
14. Increasing isolation from and fear of those who are different

In addition to these major trends there are issues that need to be considered. How are the above trends illustrated with information from the following?

1. The Cold War
2. Specific foreign policy actions by each postwar president from Truman to George W. Bush
3. The Civil Rights Movement and the emergence of minority organizations
4. The Vietnam War and its impact on government and society
5. Johnson's Great Society
6. Changing economic policies of the federal government, including Reaganomics, welfare, health care, Social Security, and taxes
7. Social, economic, and political divisions in the nation manifested in such issues as civil rights, abortion, the widening gap between rich and poor, legislative gridlock in Washington, the "politics of personal destruction," and the aftermath of the terrorist attack of September 11, 2001.
8. The most significant contributions to and changes in American social and intellectual history

Some of your study may have to be done in contemporary sources, as some texts will not go up to the present. In fact, if you get in the habit of reading the newspapers and newsmagazines, this reading will give you a lot of information on recent history, will help your understanding of charts, graphs, and maps, and will often make you aware of past events, since such events are often referred to in articles. Such reading of newspapers and newsmagazines is strongly recommended.

Sample Essay Question—Review

In Chapters 1 through 7 we have presented and analyzed different types of essay questions. We have illustrated the fact that different types of questions are often combined. This means there are innumerable combinations of questions and directions, but in what we have discussed so far, you have been presented with the most important types of essay questions found on the Advanced

Placement exam. Rather than discuss and analyze another type of essay question in this last chapter, we will present two different questions and one student answer to each. As in all cases so far, we suggest that you write an answer to the question before you read the sample answer and the teacher comments.

Sample Question A

"The Supreme Court's interpretation of the Constitution in the years before the election of Franklin Roosevelt in 1932 made it difficult for the federal government to legislate social policy and changes at the national level, yet from that time until the election of Ronald Reagan in 1980 the situation was reversed." *Assess the validity* of this quotation.

Sample Answer A

The Supreme Court is a very powerful part of the federal government. In many ways it is the most powerful of the three branches, since the president and Congress must abide by its decisions. These decisions are based on the Court's philosophy and interpretation of the Constitution and can change from time to time. Before the New Deal the Court was conservative but after 1937 it became more liberal in its interpretation of social issues.

Until the late 1930s the philosophy of the Supreme Court judges and their interpretation of the Constitution made it almost impossible to have any social legislation passed by the federal government upheld by the Court. By social legislation, we mean national laws regulating social and economic relations between individual people, possibly an employer and employee, businessperson and consumer, or starving individuals and those to whom they were forced to turn for handouts.

In 1890 Congress passed the Sherman Act, which forbade any business combination in restraint of (interstate) trade. This act was intended to break up monopolies. In *United States v. E. C. Knight*, the Sugar Trust, a manufacturing company that controlled the sugar industry and whose goods were traded in interstate commerce, was said not to affect interstate commerce since control of manufacture did not mean control of trade. Similar interpretations invalidated the Clayton Antitrust Act passed by Congress in 1914. Thus, Supreme Court decisions in the early part of the 20th century blocked federal legislation to control big business for the benefit of the people.

In 1916 Congress passed the first child labor act forbidding a company to ship goods in interstate commerce if the company employed children. In *Hammer v. Dragenhart*, a year later, the Court struck down the law as an unjustifiable use of the commerce power to control local labor conditions. A year after that, Congress passed a law taxing companies employing child labor. In *Baily v. Drexel Furniture Company*, the Court again struck down the social legislation. Most states eventually forbade child labor, but the Supreme Court had effectively blocked national social legislation in this area.

Even in 1934, at almost the peak of our country's depression, the Court struck down Roosevelt's NIRA in *Schechter Poultry v. United States*. The NIRA had among other things set a minimum wage and a code of fair labor and price policies. This was needed and was beneficial social legislation for the United States, but the Court again seemed to interpret only the literal meaning of the Constitution. Schechter didn't affect interstate commerce directly and therefore the law, which was derived from Congress's commerce power, was unconstitutional.

There were two reasons why the Court had not let Congress pass social legislation. One was because in almost all the laws for social reform, some part or wording of the Constitution was being stretched or broadened. For example, Congress claimed that because the Constitution said "Congress shall have the power to regulate interstate commerce," they had the right to regulate any company involved in interstate commerce. They felt that if they once gave such a loose interpretation to the Constitution, Congress would soon be able to justify any law it wished to pass, which would be wrong.

The other reason was that the Court was dominated by rather conservative justices who were influenced by the philosophy of Social Darwinism and a laissez-faire approach to economics. These attitudes prevented the Court from regarding social legislation as beneficial to the country.

In the early 1930s the Court continued to uphold its rather literal interpretation of the Constitution. Thus, almost no social legislation was approved but most of the decisions were by a 5–4 vote. After the Court invalidated several other items of New Deal legislation, such as the AAA in 1937, Roosevelt attempted to pack the Court, which, although not passed by Congress, scared the Court. Also, one of the elder judges retired and was replaced by a supporter of FDR; thus we began to see 5–4 and 6–3 decisions in favor of Roosevelt's social legislation.

The most obvious change in the Court's decisions was in the Bituminous Coal Board case, which said that Congress could regulate the working hours of miners, their pay, and the price of coal. In 1941, in *Darby v. United States*, the Court validated a law forbidding child labor, thus reversing its previous position. *Commerce* was now defined as totally under congressional control, thus breaking down barriers between state and federal areas of control.

The climax in the Court's change of opinion as to how to interpret the Constitution probably is marked by *Brown v. Board of Education*, which struck down segregated schools. Although the decision did not involve federal social legislation, it involved the relations between individuals as established by state and local laws. The Court interpreted the Constitution loosely and largely based its decision on psychological evidence. Under the leadership of Chief Justice Warren several important decisions, such as that in the Gideon case, gave strong protection to the rights of the individual in opposition to the rights of the state. Later in *Roe v. Wade*, a woman's right to an abortion was upheld. This case continued the trend established in the 1930s of using the power of government, in this case the courts, to support the individual. After his election, Ronald Reagan called for more conservative decisions, and with his court appointments the court began to reverse itself. The abortion cases of the 1980s and early 1990s clearly illustrate the conservative trend.

The Supreme Court effectively prevented national social legislation in the early years of the 20th century. After an apparent total reversal of opinion, the Warren Court appeared to be ready not only to approve social legislation passed by Congress, but even to take the lead in bringing on social change, which illustrates that the Court is an important and powerful branch of the federal government.

Teacher Comments on Sample Answer A

"This is an excellent answer to the question on social legislation and the Supreme Court. It is well organized, presents a thesis that is well developed, and contains fine factual details from one of the more specialized areas of

American history—legal history. The student's definition of social legislation is adhered to in the essay and his or her thesis on the philosophy of the judges and their interpretation of the Constitution is well supported. Only at the end does he or she depart from examples drawn from cases involving strictly social legislation. The student is aware of this departure and carefully states what might be expected from the Court in the future. The conclusion is well presented as is the introduction, both of which follow well-established techniques for essay writing. This essay would have received a top grade as an answer to this question."

Did you agree with the teacher comments? It is longer than those usually written on the AP but was included to illustrate how legal history can be used and to provide you with information on the Court. This answer is one of the best sample essay answers in the book and was placed here to provide a high standard for comparison now that you have almost completed your study and you have had extended experience writing essays. How did your essay compare with this one?

This is a typical *Assess the validity* type of question. What the question was asking for should not have been difficult for you to analyze. Whether you were as well prepared to discuss Court cases and decisions as the writer of the sample essay will depend on how much time you devoted to legal history. You could write an effective answer putting greater emphasis on social legislation and explaining why you believe the trend changed. The directions to the question illustrate how information from the most recent period covered on the exam may be included. It does not ask you to deal with changes in the Court's decisions that began with the appointment of several conservative judges by President Reagan.

Now let us look at another question and a sample student answer. This question is a good example of the type of essay question you might get on recent history. The question is confined to the post-World War II era and is a clear indication of what a student is expected to know about the period after 1945.

Sample Question B

> In what ways did the administrations of Presidents Eisenhower, Kennedy, Johnson, and Nixon continue the containment policy of President Truman?

Sample Answer B

Americans seem to have a basic fear of those who are different. The foreign policy known as *containment,* developed in the Truman years following the ideas expressed in the famous "*X*" article in *Foreign Affairs,* was a reflection of the fears of the American people and government that the Communist Soviet Union (and later China) was a threat to America. The containment policy set by the Truman administration remained the basic foreign policy of the Eisenhower, Kennedy, Johnson, and Nixon administrations.

The containment policy held that the West should meet every aggressive Communist move with equal pressure. It became clear that Europe would have to be rebuilt if it were to help in applying this pressure. The Marshall Plan was developed in 1947 to do this. The first clear statement of containment was the Truman Doctrine, which, following an apparent Soviet threat to Greece and Turkey, stated the United States would aid any nation in Europe threatened by Communist power internally or externally. When the Soviet Union blocked the land transportation routes to Berlin in 1948, the Truman administration pushed for the establishment of the North Atlantic Treaty Organization, a mutual defense pact eventually subscribed to by most of the nations ringing the Atlantic area and extending through the Mediterranean to Turkey.

A major test of the containment policy was the Korean War. Truman responded to the invasion of South Korea by sending U.S. troops into battle. Later the United Nations approved of this act and war was fought under the auspices of the U.N. But it was really a U.S. act of containment of Communism.

One primary proponent of the policy of containment was John Foster Dulles, Eisenhower's secretary of state. It was Dulles who formed the Southeast Asia Treaty Organization and the Central Treaty Organization, both modeled after NATO and devoted to the purpose of surrounding the Soviet Union and China with U.S. allies.

It was under Eisenhower that the Domino Theory was first expressed. The theory held that if one country in Southeast Asia fell to Communism, the other countries would fall like dominoes. The French in Indochina were aided under this reasoning. This was the beginning of the long U.S. involvement in Indochina to prevent a Communist government in Vietnam, Laos, and Cambodia. Other examples of containment at work under the Eisenhower administration were the rearmament of Germany and its admittance into NATO, the maintenance of Chiang Kai-shek on Formosa, the sending of Marines to Lebanon in 1957, and the development of extensive spying techniques such as the U-2. Although there were moves for rapprochement with the Soviet Union toward the end of Eisenhower's administration, the basic foreign policy of the Eisenhower administration was containment by *Brinkmanship,* Dulles' idea of threatening nuclear retaliation for any aggressive Communist moves. We were guided by fear of those who were different from us.

Kennedy enlarged the foreign aid program first used by President Truman to win friends in undeveloped countries. The Peace Corps and an increased emphasis upon the Good Neighbor Policy in South America were part of the aid policy. It was rooted in America's fear that Castro's Cuban Communism would spread to South America if not blocked by U.S. money. The Cuban missile crisis brought the world to the brink of war, but Kennedy proved that the United States would not permit the Soviet Union to establish a military base in this hemisphere. It was a classic example of the containment policy at work and was designed to keep those who are different out of the hemisphere.

Kennedy's foreign policy program, cut short by his death, was inherited by Johnson, his successor. The Johnson years were primarily the time of an enlargement of the Vietnam conflict into a full-scale bloody war albeit localized. The Vietnam War is an excellent example of the containment policy. Other examples of Johnson's pursuing this policy can be seen in the Middle East and in Central America where troops were sent into the Dominican Republic.

Nixon's efforts to end the Vietnam War, to establish good relations with China, and détente with the Soviet Union may appear to go against containment. In reality they were merely other ways of achieving the same goal. Nixon hoped China and the Soviets would contain each other if we were friendlier with each of them and could thus play one off against the other.

Under these four presidents, containment became our worldwide policy. It ranged from Eisenhower's decisions over financing Egypt's Aswan Dam project and our involvement in supplying arms to Israel to Kennedy's aiding newly independent African nations to keep them from forming Communist governments.

In conclusion, then, the Eisenhower through Nixon administrations saw the enlargement of the containment policy to include not only Western Europe and the Far East, but Southeast Asia, the Middle East, Africa, and South America as well. The motive behind the policy was to block the spread of that fearful quantity known as Communism. Each administration enlarged upon the policies of the previous administration, which served to establish America's position as "police officer of the world." America's motivation in this move to a police officer's role began in fear—fear of international Communism.

Teacher Comments on Sample Answer B

"The student essay is a very fine answer to the question. He or she defines the containment policy of the Truman administration and goes on to present excellent examples of the policy in operation under the Eisenhower, Kennedy, Johnson, and Nixon administrations. The student states the thesis in the introduction and develops the essay to support it all the way through. The conclusion brings the reader back to the thesis and completes a very effective organization for the paper. Although there are some foreign policy developments in these years that negate the thesis, the student has chosen to ignore them and to pick very effectively a variety of factual details that do support the thesis. The interpretation of Nixon's goal in pursuing détente may be questioned, but it is an example of interpreting information to support your view. The essay is perhaps longer than the average one, but it is the quality of expression and argument, not the length, that makes this an outstanding answer."

Would you have made the same comments as the teacher did on this answer? As with the first essay, it is a good answer and was placed here to provide a high standard for you as you finish the book. It demonstrates what a student can do with a question based on post-World War II material. The answer is a bit long. It could be condensed by including fewer examples from each administration but if you have the time, include all the evidence you can but do not simply give a laundry list of facts—interpret the question and pick the facts that relate to it.

As you realize, question B is a version of the *What?* type of essay question. You should have had no difficulty in analyzing and answering the question. By now, with our consideration of basic types of essay questions and with the many essays you have written, you should be well prepared for the essay and DBQ parts of the Advanced Placement exam. You can test your readiness by taking the sample exams in Part Four. While you are using them and when you take the Advanced Placement exam in U.S. History, never fail to use the Seven Basic Steps in Essay Writing:

First—Analyze the question
Second—Collect and sort information
Third—Develop your thesis
Fourth—Write the introduction
Fifth—Write the body of the essay
Sixth—Write the conclusion
Seventh—Reread the essay—Introduction, Body, Conclusion

And do not forget the flashlight image.

Practice Essay Questions

The following practice essay questions require knowledge of the period since 1945 and one other period from American history. The questions represent different types of essay questions presented in the text. These five questions thus provide an excellent review for the Advanced Placement examination.

1. ". . . almost all the defects inherent in democratic institutions are brought to light in the conduct of foreign affairs." Evaluate this statement from *Democracy in America* by Alexis de Tocqueville (1835) by comparing the conduct of U.S. foreign affairs from 1961 to 1973 with its conduct from 1931 to 1941.

2. How do you account for the fact that in the Populist Era both state legislation and federal Supreme Court decisions went against the civil rights of minorities, whereas in the period 1954–1980, both national legislation and federal Supreme Court decisions supported the civil rights of all Americans?

3. Describe three economic reform measures passed as part of the New Deal Program of the 1930s and explain their importance to the economic growth of the post-World War II period.

4. Compare the efforts for international cooperation and peace in the 20 years after World War I with those efforts for international cooperation and peace pursued in the 20 years after World War II. Why do you believe the latter were more successful in preventing a world war?

5. "Americans have learned that, when the nation is divided in its support of military activity, the social fabric of a democratic society is weakened, which results in moral and ethical decline." Assess the validity of this quotation by using information from TWO of the following:
    World War I
    World War II
    Vietnam War

**Comments on
Question 1**

The first sample essay question is a standard combination type in which an *Evaluate This Statement* type is combined with a *Compare* type. The *Compare* part provides specific directions as to what periods of time you are to consider. You may use a chronological approach or a compare and/or contrast of similar situations approach.

The two time periods are interesting and provided real tests of American democracy. The 1930s saw the rise of Hitler and the Japanese aggression in Asia, America's response of neutrality, and Roosevelt's support of the Allies. The 1960s included the Vietnam War, which split the nation, the intensification of the Cold War under Kennedy and Johnson, Nixon's move to détente, and Carter's response to the Iranian hostage crisis of 1979.

The quotation is an observation by that most astute and perceptive Frenchman, Alexis de Tocqueville, who wrote an outstanding commentary of American life in 1835. His *Democracy in America*, although rather slow reading for present-day students, should be read by all who consider themselves scholars of America's past. This quote is typical of his sharp analysis and clear perception of life in the United States in the Jackson era, much of which is still applicable to the nation today. Do you agree with this statement of de Tocqueville's? What will your thesis be?

**Comments on
Question 2**

The second question is the familiar *How do you account?* type. This question asks about the change in attitude toward civil rights and minorities as seen in legislation and Supreme Court decisions between the Populist Era (1890–1898) and the period 1954–1974. Two words—*state, national*—in the question may provide a key to interpretation. For the Populist Era, *state* legislation is mentioned; for the more recent period, *national* legislation is referred to. Why? When you decide on your answer to that, you will probably have both your thesis and very likely your organizational pattern. The question focuses on a very important aspect of recent history. You will want to include the 1896 *Plessy v. Ferguson* Supreme Court decision that accepted the "separate but equal" concept in race relations as established in state law, thus making it national policy. At the time, Social Darwinsim with its idea of "survival of the fittest" still prevailed in the nation. In contrast, you should include both the civil rights legislation of the Johnson era and the Supreme Court decision in the 1954 *Brown v. Board of Education* case (desegregation of schools). An exciting answer would extend civil rights to include the rights of the suspect, the Miranda case, and women's rights to privacy and abortion upheld in *Roe v. Wade* in 1974.

**Comments on
Question 3**

Question 3 is a *Describe . . . explain* question that asks you to analyze the economic reforms of the New Deal in light of the importance of recent economic history. It will probably force you to take a new and different look at both the New Deal and recent economic history before you will be ready to answer the question. There has not been a great deal of emphasis placed on cause-and-effect relationships between the New Deal reforms and postwar prosperity. It appears to be a rather difficult, narrow, and specialized question, but the general topic— economic history—has been very important in the past 70 years. How much have you learned? Are you ready yet to answer this question? The wording of the question is not complicated, so your analysis should not be difficult, but you may have real difficulty making brief notes without further research. Do not worry if you are not ready to answer this question. On the exam you can assume there will be at least one question on a topic with which you are not familiar, so do not get upset when you find a question you cannot answer.

Comments on Question 4

The fourth question focuses on the important issue of international cooperation and peace and uses a *Compare* type of question to get you to make decisions about international cooperation after the two world wars of this century. The question concludes with a second part, a *Why?* part, which forces you to make a judgment as to why we have been able to avoid World War III. The information needed to answer the question should be part of your knowledge of the history of this century. What your thesis will be, however, and how you organize the materials is open to many possibilities. The question falls easily into a description of post–World War I and then post–World War II methods followed by your reasons for the latter avoiding World War III. On the other hand, you might begin with how war has been avoided and use illustrations, such as actions of the League of Nations and the United Nations, from the postwar periods to explain the failure in one era and success in the other in avoiding war. This latter organization would provide an exciting essay, but it would require careful thought before writing. This is a good question for 20th-century history.

Comments on Question 5

The last sample question is based on a quotation dealing with the social and moral as well as the political life of our nation. The familiar directions *Assess the validity* have been expanded to include directions to use information from two wars chosen from a list of three. The wars divided the nation in varying degrees. The nation is still experiencing the aftermath of the very divisive Vietnam War. There was widespread opposition to U.S. involvement in World War I and also in World War II until the Japanese attack on Pearl Harbor brought general support to the war effort. Thus, all three wars had divisive aspects, but did they weaken the social fabric and lead to moral and ethical decline? That you need to decide, but the 1968 riots at the Democratic Convention and the Watergate incident suggest changes in the social fabric after the Vietnam War. What about after World Wars I and II?

The question should not be hard to analyze, although the phrase *social fabric* may not be familiar. It refers to the underlying structure of society—all those elements that weave it together. No dates are given so you must recall the time period of each war—this is why a timeline is important. The question focuses on social rather than the more familiar economic or political history. You can expect at least one question on the Advanced Placement examination to deal with aspects of social history. If you have included any social history in your study, you should be able to deal with this question. The question certainly invites a range of theses and a variety of organizations. It is a wide-open question dealing with the important issue of war and social life and morality—crucial and recurring issues in history and thus a very good one with which to end this study of essay questions based on U.S. history.

These five questions, as well as those in Chapter 7, provide an excellent review of U.S. history. If you are able to answer them in effective, well-organized essays without additional research, you should be suitably prepared for the Advanced Placement exam.

Multiple-Choice Questions—Vocabulary

Throughout this book we have taken care to define special words used in the questions. Every student of history must know the vocabulary used by the historian. In Part One we suggested keeping a vocabulary list. Throughout the book, questions, both essay and multiple-choice, have been introduced that indirectly tested your specialized history vocabulary.

Every subject has its own vocabulary. You become particularly aware of this when you study a foreign language or begin studying a new field—biology, for instance, has a very specialized vocabulary. Often, students studying history or English do not realize that there is a specialized vocabulary for these subjects because they have usually used or heard the words all their lives. We have saved this topic for last because most of the vocabulary you will need will have been absorbed without effort, and there is no need to make an issue of an obvious matter. We have defined some terms, such as *embargo*, and to aid you in your vocabulary development, there is a Glossary included at the end of the book. It is not a list to memorize, but it illustrates the types of words you should know and provides a starting place for expanding your vocabulary. If you followed the suggestions for vocabulary building in Part One, you should have your own extensive list by now that should enable you to answer the sample questions below.

The following multiple-choice questions illustrate several ways in which your knowledge of historical terms may be tested directly on the Advanced Placement exam. It should be obvious, however, that your vocabulary will be tested throughout the exam on every question.

Sample Question 1

> 1. One who moves from place to place seeking agricultural employment is referred to as a (an)
>   (A) displaced person
>   (B) serf
>   (C) migrant worker
>   (D) agriculturist
>   (E) veteran

Comments on Question 1

Question 1 is a straightforward one in which a definition of a word is presented followed by five choices of words for which you are to pick the correct word for the definition. You are probably familiar with this type of question from English examinations. In this question the correct answer is "migrant worker." If you did not know the term, you might have known other words related to *migrant,* such as *migratory, migration,* or *immigration.* In all three words, movement is involved; the phrase *moves from place to place* in the definition might lead you to the word *migrant.* Combining with this the fact that *employment* means work, you would have a good chance of picking "migrant worker" as the correct answer. You might also know the meaning of the other words, thus eliminating them. You can check the meaning of these other words in the Glossary.

Sample Question 2

> 2. A scalawag was a Southern white who, after the Civil War, believed
>   (A) in segregation
>   (B) in cooperation with former slaves and Northerners
>   (C) all Southern whites should be paid for their freed slaves
>   (D) secession was still legal
>   (E) all former slaves should be sent back to Africa

Comments on Question 2

The second question reverses the order of the first and provides a term in the question and five choices for a correct definition. The term *scalawag* was applied to Southern whites who cooperated with the former slaves and Northerners in the period after the Civil War. The term is often used in discussing the Reconstruction period. The chances are that to answer this question you would have to know the term *scalawag*. It is specialized, but you might have been able to deduce the definition by eliminating several of the choices.

Sample Question 3

> 3. Which of the following terms is used to refer to the foreign policy of the United States in the years 1844–1850?
>   (A) Manifest Destiny   (D) Isolationism
>   (B) Détente   (E) Brinkmanship
>   (C) Alliance for Progress

Comments on Question 3

The third question combines a knowledge of historic periods with a definition of terms. In order to answer the question you must know what the foreign policy of the United States was during the years 1844–1850 and then you must be able to relate it to a specific word. All the choices relate to American foreign policy at different periods. You should recognize them and thus you would have no trouble identifying "Manifest Destiny" as the correct answer. This is a very common expression used in texts to describe U.S. foreign policy of the mid-1840s. The other words can be found in the Glossary. Before studying American history you were probably not familiar with these terms and you would have had difficulty with the question, but the chances are you know all or enough of them now so that you could eliminate most of the choices.

Sample Question 4

> 4. If you lived in a city slum in the 1890s, the building in which you lived would most likely be a
>   (A) megalopolis   (D) trust
>   (B) condominium   (E) tenement
>   (C) skyscraper

Comments on Question 4

Again, question 4 combines a knowledge of specific historic periods with an understanding of words. As in the first and third questions, the definition is given in the question and the choices are of words to fit the definition. In this question the words *city, slum, 1890s,* and *building* should combine to give you the answer—"tenement." *Condominium* is a more recent word for middle- and upper-class apartment houses. A skyscraper, a particular type of tall building usually used for offices, was developed in the 1890s, but not in slums. Trusts were formed in the 1890s, but they were large businesses, and *megalopolis* is a 20th-century term used to describe a huge, sprawling urban center and not a building. If you could not immediately identify "tenement" as the correct answer, you could probably arrive at the answer by eliminating the other terms, which should be part of your specialized history vocabulary.

Sample Question 5

5. Since the Civil War and especially in the latter half of the 20th century, those individuals supporting states' rights turned to which ONE of the following to gain support for their view?
   (A) The federal bureaucracy
   (B) The Defense Department
   (C) The Supreme Court
   (D) The National Democratic Party
   (E) The Civil Rights Movement

Comments on Question 5

The last question is a little more complicated in form, but essentially it does what question 2 did. A word is presented in the question and the choices test your understanding of the word. States' rights advocates believe each state is sovereign—has the right to rule itself. They believe the Constitution was formed and ratified by the states. They emphasize the amendment of the Constitution that reserves powers not delegated to the federal government to the states. State vs. federal power has always been an issue in U.S. history. Since the Civil War states' rights advocates have appealed to the Supreme Court for support. The four other choices all have supported and/or used the federal government to gain support for the ideas they support. This question tests a very specialized understanding of a very important word.

These five examples illustrate ways in which vocabulary can be specifically tested on the Advanced Placement examination. It is important to remember, however, that all questions on the exam will require a history vocabulary, so be sure to study the Glossary and develop your own vocabulary list.

Practice Multiple-Choice Questions

The following questions illustrate the type of questions one might be asked concerning events since World War II. Remember, however, that only one-third of the multiple-choice questions on the examination will be on the post-1914 period (1915–present) and that not many will be on the post-1980 era although there may be questions up to the present.

These are the last practice multiple-choice questions in the book. As you begin this final set of practice questions, remember that it is important to read the entire question and all the answers carefully. Do not guess at answers unless you can eliminate several of the possible choices.

1. All of the following individuals are correctly paired with the organization with which they are usually connected EXCEPT
   (A) Martin Luther King, Jr.—Southern Christian Leadership Conference
   (B) Ralph Nader—Black Panthers
   (C) Malcolm X—Black Muslims
   (D) César Chavez—United Farm Workers of America
   (E) Betty Friedan—National Organization for Women (NOW)

2. The Cold War included many events, among which are the
   I. Truman Doctrine
   II. U-2 incident
   III. Marshall Plan
   IV. Korean War
   (A) I and II
   (B) I, II, and III
   (C) I, III, and IV
   (D) I and IV
   (E) I, II, III, and IV

3. Since World War II, U.S. troops have been sent to the Middle East to protect U.S. interests in Lebanon and the Persian Gulf by United States presidents
   (A) Eisenhower, Nixon, George W. Bush, and Clinton
   (B) Eisenhower, Kennedy, Nixon, and George H. W. Bush
   (C) Eisenhower, Ford, Reagan, and George H. W. Bush
   (D) Eisenhower, Reagan, George W. Bush, and Clinton
   (E) Kennedy, Carter, George H. W. Bush, and Clinton

4. In retaliation for a supposed attack on U.S. destroyers, the U.S. Congress authorized President Johnson to take any action he deemed necessary to deal with the crisis when they voted for
   (A) My Lai
   (B) the War on Poverty
   (C) support of Escobedo and Miranda
   (D) ICBMs
   (E) the Tonkin Gulf Resolution

5. On the map at the right, Vietnam
    is numbered
    (A) 1 and 2
    (B) 2, 3, and 4
    (C) 2 and 4
    (D) 1, 2, 4, and 5
    (E) 4 and 5

6. The 1973 Supreme Court decision in the case of *Roe v. Wade*
    (A) marked the end of the Court's liberal view in support of the rights
         of suspected criminals
    (B) was strongly opposed by the National Rifle Association
    (C) was very controversial and precipitated strong political reactions
         both pro and con
    (D) has been supported by each president since 1973
    (E) was the Court's most sweeping decision in favor of the civil rights
         of African Americans

7. The most recent event to occur was
    (A) Castro's taking power in Cuba
    (B) The overthrow of the Shah of Iran
    (C) The Iran-Contra Affair
    (D) The fall of the Berlin Wall
    (E) The Vietnam War

8. All of the following were characteristic of the 1960s EXCEPT
    (A) increasing computerization of industry
    (B) pop art
    (C) the Beatles and rock and roll
    (D) adult movies stressing sex and nudity
    (E) an increase in the quality and number of dramatic programs pro-
         duced by American TV

9.   **PERSONS IN POVERTY**

Family Situation	Number of persons in millions in given family situations living in poverty over total number of persons in that situation.		
	White	Nonwhite	Total: All Races
Individuals Living Alone	4.0 / 10.8	.8 / 1.6	4.8 / 12.4
Members of Family Units	16.3 / 159.6	8.5 / 21.4	24.8 / 181.0
TOTAL Both Situations	20.3 / 170.4	9.3 / 23.0	29.7 / 193.4

According to the table above for 1966 during Lyndon Johnson's "War on Poverty," all of the following statements are true EXCEPT
- (A) There were more whites living in poverty than nonwhites.
- (B) If you are nonwhite and live alone, you have a 50-50 chance of living in poverty.
- (C) Your best chance of avoiding poverty is to be born in a white family.
- (D) More individuals living alone live in poverty than do members of families.
- (E) Although the total number in poverty for whites is greater, there is a higher percentage of poverty among nonwhites.

10. The presidency of William Jefferson Clinton included all of the following EXCEPT
- (A) an impeachment trial of the president in the United States Senate
- (B) the loss of a Democratic Party majority in the House of Representatives
- (C) a major effort to reform the health care system for the nation
- (D) efforts by the president to increase federal spending on schools and education
- (E) a steady reduction in the appropriations made for the Department of Defense

11. All of the following occurred during the presidency of Richard Nixon EXCEPT
- (A) the fall of Saigon to the North Vietnamese
- (B) the Watergate break-in and consequent congressional hearings
- (C) the resignation of Vice President Agnew
- (D) diplomatic overtures to the People's Republic of China, including a presidential visit
- (E) an attempt to end the Arab-Israeli conflict in the Middle East through shuttle diplomacy

12. Which of the following was a result of the supply-side economic policies adopted during the presidency of Ronald Reagan?

(A) A large decrease in the trade deficit

(B) A large increase in the national debt

(C) A steady decline of the Dow Jones stock index

(D) A rapid increase in the rate of inflation

(E) An agreement to reduce military expenditures during his presidency

Answers and Answer Explanations

1.	B	2.	E	3.	D	4.	E
5.	C	6.	C	7.	D	8.	E
9.	D	10.	E	11.	A	12.	B

1. (B) Ralph Nader founded Public Citizen, Inc., an organization that focused on consumer protection. He was not connected with the Black Panthers, who were organized as an activist Black Power group by H. Rap Brown. The other individuals are correctly linked with their organizations, all of which were very important in the Civil Rights Movement of the 1960s and 1970s.

2. (E) The Truman Doctrine proclaiming support for Greece and Turkey against Communist attack, the U-2 spy plane incident during President Eisenhower's administration, the Marshall Plan begun under President Truman, and the Korean War fought under Presidents Truman and Eisenhower were all incidents of the Cold War.

3. (D) Since World War II, U.S. troops have been sent to Lebanon and the Persian Gulf by Presidents Eisenhower, Carter, Reagan, George H. W. Bush, Clinton, and George W. Bush. Ford and Nixon did not send troops to these areas. Eisenhower declared the Eisenhower Doctrine to protect our interests in the Middle East and sent troops to Lebanon. Carter sent a helicopter mission to rescue American hostages in Teheran, Iran, but it was brief, unsuccessful, and not as significant as the military missions sent by Eisenhower, Reagan, both Bushes, and Clinton. Reagan again sent troops into Lebanon. George H. W. Bush organized Operation Desert Storm through the United Nations and sent troops to force Iraq out of Kuwait. After the end of hostilities, United Nations Weapons Inspection Teams were expected to destroy the nuclear and biological weapons of Iraq. When President Saddam Hussein refused to cooperate with the United Nations, President Clinton sent U.S. forces to join Great Britain in a massive bombing attack on Iraq in December 1998. This proved unsuccessful, and George W. Bush, after failing to gain full U.N. support, attacked Iraq in March 2003 with the military support of Great Britain and Australia, and the support of a number of smaller nations, called the coalition of the willing.

4. (E) The Tonkin Gulf Resolution, passed by the U.S. Congress in August 1964 after it was reported that two U.S. destroyers were attacked in the Tonkin Gulf, gave the president authority to take any action he deemed necessary for dealing with the crisis. The resolution was used to justify the entire U.S. involvement in Vietnam without a declaration of war. The other items relate to different developments since 1960.

5. (C) On the map of the Indochina Peninsula, 2 is the former North Vietnam and 4 is the former South Vietnam so the correct answer is C—Vietnam consists of both the former North and South Vietnam. It does not include Cambodia, which is number 5, and Laos, which is number 1. Number 3 is Thailand.

6. (C) The Supreme Court decision in *Roe v. Wade* supported a woman's right to abortion during the first trimester of pregnancy. It was a very controversial decision and brought reaction in the political arena where pro-life and pro-choice groups became active. The decision was based on the "right to privacy" and not civil rights. It had nothing to do with the rights of suspected criminals. The National Rifle Association, although an active pressure group, has not lobbied against this decision. Presidents Reagan and the two Bushes opposed the decision and worked to have it overturned.

7. (D) These items relate to the Cold War and concern over Communism. Fidel Castro took power in Cuba in 1959 turning Cuba into a Communist nation and posing a potential threat to American security during the Cold War. The overthrow of the Shah of Iran in 1979 meant the loss of an American ally in the Persian Gulf area and threatened the oil supplies from the area. A strict Islamic Republic was established. Members of Reagan's administration developed the idea of Iran-Contra in the mid-1980s. The plan called for supplying arms to Iran for its use in its war against Iraq. The goal was to gain favor with Iran, to obtain the release of hostages in Lebanon, and to use secretly the money obtained from the sale of weapons to support the Contras fighting against the government of Nicaragua. That government was seen as too supportive of Communist ideas and potentially another Cuba. Congress had refused to fund the Contras. The Berlin Wall fell in 1989 and is the correct answer, since the Vietnam War took place in the 1960s and 1970s.

8. (E) Increased use of computers, pop art, rock and roll, and adult movies were all characteristic of U.S. culture in the 1960s; higher-quality dramatic TV programs were not.

9. (D) The table presents information by two categories—first white and nonwhite, second, living alone and in family units. Information about the totals in these categories is presented for all races and both living situations and finally, in the lower right-hand corner, there is a grand total indicating all those in poverty. If you read the titles of each column carefully and understand that the fraction represents the total number of persons in each category as the denominator (bottom number) and the number of persons in poverty in each category as the numerator (top number), then you would realize that all the choices except D, "more unrelated individuals live in poverty than do members of families," are correct. It was information of this type that led President Johnson to undertake the War on Poverty as part of his Great Society.

10. (E) In 1998 President Clinton was impeached by the House of Representatives and was found not guilty after a month-long trial in the Senate. In the election of 1994 the Democratic Party lost its majority in the House of Representatives for the first time since 1954. In his first term the president appointed his wife, Hillary Rodham Clinton, to pursue a major reform of the health system, but it was defeated in the Congress. He then focused on increasing spending for schools and education, and in 1999, with a budget surplus, asked for increased, not less, spending for the military.

11. (A) The Nixon administration negotiated a cease-fire and a settlement to the Vietnam War. Saigon, the capital of South Vietnam, did not fall to the North Vietnamese until 1975 during the presidency of Gerald Ford. The other events took place during the Nixon years.

12. (B) The supply-side economic policies adopted by the Reagan administration resulted in a large increase in the national debt. Budgets remained unbalanced until 1998. The trade deficit increased, the Dow Jones stock index rose, although somewhat erratically, and the rate of inflation declined during his presidency. Reagan increased military expenditures.

Bibliography

Acuna, Rodolfo. *Occupied America: A History of Chicanos*. Reading, MA: Addison-Wesley Educational, 1999.

Bernstein, Carl, and Bob Woodward. *All the President's Men*. New York: Touchstone Books, 1994.

Brinkley, Alan. *Liberalism and Its Discontents*. Cambridge: Harvard University Press, 2000.

Donovan, R. J. *Tumultuous Years: The Presidency of Harry S. Truman 1949–1953*. Columbia, MO: University of Missouri Press, 1996.

Gaddis, J. L. *We Now Know: Rethinking Cold War History*. New York: Oxford University Press, 1998.

Goodwin, Doris Kearns. *Lyndon Johnson and the American Dream*. New York: St. Martin's Press, 1991.

Halberstam, David. *The Best and the Brightest*. New York: Fawcett World Library, 1993.

——. *War in a Time of Peace: Bush, Clinton and the Generals*. New York: Scribner, 2001.

Halle, Louis J. *Cold War as History*. New York: HarperCollins, 1991.

Harrington, Michael. *The Other America*. Old Tappan, NJ: Touchstone Books, 1997.

Karnow, Stanley. *Vietnam: A History*. New York: Penguin, 1997.

Kennedy, R. F. *Thirteen Days*. New York: W. W. Norton & Co., 1999.

King, M. L., Jr. *Why We Can't Wait*. New York: Signet Classics, 2000.

Leuchtenburg, W. E. *In the Shadow of FDR: From Harry Truman to George W. Bush*. Ithaca, NY: Cornell University Press, 2001.

Marton, Kati. *Hidden Power*. New York: Pantheon Books, 2001.

Nash, G. H. *The Conservative Intellectual Movement in America*. Wilmington, DE: Intercollegiate Studies Institute, 1998.

Putnam, R. D. *Bowling Alone: The Collapse and Revival of the American Community*. New York: Touchstone Books, 2003.

Schlesinger, A. M. Jr. *A Thousand Days: John F. Kennedy in the White House*. New York: Mariner Books, 2002.

Takaki, Ronald. *Strangers from a Different Shore: A History of Asian Americans*. Boston: Back Bay Books, 1998.

Williams, Juan. *Eyes on the Prize*. New York: Penguin, U.S.A., 1988.

Woodward, Bob. *Bush at War*. New York: Simon & Schuster, 2002.

Memoirs

Acheson, Dean. *Present at the Creation*. New York: W. W. Norton & Co., 1987.

Bush, Barbara. *A Memoir*. New York: St. Martin's Press, 1995.

Blumenthal, Sidney. *The Clinton Wars*. New York: Farrar, Straus & Giroux, 2003.

Carter, Jimmy. *Keeping Faith: Memoirs of a President*. Toronto: Bantam Books, 1982.

Clinton, Hillary R. *Living History*. New York: Simon & Schuster, 2003.

Fitzwater, Marlin. *Call the Briefing!: Bush and Reagan, Sam and Helen: A Decade with Presidents and the Press*. Holbrook, MA: Xlibris Corp., 2000.

Graham, Katharine. *Personal History*. New York: Vintage Books, 1998.

Johnson, Lyndon Baines. *The Vantage Point*. New York: Henry Holt and Co., 1971.

Malcolm X. *Autobiography*. New York: African American Images, 1989.

McNamara, Robert. *In Retrospect: The Tragedy and Lessons of Vietnam*. New York: Vintage Press, 1996.

Meese, Edwin. *With Reagan: The Inside Story*. Washington, D.C.: Regnery Publishing, Inc., 1992.

Nixon, Richard. *R. N.: The Memoirs of Richard Nixon*. New York: Simon and Schuster, Inc., 1990.

Reston, James B. *Deadline*. New York: Times Books, 1992.

Robinson, Jackie. *I Never Had It Made: An Autobiography of Jackie Robinson*. New York: Ecco, 2003.

Fiction

Kerouac, Jack. *On the Road*. New York: Viking, 1997.

Salinger, J. D. *The Catcher in the Rye*. Boston: Back Bay Books, 2001.

Updike, John. *Rabbit Run*. New York: A. A. Knopf, 1960.

Wolfe, Tom. *The Bonfire of the Vanities*. New York: Farrar, Straus & Giroux, 1987.

A Summary of Things to Remember and to Do

Points to Remember About the Exam: A Summary

Multiple-Choice Section

The Questions

The exam consists of 80 multiple-choice questions. You have 55 minutes in which to answer them. You should keep moving through the questions at a steady pace. If you come to a question that is difficult or confusing, make a checkmark (✔) by the question in your question booklet and go on to the next question. When you have finished the 80 questions, you can come back to those you have skipped. The checkmark by the question will help you quickly identify those you skipped. **When you skip a question, be careful to mark the answer to the next question in the correct space on your answer sheet.**

Material Covered

The questions will test factual knowledge and, in the "stimulus" questions, analytical skills. Approximately 35 percent of the questions will cover political history, 35 percent will cover social history, 15 percent will cover foreign policy and diplomatic history, 10 percent will cover economic history, and 5 percent will cover intellectual history. One-sixth of the multiple-choice questions will come from the period prior to 1789, one-half will come from 1789–1914, and one-third will come from 1914 to the present.

Grading

The multiple-choice questions are designed to present a range of difficulty. The level of difficulty is such that if you answer about 60 percent correctly, you'll receive a grade of three, which ranks you as "qualified" on the AP examination.

Thoughtless guessing of answers should be avoided, as one-fourth of a point is deducted for each incorrect answer. However, if in analyzing the question you can eliminate one or two of the five possible choices, selecting what appears to be the best answer from the three or four choices remaining is recommended.

The Answer Page

Answers to the questions are indicated on your answer page by filling in a small space with a number 2 lead pencil. You should bring at least two sharpened number 2 pencils with erasers to the exam. When you skip a question, be sure to leave that space blank on the answer sheet until you come back later. If you realize you have made an error in filling in the spaces, do not panic. Make a note where you realized your mistake, start marking the answers correctly at that point and finish the multiple-choice section. Speak to the test administrator when the multiple-choice question part of the exam is over and tell your teacher when you next attend class. If the Advanced Placement Program Director at the College Board is notified immediately, preferably by phone, your answer sheets will be hand corrected, not machine corrected.

Essay or Free-Response Section

Time

There are three essays to be written in Section 2 of the examination. There is a 15-minute required period in which you should read the questions, analyze the documents, and briefly outline your answer(s). You then have 45 minutes to write your answer to Part A—the DBQ—and 70 minutes to write your answers to Part B—two essay questions, one from Group 1 and one from Group 2. There is a total of 2 hours and 10 minutes on the essay section. You should bring two pens to the exam, since you should write the essays in ink.

DBQ: Section 2, Part A

Remember, the purpose of the DBQ is to test your analytical skills *and* your understanding of "mainstream" American history. You must analyze the question, then read the documents and determine how they relate to the question and to the traditional, chronological history of the period from which they come. In your answer you need to weave together information from **both** these sources. You should not simply recite what is in the documents.

In writing your DBQ answer you should refer to the documents by the author or sources but try not to quote long passages. Paraphrase the main ideas and discuss **how** they relate to the question and to the political, economic, diplomatic, or social history of the period. A listing of the documents and recitation of what each one says is referred to by the correctors as a "laundry list" and is not well regarded by these readers.

Essay or Free-Response Questions— Section 2, Part B

Remember that you are to select one question from Group 1 and one from Group 2. The purpose of the questions is to test your knowledge of American history, your ability to think as an historian, and your writing skills. Read and analyze the four questions carefully before making your choice. You will have 5 minutes to make a brief outline and 30 minutes to write each answer. Follow the suggestions presented in this book. Remember the Seven Steps in Essay Writing and the image of the flashlight as you write your essay.

Reviewing the Week Before the Examination

The most important thing to remember as you begin to review for the AP examination is that you have been preparing since you first picked up this book or began your study of American history. Have confidence in yourself and rely on the work you have done all year. **A planned review can be helpful but cannot replace the confidence gained by systematic work over a year. Last-minute cramming of factual information can be counterproductive and confusing.**

A One-Week Review Plan

Develop a plan that fits your own time schedule. A little review each day or evening is best—an hour should be plenty of time if used well. If you have not yet taken the practice Advanced Placement exam that follows, you should begin your review by doing that. First read this section and then set aside three hours in which to take the model exam.

In planning a five-day review, an easy approach is to review two chapters in Part III each day and use the fifth day for an overview. Each day of the four, begin by going over the sample multiple-choice questions in the two chapters and see how well you do. Then read the appropriate sections in Part V or study your own time line and notes. Do *not* try to reread the whole text but use *your* notes. Finally, you will want to read over the sample essay questions in the two chapters under review that day and think about answers to them. What your goal is for this review is to get your mind turning again, thinking over material you studied several months ago.

Reviewing with a Friend	One excellent way to review is to work with a friend. If this can be arranged, after you have both read over your own notes and answered the multiple-choice questions, discuss possible approaches to the five essays. Share your knowledge. Remember that your AP examination results will be reported by the College Board as a ranking on a scale of 5 to 1. You are not competing with your friends for the one top grade in the class. Instead you are going to be ranked in five categories with more than 200,000 students who will take the Advanced Placement exam. A score of 5 means you are "extremely well qualified" and there will be many who achieve this score. Therefore, work together to support each other's efforts to reach a rank of 5. Thirty minutes a day spent reviewing your notes and multiple-choice questions and 30 minutes spent discussing the essay questions and your notes with a friend will prove an excellent five-day review pattern. On the fifth day you can review whatever information seems appropriate at that time—your own notes, your lecture notes, old tests.

Taking the Exam

The Night before the Exam	The night before the exam is a time to relax and get a good night's sleep. Some students have found seeing a good movie or watching a favorite TV show a better preparation than last-minute studying. Other students look over special notes or review the chapters that gave them the most difficulty in the final week's review. Another excellent option for this last-night review is to read again one of the model Advanced Placement exams included in Part Four. What is most important, however, on this night is to get a good rest and have confidence that you have prepared well throughout the year. There is nothing worse than to spend all night before the exam cramming facts into your head—facts that only end up being jumbled by morning.
The Day of the Exam	Just as a good night's sleep is most beneficial, a good breakfast is important. If you are a coffee-only, non-breakfast person, take time to eat something on the morning of the exam. Three hours of exam taking is very draining and you need the energy a good breakfast will supply.
Being Ready Early	Plan to be at school or the exam location in plenty of time. Hunting for a parking spot can be distracting and you want to be focused on American history on this day. Follow whatever directions you have been given by your teacher or guidance counselor about when to report and what to bring to the exam in the way of I.D. material or other information. Remember you will need several number 2 pencils and two pens.
Starting the Exam	Once you arrive at the exam room, find a seat where you will feel comfortable. Sitting toward the front often makes it easier to hear all the directions and there

will be many instructions given by the person administering the exam. You will have identification material to fill out before beginning the exam. There will normally be a short break between Sections 1 and 2 of the examination. Instructions will be given for both sections. Pay attention but do not hesitate to ask if there is something you do not understand.

Exercises

For many students the 3 hours and 5 minutes of the Advanced Placement exam will be the longest exam time they have experienced. Both the body and mind can get tired. You want to keep your blood circulating and plenty of oxygen coming into your lungs while you are working on the examination. There are several simple exercises you can do that help to achieve these goals during long examinations. While writing, you can clench your fists several times and release them quickly, and squeeze your toes hard and release them several times. These two exercises will get the blood flowing to your extremities. Another excellent exercise is to make what is known in yoga as the Lion's Face. Stick your tongue out as far as you can and open your mouth and eyes as wide as you can. This will get circulation going in your face. These three exercises can be done while you are writing. A fourth exercise is a gentle finger massage of the temples and over the eyes and cheeks; this will help relieve tension and focus your thoughts. It requires putting the pencil or pen down and gently rubbing your fingers over your temples and then the palm of your hands gently over your eye sockets. Some find gently rubbing the cheekbones and forehead also helpful. A minute or less doing this simple tension-releasing exercise will be time well spent. These simple exercises should be done when you seem to be getting tired. They are not distracting to others and can be helpful to you. If you are allowed to stand at the break between sections of the examination, bend over to touch your toes several times and stretch. Such simple exercises between sections of the examination, plus some good deep breathing spaced through the exam, can make taking the exam much easier.

Sugar Boost

Some people bring several pieces of hard candy or a candy bar to eat at the break for quick energy. As we now know, a sugar high does not have a long-lasting effect but can be very helpful in the middle of the examination. However, check whether eating is permitted by the test administrator before opening your candy bar.

These hints may seem strange and you may feel awkward making a Lion's Face in the middle of the Advanced Placement examination, but such actions can keep you fresher and your mind working, which is important during the long 3 hours and 5 minutes of the examination. You should practice these exercises as you take the model exams that follow.

After the Exam Ends

Follow the directions given by your test administrator at the end of the examination. Ask any questions you have before leaving.

The essays on the Advanced Placement examination are read in mid-June by a large group of experienced college and high school teachers. After careful preparation to establish standards, these Faculty Consultants read and rank all the free response questions. The multiple-choice questions are machine corrected. Then the Chief Reader, working with a team, determines where each exam ranks. You will hear your results in the summer so you should relax and get on with the rest of your schoolwork. Do not worry about how you did on the Advanced Placement examination. If you have worked steadily all year and reviewed with this book, you have done all you can to do well on the examination.

ANSWER SHEET FOR THE MODEL A
ADVANCED PLACEMENT EXAM IN PART FOUR

Name _____

Date _____

Grade _____

FOR SECTION I—MULTIPLE CHOICE

Sample: 1. The American Declaration of Independence was signed in   1. (A)(B)(C)●(E)

(A) 1789   (D) 1776

(B) 1763   (E) 1667

(C) 1976

Box D is filled in since the correct answer for the sample question 1 is D.

1. (A)(B)(C)(D)(E)	21. (A)(B)(C)(D)(E)	41. (A)(B)(C)(D)(E)	61. (A)(B)(C)(D)(E)
2. (A)(B)(C)(D)(E)	22. (A)(B)(C)(D)(E)	42. (A)(B)(C)(D)(E)	62. (A)(B)(C)(D)(E)
3. (A)(B)(C)(D)(E)	23. (A)(B)(C)(D)(E)	43. (A)(B)(C)(D)(E)	63. (A)(B)(C)(D)(E)
4. (A)(B)(C)(D)(E)	24. (A)(B)(C)(D)(E)	44. (A)(B)(C)(D)(E)	64. (A)(B)(C)(D)(E)
5. (A)(B)(C)(D)(E)	25. (A)(B)(C)(D)(E)	45. (A)(B)(C)(D)(E)	65. (A)(B)(C)(D)(E)
6. (A)(B)(C)(D)(E)	26. (A)(B)(C)(D)(E)	46. (A)(B)(C)(D)(E)	66. (A)(B)(C)(D)(E)
7. (A)(B)(C)(D)(E)	27. (A)(B)(C)(D)(E)	47. (A)(B)(C)(D)(E)	67. (A)(B)(C)(D)(E)
8. (A)(B)(C)(D)(E)	28. (A)(B)(C)(D)(E)	48. (A)(B)(C)(D)(E)	68. (A)(B)(C)(D)(E)
9. (A)(B)(C)(D)(E)	29. (A)(B)(C)(D)(E)	49. (A)(B)(C)(D)(E)	69. (A)(B)(C)(D)(E)
10. (A)(B)(C)(D)(E)	30. (A)(B)(C)(D)(E)	50. (A)(B)(C)(D)(E)	70. (A)(B)(C)(D)(E)
11. (A)(B)(C)(D)(E)	31. (A)(B)(C)(D)(E)	51. (A)(B)(C)(D)(E)	71. (A)(B)(C)(D)(E)
12. (A)(B)(C)(D)(E)	32. (A)(B)(C)(D)(E)	52. (A)(B)(C)(D)(E)	72. (A)(B)(C)(D)(E)
13. (A)(B)(C)(D)(E)	33. (A)(B)(C)(D)(E)	53. (A)(B)(C)(D)(E)	73. (A)(B)(C)(D)(E)
14. (A)(B)(C)(D)(E)	34. (A)(B)(C)(D)(E)	54. (A)(B)(C)(D)(E)	74. (A)(B)(C)(D)(E)
15. (A)(B)(C)(D)(E)	35. (A)(B)(C)(D)(E)	55. (A)(B)(C)(D)(E)	75. (A)(B)(C)(D)(E)
16. (A)(B)(C)(D)(E)	36. (A)(B)(C)(D)(E)	56. (A)(B)(C)(D)(E)	76. (A)(B)(C)(D)(E)
17. (A)(B)(C)(D)(E)	37. (A)(B)(C)(D)(E)	57. (A)(B)(C)(D)(E)	77. (A)(B)(C)(D)(E)
18. (A)(B)(C)(D)(E)	38. (A)(B)(C)(D)(E)	58. (A)(B)(C)(D)(E)	78. (A)(B)(C)(D)(E)
19. (A)(B)(C)(D)(E)	39. (A)(B)(C)(D)(E)	59. (A)(B)(C)(D)(E)	79. (A)(B)(C)(D)(E)
20. (A)(B)(C)(D)(E)	40. (A)(B)(C)(D)(E)	60. (A)(B)(C)(D)(E)	80. (A)(B)(C)(D)(E)

Practice Advanced Placement United States History Examination Model A

The following is a typical Advanced Placement examination in United States history. After you have completed your review of the subject and have studied and analyzed the various types of questions that may appear on the actual exam, take this model examination and get a preview of how you will fare on the real examination in May. Be sure to use the answer sheet on the previous page because it does take a little longer to mark answers on a separate sheet.

Section 1

You will be allowed 3 hours and 5 minutes for the entire examination. Section 1, the Multiple-Choice Section, includes 80 questions to be answered in 55 minutes. This gives you 45 seconds for each question. Since one-fourth of the number of questions you have incorrect will be subtracted from the total number of your correct answers, guessing haphazardly will detract from your score. However, if you can narrow your choices down to two or three because of your general knowledge of the subject, then it may help your score if you pick an answer. You should work quickly. If the question is difficult for you, do not waste time on it but move on to the next question. You may return to the questions you skipped if there is time left after you have gone over all 80 questions. Since preparation varies from school to school, very few students can answer all the questions, so do not be discouraged.

Section 2

Section 2, the Essay Section, includes the DBQ and two other essay questions to be selected from four questions. These are to be answered in 2 hours and 10 minutes. The first 15 minutes consists of a reading period in which you will read the DBQ and prepare notes for your answer. If you have time, you may select and make notes on the two other free response questions you will answer. However, from the total time given for the two essays, each of them is allotted 5 minutes for preparing notes. You then have one hour and 55 minutes to write your answers. It is suggested that this time be divided, with 45 minutes for the DBQ, 10 minutes for planning answers for the two free response questions, and 30 minutes to write each of the two essays. At the examination you will be supplied a small booklet of $8\frac{1}{2}'' \times 11''$ lined pages on which to write your answers. For this sample examination you will want to use your own paper. You should write your essay answers in black or blue ink. Pencils should not be used as they make reading difficult.

Now tear out the multiple-choice answer sheet or xerox a copy of it. Get some lined paper, pencils and pens, and a timer, and sit down ready to spend 3 hours and 5 minutes on this practice exam. If you need to, you may take breaks between the sections and/or between the three essays. It would be best to find a quiet place with a desk and to work uninterrupted.

Model Exam A

Section I
Multiple-Choice
Questions

Time: 55 minutes

Number of Questions—80 MULTIPLE CHOICE

Directions: Each of the questions or incomplete statements below is followed by five suggested answers or completions. Select the one that is best in each case and then blacken the corresponding oval on the answer sheet.

1. "The [American] people, . . . to a greater extent than any other, realize that surplus wealth is but a trust to be administered during life for the good of the community. Nowhere are there so many philanthropic agencies at work."
    The above statement would describe the attitudes most likely held by all of the following at the end of the 19th century EXCEPT
    (A) a Social Darwinist
    (B) Andrew Carnegie
    (C) a successful businessperson
    (D) John D. Rockefeller
    (E) Eugene V. Debs

(Question 2)

EUROPEAN IMMIGRATION 1820—1957

Legend
· · · · · · · Ireland
————— Northern Europe Great Britain, Scandinavia, Germany, and other northwestern nations
— — — — Southern and Eastern Europe Poland, Russia, Baltic States, Italy, other Eastern and Southern nations
(1) immigration from Southern and Eastern Europe was insignificant prior to 1870
(2) Irish immigration has not exceeded 10,000 per year since 1930

Sources: Historical Statistics of the United States
Statistical Abstractst of the United States

Source: U.S. Bureau of the Census, *Historical Statistics of the U.S., Colonial Times to 1957.*

2. According to the chart showing European immigration,
    (A) the period of greatest yearly immigration from northern Europe was 1905–1910
    (B) more Irish came to America in 1850–1855 than in 1885–1890
    (C) immigration from southern and eastern Europe was insignificant prior to 1930
    (D) northern Europe includes Great Britain, Scandinavia, and the Baltic States
    (E) the period of greatest immigration from southern Europe was after 1945

3. Which one of the following events occurred most recently?
    (A) The ratification of the Articles of Confederation
    (B) The presentation of the Connecticut Compromise
    (C) The introduction of the Virginia Plan
    (D) The drafting of the Declaration of Independence
    (E) The offering of the New Jersey Plan

4. Which one of the following groups includes individuals all of whom supported the ratification of the U.S. Constitution by the states?
    (A) Thomas Jefferson, Patrick Henry, Melancthon Smith
    (B) John Jay, Alexander Hamilton, Patrick Henry
    (C) James Madison, John Jay, Alexander Hamilton
    (D) Thomas Jefferson, James Madison, Andrew Jackson
    (E) James Madison, Daniel Webster, Alexander Hamilton

5. Which of the following was NOT offered by Americans as a solution to the problems of the Great Depression?
    (A) WPA   (D) NATO
    (B) "Share the Wealth"   (E) NIRA
    (C) EPIC

6. The Palmer Raids
    (A) created a climate of opinion in which Senator Joseph McCarthy could capture the attention of the American people
    (B) identified over 400,000 Communists who were exiled to the Soviet Union
    (C) exposed the attorney general to such publicity that he was able to capture the Republican nomination for president in 1924
    (D) united the country in opposing the Fascist threat of Italy and Germany in the 1930s
    (E) reflected the anticommunist hysteria of the post-World War I period

7. Which of the following ideas was NOT incorporated in Frederick Jackson Turner's thesis on the influence of the frontier on America?
   (A) "The complex European life" had continual impact on America since the "Atlantic Coast . . . was the frontier of Europe."
   (B) There is a "new product that is American."
   (C) The frontier is the "outer edge . . . the meeting point between savagery and civilization."
   (D) A "frontier settlement" had existed until 1890.
   (E) "Democracy born of free land, strong in selfishness and individualism," has its "dangers as well as its benefits."

8. ". . . and he [the president] shall nominate, and by and with the advice and consent of the Senate, shall appoint . . . judges of the Supreme Court . . ."

   The passage above from the Constitution best illustrates the concept of
   (A) the power of the purse
   (B) executive privilege
   (C) checks and balances
   (D) judicial review
   (E) due process

9. "I will not, I cannot, give up my belief that America must, not alone for the happiness of her own people, but for the moral guidance and greater contentment of the world, be permitted to live her own life. Next to the tie which binds a man to his God is the tie which binds a man to his country, and all schemes, all plans however ambitious and fascinating they seem in their proposal, but which would embarrass or entangle and impede or shackle her sovereign will, which would compromise her freedom of action I unhesitatingly put behind me."

   The writer is making a statement that could best be summarized as in favor of
   (A) isolationism and Christianity
   (B) sovereignty and socialism
   (C) freedom and nationalism
   (D) socialism and Christianity
   (E) isolationism and nationalism

(Question 10)

Source: *World Telegram*, August 11, 1934

10. In the cartoon above the artist is
  (A) suggesting the Republican Party has no effective solution to the depression
  (B) supporting the anticommunist crusade of the 1920s
  (C) advocating Social Darwinism as a policy
  (D) indicating he believes in nonviolent protest
  (E) implying that the GOP is being robbed by Wall Street and Rugged Individualism

(Question 11)

11. On the above map, the areas colored black illustrate the
    (A) region divided into camps at the Yalta Conference
    (B) members of the Common Market
    (C) Central Powers in World War I
    (D) greatest extent of Nazi control in World War II
    (E) regions subjected to terrorist attacks during the Cold War

12. All of the following are true of the 1994 Congressional elections EXCEPT
    (A) The Republicans gained control of the House of Representatives for
        the first time since Eisenhower's presidency.
    (B) The Democrats lost control of the Senate.
    (C) President Clinton refused to campaign for members of his party.
    (D) The Republicans based their campaign for the House of
        Representatives on a Contract with America, which they promised
        to bring to a vote within 100 days.
    (E) Newt Gingrich, then minority leader of the House of Representa-
        tives, helped plan the Republican campaign.

13. Which of the following would NOT be considered part of the Cold War?
    (A) The U-2 incident
    (B) The Truman Doctrine
    (C) The U.N. intervention in the Congo
    (D) The attempts to impeach Earl Warren
    (E) The Bay of Pigs affair

14. William Jennings Bryan's Cross of Gold speech addressed economic issues and helped him

    (A) be appointed Secretary of State

    (B) express his views on evolution at the Scopes Trial .

    (C) gain support of Republican business leaders

    (D) win the Democratic Party presidential nomination

    (E) found the Populist Party

15. Which of the following is a correct statement regarding the Vietnam War?

    (A) U.S. involvement in Vietnam began with John F. Kennedy.

    (B) President Lyndon Johnson decided to withdraw from the presidential race because of his stand on Vietnam.

    (C) U.S. forces never attacked outside the borders of Vietnam.

    (D) The Gulf of Tonkin Resolution made the Vietnam conflict legal in international law as it declared war on North Vietnam.

    (E) Throughout the war the areas controlled by each side were clearly identifiable.

16. An economic system in which a nation seeks to accumulate precious metals by maintaining a favorable balance of trade is most descriptive of

    (A) capitalism   (D) feudalism

    (B) socialism   (E) fascism

    (C) mercantilism

17. Under the Articles of Confederation, sovereignty was in the hands of the

    (A) executive   (D) town meetings

    (B) Congress   (E) revolutionary army

    (C) states

18. A person supporting the concept of implied power in regard to the U.S. Constitution would be a believer in

    (A) limited executive power   (D) loose constructionism

    (B) strict constructionism   (E) states' rights

    (C) Jeffersonianism

19. The principal reason for the Era of Good Feeling during the presidency of James Monroe was

    (A) relative peace in the world

    (B) great economic development and general prosperity at home

    (C) a great religious revival that de-emphasized political considerations

    (D) a very weakened opposition political party

    (E) his strong stand in favor of Latin America stated in the Monroe Doctrine

20. The main purpose of Henry Clay's American System was to
   (A) advance and implement Manifest Destiny
   (B) develop an interdependent economic system tying the East, West, and South together
   (C) curtail immigration in favor of large native population growth
   (D) integrate the Native American into U.S. society
   (E) expand American investment abroad

21. Transcendentalist writers found their major source of truth and inspiration in
   (A) church dogma   (D) nature
   (B) the Bible   (E) history
   (C) the political situation of the time

22. The Age of Jackson is noted for all of the following events EXCEPT
   (A) Jackson's refusal to accept the Supreme Court's decision concerning the land claims of the Cherokee Indian Tribe
   (B) the publication of the South Carolina "exposition and protest"
   (C) the veto of the bill rechartering the Second Bank of the United States
   (D) the meeting of the Hartford Convention
   (E) the passage of the Force Act

23. The event in the western theater during the Civil War that had the effect of splitting the Confederacy in half was the
   (A) Battle of the Wilderness   (D) Battle of Gettysburg
   (B) Capture of Vicksburg   (E) Siege of Petersburg
   (C) Battle of Antietam

24. The political leader most responsible for securing the passage of the Civil Rights Act of 1964 was
   (A) John F. Kennedy   (D) Andrew Young
   (B) Lyndon B. Johnson   (E) George Wallace
   (C) Adam Clayton Powell

25. Of his Fourteen Points, Wilson was most concerned with establishing
   (A) Point I: Open covenants, openly arrived at
   (B) Point II: Absolute freedom of navigation upon the seas
   (C) Point IV: Adequate guarantees given and taken that national armaments will be reduced to the lowest point consistent with domestic safety
   (D) Point V: A free, open-minded and absolutely impartial adjustment of all colonial claims
   (E) Point XIV: A general association of nations formed to provide political independence and territorial integrity of all nations

26. The Creel Committee during World War I represented the United States' first successful attempt at large-scale governmental
    - (A) armament manufacture
    - (B) food production
    - (C) shipbuilding
    - (D) propaganda
    - (E) railroad management

27. "We had a chance to gain the leadership of the world. We lost it, and soon we shall be witnessing the tragedy of it all."

    Which American leader during the 20th century would most likely have made the above statement?
    - (A) Theodore Roosevelt
    - (B) Woodrow Wilson
    - (C) Franklin Roosevelt
    - (D) John F. Kennedy
    - (E) Lyndon B. Johnson

28. Which of the following New Deal legislation was a basic reform measure dealing with banking?
    - (A) Public Works Administration
    - (B) Federal Deposit Insurance Corporation
    - (C) Civilian Conservation Corps
    - (D) National Industrial Recovery Act
    - (E) Agricultural Adjustment Administration

29. "With millions of men and women still unemployed and the whole industrialized world critically dependent upon the scope and vigor of the American economic recovery, a veto of the tax cut would be poor public policy, which political headline-hunting could not justify."

    The quotation suggests all of the following EXCEPT
    - (A) The United States continues to be in a depression.
    - (B) A presidential veto would be harmful to the nation.
    - (C) Other nations are heavily affected by the U.S. economy.
    - (D) In determining policy, the president should be guided solely by the political impact of the policy.
    - (E) The unemployment rate is high in the nation.

30. Which one of the following accurately describes the president's cabinet?
    - (A) It is fully described in the United States Constitution.
    - (B) Members are not approved by the United States Senate.
    - (C) Members of the cabinet serve at the pleasure of the Chief Executive.
    - (D) The cabinet must meet every Thursday.
    - (E) The number of Executive Departments headed by cabinet officers can be changed by the president as he wishes.

31. The political Reconstruction of the South was ended after
     (A) the impeachment of President Johnson
     (B) the Democratic presidential victory in 1884
     (C) an agreement was arranged that allowed Republican Rutherford B.
          Hayes to become president
     (D) the Southern states indicated they welcomed military occupation
     (E) the grandfather clause as a voting requirement was outlawed by the
          Supreme Court

32. When the New Deal program of Franklin D. Roosevelt was threatened by
     Supreme Court decisions against New Deal measures, the president
     responded by
     (A) giving his famous "my dog Falla" speech, which compared the
          Supreme Court to his dog
     (B) calling on Congress to increase the size of the Supreme Court so that
          he could appoint new members who approved of New Deal legislation
     (C) ordering impeachment proceedings against members of the Court
     (D) ignoring the Court decisions following the precedent set by Andrew
          Jackson
     (E) calling on the American people to elect only Democrats to Congress

33. Which of the following did NOT contribute to the bad relations between
     Native Americans and the U.S. government in the 40 years following the
     Civil War?
     (A) The slaughter of the buffalo
     (B) The corruption of many Indian Agents
     (C) The discovery and exploitation of gold in the Black Hills of South
          Dakota
     (D) The publication of works such as Helen Hunt Jackson's *A Century
          of Dishonor* and *Ramona*
     (E) The disregard of treaty arrangements

34. All of the following would be considered a victory for organized labor
     EXCEPT the
     (A) Taft-Hartley Act
     (B) Wisconsin Unemployment Insurance Law
     (C) establishment of a national minimum wage
     (D) Wagner Act
     (E) Anthracite Coal Strike of 1902

35. Which one of the following transportation developments affecting U.S.
     history took place in the 20th century?
     (A) Opening of the transcontinental railroad
     (B) Organization of local canals to support manufacturing
     (C) Introduction of steamboats on the Mississippi River
     (D) Establishment of air mail service
     (E) The Pony Express mail service

36. The English colony first settled by the Dutch was
    (A) New York   (D) Pennsylvania
    (B) Jamaica   (E) Delaware
    (C) Canada

37. The principal motivation for the settlement of the Plymouth Bay Colony was
    (A) economic   (D) social
    (B) political   (E) cultural
    (C) religious

38. Which of the following best explains why the earliest factories in the United States were located in New England?
    (A) Its easy access to large quantities of coal
    (B) Abundant water power
    (C) The availability of cheap labor
    (D) A well-developed system of canals
    (E) Good harbors

39. *The Sovereignty and Goodness of God or Narrative of the Captivity and Restoration of Mrs. Mary Rowlandson* was
    (A) an account of the Salem Witch Trials
    (B) a sermon by Jonathan Edwards, which precipitated the Great Awakening
    (C) an argument used by the Abolitionists in attacking slavery
    (D) the most popular story about Native Americans written in the English colonies
    (E) a statement in favor of temperance

40. The era of Prohibition in the 1920s created which of the following?
    I. A general breakdown or change in the moral attitudes of Americans
    II. An increase in the number of gangsters and bootleggers
    III. Strong support for repeal of Prohibition throughout the South
    IV. An awareness of the weakness of the federal government in controlling private habits of its citizens
    (A) I and II
    (B) I, II, III
    (C) II, III, IV
    (D) I, II, IV
    (E) I, II, III, IV

41. The fundamental thesis of Keynesian economics is that
    (A) the government should tax highly in times of inflation and the government should spend extensively in times of deflation
    (B) the government should keep "hands off" all economic activity
    (C) successful businessmen should run the government
    (D) the wealth of a nation is measured by the amount of gold it holds
    (E) the Federal Reserve Board should control economic policy

42. Which of the following events occurred under the government of the Articles of Confederation?
   (A) The repeal of the Stamp Act
   (B) Shays' Rebellion
   (C) The Whiskey Rebellion
   (D) Daniel Boone's first trip to Kentucky
   (E) The Boston Massacre

43. Jefferson is often accused of political inconsistency since he apparently supported states' rights in the Kentucky and Virginia resolves but acted as a supporter of federal power and loose construction of the Constitution when he did all of the following EXCEPT
   (A) arranged the Louisiana Purchase
   (B) sent the United States Navy to attack the Barbary Pirates
   (C) ordered Lewis and Clark to explore the West
   (D) proclaimed the Embargo in 1807
   (E) supported the French in the XYZ Affair

44. In the years immediately after 1825 the pattern of western settlement was greatly affected by the
   (A) aftermath of the Battle of the Little Big Horn
   (B) opening of the Erie Canal
   (C) purchase of Alaska
   (D) discovery of gold in South Dakota
   (E) the clipper ship trade with China

45. The Pendleton Act was passed by Congress as a response to
   (A) the assassination of President Garfield
   (B) the Cross of Gold speech by William Jennings Bryan
   (C) the declaration by the Supreme Court that the Granger Laws were unconstitutional
   (D) the election of Theodore Roosevelt as vice president
   (E) the annexation of Hawaii

46. Which of the following was NOT a major issue during the presidency of Jimmy Carter?
   (A) The Iranian hostage crisis
   (B) Inflation
   (C) the number of U.S. troops in Europe
   (D) SALT negotiations
   (E) Human rights

47. All of the following were actions by the United States federal government to deal with the money supply EXCEPT the
   (A) Sherman Silver Purchase Act
   (B) Social Security Act
   (C) establishment of the Commodity Dollar
   (D) Federal Reserve Act
   (E) Specie Circular

48. In the 40 years following the end of Reconstruction, fundamental changes in the American system were brought about as a result of federal legislation in all of the following EXCEPT
    (A) immigration
    (B) civil service
    (C) civil rights
    (D) interstate commerce
    (E) monetary policy

49. All of the following contributed to the decision of the United States to declare war on Spain in 1898 EXCEPT
    (A) The sinking of the battleship *Maine*
    (B) The De Lome Letter
    (C) The stimulation of public opinion by the Yellow Press
    (D) The acquisition of Pago Pago
    (E) The need to protect American economic investments

50. The purpose of the "gag rule" adopted by the U.S. Senate was to
    (A) encourage full participation in debate by all members of the Senate
    (B) control unlimited filibuster
    (C) limit debate on attempts to override presidential vetoes
    (D) prevent debate of abolitionist proposals
    (E) discourage criticism of U.S. foreign policy

51. All of the following occurred during George Washington's two terms EXCEPT
    (A) the election of John Adams to the presidency
    (B) the resignation of Thomas Jefferson as Secretary of State
    (C) the XYZ Affair
    (D) Hamilton's and Jefferson's letters on the constitutionality of the Bank of the U.S.
    (E) the negotiation of the Jay Treaty

52. Which of the following acts established the concept of surveying land into six-square-mile townships and the sale of land at public auction?
    (A) Homestead Act
    (B) Pacific Railway Act
    (C) Land Act of 1796
    (D) Desert Land Act
    (E) Surplus Revenue Act

53. Which of the following events finally precipitated the military activity of the Civil War?
    (A) The establishment of the state of West Virginia
    (B) Secession of South Carolina
    (C) The action at Fort Sumter
    (D) The first election of Lincoln to the presidency
    (E) The Emancipation Proclamation

(Question 54)

THE DEFENDER OF TRUSTS.

J. G. B. "This is only a little private matter, officer, with which you have nothing to do."

Source: Harper's Weekly, September 1, 1888

54. All of the following ideas are presented by the cartoonist EXCEPT
   (A) Several American industries are organized as trusts
   (B) The American market at the time the cartoon was drawn was oper-
        ated under the emblem of freedom and equality
   (C) Trusts are robbing competition in the American market
   (D) A well-dressed gentleman does not believe the police officer should
        interfere with the robbery
   (E) The law is not prepared to become involved

55. Which of the following is NOT true regarding Dollar Diplomacy?
    (A) Investments were encouraged in both the Far East and in countries near the Panama Canal.
    (B) It allowed Taft to spend less on the Navy.
    (C) It eliminated armed intervention by United States forces in the Caribbean.
    (D) Woodrow Wilson reluctantly continued the policy after his election to the presidency.
    (E) United States money was used to support governments in the Caribbean and Central America.

56. "For upwards of half a century the republics of the Western world have been working together to promote their common civilization under a system of peace. That venture, launched so hopefully fifty years ago (in 1889), has succeeded; the American family is today a great co-operative group facing a troubled world in serenity and calm . . ."

    To which of the following organizations is the author referring?
    (A) Economic Development Council (EDC)
    (B) Pan-American Union
    (C) Contradora Group
    (D) League of Nations
    (E) NATO

57. United States society in the period from the end of World War II until the election of President John F. Kennedy was characterized by all of the following EXCEPT
    (A) a new attitude toward segregation precipitated by Supreme Court decisions
    (B) a concern over Communist (Soviet) infiltration into the U.S. government bureaucracy
    (C) the start of a new movement of popular music
    (D) a mood of conformity and uncritical support of government policies
    (E) a major economic recession with high unemployment for all Americans

58. "In the discussions to which this interest has given rise . . . the occasion has been judged proper for asserting, as a principle in which the rights and interests of the United States are involved, that the American continents, by the free and independent condition which they have assumed and maintain, are henceforth not to be considered as subjects for future colonization by any European powers . . ."

The principles articulated in the above passage are often considered the key point in the

(A) Stimson Doctrine
(B) Eisenhower Doctrine
(C) Roosevelt Corollary
(D) Monroe Doctrine
(E) Truman Doctrine

(Question 59)

Source: Los Angeles County Natural History Museum Foundation, History Fund

59. The scene in the photograph above is most likely of
(A) Hispanic Americans in Los Angeles
(B) San Francisco during the Gold Rush
(C) the south side of Chicago during the days of African American migration to the cities
(D) Native Americans settled in Sioux City
(E) immigrants in New York City

60. The economic program introduced during the presidency of Ronald Reagan and often referred to as Reaganomics resulted in which one of the following items?
    (A) Tax increases for all payers of federal income taxes
    (B) Decreased expenditures for military defense
    (C) Elimination of government cabinet-level departments
    (D) A rapidly increasing federal deficit
    (E) Large increases in federal expenditures for social services

(Question 61)

Getting Back to a Competitive Basis

Source: *Saturday Evening Post*, June 6, 1914

61. The political cartoonist who drew this picture was making a comment about the
    (A) popularity of organ grinders
    (B) attempt to win people's support for animal rights
    (C) seeking by Theodore Roosevelt and Woodrow Wilson of popular support for their political reform programs
    (D) way every product in America is advertised as "new"
    (E) rivalry of political candidates

(Question 62)

Source: Harper's Weekly, March 9, 1912

62. The tall building in the middle of the photograph reflects the architectural style of
    (A) English Georgian architects
    (B) the Greek Revival movement
    (C) Frank Lloyd Wright
    (D) Henry Hobson Richardson
    (E) Eino Saarinen

63. All of the following occurred during the presidency of Jimmy Carter EXCEPT
    (A) the imposition by OPEC of its first oil embargo to force oil prices to rise
    (B) the seizure of Americans by Iranians and the holding of them as hostages in Teheran
    (C) the signing of the Camp David Peace Accord
    (D) the strong support for human rights and the Helsinki Accord by the president
    (E) the negotiation of a treaty with Panama that would return the Canal to Panama

64. "If the *British* Parliament has a legal authority to issue an order that we shall furnish a single article for the troops here, and to compel obedience to *that* order, they have the same right to issue an order for us to supply those troops with arms, clothes, and every necessary; and to compel obedience to *that* order also; in short, to lay any burthens they please upon us. What is this but taxing us to a certain sum, and leaving us only the manner of raising it?"

    The argument presented by the author of the above statement could best be summarized as
    (A) The British Parliament has no authority to compel Americans to supply goods for troops.
    (B) The Stamp Act is intolerable and should be repealed immediately.
    (C) Americans should supply British troops with clothes, arms, and all other necessities.
    (D) Americans should determine the sum by which they will be taxed by Parliament.
    (E) Americans should pay more taxes to help the British.

65. All of the following are characteristic of the African slave trade in the 18th century EXCEPT
    (A) Kings of African nations along the coast sold slaves to white traders.
    (B) During the "middle passage" slaves were chained and kept below deck most of the time.
    (C) Degradation and psychological damage occurred to all those involved, according to scholars today.
    (D) The colonists relied on the English traders to supply slaves.
    (E) Most of the slaves sold in the Southern colonies were imported directly from Africa.

66. Which of the following best describes the events of the Cuban Missile Crisis during John F. Kennedy's presidency?
    (A) The presence of Soviet missiles in Cuba was discovered accidentally.
    (B) The president of the United States overreacted and was restrained by his advisors from taking steps that would have meant war.
    (C) Both sides displayed a sober approach and made concessions to overcome dangerous developments.
    (D) Nikita Khrushchev refused to accept a U.S. naval quarantine of Cuba and forced the U.S. to board Soviet ships to resolve the crisis.
    (E) Fidel Castro was consulted by the Soviets and followed the Soviet lead in all responses to the United States' actions during the crisis.

(Question 67)

IMPROVEMENTS IN AMERICAN HOMES

TOWN AND CITY HOMES

| | WITH IMPROVEMENT | WITHOUT IMPROVEMENT |

Running Water

Electric Lighting

Private Indoor Water Closet

Bathtub or Shower

Central Heating

FARM HOMES

| WITH IMPROVEMENT | WITHOUT IMPROVEMENT |

Running Water

Electric Lighting

Private Indoor Water Closet

Bathtub or Shower

Central Heating

Each unit represents 10 percent of all homes

Source: Building America

67. Considering the items chosen for comparison in the above chart and the quantitative relationship between farm and city homes, one would assume the information in the chart dates from the
   (A) post-World War II period
   (B) Populist Era
   (C) Civil War years
   (D) Great Depression
   (E) Jacksonian period

68. According to the Constitution, in an impeachment trial of a president
   (A) the evidence against the president should be gathered by an independent counsel
   (B) the president may be impeached by a majority vote of the Senate
   (C) punishment for an impeached and guilty president is removal from office and disqualification to hold other offices
   (D) witnesses against the president must be questioned before the entire Senate
   (E) the House of Representatives must approve the Articles of Impeachment by a two-thirds vote

(Question 69)

THE IRREPRESSIBLE INDEPENDENT.

Source: Harper's Weekly, October 20, 1888

69. In the cartoon above, the Spoils System referred to on the Tammany booth indicates the political system of
    (A) honoring opponents with at least one appointed office
    (B) rewarding supporters with appointed offices
    (C) declaring openly who one's political supporters have been
    (D) appointing one's campaign manager to the cabinet
    (E) pointing out how one's opponents spoiled one's opportunity for election

(Question 70)

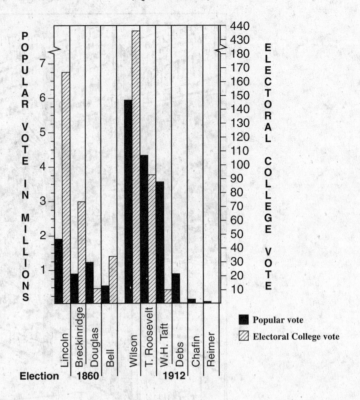

70. The bar graph above proves that
     (A) the electoral college is unjust
     (B) any of the three top candidates in the 1912 election, if they had run
          in 1860, would have defeated Lincoln
     (C) popular candidates cannot win in the electoral college
     (D) Bell was a better candidate than Douglas
     (E) Lincoln and Wilson were both minority presidents according to the
          popular vote, but received a majority of votes in the electoral college

71. Which statement is INCORRECTLY paired with the man who stated it?
     (A) John C. Calhoun—"Liberty and union, now and forever, one and
          inseparable"
     (B) Patrick Henry—"Give me liberty or give me death"
     (C) Thomas Jefferson—"We hold these truths to be self-evident"
     (D) Andrew Jackson—"Our federal union, it must be preserved"
     (E) Franklin D. Roosevelt—"The only thing we have to fear is fear itself"

72. Which one of the following American authors was LEAST concerned with
     social criticism of America?
     (A) John Steinbeck   (D) Upton Sinclair
     (B) Frank Norris   (E) Jacob Riis
     (C) Booth Tarkington

73. The term *impressment* as used by the United States in the period before the War of 1812 referred to
    (A) the foreign policy concept of shunning alliances with other countries
    (B) a combining together of nations in an effort to provide greater protection from attacks of the British
    (C) the British practice of forcing American sailors into service on British warships
    (D) an agreement temporarily uniting two or more countries
    (E) a written plea from an individual protesting a wrong as a result of the actions of the British

74. "... Whereas ... [the colonies] have freely declared ... that a most flourishing civil state may stand and best be maintained ... with a full liberty in religious concernments ...
    "... we, being willing to ... secure them [the people] in the free exercise and enjoyment of all their civil and religious rights ... do hereby publish, grant, ordain, and declare ... that no person with the said colony, at any time hereafter, shall be any wise molested, punished, disquieted, or called in question for any differences in opinion in matters of religion."

    The above quotation is most likely taken from
    (A) the Mayflower Compact
    (B) the Rhode Island colonial charter
    (C) a speech to Parliament by King James I
    (D) the Albany Plan of Union
    (E) the transcript of the trial of Peter Zenger

75. If a historian doing original research wished to analyze the changes made in Thomas Jefferson's original draft of the Declaration of Independence by the Committee of Five and by the members of the Continental Congress, the best way to begin would be to
    (A) call the Library of Congress and ask for advice
    (B) consult the final version signed by members of the Continental Congress and the letters they wrote about the Declaration
    (C) visit the National Archives to study the original draft and other early copies of the Declaration, including the version signed by the members of the Congress
    (D) read a book on the writing of the Declaration of Independence and analyze the author's conclusion
    (E) put out a message on the Internet asking historians what they believe the changes were

76. "The history of mankind is a history of repeated injuries and usurpations on the part of man toward woman, having in direct object the establishment of an absolute tyranny over her. To prove this, let facts be submitted to a candid world.

    "Having deprived her of this first right of a citizen, the elective franchise [right to vote], thereby leaving her without representation in the halls of legislation, he has oppressed her on all sides.

    "*Resolved,* That it is the duty of the women of this country to secure to themselves their sacred right to the elective franchise."

    The above statement would NOT be needed to have been written after
    (A) 1828
    (B) 1848
    (C) 1870
    (D) 1919
    (E) 1971

77. All of the following reform movements of the pre-Civil War period are correctly paired with a leader of the movement EXCEPT
    (A) Care of the insane—Dorothea Dix
    (B) Abolition—Harriet Beecher Stowe
    (C) Women's Rights—Lucretia Mott
    (D) Education—Brigham Young
    (E) Prohibition— Neal S. Dow

78. All of the following major U.S. Supreme Court decisions are correctly paired with the decision handed down by the Supreme Court in the case named EXCEPT
    (A) *McCulloch v. Maryland*—upheld Maryland's right to tax the Bank of the United States
    (B) *Schechter v. United States*—declared the NIRA invalid, thus ending the first phase of the New Deal
    (C) *Plessy v. Ferguson*—upheld Louisiana law requiring segregated trains
    (D) *Munn v. Illinois*—upheld an Illinois law fixing maximum rates for grain storage
    (E) *Mueller v. Oregon*—upheld an Oregon law limiting the maximum working hours for women

79. Which of the following events connected with the Civil Rights Movement of the post-World War II period occurred first?
    (A) The lunch counter sit-ins
    (B) The decision in *Brown v. Board of Education*
    (C) The assassination of Martin Luther King, Jr.
    (D) Montgomery, Alabama, bus boycott
    (E) The twenty-fourth Amendment (anti-poll tax) to the Constitution

80. "Now the trumpet summons us again—not a call to bear arms, though arms we need—not a call to battle, though embattled we are—but a call to bear the burden of a long twilight struggle, year in and year out, 'rejoicing in hope, patient in tribulation'—a struggle against the common enemies of man: tyranny, poverty, disease and war itself"

Based on the above quotation, the author would most likely have supported all of the following EXCEPT
(A) the War on Poverty
(B) the Peace Corps
(C) the establishment of Communist rule in Vietnam
(D) Medicare
(E) the SALT disarmament agreements

**Section II
DBQ**

The free-response section consists of two parts. All students must answer the DBQ in Part A. Part B includes two groups of essay questions and students must answer one question from each group.

You have a 15-minute reading period to read the documents and prepare your answer.

Part A: Document-Based Essay Question (DBQ)

Writing time—45 minutes

Directions: The following question requires you to construct a coherent essay that integrates your interpretation of documents A–H **and** your knowledge of the period referred to in the question. In order to earn a high score you must cite key pieces of evidence from the documents and draw on your knowledge of the period.

1. Between 1900 and 1918 to what degree did the attitudes expressed in Supreme Court decisions concerning government regulation of business and working conditions reflect the attitudes of the political leaders of the nation? Why or why not were they in agreement?

Document A

Source: **Oliver Wendell Holmes' Dissenting Opinion in U.S. Supreme Court Case *Lochner v. New York*, 1905. In this case the majority of the Court declared unconstitutional a New York State law limiting the number of hours bakers could work each week.**

It is settled by various decisions of this court that state constitutions and state laws may regulate life in many ways which we as legislators might think as injudicious or if you like as tyrannical.

The liberty of the citizen to do as he likes so long as he does not interfere with the liberty of others to do the same, which has been a shibboleth (accepted truth) for some well-known writers, is interfered with by school laws, by the Post Office, by every state or municipal institution which takes his money for purposes thought desirable, whether he likes it or not.

A constitution is not intended to embody a particular economic theory, whether of paternalism and the relation of the citizen to the State or of laissez-faire. It is made for people of fundamentally differing views.

Document B

Source: John Spargo, *The Cry of the Children,* 1906

. . . in the spinning and carding rooms of cotton and woolen mills, where large numbers of children are employed, clouds of lint-dust fill the lungs and menace the health. The children have a distressing cough, caused by the irritation of the throat, and many are hoarse from the same cause. In bottle factories and other branches of glass manufacture, the atmosphere is constantly charged with microscopic particles of glass.

The children who are employed in the manufacture of wall papers and poisonous paints suffer from slow poisoning. The naphtha fumes in the manufacture of rubber goods produce paralysis and premature decay.

Document C

Source: United States Senator Nathan B. Scott of West Virginia, from a Speech in the U.S. Congress, 1906

. . . A gentleman by the name of Markham, writing a magazine article not long ago, said that he had visited the glasshouses and had seen children—boys and girls—with emaciated forms, with their eyes, as it were, protruding from their sockets, all due to overwork. He spoke of their little bodies being blistered by the hot furnaces, and a lot more of that kind of magazine stuff, for it is nothing but stuff.

I have been engaged in the manufacture of glass for thirty-five years and if Mr. Markham had come to see my factory . . . (he) would not (have seen) anything like that which he described in his magazine article.

. . . The glasshouse boy of today becomes the glass manufacturer of tomorrow.

Document D

Source: **Library of Congress**

Young boy working in canning factory. Early 1900s.

Document E

Source: **Majority opinion in Supreme Court *Mueller v. Oregon*, 1908. In this case the Court upheld an Oregon law limiting to ten a day the hours of labor for women employed in factories. Scientific, psychological, and sociological evidence was introduced by Louis B. Brandeis in winning the case.**

Constitutional questions are not settled by even a consensus of present public opinion, for it is the peculiar value of a written constitution that it places in unchanging form limitations upon legislative action, and thus gives a permanence and stability to popular government which otherwise would be lacking.

As argued in this case, the two sexes differ in structure of body, in the functions to be performed by each, in the amount of physical strength, in the capacity for long-continued labor, particularly when done standing, in the influence of vigorous health upon the future well-being of the race. This difference justifies a difference in legislation.

For these reasons the act in question is not in conflict with the federal Constitution as it respects the limitation of the hours of work done by a female in a laundry.

Document F

Source: **Speeches by Woodrow Wilson, 1912 and 1913**

—In this new age we find, for instance, that our laws with regard to relations of employer and employee are in many respects wholly antiquated and impossible . . .

—We used to think in the old-fashioned days when life was very simple that all the government had to do was to put on a policeman's uniform, and say, "Now don't anybody hurt anybody else." We used to say that the ideal of government was for every man to be left alone and not be interfered with, except when he interfered with somebody else. But we are coming now to realize that life is so complicated that we are not dealing with the old conditions, and that the law has to step in and create new conditions under which we may live, the conditions which will make it tolerable for us to live.

—We have been proud of our industrial achievements, but we have not hitherto stopped, thoughtfully enough to count . . . the fearful physical and spiritual cost to the men and women and children upon whom the dead weight and burden of it all has fallen pitilessly the years through.

Document G

Source: **Speeches by Theodore Roosevelt, 1910 and 1912**

The American people are right in demanding that new nationalism, without which we cannot hope to deal with new problems. . . . This new nationalism regards the executive power as the steward of the public welfare. It demands of the judiciary that it should be interested primarily in human welfare rather than in property, just as it demands that the representative body shall represent all of the people rather than any one class or section of people. . . .

One of the fundamental necessities of a representative government such as ours is to make certain that the men to whom people delegate their power shall serve the people by whom they are elected, and not the special interests . . . The object of government is the welfare of the people . . . No matter how honest and decent we are in our private lives, if we do not have the right kind of law and the right kind of administration of the law, we cannot go forward as a nation.

A National Industrial Commission would be created . . . [to] deal with all the abuses of the Trust, such supervision would put a stop to exploitation of the people by dishonest capitalists.

Document H

> *Source:* **Majority opinion in U.S. Supreme Court [*Hammer v. Dagenhart*], 1918. In this case the Court declared unconstitutional the Keating-Owen Child Labor Act.**
>
> . . . In the present case . . . The Act, in effect, does not regulate transportation among the states, but aims to standardize the ages at which children may be employed in mining and manufacturing within the states.
>
> That there should be limitations upon the right to employ children in the mines and factories in the interest of their own and the public welfare, all will admit . . . [However,] in our view, the necessary effect of this Act is, by means of a prohibition against a movement [of commodities] in interstate commerce . . ., to regulate the hours of labor of children . . ., [which is] a purely state authority . . . The Act . . . is repugnant to the Constitution. It not only transcends the authority delegated to Congress over commerce, but also exerts a power as to a purely local matter to which the federal authority does not extend.

**Section II
Free-Response
Questions 2–5**

Essay Questions

Writing time—70 minutes

Directions: You are to answer *two* of the following questions—one from Part B and one from Part C. Carefully choose the question that you are best prepared to answer. Cite relevant historical evidence in support of your generalizations and present your arguments clearly and logically. When you finish writing, check your work if time permits. Make certain to number your answer as the question is numbered below. You should write your answer in pen.

Part B: Choose ONE question from Part B. It is suggested that you spend 5 minutes organizing your answer and 30 minutes writing it.

2. "Events on the frontier between 1763 and 1788 and the development of government policies in response to them were more significant for the development of the United States than the events that took place in the settled areas of the eastern seaboard between 1763 and 1788." Evaluate this statement.

3. "American history reveals that government by the majority can be divisive and that the views of the minority must be considered in executing policy." Assess the validity of this statement for the period 1793–1812.

Part C: Choose ONE question from this group. It is suggested that you spend 5 minutes organizing your answer and 30 minutes writing it.

4. In what ways was the change in the political control of the federal government a result of economic issues in TWO of the following presidential elections?

   McKinley's defeat of Bryan in 1896

   Wilson's defeat of Taft in 1912

   Roosevelt's defeat of Hoover in 1932

   Reagan's defeat of Carter in 1980

5. Compare and contrast the issues that led to reform and the reforms that were introduced in TWO of the following periods.

   The Jacksonian Era

   The New Deal period

   The Kennedy/Johnson years

End of Examination   At the end of the exam you will be directed to circle on the back of your essay answer booklet the numbers of the two questions you answered.

Comments and Answers to Questions on Practice Advanced Placement Examination—Model A

In this section you will find answers and answer explanations for the 80 multiple-choice questions of the model exam. The explanations of the multiple-choice questions indicate which answer is most correct and, in most cases, why the other choices should be eliminated. By reading all 80 statements, you will get a quick summary of the highlights of American history.

1. E	21. D	41. A	61. C
2. B	22. D	42. B	62. D
3. B	23. B	43. E	63. A
4. C	24. B	44. B	64. A
5. D	25. E	45. A	65. D
6. E	26. D	46. C	66. C
7. A	27. B	47. B	67. D
8. C	28. B	48. C	68. C
9. E	29. D	49. D	69. B
10. A	30. C	50. D	70. E
11. D	31. C	51. C	71. A
12. C	32. B	52. C	72. C
13. D	33. D	53. C	73. C
14. D	34. A	54. E	74. B
15. B	35. D	55. C	75. C
16. C	36. A	56. B	76. D
17. C	37. C	57. E	77. D
18. D	38. B	58. D	78. A
19. D	39. D	59. E	79. B
20. B	40. D	60. D	80. C

**Comments on
Multiple-Choice
Answers**

1. (E) The statement is typical of the Social Darwinist point of view. A Social Darwinist, Andrew Carnegie, a successful businessperson, and John D. Rockefeller would have all shared this viewpoint at the end of the last century. Eugene V. Debs, an American Socialist, would not have supported the view.

2. (B) For this question, you need to be able to read the chart and to understand the key. The only statement that is correct is the one about more Irish coming to America in 1850–1855 than in 1885–1890.

3. (B) This is a simple chronological question. The Connecticut Compromise was a compromise between the Virginia Plan and the New Jersey Plan at the Constitutional Convention, and it came last. The first event was the Declaration of Independence, and then the government under the Articles of Confederation was established. This government was changed by the Constitution.

4. (C) James Madison, John Jay, and Alexander Hamilton authored *The Federalist Papers* together. They all supported the Constitution. Thomas Jefferson, Patrick Henry, and Melancthon Smith all opposed the Constitution. Andrew Jackson and Daniel Webster were not involved in its ratification as they were members of the next generation.

5. (D) NATO (North Atlantic Treaty Organization) was a post-World War II development. The other four choices were offered as solutions to the problems of the Great Depression. The WPA (Work Progress Administration) and the NIRA (National Industrial Recovery Act) were part of Roosevelt's solution to the problems of the Great Depression. EPIC (End Poverty in California) and the "Share the Wealth" movement were offered in opposition to Roosevelt's ideas.

6. (E) The Palmer Raids, led by the attorney general, reflected the anti-communist hysteria of the post-World War I period. The raids created a climate of opinion similar to that created by Senator Joseph McCarthy in the 1950s.

7. (A) The American historian Frederick Jackson Turner, in his thesis on the influence of the frontier on America, stated all four points except the idea that "'The complex European life' had continual impact on America." In his article, Turner emphasized the uniqueness of America and the importance of the frontier in developing the American.

8. (C) The quotation from the Constitution is a clear example of checks and balances.

9. (E) The concepts expressed in the passage are those of isolationism and nationalism. Isolationism calls for separation of America from other nations. Nationalism contains the idea that your country is the best, and its sovereign will should not be compromised in any way by following other nations. The writer is certainly in favor of freedom, but there is less emphasis on that concept than upon isolationism. Christianity, sovereignty, and socialism are irrelevant to the quotation.

10. (A) The cartoon from the *World Telegram* of August 1, 1934, clearly suggests that the Republican Party, represented as the old man with the letters G.O.P. on his vest, has no effective solution to the Great Depression. The only ideas offered are those of a return to the programs of 1929, which were in effect under President Hoover at the time of the "great crash." It might appear that the G.O.P. is being robbed by Wall Street and Rugged Individualism, but these two figures represent the G.O.P.'s major support. They are holding on to the G.O.P. for support; they are not robbing him. To be able to interpret this cartoon, one needs an understanding of the economic situation in the United States from 1929 to 1934 and to know that G.O.P. (Grand Old Party) refers to the Republican Party.

11. (D) The areas colored black on the map represent the greatest extent of Nazi control in World War II. The names of the countries on the map should help you to identify what the black represents. The name of the city of Stalingrad may be the best clue. It was at Stalingrad that the Russians finally stopped the German advance.

12. (C) President Clinton campaigned for Democrats in the 1994 congressional elections, although some candidates preferred that he did not because of his lack of popularity at that time. The other four selections are true about the 1994 election.

13. (D) The attempt to impeach Chief Justice of the U.S. Supreme Court Earl Warren during the 1950s related to domestic issues and not to issues of foreign policy. Therefore, it would not be considered part of the Cold War. The other four events involved international conflicts between the United States and its allies and the communist nations under the leadership of the Soviet Union.

14. (D) William Jennings Bryan's Cross of Gold speech helped gain him the Democratic Party presidential nomination. After Bryan ran for president three times, Wilson appointed him Secretary of State, and he did testify at the Scopes Trial, but these events happened many years later. The Populists nominated him for president, but he was not a founder of the party, and Republicans never supported his views on free and unlimited coinage of silver.

15. (B) President Lyndon Johnson withdrew from the presidential race after his defeat in the New Hampshire primary in 1968. His withdrawal was attributed to the public's rejection of his policy in Vietnam. President Johnson had expanded America's commitment to that nation. U.S. involvement began under President Eisenhower with his support of the French in that country. U.S. forces attacked both Cambodia and Laos outside the Vietnam borders and also bombed North Vietnam. The Gulf of Tonkin Resolution authorized retaliation by President Johnson but was not a declaration of war and did not legalize the conflict internationally. One of the identifying features of the Vietnam War was the inability to identify the enemy. There were no clear battle lines.

16. (C) The statement is a definition of mercantilism. Check the Glossary for definitions of the other terms.

17. (C) Under the Articles of Confederation, the states exercised sovereignty. This was the greatest weakness of the Articles of Confederation because the central government was unable to make and enforce decisions for all of the states.

18. (D) A "loose constructionist" believes that the U.S. Constitution should not be read strictly and that when you find a power that is implied by the wording of the Constitution, that power is a legitimate power for the government to exercise. The four other choices all share the concept of "strict construction" under which the Constitution must be read literally and no extension of powers made.

19. (D) The presidential years of James Monroe have often been referred to as the Era of Good Feeling. The Federalists, or the opposition political party, had been badly weakened by its failure to support the War of 1812. Thus, President Monroe had little resistance to his measures, something that made his presidency appear as a period of "good feeling."

20. (B) The main purpose of Henry Clay's American System was to develop an interdependent economic system tying the East, West, and South together. He offered it after the Era of Good Feeling at a time when sectionalism was beginning to grow. The other four choices had nothing to do with his American System.

21. (D) The Transcendentalist writers of New England, of whom Ralph Waldo Emerson is the most noteworthy, found their major source of truth and inspiration in nature. The writers—centered in Concord, Massachusetts, in the 1830s and 1840s—are considered to have begun the first truly American philosophical movement, although this movement had close connections with the Romantic Movement in England.

22. (D) Jackson refused to accept the Supreme Court decision, which led to the Cherokee Trail of Tears. The South Carolina "exposition and protest" was written but not signed by Calhoun. It supported the South Carolina legislature's resolutions declaring the Tariff of Abominations unconstitutional, unjust, and oppressive to the interest of the South. The Tariff of Abominations, passed in 1828, supported the protective concept. It was a political move by Jackson's supporters to undercut President J. Q. Adams and work for the election of Jackson. This was one step in the slow alienation of South Carolina from the Union, which culminated in secession in 1860. The Force Act was Jackson's response to the "exposition and protest." A major issue of Jackson's presidency was the rechartering of the Second Bank of the United States, which he vetoed. The Hartford Convention was called to protest the War of 1812.

23. (B) After the capture of Vicksburg in the West, the Confederacy was split in half. The other four choices are important battles of the Civil War in the East.

24. (B) The person usually given credit for the passage of the Civil Rights Act of 1964 is Lyndon Baines Johnson. In 1964 he was president of the United States. John F. Kennedy had been in favor of civil rights legislation, but couldn't get it through Congress. With the impact Kennedy's assassination had on the country, President Johnson was able to get passed not only the Civil Rights Act of 1964 but many of the things President Kennedy believed in. African Americans Adam Clayton Powell, formerly an important member of the House of Representatives, and Andrew Young, U.S. Ambassador to the United Nations under President Carter, were not involved with the congressional passage of the Civil Rights Act of 1964. George Wallace, Governor of Alabama, opposed civil rights legislation in the 1960s.

25. (E) Wilson announced his Fourteen Points as a possible formula for peace at the end of World War I. He was most concerned about establishing a League of Nations, as suggested in Point XIV. The League was incorporated into the Treaty of Versailles, and the Treaty was rejected by the Senate. The other points are important ones, but Wilson was more prepared to compromise on them than on the League. He believed that if there was a League, other issues could be resolved by it before war broke out.

26. (D) The Creel Committee organized during World War I by the U.S. government had propaganda as its purpose. During the war, the government was concerned about the four other issues, but other committees and commissions took care of those matters.

27. (B) Woodrow Wilson would most likely have commented on the lost opportunity of the United States to take world leadership. He had hoped the United States would take the lead in the League of Nations after World War I, and this was rejected. The idea expressed was too early for the period of Theodore Roosevelt, who was more an American nationalist than an internationalist. John F. Kennedy and Lyndon B. Johnson both rose to importance as political leaders after World War II, when America had already taken on world leadership. One might think that Franklin Roosevelt was the author, but during his administration he slowly moved the United States into a position of leadership and saw the United States through the "tragedy" of World War II.

28. (B) Although all five choices present New Deal legislation, the only one dealing with banking is the Federal Deposit Insurance Corporation.

29. (D) A careful reading of the quotation will show that the author suggests that the United States continues to be in a depression, that a veto of the tax cut would be harmful to the nation, that other nations are heavily affected by the U.S. economy, and that the unemployment rate in the country is high. The issue under discussion is a tax cut to create economic recovery at a time of high unemployment. The author does not suggest that the political impact of the policy should be the sole guide in determining policy.

30. (C) Changes in the number and function of executive departments must be approved by Congress, not the president alone, and no law states when the cabinet must meet. The president's cabinet is not described in the Constitution. However, the Constitution states that members of the executive branch should be appointed by the president and confirmed by the Senate. During President Andrew Johnson's administration, the Senate tried to make this constitutional provision also apply to the firing of cabinet members. This was rejected and the idea that members of the executive branch serve at the pleasure of the chief executive— the president—was reestablished and remains in force. So C is the correct answer.

31. (C) The Joint Electoral Commission Report on the disputed election of 1876 between Samuel J. Tilden and Rutherford B. Hayes was accepted in 1877, making Hayes president. As part of the report, Republicans promised to withdraw federal troops from the South and appoint at least one Southerner to the cabinet. This has traditionally been interpreted to indicate the end of the political Reconstruction of the South. The South never welcomed military occupation. The other three choices all deal with post-Civil War matters but do not mark the end of Reconstruction.

32. (B) The plan that Franklin D. Roosevelt introduced to force the Supreme Court to change its decisions and begin to accept the New Deal program consisted of a proposal to the Congress that the Court be increased in size. The Constitution gives to Congress the power to set the number of judges on the Court. The plan is often referred to as the Court Packing Plan. The famous "My dog Fala" speech was a humorous speech given by Roosevelt mocking the Republicans who were attacking not only his plans and policies but his family and even his dog. This was part of the presidential campaign of 1940. The president has no power to order impeachment proceedings, the president did not ignore the Court decisions but tried to get them reversed, and he did not call on the American people to elect only Democrats to Congress as a response to the decisions by the Supreme Court.

33. (D) Helen Hunt Jackson's books *A Century of Dishonor* and *Ramona* pricked the conscience of Americans and led to a new approach to Native Americans that was incorporated in the Dawes Severalty Act of 1887. The goal of the act was to assimilate Native Americans into the mainstream of American life by making them citizens. The other four choices were among the causes of the intense antagonisms between the Native Americans and the U.S. government that led to warfare between the two.

34. (A) The Taft-Hartley Act of 1947 banned the closed shop, permitted employers to sue unions for broken contracts, required unions to abide by a 60-day "cooling-off period" as part of strike procedures, required unions to make public their financial statements, forced union leaders to sign a non-communist oath, and forbade unions to support political campaigns with monetary contributions. Because of these features, the act is not considered a victory for organized labor. The other four choices are. Wisconsin passed one of the first unemployment insurance laws in the country that helped workers who lost jobs or were injured; the establishment of a national minimum wage law helped increase workers' wages; the Anthracite Strike of 1902 was settled by Teddy Roosevelt in favor of the workers, using the authority of the federal government to support labor; and the Wagner Act of 1935 was one of the highlights of the New Deal labor legislation. It defined unfair labor practices on the employers' part and upheld the right of employees to join unions and to bargain collectively.

35. (D) Air mail service was not developed until the 20th century. The other four choices were developed in the 19th century or earlier.

36. (A) New York was first settled by the Dutch. Delaware was first settled by Swedes, Pennsylvania by the English, Jamaica by the Spanish, and Canada by the French.

37. (C) The traditional interpretation of the founding of the Plymouth Bay Colony is that it was founded *primarily* for religious purposes. To some degree, the reasons were also political, social, cultural, and economic, but the religious were the most important ones.

38. (B) Although all the choices are important for the development of factories, it was because of abundant water power that the earliest factories in the United States were located in New England. They were founded at a time when water power was used to drive the machinery. As farming declined in northern New England with the opening of the West, and as factories grew, especially along the Merrimack River (Lowell, Manchester), many young women born on the farms found jobs in the factories.

39. (D) *The Sovereignty and Goodness of God or Narrative of the Captivity and Restoration of Mrs. Mary Rowlandson* was the most popular story about Native Americans written in the English colonies.

40. (D) The South strongly supported Prohibition and even today regions of the South have Prohibition laws. The other three choices are characteristic of the Prohibition Era of the 1920s.

41. (A) Keynes developed his economic theories in the post-World War I period, and they have had a profound impact on Western society since then. The general concept is that the government should interfere in the business cycle to counteract the highs and lows of inflation and deflation. To smooth out the extremes of the business cycle, the government should tax highly in times of inflation and should spend extensively in times of deflation. In theory, the high taxes will cut down the rate of inflation, and the government spending in times of deflation would create jobs and counterbalance the deflationary cycle. The government has found it much easier to spend extensively in deflationary times than it has to tax highly in times of inflation. The other choices present other economic theories. Laissez-faire economics believes that government should keep hands off all economic activity. Social Darwinists believe successful individuals who have proven they have the ability to survive, such as business leaders, should run the government. Under mercantilist economic theory the wealth of a nation is measured by the amount of gold it holds. The Federal Reserve Board sets the interest rates banks must pay to borrow money from the Federal Reserve Bank, which in theory provides some control over inflation.

42. (B) Shays' Rebellion occurred in western Massachusetts in 1786 under the government of the Articles of Confederation. It was one of the events that led to the calling of the Constitutional Convention in 1787. The Stamp Act was repealed in 1766, Daniel Boone took his first trip to Kentucky in 1767, and the Boston Massacre occurred in 1770, all before independence was declared. The Whiskey Rebellion took place in western Pennsylvania during Washington's first term as president under the Constitution. Farmers protesting a tax on whiskey were crushed by the new federal government.

43. (E) Jefferson is often considered a states' rights supporter and strict constructionist. As president, however, he often acted beyond the authority strictly given to the president in the Constitution. During his presidency, he undertook the first four events mentioned. All stretched the power of the presidency and the Constitution, especially the purchase of Louisiana. Although often a supporter of the French, he did not support the XYZ Affair.

44. (B) The opening of the Erie Canal in 1825 had an important effect on the settlement of the West, since it provided an easy water route west of the New England and New York areas. The canal increased the settlement in the Northwest territories greatly. The other events had limited impact on the pattern of western settlement.

45. (A) The Pendleton Act (Civil Service Act of 1883) was passed as a response to the assassination of President Garfield. The act set up a three-person Civil Service Commission with the responsibility of administering competitive examinations so that federal office holders could be appointed on a merit basis. President Garfield had been assassinated by Charles Guiteau, who was a disappointed office seeker and mentally unstable.

46. (C) During the presidency of Jimmy Carter there was talk of the possibility of reducing not increasing the number of U.S. troops in Europe, but U.S. troops were not withdrawn. Strategic Arms Limitation Talks (SALT) were held during his presidency, inflation was a major problem, human rights were the guiding principle of U.S. foreign policy, and American hostages were seized after the overthrow of the Shah of Iran and the establishment of the Khomeini government. The hostages were not released until the day of the inauguration of Carter's successor, Ronald Reagan.

47. (B) The Social Security Act of 1935 passed as part of the New Deal provided retirement pensions and unemployment payments. While it provided an income for the old, disabled, and unemployed, its purpose was not to control the money supply. The other four choices, the Specie Circular of 1836, the Sherman Silver Purchase Act of 1890, the Federal Reserve Act of 1913, and the establishment of the Commodity Dollar in 1933, all had as their purpose the control of the money supply in some way.

48. (C) From the end of Reconstruction in 1877 to the outbreak of World War I in 1914, fundamental changes in the American system were brought about by federal legislation in all areas mentioned except civil rights.

49. (D) The acquisition of Pago Pago by a treaty negotiated with the chiefs of the island of Tutuila in the Samoan Islands had nothing to do with the U.S. entry into the Spanish-American War. The other choices are often given as reasons for the U.S. entry into the Spanish-American War, the sinking of the battleship *Maine* being considered the final justification for war.

50. (D) The "gag rule" was adopted by the U.S. Senate in 1836 to prevent debate of abolitionist proposals requesting the ending of slavery. The rule provided a complicated formula by which abolitionists could petition the Senate, but the petition would not be debated.

51. (C) The XYZ Affair occurred during John Adams's administration. The other events occurred during Washington's administration. The XYZ Affair of 1797 involved a demand by French ministers for a large bribe from U.S. representatives who were in France seeking to improve relations between the two countries. Relations with France were strained as a result of Jay's Treaty and French interference with U.S. trade. Secretary of State John Jay negotiated the Jay treaty with the English in 1795. The treaty resolved issues left over from the Revolution. John Adams was elected to succeed Washington while Washington was still president. Jefferson resigned in part because his views on the Bank of the United States were rejected while Hamilton's views were accepted by Washington.

52. (C) All five choices are acts passed by the U.S. Congress dealing with land. The Land Act of 1796 called for rectangular survey and sale of land at public auction at a minimum price of two dollars an acre. Townships were set at six square miles each, and they were subdivided into sections. The smallest section one could purchase under the act was 640 acres.

53. (C) These five events all relate to the Civil War. The event that occurred first is Lincoln's first election to the presidency in November of 1860. South Carolina seceded at the end of the year; Fort Sumter was fired upon in 1861, beginning the military activity. The Emancipation Proclamation, which freed slaves in states still in rebellion against the United States, was a wartime measure announced in 1862 and it went into effect in 1863. West Virginia was admitted to the Union as a state on June 20,1863. (West Virginia consisted of the 50 western counties of Virginia that had refused to acknowledge the secession of Virginia from the Union.)

54. (E) If you carefully study the cartoon from *Harper's Weekly* of September 1, 1888, you can tell that the well-dressed gentleman was trying to prevent the law, as represented by the policeman, from interfering. The gentleman does not believe the police officer should interfere, but the cartoonist suggests he is prepared to do so by both the statement under the cartoon in which the well-dressed man wants to keep the police out and by the upraised billy club held ready for use. The individual being robbed is competition, and it is being robbed by American industries, which are organized as trusts. The American market is advertised as operating under freedom and equality.

55. (C) In spite of Taft's replacement of Theodore Roosevelt's "Big Stick" policy with Dollar Diplomacy, the United States continued to intervene militarily in the Caribbean (Cuba and Santo Domingo) and in Latin America (Nicaragua and Honduras). The other statements are all true concerning the concept of Dollar Diplomacy. Investments were encouraged in the Far East, especially China, and in Latin America. Because the policy was to secure a peace through business investment, less money was spent on military defense. Wilson continued the policy although philosophically he opposed it.

56. (B) The author of the quotation is referring to the Pan-American Union, the oldest and most successful association of sovereign governments in the world, which is now known as the Organization of American States (OAS). Its members are the nations of North and South America. The League of Nations was part of the Treaty of Versailles. The EDC and NATO were formed after World War II in Europe. The Contradora Group, the most recent, was formed in 1985 to bring peace to Nicaragua and end the fighting between the Contras and the Sandinista government of Nicaragua.

57. (E) All of the items except E—a major economic recession with high unemployment for all Americans—were characteristic of the period in U.S. society between the end of World War II and the election of President John F. Kennedy. The Supreme Court knocked down segregation in the public schools in the famous *Brown v. Board of Education* decision in 1954. The McCarthy era in the late 1940s and early 1950s was another Red Scare. The start of rock and roll symbolized by Elvis Presley and the introduction of other types of popular music has changed American society considerably. Finally, the 1950s has often been characterized by historians as a period of conformity and uncritical support of government policies.

58. (D) The passage states the important points found in the Monroe Doctrine of 1823 that the American continents are not open for colonization and that the nations on the continents are free and independent states. Theodore Roosevelt interpreted the Monroe Doctrine to allow for the United States' intervention to maintain order in the Americas and to collect debts owed other nations. This concept of America acting either on behalf of its own nationals or the other nations of the world to collect debts and maintain order has been called the Roosevelt Corollary to the Monroe Doctrine. It is a stretching of the original doctrine and its concept as presented in the passage. The other doctrines do not relate to the Americas so the quote would not relate to them.

59. (E) The photograph from the *Los Angeles County Natural History Museum Foundation* shows immigrants living in New York City. The time as revealed by the clothing is the turn of the century. Hispanic migration to Los Angeles was later than that. The population is clearly not African American. The names on the buildings, the tenement-style buildings, and active life on the street all point to immigrants in New York City.

60. (D) The economic program known as Reaganomics followed the theory of supply-side economics. It called first for tax cuts, which were to stimulate the economy so no revenue would be lost to the government. Reaganomics also included increased military expenditures and reduced expenditures for social services. The program resulted in unplanned massive increases in the federal debt since the economy did not respond as anticipated and the Congress refused to cut social services. No cabinet-level departments were eliminated.

61. (C) In the cartoon from the *Saturday Evening Post* of June 6, 1914, the main point the cartoonist is making is that Theodore Roosevelt and Woodrow Wilson are again seeking popular support for their political reform programs. Roosevelt had run for president on the "Bull Moose" ticket in 1912, and in doing so split the Republican Party, which renominated President Taft. Eugene V. Debs ran as a Socialist. With these three candidates in the field, Woodrow Wilson, the candidate of the Democratic Party, was able to win. The New Nationalism was the reform program advocated by Roosevelt, and the New Freedom was the reform program advocated by Wilson in that election. Wilson won and began his reforms. Choice E, "rivalry of political candidates," has truth in it, but C is a better answer. The other choices are irrelevant.

62. (D) The office building in the center of the photograph from *Harper's Weekly,* March 9, 1912, shows the influence during the last quarter of the 19th century of the outstanding American architect, Henry Hobson Richardson. Richardson was strongly influenced by the Romanesque architecture of southern France. He is known for his use of Romanesque elements (one being the arch) and for imaginative treatment of ornament, both of which can be seen in this photograph.

Frank Lloyd Wright's work is characterized as natural. He often blended his houses into the natural surroundings and used local materials. He was deeply concerned about the materials used and about the functional qualities of his buildings. He is considered by many to be the outstanding American architect of the first half of this century, with a strong influence on many others.

Eino Saarinen is remembered for his imaginative qualities, as seen in the residential colleges at Yale, which remind one of Italian hill towns. He, too, was concerned with structure and function. He is remembered as one of the outstanding mid-20th-century American architects.

Buildings in the Greek Revival style of architecture incorporate many elements of classical Greek temples. It became the style used in public buildings and homes after the establishment of the new federal government. Columns with Doric, Corinthian, or Ionic capitals; friezes and carvings with egg and dart designs; and porticoes with columns two stories high characterize this architecture.

The Georgian style was developed in England in the 18th century during the reigns of the first three Georges. In the colonies the finest public buildings, such as those at Williamsburg, the homes of wealthy colonists in Boston, Philadelphia, and Charleston, and plantation homes such as Westover in Virginia were built in the Georgian style. These constructions are all characterized by balance and symmetry and a strong emphasis on the horizontal line. In many cases, there are pediments or decorative devices above the windows and pilasters and pediments beside and above the doors.

63. (A) The first oil embargo imposed by OPEC in order to raise oil prices occurred in 1973 during Nixon's second term. The effect of the embargo continued to be felt during the Carter and Reagan administrations. The other events all occurred during Carter's presidency and were important foreign policy issues of the period.

64. (A) In the quotation the most important argument being presented is that the British Parliament has no authority to compel the obedience of any law that forces them to supply goods. The concern is that if Parliament can force the colonists to carry out this order, then they can force the colonists to do everything—pay taxes, clothe and house troops—and the colonists rebelled against this concept.

65. (D) The American colonists, especially merchants from Newport and Bristol, Rhode Island, and some from Boston and Salem, Massachusetts; Providence, Rhode Island; Portsmouth, New Hampshire; and New London, Connecticut, all participated in the profitable slave trade along with many English merchants. The other statements are all true concerning the slave trade in the 18th century.

66. (C) Both sides did make concessions during the Cuban Missile Crisis that averted a move to World War III. Both Kennedy and Khrushchev said this in reflecting upon the crisis. Recent studies show Castro did not follow every lead of the Soviets, and Khrushchev did honor the U.S. quarantine. Some believe Kennedy overreacted but that is not generally accepted and even if it were, it is not as full a description of the event as is choice C. The missiles were discovered by U.S. planes flying over Cuba. The flights were part of regular U.S. surveillance and the sighting of missiles was a surprise. Recently it has been learned that those working at the missile sites disobeyed Soviet orders to camouflage the construction sites. The discovery was a surprise but that fact is certainly not the best way to characterize the missile crisis. In this question as in many others, there is some truth in the choices and you must pick the choice that "best" describes the situation based on recent study.

67. (D) The chart from *Building America* dates from the Great Depression of the early 1930s. Electric lighting proves a particularly helpful clue for dating the chart. Electric lighting was not developed until the 1870s, with Philadelphia getting the first electric street lights in 1878. It had not spread widely by the time of the Populist Era in the 1890s. The New Deal through REA (Rural Electrification Administration) worked hard to bring electric power to rural areas, and it succeeded. Therefore, by the post-World War II period, there would be much more electric lighting in farm homes than is indicated by the chart. The Civil War years were the first half of the decade of the 1860s, and the Jacksonian period centered on the two terms of President Andrew Jackson, 1829–37, both prior to the development of electric lighting.

68. (C) The Constitution makes no provision about how the facts in an impeachment case are to be gathered or where or what witnesses are to be heard. The Senate and House can make their own rules on these matters. The House can approve Articles of Impeachment by a majority vote, but it takes a vote of two-thirds of the Senate to find an impeached individual guilty. If found guilty, according to the Constitution, the judgment against the president "shall not extend further than to removal from office and disqualification to hold and enjoy an Office of Honor, Trust or Profit under the United States." Article I, Section 3.

69. (B) In the cartoon, *The Irrepressible Independent,* by W. A. Rogers, the Spoils System referred to on the Tammany booth indicates the political system of rewarding supporters with appointed offices. Tammany was a political machine that ran New York City and was noted for its system of rewarding its workers with political jobs. The other choices do not apply. This question is simply a case of knowing the definition of a political term.

70. (E) The only thing that can clearly be proven by the bar graph is that Lincoln and Wilson were both minority presidents according to popular vote, but received a majority of votes in the electoral college. The chart cannot prove that the electoral college is unjust, although many may feel that is true. Nor can it prove that Bell was a better candidate than Douglas, or that someone running in 1912 would have done as well if he had run in 1860. Finally, the chart cannot prove that popular candidates cannot win in the electoral college.

71. (A) The quote "Liberty and union, now and forever, one and inseparable," was said by Daniel Webster, not John C. Calhoun. Calhoun was a states' rights advocate and would not call for union in such strong terms. His famous quotation is "The union, next to our liberty, the most dear." This is a very different idea from the Webster quote. The other quotes are correctly paired and represent the position held by the speaker. Patrick Henry, speaking about the rebellion against England, Thomas Jefferson in writing the Declaration of Independence, Andrew Jackson speaking about the Nullification Crisis, and Franklin Roosevelt speaking about the Great Depression made the statements ascribed to them in this question.

72. (C) This question requires you to know what these American authors wrote about. Of the five, Booth Tarkington is the one who was least concerned with social criticism of America. In fact, he is best characterized as a Victorian sentimentalist. On the other hand, Steinbeck, Norris, Sinclair, and Riis are noted for their writings of social criticisms. John Steinbeck in *The Grapes of Wrath* described conditions in Oklahoma and California during the dust bowl years of the 1930s. Frank Norris in *The Octopus* depicted the human drama arising from the raising, selling, and consumption of wheat. Upton Sinclair in *The Jungle* wrote of conditions in the meatpacking industry in Chicago at the beginning of the 20th century. Jacob Riis in *The Shame of the Cities* described tenement and slum life in New York, again in the early 1900s.

73. (C) The term *impressment* means to take by force for public service, especially naval service. As used by the United States in the period before the Revolutionary War of 1812, the term referred to the British practice of forcing American sailors into service on British warships. This British practice was one of the causes of that war.

74. (B) The quotation is taken from the Rhode Island colonial charter. The founders of Rhode Island were particularly concerned about both civil and religious rights. King James I believed in the divine right of kings, which is not upheld by this quotation; the Albany Plan of Union was proposed by Benjamin Franklin as the political, not religious, framework for colonial unity at the time of the French and Indian War; the trial of Peter Zenger is famous for establishing a free press and not religious liberty; and the Mayflower Compact established a political framework of government for the Pilgrims.

75. (C) If you are doing original research, the best way to begin is to go to the original sources and find what is said there. The National Archives contain the important documents of American history so that would be the best place to start. If you are an amateur, you might not know this and would need to consult a librarian, put out inquiries on the Internet, or read someone else's book (a secondary source) to start. At some point, a researcher might wish to consult the letters of the signers of the Declaration but they may not comment on any changes made. Also, it is always helpful to consult other historians about their opinions but opinions are no substitute for the information you can find in original sources.

76. (D) The statement is from the Seneca Falls Convention which was held in New York State, in 1848 under the leadership of Lucretia Mott and Elizabeth Cady Stanton. If you cannot identify this statement and its date, you would know it would not have been made after 1919 because in that year the 19th Amendment to the Constitution, which provided for women's suffrage, was declared ratified. The last paragraph in the statement is calling for suffrage for women and would not have been needed after 1919.

77. (D) All of the movements are correctly linked with their leaders except for education. Although a university is named after him, Brigham Young is noted as the leader of the Mormons, not of educational reform. Horace Mann, Henry Barnard, Elizabeth Peabody, and Mary Lyon are some noted leaders of educational reform in the pre-Civil War period.

78. (A) The last four choices correctly link the case with the decision reached. *McCulloch v. Maryland* denied the right of the state of Maryland to tax the Bank of the United States. In this famous case of 1819, Chief Justice John Marshall established the concept of loose construction of the Constitution. Although the Constitution does not give Congress the power to establish a bank, the power, according to Marshall, is implied. He went on to say that no state could tax an organ (agency) of the federal government.

79. (B) The decision in the *Brown v. Board of Education* case came in 1954. The other events in the Civil Rights Movement of the post-World War II period occurred after that date.

80. (C) The quotation from John F. Kennedy's inaugural address suggests that he would have supported all four points except the establishment of a communist government in Vietnam that he would have viewed as a tyranny.

Practice Advanced Placement Examination Section II The Free-Response Questions

Comments follow on the five sample essay questions of Part A and B of Section II of the exam. For each essay question, there is a general analysis that is similar to those given for the sample essay questions in each chapter of Part Three. In addition to the analyses, two sample answers—one for the DBQ (Part A) and one for the first standard essay question (Part B)—are included. In the left margin of the two sample answers there are comments on certain noteworthy elements of the answers.

You must be aware, as all of the analyses of essay questions have indicated, that there are many possible ways to answer each essay question—theses will differ, organizational schemes will differ, and the facts chosen to prove a point will differ. The two sample answers illustrate only one of the many possible ways to write good answers.

Analysis of the DBQ (Part A)—Question 1

The DBQ is a straightforward *To what extent (degree)?* type of question (see Part Three, Chapter 4). You are asked to analyze how Supreme Court decisions and the views expressed by political leaders are related. The second sentence of the question adds a *Why?* (see Part Three, Chapter 3) aspect to this simple *To what extent?* question. This should present no particular problem, since it merely requires that in your answer, after you have analyzed the relationship between the Court decisions and the views of the political leaders, you explain the reasons for this relationship. You will want to keep this in mind as you analyze the question and prepare an outline of your answer.

Although the documents are chosen from 1905–1918, the time period 1900–1918 is stated in the directions. Directions are extremely important, and the time periods presented must be followed. You should give some background information from the beginning of the 20th century. The vocabulary used in the question should present no difficulties.

This DBQ asks you to deal with a perennial issue of American history, that is, do or should the decisions of the Supreme Court follow or lead public opinion? As the DBQ is worded, public opinion is equated with the statements of political leaders. You should have discussed this matter at some time in your study so you should come to the question with some thoughts on the issue.

As indicated in Chapter 5, the DBQ on the AP examination will relate to the "mainstream" of American history. This question certainly does that, since it asks the student to focus on one crucial aspect of that important era of reform, the Progressive Era. Several of the documents are statements from presidents who led the political reforms of the age. Nothing could be more mainstream than Theodore Roosevelt and Woodrow Wilson—two presidents who would be studied in every American history course. The other documents may be less obvious and you may not have studied these particular Supreme Court cases but enough information about the cases is included for you to understand them. You should have no difficulty relating them to the main developments from 1900 to 1918.

As you are aware, it is necessary to introduce in your answer information **not** found in the documents but that is relevant to the question. In this question, knowledge from many sources might be introduced to illustrate your understanding of the "mainstream" of American history in the Progressive Era. Some information you introduce might be on the Muckrakers who, at the turn of the century, pointed out unsavory working conditions and political corruption, thus paving the way for many reforms. You might use some of this legislation such as the Pure Food and Drug Laws of T. Roosevelt's presidency to the Adamson Act (eight-hour day for railroad workers) of Wilson's presidency to illustrate one attitude of the public as expressed by legislators. On the other side, mention might be made of the attitude of Social Darwinists who supported laissez-faire government and opposed government regulation of business. Comments on Roosevelt and Wilson—their styles of leadership as president, their goals as developed in the New Nationalism and New Freedom Programs, legislation they supported and their views toward the individual—might be included to provide the background to the issues addressed in the documents. In your answer you need to relate this information to the documents.

Organizing is a crucial step in essay writing, as has been emphasized throughout the book (see "Seven Steps in Essay Writing" in Part Two, Steps 1–3). You must decide on a thesis before you begin to write.

Sample Answer for the DBQ

Opening sentence introduces broad topic of the question.

Thesis on the *To what degree?* aspect of the question.

Two reasons that respond to the *Why?* part of the question follow.

Two documents are mentioned as evidence, and dates are given, setting the time period of the question.

Information from the "mainstream" of American history is introduced to support ideas in the documents.

Uses information in the document, but does not repeat the content of the document, thus indicating an understanding of and ability to use the information.

A continual issue in U.S. history has been how to get the Supreme Court to work together with the executive and legislative branches and not to block their desires. This was an important issue in the years 1900–1918, when decisions of the Supreme Court were not in agreement with the views of the best-known political leaders. Two reasons can be given for this situation: first, Court members were confirmed by the conservative Senate, which was out of touch with the country and its changing political attitudes and second, the ideas of Wilson and Roosevelt were ahead of those of most political leaders.

The decisions of the Supreme Court in *Lochner v. New York* in 1905 and in *Hammer v. Dagenhart* in 1918 indicate that the Court upheld the conservative ideas of the Social Darwinists throughout the period 1900–1918. Social Darwinists applied the idea of survival of the fittest to business and wanted no government interference in the economic life of the nation. Of course, not every judge believed in Social Darwinism, as seen in Mr. Holmes's dissent in 1905 in which he is complaining about that concept. Also, a good lawyer such as Mr. Brandeis, by using special arguments, could persuade the Court to allow the regulation of the working conditions of women by a state government. But this is a major exception to the general views

Poor linking of paragraphs. Ideas introduced appear separated from documents, but writer ties mainstream information to documents in last sentence to support point 1 of reasons for *Why?* part of question.

held by the Court.

Until 1913 the United States senators were elected by state legislatures, which were often controlled by business interests. For example, the Boston and Maine Railroad controlled the New Hampshire legislature. U.S. senators confirmed members of the Supreme Court, and the conservative views of business were thus represented both in the Senate and on the Court. This conservative view is seen in Senator Scott's statement on the working conditions he has seen—a personal view that is not a very reliable historical source, but in this case is illustrative of a widely held view.

Good comment on value of sources.

Documents may be referred to by letter, but better to use author's name or some other specific identification from the document. Good use of "mainstream" history.

Document B presents a view of the Muckrakers, a group of writers who pointed out the political corruption in the cities, the power of business monopolies (Tarbell and Standard Oil), and the horror of working conditions. These writers had an impact on certain men, such as Roosevelt, who became the leaders of the Progressive Movement, a reform movement of the first two decades of this century.

Repetition of "Roosevelt" helps link paragraphs.

Roosevelt became president by a fluke—he was on the Republican ticket to win votes and did not represent the views of the leadership. He became president when McKinley was assassinated, and he worked for better labor conditions, as can be seen in his settlement of the coal strike. But at the same time, the Court remained conservative as seen in the Lochner decision in 1905. When Taft did not support Roosevelt's ideas, T. R. ran for president in 1912 on the Bull Moose ticket. As seen in his speeches, he campaigned for the "welfare of the people" and for the judiciary to respond to the needs of all the people, and not just for special interests. Roosevelt's campaign split the Republican Party, allowing the Progressive Democrat, Woodrow Wilson, to win. Wilson, a minority president, was able to get some legislation passed to improve working conditions (Adamson Act), but the Supreme Court continued to lag behind the executive and legislative branches of government with its conservative, Social Darwinist attitude expressed in *Hammer v. Dagenhart*. This decision forbid federal regulation of child labor. The Court thus remained conservative in spite of the election of Wilson, who in speeches in 1912–1913 had expressed his desire to have the law "step in and create new conditions under which we may live."

Use of abbreviation "T. R." is not formal essay style, but permissible if time is running out.

Effective weaving together of information in documents, and knowledge *recalled* from study of main issues in U.S. history—supporting point 2 of reasons for *Why?* part of question.

Good use of document—brief quote with source stated is effective.

Repeats thesis.

The documents presented help to make it clear that the decisions of the Supreme Court were not in agreement with the expressed views of the leaders of the executive branch of government. The Supreme Court remained conservative while the Progressive, Woodrow Wilson, was president. The period 1900–1918 clearly illustrates the adage that the Supreme Court lags behind the executive and legislative branch of government in its decisions and understanding of the needs of the people.

Brings paper back to broad topic of opening sentence.

Comment on the Sample Answer for the DBQ

The essay is a good example of what should be done with the DBQ. The writer makes use of all the documents except D. They are not discussed in order, but are used in different combinations to illustrate points. The writer uses considerable information from the period 1900–1918 to support the thesis and weaves it in well with the documents. He or she assumes the reader understands the content of the documents, so there is no need to summarize or quote them extensively. The writer uses one **short** quote from Wilson's speeches in Document F, which is an effective way to show a clear understanding of the document. In summary, the sample answer for this DBQ makes good use of the documents and includes sound information from American history to support the thesis presented. This answer would qualify for a high score on the examination.

Comments on Free-Response Essays

Comments on Question 2 of Section II

The second question is a typical *Evaluate This Statement* question (see Part III, Chapter 1). The quotation presents a most unusual interpretation of the era of the American Revolution, suggesting that the events in the West (frontier) were more "significant" for the development of the United States than events on the eastern seaboard (Boston, Philadelphia, Virginia) in the years from the Peace of Paris, which ended the French and Indian War in 1763, to the establishment of the government under the Constitution in 1788. The wording of the quotation should present no problem, and most students should quickly recall many events of the era under consideration. The question lends itself to a chronological organization, discussing events on the frontier before 1776 first, and then those after 1776, with references to events on the eastern seaboard woven in. The events you pick will be ones to support your thesis.

Remember, you are free to agree or disagree with this quotation. Most students will probably disagree, citing events such as the Stamp Act crisis; the Boston Massacre; the closing of the port of Boston; the reaction in New York to the Quartering Act; the meetings of the Continental Congresses; the writing and approval of the Declaration of Independence; the fighting at Bunker Hill, Saratoga, and Yorktown; the economic crisis under the government of the Articles of Confederation; and Shays' Rebellion, which led to the Constitutional Convention. To illustrate that there are arguments on the other side of the question, the following sample answer supports the quotation. Again, in the left-hand margin are comments pointing out good aspects of the answer. This answer presents only *one* of many possible approaches to a very interesting and provocative *Evaluate This Statement* type of question.

Sample Answer for Standard Essay Question 2

Opening comment is broad—catches attention—flashlight beam image of Seven Steps in Essay Writing.

Links opening comment to thesis, and introduces the **Topic** of the essay.

The role of the historian is to determine what events of the past are significant and explain to his generation why they are. For many years American historians have concentrated on the events that took place on the eastern seaboard between 1763 and 1788, suggesting that for American history they were the most significant events of those decades. These

Clearly stated **thesis** using quote from the question.

> historians have often ignored the events on the western frontier in those years—events that were "more significant for the development of U.S. history" than happenings in the East.

Admits evidence exists that might refute the stated thesis. →

Main idea of paragraph

Introduces factual refutation of the evidence given at start of the paragraph—important to admit and then to refute other views whenever possible.

> Granted that many significant events from the Stamp Act Crisis of 1765 to Shays' Rebellion of 1786 took place in the East. Granted also that the Declaration of Independence was signed, the Continental Congresses met, and many battles of the Revolutionary War were fought in the East, but *all of these were affected by events in the West.* It must be remembered that the Peace of Paris in 1763 ended a war fought basically for possible session and/or control of the Northwest Territory (Ohio, Michigan, etc.) and of the Mississippi Valley. It was in this war that George Washington gained his colonial reputation that allowed him to become the leader of the colonial army. Without his Western military experience, where would the colonial armies have been? More significantly, the entire taxation issue that was argued in the East was precipitated by the need of the British to pay the expenses they incurred in the French and Indian War. Without that war, *a result of British policy on the frontier*, there would have been no need for the taxes—Stamp Act, Townshend Acts, Tea Act—which stirred up the East, and led to the cry, "No taxation without representation" and ultimately to independence.

Points out an understanding of geography in parenthetical expression.

Paragraph is structured so major point of refutation appears at the end of paragraph. Ties facts back to topic and thesis.

Word *independence* links paragraphs.

Shifts argument to events that actually took place in the West. Shows understanding of the two major laws dealing with the Northwest.

> One often-forgotten event leading to American independence is the British Proclamation Line of 1763, which closed the Northwest Territory to colonial settlement. American leaders such as Washington and Franklin had committed money to companies to organize this territory. When the British stopped this settlement, colonists had an important motive for leading an anti-British movement in the East. In 1774 the English made matters worse for colonial leaders when by the Quebec Act they extended the boundaries of the former French province of Quebec to include the Northwest and established a form of government for the area putting it under different laws than the British colonies.

Good linkage of paragraphs as point of argument is shifted to government.

Student's grammar is somewhat scrambled, but the point is made. Minor grammatical errors can be expected when writing under intense pressure.

> Many of these colonies, such as Virginia and Connecticut, claimed control of the Northwest. After the Declaration of Independence, as the Continental Congress struggled to govern the colonies, Maryland refused to ratify the new government arrangement—the Articles of Confederation—until all colonies gave up their claims to Western lands. When Virginia finally did cede her claim in 1781, the Articles were ratified, and so, again, the West played a significant role in Eastern events.

Again, ties facts to topic and thesis.

Repeated word again links paragraphs as several new arguments are added. →

Cleverly presents many facts centered on the military significance of the West and its place in U.S. foreign policy.

> Many other illustrations could be given of the *significance* of the West: the British plan to split the West from the seaboard colonies, which was frustrated by the colonial victory at Saratoga, and victories on the frontier in Carolina, which led to Yorktown. Also, during the negotiations for peace, the United States won control over the land from the Appalachians to the Mississippi because of the victories of George Rogers Clark in

Another good link but wordy for a short essay.

Saves major point to the last paragraph so that reader is left with this crucial point of the argument in favor of the thesis.

Good, brief summary of important document shows writer knows the facts, not just the name of the document.

Grammatically a little confusing but presents important ideas.

Again, acknowledges events in the East, but restates thesis, and adds an interpretation of history to reinforce it.

Ends by moving back to broad topic of the opening, thus framing the essay and tying it together.

the Northwest. The British refused to evacuate forts and the resulting diplomatic struggle to gain control of the frontier region was the major foreign policy issue between 1783 and 1788.

All of these illustrations of the significance of the West for U.S. history pale by comparison to the great issue that was solved by the Continental Congress, that is, *how to organize and govern the frontier region.* The plan of organization was first set forth in the Basic Land Ordinance of 1785 and developed fully in the Northwest Ordinance of 1787. This document set the pattern for the future expansion of the United States in creating new states coast to coast. It abolished slavery in the territory and established trial by jury and freedom of religion. Nothing could be more significant to the development of the United States than the establishment both of the idea that these principles would be extended to new territory, which might have been treated as colonies, and of the plan for the expansion of the United States coast to coast.

Certainly, the East was important in American history from 1763 to 1788, but the events in the West were more significant. They provided the cause for so many events, and history is a cause-and-effect relationship. One must admit that the cause of events is more significant than the effects, and American historians should take more time to explain why from 1763 to 1788 the events of the frontier are more significant than those in the East.

Comment on the Sample Answer for Standard Essay Question 2

This was a very good answer to the question. The writer introduces the topic with a broad statement and narrows it down to a clearly stated thesis in which the question is quoted. The thesis is the last sentence of the opening paragraph. As you are aware, you may argue on any side of the question, and in this case, the writer has taken the less accepted view. Since most individuals would believe that events in the East were more important and would be aware of these events, the writer refutes these in the second paragraph. This, then, paves the way for the positive data the writer will use. The most important point the writer has is kept for the last paragraph, which is a very effective technique. The organization used is basically chronological, but there is some movement back and forth in time as the main topic under discussion (war, government, land organization) is shifted. The conclusion restates the thesis and moves back to the more general topic introduced in the opening sentence of the essay. This frames the essay effectively. The "Seven Steps in Essay Writing" have been well used by this author.

Comment on Standard Essay Question 3

This third question from the sample exam is an example of an *Assess the validity* type of question (see Part Three, Chapter 1), a type of question that has been used on many United States History AP examinations.

The first step in answering the question will be to analyze the quotation. It raises the eternal issue of democratic government—the conflict between the power of the majority and the rights of the minority. The question provides an unusual twist when it applies this issue to foreign policy. The quote states that minority rights ("views") cannot be ignored by a democratic society (the United States) when "executing foreign policy." You must decide if the statement is true or not, but, more than that, whether it is true or not for a very specific time period in American history. Once you have analyzed the quotation, you need to think about or brainstorm what factual information you could include in your answer. The time period includes the establishment of the government under Washington, Jay's Treaty with England and Pinckney's Treaty with Spain both of which angered many, the XYZ Affair, the Alien and Sedition Acts, the Louisiana Purchase, the Embargo of 1807, and the U.S. involvement in the War of 1812. In each of these issues there were majority and minority views. You must focus on the foreign policy side of these events. You must decide if the minority views were considered and what the results would have been if they were or were not considered. Is there a lesson to draw from how the issues were handled? Your answer to this question should help supply your thesis.

To prove your thesis, you must select several issues and not try to cover everything in the time period. You might decide on a chronological approach or you might use examples where the minority views were or were not considered thus using a topical approach. In any case it is an interesting question, which raises an important issue in a slightly different way. Questions on the AP examination will often ask you to use your knowledge in this way.

As in all essay answers, there are many ways to approach the question and no one way is best. What is important is that you follow the Seven Steps in Essay Writing and that you use specific facts carefully selected from your study of American history to prove your thesis.

Comment on Standard Essay Question 4

This is a typical *In what ways?* question (see Part Three, Chapter 4). The wording of the question links economic and political history. You are given a choice of four presidential elections from which you must pick two for information to prove your thesis. One election choice is after 1970, which illustrates how this later period may be used on the AP exam. If you know nothing of the 1980 election, your choices are more limited but you can still answer the question. Many students will know something of 1980 because of current events or comparisons made to recent events when studying the past. Consider your choice of elections carefully. Each had important economic aspects. In 1896 there was depression on the farms, the Panic of 1893, and the following gold crisis. The aftermath of the Panic of 1907 and the issue of the role of government in economic activity were discussed in the 1912 election. The election of 1932 was preceded by the Stock Market Crash and Great Depression. The inflationary crisis of the late 1970s and the impact of OPEC were important in the 1980 election as well as Reagan's solutions referred to as Reaganomics. Once you decide on the two elections you will discuss and the economic issues involved, you will need to consider noneconomic issues that might have been the cause for the change in political control. Among issues to consider would be U.S. expansion in the Pacific and concern over Cuba in 1896, differing views of the role of government and reform movements in 1912, the impact of the Roaring Twenties and post-World War I issues in 1932, and the aftermath of the Vietnam War and Watergate and the continuing Cold War in 1980.

You can organize the question in several ways. Least effective would be to simply write about two elections separately. More effective would be to group political and/or economic information from the two periods together.

Whether you emphasize the political or economic aspects may well depend on the emphasis given to these factors in your study of American history. The question expects you to establish a relationship between these two forces in history. Your perception of the relationship should be stated in your thesis. While deciding on your thesis, you will have recalled many events, and as always, you should use those events that you are most familiar with to prove your thesis.

**Comment on
Standard Essay
Question 5**

This is a good question that has a clear focus on one type of information—reform. In answering this *Compare* and *Contrast* question (see Part Three, Chapter 6), the first thing you must do is to determine what reform periods you will discuss. The three choices are the Jacksonian Era (1828–1840), the New Deal (1933–1940), and the Kennedy/Johnson years (1961–1968). Are there factors that these periods have in common? How do they differ? What were the main issues addressed in each period? What role did the president play in each period? Did they respond to public pressures or did they lead? Were the reforms primarily economic, social, or political or were they a combination?

One important point to note about this question is that it involves what is now called social history. It illustrates how the AP exam has questions on different types of history. Thirty-five percent of the multiple-choice questions are on social history, and this will be reflected in the free-response questions. In discussing reform movements, you should mention several specific reforms of a social nature: for example, the reforms in education in the 1830s and 1840s, the laws affecting conditions of employment passed in the 1930s, the legislation concerning the improvement of the environment passed in the 1960s. These social reforms are all interwoven with economic and political history, and you should include some economic and political history in your answer even if you wish to focus on the social aspects of reform.

There are obviously other matters one might consider in an analysis of the question. Once you have done your own analysis, an effective thesis should follow. The thesis must address both the comparison of the two periods **and** the contrast between them, as asked for in the question.

There are many ways to organize the answer to this question. It might be chronological, with one movement following the next, or you might trace one or two issues through the two periods of reform. However you structure your answer, you must remember to include specific information on reforms in both periods.

ANSWER SHEET FOR THE MODEL B
ADVANCED PLACEMENT EXAM IN PART FOUR

Name _____

Date _____

Grade _____

FOR SECTION I—MULTIPLE CHOICE

Sample: 1. The American Declaration of Independence was signed in   1. Ⓐ Ⓑ Ⓒ ● Ⓔ

        (A) 1789   (D) 1776

        (B) 1763   (E) 1667

        (C) 1976

Box D is filled in since the correct answer for the sample question 1 is D.

1. Ⓐ Ⓑ Ⓒ Ⓓ Ⓔ	21. Ⓐ Ⓑ Ⓒ Ⓓ Ⓔ	41. Ⓐ Ⓑ Ⓒ Ⓓ Ⓔ	61. Ⓐ Ⓑ Ⓒ Ⓓ Ⓔ
2. Ⓐ Ⓑ Ⓒ Ⓓ Ⓔ	22. Ⓐ Ⓑ Ⓒ Ⓓ Ⓔ	42. Ⓐ Ⓑ Ⓒ Ⓓ Ⓔ	62. Ⓐ Ⓑ Ⓒ Ⓓ Ⓔ
3. Ⓐ Ⓑ Ⓒ Ⓓ Ⓔ	23. Ⓐ Ⓑ Ⓒ Ⓓ Ⓔ	43. Ⓐ Ⓑ Ⓒ Ⓓ Ⓔ	63. Ⓐ Ⓑ Ⓒ Ⓓ Ⓔ
4. Ⓐ Ⓑ Ⓒ Ⓓ Ⓔ	24. Ⓐ Ⓑ Ⓒ Ⓓ Ⓔ	44. Ⓐ Ⓑ Ⓒ Ⓓ Ⓔ	64. Ⓐ Ⓑ Ⓒ Ⓓ Ⓔ
5. Ⓐ Ⓑ Ⓒ Ⓓ Ⓔ	25. Ⓐ Ⓑ Ⓒ Ⓓ Ⓔ	45. Ⓐ Ⓑ Ⓒ Ⓓ Ⓔ	65. Ⓐ Ⓑ Ⓒ Ⓓ Ⓔ
6. Ⓐ Ⓑ Ⓒ Ⓓ Ⓔ	26. Ⓐ Ⓑ Ⓒ Ⓓ Ⓔ	46. Ⓐ Ⓑ Ⓒ Ⓓ Ⓔ	66. Ⓐ Ⓑ Ⓒ Ⓓ Ⓔ
7. Ⓐ Ⓑ Ⓒ Ⓓ Ⓔ	27. Ⓐ Ⓑ Ⓒ Ⓓ Ⓔ	47. Ⓐ Ⓑ Ⓒ Ⓓ Ⓔ	67. Ⓐ Ⓑ Ⓒ Ⓓ Ⓔ
8. Ⓐ Ⓑ Ⓒ Ⓓ Ⓔ	28. Ⓐ Ⓑ Ⓒ Ⓓ Ⓔ	48. Ⓐ Ⓑ Ⓒ Ⓓ Ⓔ	68. Ⓐ Ⓑ Ⓒ Ⓓ Ⓔ
9. Ⓐ Ⓑ Ⓒ Ⓓ Ⓔ	29. Ⓐ Ⓑ Ⓒ Ⓓ Ⓔ	49. Ⓐ Ⓑ Ⓒ Ⓓ Ⓔ	69. Ⓐ Ⓑ Ⓒ Ⓓ Ⓔ
10. Ⓐ Ⓑ Ⓒ Ⓓ Ⓔ	30. Ⓐ Ⓑ Ⓒ Ⓓ Ⓔ	50. Ⓐ Ⓑ Ⓒ Ⓓ Ⓔ	70. Ⓐ Ⓑ Ⓒ Ⓓ Ⓔ
11. Ⓐ Ⓑ Ⓒ Ⓓ Ⓔ	31. Ⓐ Ⓑ Ⓒ Ⓓ Ⓔ	51. Ⓐ Ⓑ Ⓒ Ⓓ Ⓔ	71. Ⓐ Ⓑ Ⓒ Ⓓ Ⓔ
12. Ⓐ Ⓑ Ⓒ Ⓓ Ⓔ	32. Ⓐ Ⓑ Ⓒ Ⓓ Ⓔ	52. Ⓐ Ⓑ Ⓒ Ⓓ Ⓔ	72. Ⓐ Ⓑ Ⓒ Ⓓ Ⓔ
13. Ⓐ Ⓑ Ⓒ Ⓓ Ⓔ	33. Ⓐ Ⓑ Ⓒ Ⓓ Ⓔ	53. Ⓐ Ⓑ Ⓒ Ⓓ Ⓔ	73. Ⓐ Ⓑ Ⓒ Ⓓ Ⓔ
14. Ⓐ Ⓑ Ⓒ Ⓓ Ⓔ	34. Ⓐ Ⓑ Ⓒ Ⓓ Ⓔ	54. Ⓐ Ⓑ Ⓒ Ⓓ Ⓔ	74. Ⓐ Ⓑ Ⓒ Ⓓ Ⓔ
15. Ⓐ Ⓑ Ⓒ Ⓓ Ⓔ	35. Ⓐ Ⓑ Ⓒ Ⓓ Ⓔ	55. Ⓐ Ⓑ Ⓒ Ⓓ Ⓔ	75. Ⓐ Ⓑ Ⓒ Ⓓ Ⓔ
16. Ⓐ Ⓑ Ⓒ Ⓓ Ⓔ	36. Ⓐ Ⓑ Ⓒ Ⓓ Ⓔ	56. Ⓐ Ⓑ Ⓒ Ⓓ Ⓔ	76. Ⓐ Ⓑ Ⓒ Ⓓ Ⓔ
17. Ⓐ Ⓑ Ⓒ Ⓓ Ⓔ	37. Ⓐ Ⓑ Ⓒ Ⓓ Ⓔ	57. Ⓐ Ⓑ Ⓒ Ⓓ Ⓔ	77. Ⓐ Ⓑ Ⓒ Ⓓ Ⓔ
18. Ⓐ Ⓑ Ⓒ Ⓓ Ⓔ	38. Ⓐ Ⓑ Ⓒ Ⓓ Ⓔ	58. Ⓐ Ⓑ Ⓒ Ⓓ Ⓔ	78. Ⓐ Ⓑ Ⓒ Ⓓ Ⓔ
19. Ⓐ Ⓑ Ⓒ Ⓓ Ⓔ	39. Ⓐ Ⓑ Ⓒ Ⓓ Ⓔ	59. Ⓐ Ⓑ Ⓒ Ⓓ Ⓔ	79. Ⓐ Ⓑ Ⓒ Ⓓ Ⓔ
20. Ⓐ Ⓑ Ⓒ Ⓓ Ⓔ	40. Ⓐ Ⓑ Ⓒ Ⓓ Ⓔ	60. Ⓐ Ⓑ Ⓒ Ⓓ Ⓔ	80. Ⓐ Ⓑ Ⓒ Ⓓ Ⓔ

Practice Advanced Placement United States History Examination Model B

The comments appearing in Section A and on page 215 apply to the Model B practice examination. You may wish to use Model A as a pre-test and Model B as a summary of your study. The two examinations provide both an effective review and a preparation for the AP examination. Again, it is suggested that you create a situation in which to take the exam that is as close to that in the exam room as possible. Tear out or copy the answer sheet found at the start of the exam. Find a quiet place where you can work for more than 3 hours without interruption. Get your number 2 pencils with erasers, several pens, and some lined paper for the essays. Now take the exam. Afterward correct it, read the comments, and determine the time periods of U.S. history in which you are weakest. Spend extra time on them in your final review before taking the AP exam in May.

Model Exam B

**Section I
Multiple-Choice
Questions**

Time: 55 minutes

Number of Questions—80 MULTIPLE CHOICE

Directions: Each of the questions or incomplete statements below is followed by five suggested answers or completions. Select the one that is best in each case and then blacken the corresponding oval on the answer sheet.

1. Jim Crowism refers to legislation designed to
   (A) benefit railroad workers
   (B) sell western lands cheaply
   (C) deny equality to African Americans
   (D) keep immigrants from taking jobs away from Americans
   (E) provide economic opportunity for Spanish-American War veterans

2. Which of the following legislative acts designed to regulate or control business activity was part of the New Deal legislative program?
   (A) Clayton Antitrust Act
   (B) Sherman Antitrust Act
   (C) Federal Securities Act
   (D) Federal Trade Commission Act
   (E) Pure Food and Drug Act

3. What was the key frontier post held by the British in spite of the Treaty of Paris of 1783?
   (A) Tippecanoe
   (B) Detroit
   (C) Greenville
   (D) Genet
   (E) Erie

4. The most significant difference between the Pilgrims and the Puritans is that the Pilgrims
   (A) arrived in New England first
   (B) obtained a grant of settlement from the London Company
   (C) wished to separate from the Church of England
   (D) had a strong leader
   (E) celebrated the first Thanksgiving

5. The Independent Treasury plan called for
   (A) a bank of the United States
   (B) the funding of the U.S. debt by the Treasury
   (C) the use of silver coinage for debt payment
   (D) the use of state banks by the Treasury
   (E) the deposit of U.S. tax revenues in the Treasury rather than in banks

6. The leader of the Radical Reconstructionists of the U.S. House of Representatives was
   (A) Andrew Johnson
   (B) Charles Sumner
   (C) Thaddeus Stevens
   (D) Edwin M. Stanton
   (E) Ulysses S. Grant

7. The following items all dealt with relations between the thirteen English colonies and the English government EXCEPT
   (A) Acts of Trade and Navigation
   (B) Stamp Act
   (C) Quartering Act
   (D) Quebec Act
   (E) Olive Branch Petition

8. Where did the Whiskey Rebellion of 1794 take place?
   (A) Ohio
   (B) Massachusetts
   (C) Pennsylvania
   (D) New York
   (E) Virginia

9. Which of the following was NOT the leader of the settlement paired with his name?
   (A) John Smith—Jamestown, Virginia
   (B) General Oglethorpe—Savannah, Georgia
   (C) William Penn—Philadelphia, Pennsylvania
   (D) Roger Williams—Hartford, Connecticut
   (E) William Bradford—Plymouth, Massachusetts

10. Among the scandals connected with the Grant administration are
    (A) Teapot Dome
    (B) Whitewater
    (C) Credit Mobilier
    (D) The Tweed Gang
    (E) Watergate

11. All of the following measures were enacted by Congress as part of President Lyndon Johnson's Great Society program EXCEPT
    (A) the establishment of the Department of Housing and Welfare
    (B) Operation Headstart
    (C) Voting Rights Act of 1965
    (D) The Taft-Hartley Act
    (E) Medicare

12. COMPARISON OF MANPOWER LOSSES IN WORLD WAR I

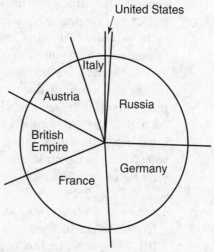

According to the chart above, manpower losses in World War I were
    (A) larger for the United States than for Austria
    (B) greater for Russia than for the British Empire, Austria, and Italy combined
    (C) approximately the same for France, the British Empire, and Italy
    (D) heaviest for the combined Central Powers of Germany and Austria
    (E) approximately equal for Russia and Germany

13. The Supreme Court decision in *Marbury v. Madison* established the
    (A) doctrine of judicial review of congressional legislation
    (B) principle of state control over local legislation
    (C) doctrine of Supreme Court review of state laws
    (D) principle of sanctity of contract
    (E) sanctity of congressional control of interstate commerce

14. Which of the following was NOT acquired by the United States as a result of involvement in the Spanish-American War?
    (A) Samoa
    (B) Hawaiian Islands
    (C) Puerto Rico
    (D) Guam
    (E) Philippine Islands

15. All of the following terms became part of the American political vocabulary in the 1960s EXCEPT
    (A) *pig*
    (B) *hippie*
    (C) *dove*
    (D) *flapper*
    (E) *black power*

16. "The object of your expedition is to try the affections of the country, to disconcert the councils of the enemy . . . and obtain large supplies of cattle, horses and carriages . . . during your whole progress your detachments are to have orders to bring into you all horses fit to mount the Dragoons (mounted infantrymen) . . . together with as many saddles and bridles as may be found . . . likewise to bring in wagons and other convenient carriages, with as many draft oxen as will be necessary to draw them . . . limit the hours of delivery and should you find it necessary to move on before such delivery (of goods) can be made, hostages of the most respectable inhabitants should be taken to secure their (delivery) next day . . . All persons acting in Committees, or any officers under direction of the Congress either civil or military, are to be made prisoners."

    The above quotation supports all of the following statements EXCEPT
    (A) these are instructions for an expedition into enemy territory
    (B) those sending the expedition are in need of additional transport
    (C) the expedition is against forces commanded by a Congress
    (D) hostages will assure the delivery of supplies
    (E) the leader of the expedition is commanded to follow a "scorched earth" policy

17. The "gag rule" passed by the House of Representatives in 1836 was passed to prevent
    (A) publication of Garrison's *Liberator*
    (B) Nat Turner's rebellion
    (C) debate of antislavery appeals
    (D) the growth of sweatshop factories in the North
    (E) organization of the Free Soil party

18. All of the following acts were part of British mercantilist policy EXCEPT
    (A) Act of Toleration
    (B) Hatters Act
    (C) Iron Act
    (D) Sugar or Molasses Act
    (E) Woolens Act

19. Theodore Roosevelt named a group of individuals Muckrakers after a character in Bunyan's *Pilgrim's Progress*, but the members of the group gained their real reputation as
    (A) the writers of local-color novels
    (B) reformers who published articles to draw attention to the evils affecting America
    (C) the ten richest men in America
    (D) leaders of conservation movements in the West, which brought national attention to conservation
    (E) members of Roosevelt's first cabinet

20. The Supreme Court under Chief Justice Earl Warren was noted for its decisions regarding segregation and the
    (A) rights of the police to punish criminals
    (B) protection of individual rights in criminal cases
    (C) defense of the death penalty
    (D) support of presidential authority
    (E) limit of federal authority in the War on Poverty

21.

Source: *Harper's Weekly,* December 13, 1862

The point the cartoon from *Harper's Weekly* is making centers on the
(A) way the British industrialists supplied arms and ships for the Confederacy
(B) way the Confederates could not make manacles for slaves and guns at the same time
(C) first time the Confederacy was personified in a cartoon as a man
(D) view of the Union concerning overfed British people
(E) great wealth and manufacturing skill of the British

22. Which of the following events occurred first?
(A) Tariff of Abominations
(B) The Force Bill
(C) South Carolina's nullification of U.S. tariff laws
(D) Clay's Compromise Tariff of 1833
(E) Calhoun's resignation as vice president

23. All of the following authors are correctly paired with one of their works EXCEPT
    (A) Ernest Hemingway—*A Farewell to Arms*
    (B) John Steinbeck—*The Grapes of Wrath*
    (C) Eugene O'Neill—*Strange Interlude*
    (D) Sinclair Lewis—*Main Street*
    (E) Langston Hughes—*The Great Gatsby*

24. The Hartford Convention of 1815
    (A) nominated candidates for president
    (B) called for repeal of the Alien and Sedition Acts
    (C) was a meeting of disaffected Federalists
    (D) rejected the Treaty of Ghent
    (E) supported another invasion of Canada

25. A major foreign policy achievement of Jimmy Carter's administration was
    (A) the withdrawal of U.S. troops from Vietnam
    (B) the breakup of OPEC
    (C) the overthrow of the Shah of Iran
    (D) the Camp David Accords for peace in the Middle East
    (E) the purchase of the Panama Canal

26. The United States' policy toward the Native American changed dramatically with the passage in 1887 of the Dawes Act, which
    (A) treated the tribes as independent nations
    (B) established new and larger reservations for all tribes
    (C) granted full citizenship to all tribal members
    (D) wiped out tribal ownership of property and granted 160 acres to heads of families
    (E) forbade selling alcohol or guns on reservations

27. "It being one chief project of Satan to keep man from the knowledge of the scriptures . . . it is therefore ordered by this court [Assembly] . . . that every township within this jurisdiction after the Lord hath increased them to the number of fifty householders, shall then forthwith appoint one within their towns to teach all such children as shall resort [apply] to him to write and read, whose wages shall be paid either by parents or masters of such children, or by the inhabitants in general . . . provided that those who send their children be not oppressed by paying much more than they can have them taught for in other towns."

    This passage sets forth basic American attitudes concerning the
    (A) separation of church and state
    (B) the power of the state over the power of Satan
    (C) political power of townships
    (D) importance of education
    (E) value of fair and equal taxation

28. Starting with the decade of 1890 until Congress passed legislation to control immigration in the 1920s, the largest number of immigrants came from
    (A) Ireland
    (B) Italy, Austria-Hungary, Russia
    (C) England, Germany, France
    (D) Norway, Sweden, Denmark
    (E) Poland

29. Which of the following would NOT be considered part of Jacksonian Democracy?
    (A) actions of Dorothea Dix to help the insane
    (B) the establishment of labor unions and their recognition by the courts
    (C) the spread of free public schools
    (D) the growth of railroads
    (E) the extension of universal male suffrage

30. The first woman to serve in the United States cabinet was
    (A) Frances Perkins
    (B) Oveta Culp Hobby
    (C) Eleanor Roosevelt
    (D) Marian Anderson
    (E) Sandra Day O'Connor

31. The National Labor Union, after winning the eight-hour day for government workers, disintegrated because of
    (A) the depression of the early 1870s
    (B) a Supreme Court ruling outlawing unions
    (C) the opposition of President Grant
    (D) the rise of the Knights of Labor
    (E) the failure to admit African Americans

32. Washington Irving is remembered as one of the first important writers of the newly established United States for his work
    (A) *Common Sense*
    (B) *Poor Richard's Almanac*
    (C) *The Legend of Sleepy Hollow*
    (D) *The Scarlet Letter*
    (E) *An American Scholar*

33. The Albany Plan was
    (A) the first plan for city development
    (B) a scheme to make money
    (C) a plan for colonial union
    (D) a plan for attack in King William's War
    (E) a plan to build a canal connecting Albany with the West

34. An agreement by one group of legislators to support or oppose a particular bill in return for support or opposition for another bill is known as
    (A) balance of power
    (B) logrolling
    (C) bilateral legislation
    (D) a social contract
    (E) a filibuster

35. In his first year in office, President Reagan tackled the issue of inflation by
    (A) establishing a Department of Energy
    (B) encouraging Congress to pass a new tax law reducing income tax
    (C) stopping U.S. military and economic aid to Taiwan
    (D) repealing the minimum-wage law
    (E) increasing military support for terrorist activities

36. "For many years numerous Americans have been living in Nicaragua, developing its industries and carrying on business. At the present time there are large investments in lumbering, mining, coffee growing, banana culture, shipping and also in general mercantile and other collateral business. In addition to these industries now in existence, the Government of Nicaragua, by a treaty entered into on the 5th day of August 1914, granted in perpetuity to the United States the exclusive proprietary rights necessary and convenient for the construction, operation, and maintenance of an oceanic canal."

    The above quotation is an example of the United States policy toward Latin America known as
    (A) the Good Neighbor Policy
    (B) the Monroe Doctrine
    (C) Dollar Diplomacy
    (D) Pan-Americanism
    (E) Alliance for Progress

37. *Common Sense* by Thomas Paine is considered a most effective
    (A) logical argument for independence
    (B) propaganda work for independence
    (C) handbook for guerrilla warfare
    (D) condemnation of Whig philosophy
    (E) attack on the Stamp Act

38. One of the chief reasons Americans were willing to join the peacetime NATO alliance was because of the
    (A) Cuban Missile Crisis
    (B) Hungarian Revolution
    (C) Berlin Blockade
    (D) Berlin Wall
    (E) Bay of Pigs

39. Each of the following men is correctly paired with an item linked with his name EXCEPT
  (A) Joseph Pulitzer—*New York World*
  (B) Louis H. Sullivan—Skyscrapers
  (C) Thomas Edison—Phonograph
  (D) Bret Harte—*Adventures of Huckleberry Finn*
  (E) Buffalo Bill Cody—Wild West Show

40. All of the following are illustrations of strong conservative attitudes in American society in the years after World War II EXCEPT
  (A) the "silent majority"
  (B) the 1994 Contract with America
  (C) the presidential nomination of Barry Goldwater
  (D) the programs offered by the "Religious Right"
  (E) the pro-choice movement

41. "There is no reason why the United States should be committed to other political units or involved in entangling alliances" expresses the view held by American
  (A) socialists
  (B) immigrants
  (C) isolationists
  (D) internationalists
  (E) clergy

42. Which of the following British acts was enacted first?
  (A) Tea Act
  (B) Intolerable Acts
  (C) Stamp Act
  (D) Townshend Revenue Act
  (E) Declaratory Act

43. Cattle raising in the semiarid lands of the West greatly increased as a result of the
  (A) Homestead Act
  (B) invention of barbed wire
  (C) building of the transcontinental railroad
  (D) cattle drives
  (E) invention of the reaper

44. "To make all laws which shall be necessary and proper for carrying into execution the foregoing powers, and all other powers vested by this Constitution in the Government of the United States" has been referred to as the
  (A) elastic clause
  (B) Bill of Rights
  (C) commerce clause
  (D) Power of the Purse
  (E) checks and balances clause

45. All of the following were provisions of the Compromise of 1850 EXCEPT
   (A) admittance of California into the union as a free state
   (B) a strict fugitive slave law
   (C) establishment of Utah and New Mexico as territories with squatter sovereignty
   (D) the redrawing of the Texas boundary
   (E) the prohibition of the slave trade in Washington, D.C.

46. All of the following occurred after the fall of the Berlin Wall in 1989 EXCEPT
   (A) the beginning of *perestroika* and *glasnost*
   (B) the breakup of the Soviet Union into separate nations
   (C) the outbreak of warfare in Yugoslavia
   (D) the Persian Gulf War
   (E) the sending of U.S. troops to Somalia in the U.N.'s Project Restore Hope

47. In the Monroe Doctrine President Monroe
   (A) introduced the concept of Dollar Diplomacy
   (B) warned European nations against interfering in South America
   (C) stated the United States would collect all debts owed by South American nations
   (D) announced the United States would seize Panama to build a canal
   (E) established a free-trade area in South America

48. United States historian Arthur Schlesinger called World War II the "greatest challenge democracy ever faced." Which one of the following events of World War II would LEAST likely be used to support this statement?
   (A) the Holocaust (killing of European Jews by the Nazis)
   (B) the ideas expressed by Hitler in his book, *Mein Kampf*
   (C) the attack on Pearl Harbor by Japan
   (D) the Allied victory in the Battle of Midway
   (E) the German defeat of France in 1940

49. The Great Depression threatened the survival of the United States capitalist, free-enterprise system because
   (A) there was no market for apples sold on street corners
   (B) business leaders moved their headquarters overseas
   (C) Communist Chinese products flooded the United States market
   (D) the balance of payment favored Asian nations
   (E) industry could not provide enough jobs for the unemployed

50. The social structure of the colonies before the American Revolution
   (A) did not support the concept that "all men are created equal"
   (B) allowed every person to rise to their fullest potential
   (C) was an exact copy of the social structure in England
   (D) did not emphasize the differences in wealth among the colonists
   (E) accepted all religious faiths as equally important

51. During World War I the massive depletion of resources and manpower led to
   (A) the establishment of new colonies in Africa
   (B) conditions that encouraged the rise of fascism and communism
   (C) the League of Nations overseeing the distribution of resources
   (D) the establishment of the Marshall Plan for European recovery
   (E) close cooperation between Europe and the United States

52. *The Jungle* by Upton Sinclair recounts the story of
   (A) Theodore Roosevelt's big-game hunting in Africa
   (B) life in the highly competitive electronics industry
   (C) growing up on an Indian reservation
   (D) corruption in the meat-packing industry
   (E) working in the business world of 1950s America

53. As Secretary of the Treasury, Alexander Hamilton introduced financial measures that benefited
   (A) publishers
   (B) merchants
   (C) small farmers
   (D) frontiersmen
   (E) slave owners

54. Which of the following means of transportation was most helpful in providing easy transport from the East to California at the time of the gold rush?
   (A) stagecoach
   (B) railroad
   (C) horses
   (D) airplane
   (E) sailing ships

55. The Treaty of Paris in 1898 ceded to the United States
   (A) Alaska
   (B) Hawaii
   (C) Puerto Rico
   (D) Midway
   (E) Samoa

56. The Missouri Compromise helped to postpone the outbreak of the Civil War by
   (A) maintaining the balance of slave and free states
   (B) admitting California into the Union as a free state
   (C) reducing the tariffs on imported manufactured goods
   (D) accepting the *Dred Scott* decision that slaves were property
   (E) prohibiting all discussion of slavery by the United States Congress

57. The World Trade Organization (WTO) has the responsibility to
    (A) maintain an equal trade balance between all nations
    (B) enforce established fair trade practices between members of the WTO
    (C) control all monetary exchanges between international corporations
    (D) manage the salary negotiations between workers and owners
    (E) supervise the accounting practices of United States firms

58. Which of the following was NOT true of life in colonial America?
    (A) slavery was accepted in all thirteen colonies
    (B) subsistence farming was common, particularly in frontier areas
    (C) trade was a major source of wealth in New England
    (D) large families were important as a source of workers
    (E) women had the same legal rights as men

59. At the Constitutional Convention there was NO need to compromise on the issue of
    (A) the counting of population in the thirteen states
    (B) the method of representation in the Senate and House of Representatives
    (C) the interests of agricultural and manufacturing states
    (D) the method of election of the president
    (E) the role of Congress in declaring war and raising an army

60. Just as computers have changed social patterns in the last twenty years, in the twenty years after World War II social patterns were changed dramatically by the increasing availability of
    (A) automobiles
    (B) microwave ovens
    (C) television sets
    (D) motion pictures
    (E) cell phones

61. The United Nations was modeled on the
    (A) Albany Plan
    (B) League of Nations
    (C) European Union
    (D) Pan American Union
    (E) United States Constitution

62. The Reconstruction of the South after the Civil War was ended by
    (A) the Radical Republican proposals passed by the U.S. Congress
    (B) the Compromise of 1877 settling the disputed election
    (C) the establishment of local government in each seceded state
    (D) the abolishment of slavery by the thirteenth amendment
    (E) the work of the Freedman's Bureau to promote free elections

63. The industrial revolution in the United States after the Civil War benefited from all of the following EXCEPT
   (A) the development of new economic structures
   (B) a rapid increase in immigration
   (C) the abundance of natural resources
   (D) the expansion of the railroad network
   (E) federal regulation exercised by the Interstate Commerce Commission (ICC)

64. The Supreme Court decision in *Brown v. Board of Education of Topeka* reversed the "separate but equal" doctrine set in the case of
   (A) *Roe v. Wade*
   (B) *Dred Scott v. Sandford*
   (C) *Marbury v. Madison*
   (D) *Plessy v. Ferguson*
   (E) *Miranda v. Arizona*

65. Considered the first popular work to publicize the environmental issue, *Silent Spring* was written by
   (A) Rachel Carson
   (B) Ralph Nader
   (C) John Muir
   (D) Tom Wolfe
   (E) Jack Kerouac

66. Martin Luther King, Jr. emerged as a leader of the Civil Rights Movement as a result of his involvement in
   (A) lunch counter sit-ins
   (B) the desegregation of the U.S. Army
   (C) the March on Washington
   (D) a drive for voter registration
   (E) the Montgomery Bus Boycott

67. President Theodore Roosevelt is considered a leader of the
   (A) Populist Movement
   (B) Transcendentalist Movement
   (C) Trust Building Movement
   (D) Westward Movement
   (E) Progressive Movement

68. As part of his progressive program, President Woodrow Wilson introduced the
   (A) Independent Treasury
   (B) Bank of the United States
   (C) Specie Circular
   (D) Federal Reserve System
   (E) Bank Holiday

69. During the period of the French Revolution and Napoleonic Wars, President Jefferson was most sympathetic to the cause of
  (A) England
  (B) Germany
  (C) France
  (D) Italy
  (E) Yugoslavia

70. The decade after the end of the Cold War was a period of
  (A) continuing confrontation between the United States and Russia
  (B) growing rivalries to build space stations
  (C) declining nationalism in southeastern Europe
  (D) increasing globalization of the world economy
  (E) failing economic growth in China

71. The Kennedy administration is noted as the time the United States committed itself to
  (A) place a man on the moon
  (B) decrease U.S. involvement in Vietnam
  (C) raise taxes to finance the government
  (D) support President Castro's rule in Cuba
  (E) reduce the size of the Peace Corps

72. By 1763 all thirteen colonies were either controlled by proprietors or were under the control of the King as
  (A) his private estate
  (B) economic centers
  (C) royal colonies
  (D) royal family colonies
  (E) military bases

73. During the Clinton presidency there were several investigations of misconduct that led to
  (A) the resignation of the Independent Counsel, Kenneth Starr
  (B) the removal of Hillary Rodham Clinton from an active role in health care reform
  (C) the failure of the Whitewater Real Estate development enterprise
  (D) the impeachment of President Clinton on charges of obstructing justice and misleading testimony
  (E) the reform of the White House staff and the use of the Oval Office

74. Before the Civil War, westward expansion was hindered by
  (A) the lack of a cross-continental railroad
  (B) the high cost of using the Panama Canal for sea transport
  (C) the support of Native American tribes in the Great Plains
  (D) the failure to find passable routes through the Rocky Mountains
  (E) the scarcity of game as a food source for the pioneers

75. Which of the following would NOT be considered part of the Cold War?
    (A) the Berlin Blockade
    (B) the Vietnam War
    (C) the founding of Israel
    (D) the fall of the Berlin Wall
    (E) Soviet invasion of Afghanistan

76. Which of the following should be considered as a step leading to the American Revolution?
    (A) the XYZ Affair
    (B) English control of frontier forts
    (C) the Articles of Confederation
    (D) the Boston Tea Party
    (E) the Northeast Ordinance

77. Opportunities for women have been greatly expanded since World War II in spite of the failure of the
    (A) Title IX program
    (B) Equal Rights Amendment (ERA)
    (C) Family and Medical Leave Act
    (D) National Organization for Women (NOW)
    (E) Women's Liberation Movement

78. The concept that those individuals who make large sums of money should become philanthropists and spend their money for the benefit of others during their lifetime is the main message of
    (A) William Jennings Bryan's Cross of Gold oration
    (B) Andrew Carnegie's Gospel of Wealth address
    (C) Horatio Alger's Rags to Riches stories
    (D) Walter Rauschenbush's Social Gospel theory
    (E) William Graham Summer's Social Darwinism concepts

79. Which of the following applies to the 1920s in the United States?
    (A) all people shared in the economic prosperity
    (B) prices for farm produce grew steadily
    (C) investments in the stock market were insured by the government
    (D) there were no indications an economic collapse might occur
    (E) speculation was widespread among investors

80. The Kansas-Nebraska Act
    (A) incorporated the concept of popular sovereignty for Kansas
    (B) maintained the 36° 30′ line of the Missouri Compromise
    (C) provided for a strict fugitive slave law
    (D) continued the concept of balance by admitting one free and one slave state
    (E) supported the decision in the Dred Scott case

**Section II
DBQ**

The free-response section consists of two parts. All students must answer the DBQ in Part A. Part B consists of two groups of essay questions, and students must answer one question from each group.

You have a 15-minute reading period to read the documents and prepare your answer.

Part A: Document-Based Essay Question (DBQ)

Writing time—45 minutes

Directions: The following question requires you to construct a coherent essay that integrates your interpretation of documents A–N **and** your knowledge of the period referred to in the question. To earn a high score you must cite key pieces of evidence from the documents and draw on your knowledge of the period.

1. Between 1789 and 1815 to what extent was the foreign policy of the United States driven by a concern for commerce?

Document A

Source: U.S. Constitution, 1789

Article I: Section 9
The Migration or Importation of such Persons as any of the States now existing shall think proper to admit, shall not be prohibited by the Congress prior to the Year one thousand eight hundred and eight, but a tax or duty may be imposed on such Importation, not exceeding ten dollars for each Person.
No Preference shall be given by any Regulation of Commerce or Revenue to the Ports of one State over those of another: nor shall Vessels bound to, or from, one State, be obliged to enter, clear, or pay Duties in another.

Document B

Source: An Act Imposing Duties on the Tonnage of Ships or Vessels, July 20, 1790

Section 1. *Be it enacted by the Senate and House of Representatives of the United States of America in Congress assembled,* That upon all ships or vessels which after the first day of September next, shall be entered in the United States from any foreign port or place, there shall . . . (pay) the several and respective duties following, that is to say: On ships or vessels of the United States at the rate of six cents per ton: on ships or vessels built within the United States after the twentieth day of July last, but belonging wholly or in part to subjects of foreign powers, at the rate of thirty cents per ton: on other ships or vessels at the rate of fifty cents per ton.

Document C

Source: The Proclamation of Neutrality 1793: A Proclamation

Whereas it appears that a state of war exists between Austria, Prussia, Sardinia, Great Britain, and the United Netherlands, of the one part, and France on the other; and the duty and interest of the United States require, that they should with sincerity and good faith adopt and pursue a conduct friendly and impartial toward the belligerent Powers; I have therefore thought fit . . . to declare the disposition of the United States to observe the conduct aforesaid towards those Powers respectfully; and to exhort and warn the citizens of the United States carefully to avoid all acts and proceedings whatsoever, which may in any manner tend to contravene such disposition.

Document D

Source: From the Letters of Thomas Jefferson

To Gouverneur Morris, Philadelphia, March 12, 1793:
We surely cannot deny to any nation that right whereon our own government is founded, that every one may govern itself according to whatever form it pleases and change these forms at its own will; and that it may transact its business with foreign nations through whatever organ it thinks proper, whether king, convention, assembly, committee, president, or anything else it may choose. The will of the nation is the only thing essential to be regarded.

To Thomas Pinckney, Philadelphia, May 29, 1797:
War is not the best engine for us to resort to. Nature has given us one in our commerce which, if properly managed, will be a better instrument for obliging the interested nations of Europe to treat us with justice.

To Benjamin Waring, Washington, March 23, 1801:
. . . the will of the people . . . is the only legitimate foundation of any government, and to protect its free expression should be our first object.

Document E

Source: Jay's Treaty, 1795

His Britannic Majesty and the United States of America, being desirous, by a treaty of amity, commerce and navigation, to terminate their difference . . . and also to regulate the commerce and navigation between their respective countries . . . , in such a manner as to render the same reciprocally beneficial and satisfactory; . . . have agreed on and concluded the following articles:

ARTICLE I:
There shall be a firm, inviolable and universal peace, and a true and sincere friendship between His Britannic Majesty, his heirs and successors, and the United States of America; . . .

ARTICLE II:
His Majesty will withdraw all his troops and garrisons from all posts and places within the boundary lines assigned by the treaty of peace to the United States . . .

Document F

Source: **Treaty of Friendship, Limits, and Navigation, signed at San Lorenzo el Real October 27, 1795**

There shall be a firm and inviolable Peace and sincere Friendship between His Catholic Majesty (King of Spain), his successors and subjects, and the United States and their Citizens without exception of persons and places.

ARTICLE II:
To prevent all disputes on the subject of the boundaries which separate the territories of the two High contracting Parties, it is hereby declared and agreed as follows: to wit: The Southern boundary of the United States which divides their territory from the Spanish Colonies of East and West Florida, shall be designated by a line beginning on the River Mississippi . . . to the Atlantic Ocean. And it is agreed that if there should be any troops, Garrisons or settlements of either Party in the territory of the other according to the above mentioned boundaries, they shall be withdrawn from the said territory . . .

ARTICLE IV:
It is likewise agreed that the Western boundary of the United States which separates them from the Spanish Colony of Louisiana, is in the middle of the channel or bed of the River Mississippi from the Northern boundary of the said States to the completion of the thirty first degree of latitude North of the Equator; . . .

Document G

Source: **Treaty of Greenville, 1795**

ARTICLE 1:
Henceforth all hostilities shall cease; peace is hereby established, and shall be perpetual; and a friendly intercourse shall take place between the said United States and Indian tribes.

ARTICLE 2:
All prisoners shall, on both sides, be restored.

ARTICLE 5:
To prevent any misunderstanding about the Indian lands relinquished by the United States in the fourth article, it is now explicitly declared, that the meaning of that relinquishment is this: the Indian tribes who have a right to those lands, are quietly enjoying them, hunting, planting, and dwelling thereon, so long as they please, without any molestation from the United States; but when those tribes, or any of them, shall be disposed to sell their lands, or any part of them, they are to be sold only to the United States; . . .

Document H

Source: **Washington's Farewell Address, 1796**

. . . The nation which indulges towards another a habitual hatred or a habitual fondness is in some degree a slave. It is a slave to its animosity or to its affection, either of which is sufficient to lead it astray from its duty and its interest. Antipathy in one nation against another disposes each more readily to offer insult and injury . . . and to be haughty and intractable, when accidental or trifling occasions of dispute occur. Hence, frequent collisions, . . . and bloody contests . . .

So likewise, a passionate attachment of one nation for another produces a variety of evils. Sympathy for the favorite nation, facilitating the illusion of an imaginary common interest in cases where no real common interest exists, betrays the former into a participation in the quarrels and wars of the latter without adequate inducement or justification . . .

Against the insidious wiles of foreign influence the jealousy of a free people ought to be constantly awake, since history and experience prove that foreign influence is one of the most baneful foes of republican government . . .

The great rule of conduct for us in regard to foreign nations is in extending our commercial relations, to have with them as little political connection as possible . . .

Harmony, liberal intercourse with all nations, are recommended by policy, humanity, and interest. But even our commercial policy should hold an equal and impartial hand; neither seeking nor granting exclusive favors or preferences; . . . define the rights of our merchants, and to enable the government to support them, establishing conventional rules of intercourse, the best that present circumstances and mutual opinion will permit, but temporary, and liable to be from time to time abandoned or varied, as experience and circumstances shall dictate; . . .

Document I

Source: John Adams—Special Message to the Senate and the House, May 16, 1797

. . . The refusal on the part of France to receive our minister is, then, the denial of a right; but the refusal to receive him until we have acceded to their demands without discussion and without investigation is to treat us neither as allies nor as friends, nor as a sovereign state.

. . . this conduct of the French Government . . . discloses sentiments more alarming than the refusal of a minister, because more dangerous to our independence and union, and at the same time studiously marked with indignities toward the Government of the United States. It evinces a disposition to separate the people of the United States from the Government, to persuade them (the people) that they have different affections, principles, and interests from those or their fellow citizens (the elected government) whom they themselves have chosen to manage their common concerns, and thus to produce divisions fatal to our peace. Such attempts ought to be repelled with a decision which shall convince France and the world that we are not a degraded people, humiliated under a colonial spirit of fear and sense of inferiority, fitted to be the miserable instruments of foreign influence, and regardless of national honor, character, and interest.

Document J

Source: Convention Between the French Republic, and the United States of America, December 21, 1801

ARTICLE I:
There shall be a firm, inviolable, and universal peace, and a true and sincere Friendship between the French Republic, and the United States of America, and between their respective countries, territories, cities, towns, and people without exception of persons, or places.

ARTICLE VI:
Commerce between the Parties shall be free . . . and in general the two parties shall enjoy in the ports of each other, in regard to commerce, and navigation, the privileges of the most favored nation.

Document K

Source: Jefferson's third message to Congress, December 15, 1803

Congress witnessed, at their last session, the extraordinary agitation produced in the public mind by the suspension of our right of deposit at the port of New Orleans . . . They were sensible that the continuance of that privation would be more injurious to our nation . . .

The enlightened government of France saw, with just discernment, the importance to both nations of such liberal arrangements as might best and permanently promote the peace, friendship, and interests of both; and the property and sovereignty of all Louisiana, which had been restored to them, have on certain conditions been transferred to the United States by instruments bearing date the 30th of April last. When these shall have received the constitutional sanction of the senate . . .

Document L

Source: James Madison First Inaugural, March 4, 1809

Indulging no passions which trespass on the rights or the repose of other nations, it has been the true glory of the United States to cultivate peace by observing justice, and to entitle themselves to the respect of the nations at war by fulfilling their neutral obligations with the most scrupulous impartiality. If there be candor in the world, the truth of these assertions will not be questioned; posterity at least will do justice to them.

Document M

Source: The Sun, Gazette and County Advertiser, Dover, N.H., Saturday, December 12, 1807

From the foregoing facts it appears . . . that the outrage committed on the frigate *Chesapeake* has been stamped with circumstances of indignity and insult of which there is scarcely to be found a parallel in the history of civilized nations, and requires only the sanction of the government under color of whose authority it was perpetrated to make it just cause of, if not an irresistible call for instant and severe retaliation . . . as other acts of aggression have been committed within our ports and waters by British ships of war as well anterior as posterior to this, some of them manifesting the same disregard of our national rights, and seeming to flow from the same contempt for the authority of our laws, and especially as the British squadron, of which the Leopard was one, after being notified of the President's proclamation ordering them to depart from the waters of the United States . . . in that situation remained capturing American vessels within our acknowledged territorial limits . . . ; impressing seamen on board American vessels, firing on vessels and boats of all descriptions having occasion to pass near them in pursuit of their lawful trade, and occasionally denouncing threats, calculated to alarm and irritate the good people of the United States, particularly the inhabitants of Norfolk and Hampton, which facts are substantiated by the accompanying documents No. 1 to 6, the committee are of opinion that . . . it is expedient to provide more effectually for the protection of our ports and harbors . . .

Document N

Source: Amendments to the Constitution Proposed by the Hartford Convention, 1814

. . . Third–Congress shall not have power to lay any embargo on the ships or vessels of the citizens of the United States, in the ports or harbors thereof, for more than sixty days.

Fourth—Congress shall not have power, without the concurrence of two-thirds of both Houses, to interdict the commercial intercourse between the United States and any foreign nation or the dependencies thereof . . .

Section II
Free-Response
Questions 2–5

Essay Questions

Writing time—70 minutes

Directions: You are to answer *two* of the following questions—one from Part B and one from Part C. Use relevant historical evidence in support of your generalizations and present your arguments clearly and logically.

Part B: Choose ONE question from Part B. It is suggested that you spend 5 minutes organizing your answer and 30 minutes writing it.

2. In what ways did federal legislation and federal judicial decisions between 1787 and 1860 affect the life of the African American in United States society?

3. Compare the presidencies of Jefferson and Jackson. To what extent were the presidencies of these two men revolutionary?

Part C: Choose ONE question from Part C. It is suggested that you spend 5 minutes organizing and 30 minutes writing your answer.

4. "The proposals of the Populists as to how to handle the economic conditions of the early 1890s were not enacted, but these proposals provided the framework for the New Deal's response to the economic conditions created by the Great Depression." Assess the validity of this generalization.

5. Evaluate THREE of the following as a factor in establishing the United States as a leader in international affairs:

    Spanish-American War

    Opening of the Panama Canal

    Defeat of the Treaty of Versailles by the United States Senate

    Outbreak of World War II

    Vietnam War

End of Examination   At the end of the exam you will be directed to circle on the back of your essay answer booklet the numbers of the two questions you answered.

Comments and Answers to Questions on Practice Advanced Placement Examination—Model B

**Section I
Model Advanced
Placement
Examination**

In this section you will find answers and answer explanations for the 80 multiple-choice questions of the model exam. The explanations of the multiple-choice questions indicate which answer is most correct and, in most cases, why the other choices should be eliminated. By reading all 80 statements, you will get a quick summary of the highlights of American history.

1. C	21. A	41. C	61. B
2. C	22. A	42. C	62. B
3. B	23. E	43. B	63. E
4. C	24. C	44. A	64. D
5. E	25. D	45. D	65. A
6. C	26. D	46. A	66. E
7. D	27. D	47. B	67. E
8. C	28. B	48. D	68. D
9. D	29. D	49. E	69. C
10. C	30. A	50. A	70. D
11. D	31. A	51. B	71. A
12. E	32. C	52. D	72. C
13. A	33. C	53. B	73. D
14. A	34. B	54. E	74. A
15. D	35. B	55. C	75. C
16. E	36. C	56. A	76. D
17. C	37. B	57. B	77. B
18. A	38. C	58. E	78. B
19. B	39. D	59. E	79. E
20. B	40. E	60. C	80. A

**Comments on
Multiple-Choice
Answers**

1. (C)   The first question requires you to define a common historic term. *Jim Crow* was a name given to the freed slave, just as John Doe has been used for whites. *Jim Crowism* refers to the legislation designed to deny equality to African Americans. Such legislation was widespread and included a great variety of laws. The laws requiring separate but equal school and railroad facilities and laws denying the vote to a person unless his grandfather had voted are examples of Jim Crowism. The U.S. Congress did not pass Jim Crow laws, but many states did. The Congress has passed laws involving the four other choices.

2. (C)   The Federal Securities Act was part of the New Deal program. The others all came earlier. The Clayton Act and the Federal Trade Commission Act were part of Wilson's New Freedom. The Pure Food and Drug Act was passed in 1906, inspired by the Muckrakers, and the Sherman Antitrust Act was passed in 1890.

3. (B)   Detroit was a key frontier post that the British refused to evacuate after 1783 in spite of the terms of the Treaty of Paris in that year. It was later evacuated according to the terms of Jay's Treaty.

4. (C)   All the choices are true, but the most significant difference between Puritans and Pilgrims lies in their relationship to the Church of England. The Pilgrims wished to separate from the church and start their own congregational form of worship. The Puritans initially were interested in purifying or reforming the Church of England.

5. (E)   The Independent Treasury Plan was Van Buren's answer to the concept of a Bank of the United States or the use of state banks by the federal government. It called for depositing federal revenue directly in the U.S. Treasury, thus ignoring banks.

6. (C)   Thaddeus Stevens was the leader of the Radical Reconstructionists in the House. He played a key role in the impeachment of Andrew Jackson and in the development of congressional reconstruction plans.

7. (D)   The Quebec Act (1774) established the framework for the government of Canada, which the British acquired by the Treaty of Paris in 1763.

8. (C)   The Whiskey Rebellion of 1794 was a protest by Pennsylvania farmers over a tax on whiskey by the federal government.

9. (D)   Roger Williams was the founder of a colony on Narragansett Bay, which joined several other colonies as the federated Colony of Rhode Island and the Providence Plantations. Connecticut was settled under the leadership of Thomas Hooker. The other men were leaders of the named colonies.

10. (C)   A number of scandals are connected with the Grant administration. The Credit Mobilier involving railroad construction and the Whiskey Ring involving the theft of some of the whiskey tax revenue from the Treasury were major scandals in Grant's administration. Teapot Dome is a scandal connected with President Harding's administration, the Tweed Gang corruptly ran New York City and was not part of the Grant administration, Whitewater was a major scandal under Clinton, and the Watergate Scandal ended Nixon's presidency.

11. (D)   President Johnson's Great Society involved many different programs including Operation Headstart, the Voting Rights Act, Medicare, and the establishment of the Department of Housing and Welfare. Although the president wanted some revisions in the Taft-Hartley Labor Act, Congress never voted for them and the act, passed over Truman's opposition in 1947, remained in force.

12. (E)   The question is based on a pie graph in which a circle is divided into pie slices, each of which represents a percentage of the whole pie. In this chart each slice represents the number of men from the nation named killed in World War I. It provides a quick comparison of the numbers killed. It should be immediately clear from comparing the sizes of the slices that the losses of Russia were greater than those of any other nation, with the United States' losses the smallest. You are not given the actual number killed, only a comparative percentage of the total killed. To compare the percentages in each slice use a ruler, piece of paper, or pencil to measure the distance between the places where the sides of each slice meet the rim of the pie. This segment provides the basis of measurement of the size of each slice. When you do this measurement and then compare the size of the pieces, you will see that the correct answer is E—losses were "approximately equal for Russia and Germany." In fact, the official count of war dead for Russia was 1.7 million and for Germany it was 1.6 million, whereas the United States lost 49,000.

13. (A) John Marshall, a Federalist, believed in strengthening the power of the federal government and of the Supreme Court within the government. The famous case of *Marbury v. Madison* established the right of judicial review of congressional legislation by the Supreme Court. Judicial review is not stated in the Constitution. It can be implied only from other stated powers and ideas included in the document. This use of implied powers allows for a loose construction or interpretation of the Constitution.

14. (A) The answer to question 14 is Samoa. It was not acquired as a result of U.S. involvement in the Spanish-American War; negotiations with Germany led to our acquisition of Samoa. We acquired Puerto Rico, Guam, and the Philippines in the peace treaty, and we annexed Hawaii to provide a fueling station for our ships supplying our troops and fleet in the Philippines. The annexation had been rejected earlier, but when we became involved in the war, the situation changed and we annexed the islands.

15. (D) *Flapper* was a term used in the 1920s to describe the ideal young woman of the period. The other terms are all from the 1960s and have political connotations. *Pig* was used to refer to police; *hippie* was used to describe those young people in the 1960s who first adopted long hair and unisex clothing and who rejected many of the materialistic values of U.S. society; a *dove*, as opposed to a *hawk*, was against U.S. involvement in Vietnam; *black power* was the slogan of some civil rights activists.

16. (E) These instructions were given to Lt. Col. Baum by General Burgoyne before the Battle of Saratoga. Lt. Col. Baum was captured at the Battle of Bennington and these orders were found and were published in Portsmouth, New Hampshire, in the *New Hampshire Gazette* of August 30, 1777. During the American Revolution the Continental Congress ran the war for the colonies. References to the enemy and the order to take prisoners confirm the orders are for movement into enemy territory. It is assumed in the orders that taking hostages will assure the delivery of confiscated goods. Although it is clear that one purpose of the expedition is to acquire horses, oxen, carriages, and wagons for transportation, there is no order to either take or burn everything, which is the meaning of a "scorched earth" policy, as used by Napoleon and General Sherman in his Civil War march through Georgia.

17. (C) The "gag rule" was passed by the House to eliminate the congressional debate of antislavery proposals, which Southerners feared would lead to federal acts against the interests of the South. Garrison's *Liberator* and Nat Turner's revolt helped provoke this fear, but the "gag rule" was not passed to prevent them.

18. (A)   The Act of Toleration was first passed in Maryland in 1649, granting religious toleration in that colony. It was soon repealed. The other acts were all passed by Parliament with the purpose of controlling trade and manufacture in the colonies.

19. (B)   Theodore Roosevelt called those "reformers who used their pens to draw attention to the evils afflicting America" "Muckrakers" after a character in John Bunyan's *Pilgrim's Progress*. The character spent so much time raking manure that he lost sight of heaven and better things. Roosevelt thought these reformers were too harsh and narrow-minded, although he supported in Congress and in the nation many of the causes these reformers supported. The other choices for question 19 have no significance for the question.

20. (B)   The so-called Warren Court is noted for its concern for the rights of all individuals. Many right-wing groups strongly opposed some of the decisions and called for the impeachment of the chief justice, but the Court continued to support the rights of individuals in criminal cases, such as the *Escobedo, Gideon,* and *Miranda* cases, and desegregation cases, such as *Brown v. Board of Education.*

21. (A)   The cartoon is from *Harper's Weekly* of December 13, 1862. John Bull represents Great Britain and is shown in front of his little shop, John Bull Variety. His customer is Mr. Confederate, who represents the Confederate states. John Bull has received money in the money bag marked CAS—Confederation of American States. Mr. Confederate is loaded up with guns, pistols, swords, and, most important, a boat representative of the *Alabama*, which was a privateer built in Great Britain and operated by the Confederacy. It did a great deal of damage to Northern shipping. The point of the cartoon is to illustrate how the British industrialists supplied arms and ships for the Confederacy. The case of the *Alabama* almost led to war between Great Britain and the Northern states. The claims against the *Alabama* were finally negotiated in 1871–1872. The cartoon required you to both interpret its parts and place them in the mainstream of American history.

22. (A)   The so-called Tariff of Abominations of 1828 set off the entire tariff, state power/federal power, nullification controversy of Jackson's administration. The other four choices all represent key aspects of this controversy.

23. (E)   The authors listed in the question are all famous writers of the period 1916–1945. Each title mentioned was written in those years, but *The Great Gatsby* was written by F. Scott Fitzgerald, not by Langston Hughes, who was noted for his poetry. Eugene O'Neill is a playwright; the others mentioned are novelists. These works all provide important insights into the attitudes of people during these years and should be read by students of United States history.

24. (C)   The Federalists of New England were opposed to the War of 1812, and when it looked as though the United States would be badly defeated, they called a secret meeting at Hartford to discuss what might be done, including the possibility of secession from the union. The Convention is considered the death knell of the Federalist Party. It never again held national political power.

25. (D) The Camp David Accords, which led to the peace treaty between Egypt and Israel, were negotiated by President Carter, using his personal persuasion. President Nixon withdrew U.S. troops from Vietnam. OPEC is still in existence as this book is being written and shows no signs of breaking up. The overthrow of the Shah of Iran is not considered an achievement of the United States, and we held the Panama Canal by treaty arrangement.

26. (D)   The Dawes Act of 1887 reversed previous policy toward Native Americans. Previously, tribes had been treated as independent nations and were placed on reservations. The Dawes Act eliminated tribal ownership of property and provided land for each head of family. It was designed to turn the natives into farmers and *eventually* into citizens. The act did nothing about guns or alcohol, but it did attempt to protect the Native Americans' claim to their 160 acres and to prepare them for citizenship. It was an attempt to deal fairly with Native Americans, but unfortunately, it was designed to turn them into whites and showed no understanding of their culture.

27. (D) Local financing and control of public education has been an important American attitude toward education since the Massachusetts Bay Colony passed this, the "Olde Deluder Satan" law.

28. (B) Question 28 focuses on the issue of the "old" and "new" immigration. The "old" immigrants formed the majority of immigrants to the United States until 1890. They came from western and northern Europe—Ireland, England, and Germany. The "new" immigrants became the majority of immigrants after 1890 and came from eastern and southern Europe—Italy, Austria-Hungary, and Russia.

29. (D) The growth of railroads had a great impact on the nation. The railroads cannot be considered a part of social democracy. The other four advanced the democratization of society and represent the great variety of reform movements begun in the 1820s and 1830s, which are considered a part of Jacksonian Democracy.

30. (A) Frances Perkins was the first woman appointed to a cabinet post by an American president. She served as Franklin D. Roosevelt's Secretary of Labor. Sandra Day O'Connor was the first woman to serve on the U.S. Supreme Court and was appointed by President Reagan. Eleanor Roosevelt, wife of the president, was active politically and served in the United States delegation to the United Nations after her husband's death. Marian Anderson is a noted African American singer who was denied the right to sing in the hall of the Daughters of the American Revolution in Washington. President and Mrs. Roosevelt were angered by this, so Mrs. Roosevelt resigned from the DAR. Oveta Culp Hobby headed the woman's branch of the Navy during World War II.

31. (A) The question asks about the decline of the first major post-Civil War labor union, the Nation Labor Union, begun in 1866. It was successful during the postwar boom years but collapsed when depression hit the country in the early 1870s. It set a recurring cycle for unions—success in prosperity but trouble during recession.

32. (C)   *The Legend of Sleepy Hollow* published in 1820 established Washington Irving as the best-known author in the new nation. *The Legend of Sleepy Hollow* was one of the stories included in Irving's *Sketch Book*. Benjamin Franklin's widely acclaimed *Poor Richard's Almanac* was printed before the Revolution, as was Thomas Paine's *Common Sense*, which stirred up sentiment in favor of independence. Nathaniel Hawthorne's *The Scarlet Letter* (1850) and Ralph Waldo Emerson's *An American Scholar* (1837) were important works of the second generation of U.S. writers. This question clearly indicates the importance of knowing both dates and cultural events.

33. (C)   The Albany Plan was drafted by Benjamin Franklin in 1754 in an attempt to get the colonies to unite for their common defense. It was not adopted, but many features foreshadowed the Articles of Confederation and the Constitution.

34. (B)   When legislators exchange support for each other's special bills, it is called logrolling. These terms are defined in the Glossary.

35. (B)   During his first year in office President Reagan successfully pressured Congress into passing a massive income tax cut—a key point of Reaganomics. It was part of his administration's attack on the high inflation rate. Reagan wanted to eliminate the Department of Energy, supported aid to Taiwan, wanted to reduce the minimum wage for teenagers but not for all workers, and wanted to block the activities of terrorists.

36. (C)   The question is from a message of President Coolidge to Congress, January 10, 1927, in which he sets forth the justification for sending U.S. Marines to Nicaragua at that time. It was a move typical of Dollar Diplomacy and of the attitude of the United States toward Latin America during much of our history.

37. (B)   Thomas Paine's pamphlet *Common Sense* is considered an excellent propaganda piece. The arguments he used in presenting his case for independence are not very logical, but they persuaded many colonists to support the rebellion.

38. (C)   The Berlin Blockade by the Russians in 1948 was met by a successful airlift of supplies to the beleaguered city. This Soviet action seemed to confirm a threat to the West and to world peace by the Communist nations. As a result, the United States joined a newly formed alliance of Britain, France, and the Benelux nations. This alliance became NATO, our first peacetime alliance since George Washington in his Farewell Address warned the nation against entangling alliances. NATO marks a major shift in U.S. foreign policy. The other items were all Cold War events that helped to confirm the need for the NATO alliance.

39. (D) In question 39 individuals who were important in other than political or economic areas are paired with items for which they are famous. Joseph Pulitzer helped to revolutionize the newspaper business as editor of the *New York World*; Louis H. Sullivan was a famous architect who designed the first skyscrapers; Thomas Edison invented the phonograph; Buffalo Bill Cody was a star of typically American Wild West shows. Bret Harte, although a famous author writing about the West, did not write *The Adventures of Huckleberry Finn*, which was written by Mark Twain.

40. (E) *Pro-choice* refers to those who support the right of a woman to choose an abortion. It is considered a liberal position. *Pro-life,* which refers to the right of the unborn fetus to live, is considered a conservative position. The other four selections all reflect conservative attitudes. The "silent majority" was President Nixon's term for those Conservatives who supported him and who were not actively involved in the agitation and turmoil of the 1960s. Barry Goldwater, a conservative Republican from Arizona, was nominated for president in 1964 and was overwhelmingly defeated, but his campaign paved the way for Nixon's victory in 1968. The 1994 Contract with America, orchestrated by House Speaker Newt Gingrich, rallied Conservatives to vote, giving Republicans control of both houses of Congress for the first time in 40 years. The "Religious Right" is synonymous with conservatism in the 1980s and 1990s.

41. (C) Question 41 summarizes the view of American isolationists. It is the opposite of what internationalists believe. Socialists also support cooperation between nations. It is impossible to group immigrants and clergy together to hold any one view.

42. (C) The Stamp Act (1765) was the first of these five acts enacted.

43. (B) As a result of the invention of barbed wire, cattle raisers could fence large enough areas of the semiarid lands of the West to make raising cattle easier. Ranges could be established with set boundaries. The reaper had no relation to cattle raising. Cattle drives to the railheads (shipping points) and the railroads were involved in cattle raising, but were not a cause of the great increase. The Homestead Act allowed for homesteads in the West, but the acreage allotment was too small for cattle raising in the semiarid areas.

44. (A) The clause from the Constitution is often referred to as the elastic clause. It has been interpreted to give extensive powers to the federal government covering all things "necessary and proper" (for example, helpful in carrying out all the other powers given to Congress).

45. (D) The Compromise of 1850 was Henry Clay's (the Great Compromiser) last contribution to national unity. It temporarily resolved the free state/slave state controversy, giving both the North and South certain points they desired. Although slavery had reappeared as a divisive issue as a result of the Texas controversy and the Mexican War, the compromise did not deal with any issue involving Texas.

46. (A)   President Gorbachev of the Soviet Union introduced his reform policies of *perestroika* and *glasnost* soon after his rise to power in 1985. Many believe these policies led to the fall of the Berlin Wall and the end of the Cold War. Soon after, the Soviet Union broke up into separate nations. Yugoslavia also broke into separate nations and warfare between them erupted. As a result of the end of the Cold War, the still united Soviet Union cooperated with President Bush in the Persian Gulf War. The sending of U.S. troops to Somalia under the United Nations was an attempt by President Bush to respond to past Cold War issues and to establish a "new world order."

47. (B)   In 1823 President Monroe warned the European powers not to interfere in South America. This, along with three other points: the Americas were not open for colonization; the American political system was different from that of Europe; the United States would not interfere in Europe or with existing European colonies, became known as the Monroe Doctrine. The other choices reflect different aspects of U.S. relations with South America.

48. (D)   The Allied naval victory at Midway reversed the string of victories by Japan that had challenged democracy in the Pacific. The other choices were antidemocratic and part of the war or steps leading to war.

49. (E)   The Great Depression's greatest threat to capitalism was the loss of jobs and industry's inability to supply jobs for the unemployed. The movement of business headquarters overseas, the flood of Communist Chinese products, and balance of trade favoring Asia all came in the late 20th century. A very small number of unemployed did sell apples during the depression and found a market.

50. (A)   The social structure of the American colonies was religiously intolerant, treated African Americans and women unequally, did not allow talent to rise easily, and, although it did not have a nobility like England, certainly did not support the concept that "all men are created equal."

51. (B)   The depletion of resources and manpower during World War I led to conditions that encouraged the rise of fascism and communism. The Marshall Plan and close U.S.–Europe cooperation came after World War II. The League never oversaw resource distribution, and no new colonies were established in Africa after World War I.

52. (D)   Upton Sinclair's *The Jungle* was an example of muckraking literature. It exposed corruption in the meat-packing industry that precipitated federal legislation.

53. (B)   Alexander Hamilton's financial measures benefited the merchants.

54. (E)   The easiest means of traveling from the East to California at the time of the 1849 gold rush were sailing ships. There were no cross-country railroads, planes had not been invented, horseback and stagecoaches were tiring, and overland travel was subject to many difficulties.

55. (C)   Puerto Rico was ceded to the United States at the end of the Spanish-American War by the terms of the Treaty of Paris in 1898.

56. (A)   The Missouri Compromise in 1820 maintained the balance between free and slave states.

57. (B)   The World Trade Organization (WTO) was established to negotiate and enforce fair trade practices between the members of WTO.

58. (E)   In colonial America women did not have the same legal rights as men. The other four choices are true.

59. (E)   Delegates to the Constitutional Convention agreed that Congress would have the power to declare war and raise an army. Compromises had to be reached on the issue of the election of the president, taxation of commerce, whether slaves would be counted in determining a state's population, and the method of representation in the Senate and House. The Constitution was created by a series of compromises.

60. (C)   In the twenty years after World War II, television dramatically changed social patterns. Motion pictures and automobiles changed social patterns before World War II. Cell phones and microwave ovens have had an effect in the same time period as computers but they have had a lesser influence than the other choices.

61. (B)   The United Nations was modeled on the League of Nations.

62. (B)   The Compromise of 1877 settled the disputed election of 1876, and the terms included the withdrawal of Northern troops from the South. This ended Reconstruction.

63. (E)   The first four answers, new economic structures such as trusts, increased immigration, abundant resources, and expanding railroads all benefited the industrial revolution in the post-Civil War United States. The Interstate Commerce Commission (ICC) was meant to regulate industry for the benefit of the public, not industry.

64. (D)   *Brown v. Board of Education of Topeka* reversed the "separate but equal" doctrine established by the Court in *Plessy v. Ferguson* and called for the end of segregation in schools. The Brown decision was a milestone in the Civil Rights Movement. The other choices are all landmark decisions of the Court.

65. (A)   Rachel Carson wrote *Silent Spring* and brought environmental issues to the attention of millions. Ralph Nader has focused public attention on many questionable business and societal practices. John Muir was a naturalist and encouraged Theodore Roosevelt's interest in conservation. Tom Wolfe (*Bonfire of the Vanities*) and Jack Kerouac (*On the Road*) are post-World War II authors.

66. (E) All five answers relate to the Civil Rights Movement of which Martin Luther King, Jr. became the most powerful spokesman. He first emerged as a leader during the Montgomery Bus Boycott.

67. (E) President Theodore Roosevelt was a leader of the Progressive Movement in the early years of the 20th century.

68. (D) As part of his progressive program, President Woodrow Wilson introduced and Congress established the Federal Reserve System that still oversees the U.S. banking system. The other choices relate to banking issues at different time periods.

69. (C) Jefferson was more sympathetic to France than to England during the French Revolution and Napoleonic Wars. The other nations did not exist at that time.

70. (D) The increasing globalization of the world economy was an important trend during the 1990s, the decade after the end of the Cold War. The United States and Russia cooperated on many issues during the decade, including building an international space station. Yugoslavia, in southeastern Europe, was torn apart by strong nationalistic sentiments. The economy of China flourished in the decade.

71. (A) John F. Kennedy committed the United States to placing a man on the moon before the end of the 1960s. The other four items are the opposite of what Kennedy supported.

72. (C) By 1763 the thirteen colonies were all either royal colonies controlled by the King or proprietary colonies controlled by descendants of individuals to whom the colony was granted by the King. Colonies had rudimentary forms of self-government, but final authority rested with the King or the proprietor.

73. (D) President Clinton was impeached on charges of obstructing justice and misleading testimony. The other choices include key words—Independent Counsel, health care reform, Whitewater, and Oval Office—but the information included about them is incorrect.

74. (A) The lack of a cross-continental railroad hindered westward expansion before the Civil War.

75. (C) The founding of Israel would not be considered part of the Cold War. However, after the establishment of the nation in 1948, the Soviet Union and the United States often disagreed on policy affecting Israel and the Middle East. The alternative choices all are considered major events in the Cold War confrontation.

76. (D) The Boston Tea Party was an important event in the series of events that led to the start of the American Revolution. The other events listed all occurred after the Revolution.

77. (B) The proposed Equal Rights Amendment to the Constitution was not approved by enough states to add it to the Constitution. Many considered this a setback for women's rights. Title IX opened up athletic opportunities for women. The Family and Medical Leave Act (signed by Clinton) allowed workers to take time off from work without being fired, allowing women, and men, to meet family and medical needs. NOW supported the Women's Liberation Movement and created greater awareness of the concerns of women, and this led to greater opportunities.

78. (B) The multi-millionaire founder of Carnegie Steel, Andrew Carnegie, set forth this view of philanthropy in his address, The Gospel of Wealth. Many 19th- and 20th-century business leaders followed this idea and gave millions to support worthy causes, from libraries to universities. The alternative answers all express important ideas. The authors were contemporaries of Carnegie. Bryan's Cross of Gold oration condemned the gold standard and won him the Democratic Party nomination for president. Alger wrote many popular stories for young people on the "rags to riches" theme. Rauschenbusch and others interpreted the Christian Gospel in terms of working actively to change and make better social conditions for the poor. Sumner applied Darwinism to the economic sphere, supporting laissez-faire and claiming that the best businessmen would naturally survive in the struggle for success if no laws restricted them.

79. (E) In the 1920s speculation was widespread among investors. The other options provide incorrect interpretations of the 1920s and in each case the opposite is true.

80. (A) The Kansas-Nebraska Act rejected the 36° 30′ line of the Missouri Compromise and introduced the concept of popular sovereignty to determine whether Kansas would be a free or slave state. The Compromise of 1850 included a strict fugitive slave law. The balance of slave and free states could be broken, depending on the vote taken under popular sovereignty. The Dred Scott case came three years after the Kansas-Nebraska Act.

Section II

Following are comments on the five free response questions from the Advanced Placement Examination Model B. There is analysis of each question, and for the DBQ, an analysis of each document.

The Free-Response Questions

Analysis of the DBQ Documents

When the consultants meet to analyze the DBQ, they develop statements for each document that summarize points and set the context in which the document was produced. These are referred to as the examinations and are judged and ranked. As a study technique such an approach is valuable. Whenever you read documents, and especially as you prepare your answer during the 15-minute reading time on the exam, you should take note of the key points in each document.

Document A—U.S. Constitution Article I, Section 8, and Article I, Section 9, 1787

In Section 8, the important "commerce clause" gives Congress the power to regulate commerce both internally and externally. Note the inclusion of the "Indian tribes." Section 9 refers to the slave trade—the words may hide that from the unskilled reader. Immigrants migrated to the United States of their own free will. Some made arrangements to travel as indentured servants and were imported under these agreements. Slaves were imported against their will. The clause guaranteed the federal government would not interfere with the slave trade for twenty years. This compromise allowed the slave owners to accept the Constitution.

Points to note:

The Constitution gives Congress power to regulate commerce.

Slave trade (importation of peoples) cannot be controlled by the Congress until 1808.

Control of commerce was a concern in 1787 at the Constitutional Convention.

Document B—Act Imposing Duties on the Tonnage of Ships or Vessels, 1790

The Congress quickly moved to exercise its power to control commerce by establishing duties on shipping. These duties would be an important source of revenue for the new government.

Points to note:

Within months of the establishment of the new government Congress exercises its power to regulate commerce.

Foreign vessels pay higher duties (50 cents per ton) than U.S.-owned vessels (6 cents per ton)—a potential for conflict.

Foreign powers are encouraged to have ships built in the United States, because duties are less than for foreign built ships.

Document C—Proclamation of Neutrality, 1793

As the French Revolution became more violent in the years after its start in 1789, European powers joined to restore the royal family in France. The United States had a treaty with France, which had helped us win independence. However, Washington decided to declare neutrality and remain out of the conflict. His argument was that our treaty had been signed with the King's government and not the new revolutionary government.

Points to note:

The United States will not take sides in the conflict between France and the listed powers, especially, Great Britain.

Citizens are warned to avoid acts that go against neutrality.

By implication, this will affect U.S. commerce with all the listed powers as they battle for victory.

Document D—From the Letters of Thomas Jefferson, 1793–1801

These three letters from before and during Jefferson's presidency provide insights into Jefferson's thinking on foreign policy. The 1797 letter mentions commerce as a better tool than war to achieve justice from other nations. The other two focus on legitimate government. The "will of the people" is the guide to legitimate government, and the latter letter says its protection should be our "first object." In the first letter Jefferson indicates there is no one type of government a nation must follow but the "will of the nation" must choose it. How does one find the will of the nation? Does Jefferson base his foreign policy on commerce or on supporting the "will of the people"? With what foreign policy events was he involved?

Points to note:

Protection of the free expression of "the will of the people (nation?)" should be the first object of the U.S. government.

There is no one perfect form of government for all people.

Control of commerce is a better instrument than war for achieving justice.

Document E—Jay's Treaty, 1795

Jay's Treaty is mentioned in all textbooks. It affirmed peace with Great Britain and dealt with issues left over from the Treaty of Paris of 1783 that ended the Revolution. What was driving the need for this treaty?

Points to note:

The treaty mentions "commerce and navigation" twice in the opening paragraph.

Withdrawal of troops and garrisons is the topic of the second article, not commerce.

Peace and friendship is emphasized between Great Britain and the United States at a time Great Britain is engaged in a war in Europe against France and the United States is neutral.

Document F—Treaty of Friendship, Limits, and Navigation, 1795

This treaty also affirms peace and friendship between the United States and a European power (Spain). In the two articles presented is the topic commerce or other issues? Why are the subjects of these two articles important for the United States? Is the United States concerned about territory or commerce or both? What was behind the need for this treaty?

Points to note:

Peace is affirmed between Spain and the United States at a time Spain is engaged in a war in Europe against France and the United States is neutral.

The southern boundary of the United States is drawn setting the line between Spanish Florida and the United States.

The western boundary of the United States is set at the middle of the channel of navigation on the Mississippi River, giving the United States the right to use the navigation channel for commerce.

Document G—Treaty of Greenville, 1795

Again this treaty is mentioned in textbooks. It ended more than twenty years of fighting in what became the Northwest Territory and ceded lands in the south-western corner of the territory to the United States. Although relations with the Native Americans are often considered as part of domestic history, the Indian Nations were free and independent, and a treaty with them should have been considered the same as a treaty with a European power. What was driving the United States to sign this treaty—land or commerce?

Points to note:

Peace with the Indian tribes is to be perpetual, and "friendly intercourse" (commerce) is to take place.

Prisoners (captives) are to be exchanged.

Land has been ceded to the United States, and if more land is to be sold, it can be sold only to the United States.

Document H—Washington's Farewell Address, 1796

This is another document that is widely mentioned in textbooks. Often some passages are quoted, so you may have seen some of these statements. What are Washington's views on foreign policy as seen in these sections? Would he have been driven by commerce in designing his foreign policy? What other factors were of concern to him?

Points to note:

Antipathy and animosity to a particular nation by a country creates an atmosphere that leads to conflicts and fighting that is often against the best interests of that country.

Too much fondness for a nation by a country can produce many evils and lead to involvement in the affairs of that nation that are often not in the best interest of the country or people.

We should have commercial relations with other nations but limited political connections.

Commercial connections should show no favoritism and should be temporary.

Document I—John Adams—Special Message to the Senate and the House, 1797

This message involves the XYZ Affair, in which the French government refused to meet with U.S. delegates sent to Paris to negotiate and resolve several disagreements particularly involving trade. The French demanded payment of bribes before negotiations could start. Adams found this insulting. The United States refused to pay a bribe. In this message Adams does not even mention the issues that originally divided the two nations but focuses on the humiliation of the delegates and the insult to the United States. What is driving Adams's policy statement? The Alien and Sedition Acts were passed soon after this incident.

Points to note:

The French government has insulted the United States and not treated her as a sovereign nation.

The French are trying to separate the people of the United States from their government, sowing the seeds of discontent, and this is more dangerous than the insult.

The United States must show the world that we will not be insulted or treated as a colonial power.

Document J—Convention Between the French Republic and the United States, 1801

This convention negotiated under Jefferson's presidency ended for the moment the tension between France and the United States. After the XYZ Affair, Congress authorized the president to use the Navy to seize French shipping and it appeared we might go to war.

Points to note:

Peace and friendship are agreed upon.

Commerce shall be free, ending the seizure of ships under a 1798 act of Congress.

Document K—Jefferson's Third Message to Congress, 1803

At this time period the president sent an annual message to Congress indicating the state of the union. Today these messages on the state of the union are delivered as a speech before Congress. This passage is from Jefferson's third such message. He reflects on the importance of the right of deposit to the nation. He also announces the possible transfer of the Louisiana Territory to the United States. Is this right of deposit and the transfer of the territory more about commerce, land, or power?

Points to note:

Denial of the right to deposit goods in transit at New Orleans without paying duties was a major issue in the West, which relied on the Mississippi for transportation of goods to overseas markets.

The French government is willing to transfer the Louisiana territory to the United States.

Both nations are promising to promote peace and friendship.

Document L—James Madison First Inaugural, 1809

In his first inaugural Madison reflects on the foreign policy of the United States. Since 1793 there had been almost continual warfare between France and the European nations. Washington had declared neutrality in 1793, and Madison is praising how the United States handled relations during those difficult years. Has "peace" driven U.S. policy during that time?

Points to note:

The United States has pursued neutrality impartially.

The policy of the United States has been to cultivate peace and observe justice and equality between combatants.

The future will prove this to be the case even if it is not believed now.

Document M—*The Sun, Gazette and County Advertiser,* Dover, N.H.—Saturday, December 12, 1807

This newspaper selection recounts the attack on the U.S. frigate *Chesapeake* by the British ship *Leopard* within the territorial limits of the United States. It was one incident in the growing tensions between the United States and Great Britain over rights of neutrals in wartime. As the Napoleonic Wars dragged on, the British tightened their attempts to control international trade. One maritime issue of concern since independence was the British seizure of seamen off U.S. ships. The British claimed that many sailors had deserted the English navy and that they were simply taking them back, but the United States disagreed. This was another concern driving U.S. foreign policy.

Points to note:

The press perceives the attack on the *Chesapeake* as aggression within the territorial waters of the United States.

The British are accused of having no respect for our laws and have not left our coast in spite of presidential orders.

U.S. seamen have been seized ("impressed") by the British.

The British fleet is alarming the coastal inhabitants by firing on shipping.

Document N—Amendments to the Constitution Proposed by the Hartford Convention, 1814

New Englanders strongly opposed to the War of 1812 met in Hartford and proposed amendments to the Constitution. These reflect the importance of trade to New England and the anger of New Englanders at the foreign policy pursued by the federal government from the time of Jefferson on, when the government tried various methods of controlling trade to avoid war.

Points to note:

Amendment Three would deny Congress the use of embargos, thus limiting Congress's control of commerce.

Amendment Four also limits Congress's power over commerce by requiring two-thirds approval for any stopping of commerce between the United States and another nation.

Both embargos and interdictions needing only a majority vote of Congress had been used by the federal government in the period 1797–1812.

Comments on the Free-Response Questions

The DBQ

The DBQ question is another *To what extent . . . ,* a popular type for the DBQ. The topic focuses on U.S. foreign policy in the first twenty-six years of the nation. During twenty-two of those years the European powers were involved in war—The French Revolution and Napoleonic Wars—and the United States attempted to maintain neutrality until war was declared on Great Britain in

1812. You are asked to determine whether commerce (trade and exchange of goods) was the issue that determined or drove U.S. foreign policy in those years. Commerce certainly was important, and many of the documents mention commerce whether the document be the U.S. Constitution (Document A), an act imposing duties on shipping (Document B), a treaty (Document E), or an attempt to amend the Constitution (Document N). Recalling the "mainstream of U.S. history" in these years there are many times that commercial activity—whether a proclamation of neutrality or an embargo—was the focus of debate in the government. However, other issues are also referred to in the documents.

Land is mentioned as a concern or the focus of several documents. The Treaty of Greenville (Document G), the Treaty of Friendship (Document F), and Jefferson's Third Message to Congress (Document K) indicate the concern of the new nation for its borders and control of land. What would have happened if the United States had not acquired the Louisiana Territory? The honor of the nation is another issue raised by the documents. The Farewell Address (Document H), Adams's Special Message to Congress (Document I), Madison's First Inaugural (Document L), and the news story (Document M) all suggest that honor and/or the integrity of the nation are of key importance. Jefferson in his letters (Document D), although mentioning managing commerce as an alternative to war, is concerned about the legitimacy of foreign governments and that they express the will of the people or the nation—what we today would call democracy. Did this idea that the newly free United States should be a beacon of freedom for the world affect U.S. foreign policy in the years 1789 to 1815?

As stated many times, there is no one answer for free response questions. Your answer will depend on the emphasis you place on these different documents and what aspects of the history of the era you wish to emphasize. If you were a New Englander depending on trade for your living, you would no doubt see trade and commerce as crucial in foreign policy and you'd emphasize Washington's neutrality, Adams's negotiations with France, the tensions with England over impressment, and finally, the Hartford Convention's proposal to limit Congress's control of commerce as key elements in U.S. foreign policy. However, if you were a frontiersman in Ohio, the treaty with the Indians giving land, the purchase of Louisiana, and the right of deposit would be key factors for you. What is your interpretation of the period?

This question introduces many documents that are mentioned in most textbooks. This is somewhat unusual but brings to the forefront the mainstream of U.S. history and forces you as the writer to fill in the background to these events. Events from that mainstream that relate to this question are neutrality; the Barbary Pirates; treaties with Indians, Great Britain, and Spain; settlement of boundaries with Great Britain and Spain; impressment; questions of national honor and the rightful place in the world of the newly independent and democratic states; the influence on the French of the American Revolution, Citizen Genet; the Alien and Sedition Acts, the XYZ Affair; financial stability of the new nation; tariffs; the embargo; and the War of 1812. All of these events connect to U.S. foreign policy. As you decide your thesis, you must pick information from these events to support it and to enhance the information you choose to use from the documents.

Comments on the Free-Response Essays

This is a straightforward *In what ways . . .* type of question, and these were discussed in Chapter 4 in Part Three. There is a clear time period. The Constitution was written in 1787. The Constitutional Convention debated the issue of slavery at length, and in Article I, Section 9 the Constitution prohibited any congressional interference with the slave trade until 1808. The document also counted a slave as three-fifths of a person in counting the population of states to determine representation in the Congress. These two points provide a starting place for a discussion of this question Lincoln was elected in 1860, and that set the stage for the Civil War. In between those dates what federal legislation or judicial decisions had an effect on the life of the African American? This requires factual recall. Among the legislation and decisions you should include are the following:

The Constitution (mentioned above)

The Abolishment of the Slave Trade in 1808

The Missouri Compromise of 1820 (keeping the balance between slave and free states and prohibiting "forever" slavery north of the line 36° 30′)

"Gag Rule," 1835

Compromise of 1850 (including the fugitive slave bill)

Kansas-Nebraska Act, 1854 (replacing the 36° 30′ line of the Missouri Compromise with the concept of "popular sovereignty")

Dred Scott Supreme Court Decision, 1857

In addition to the above, three items discussed in Congress are relevant to the question.

Tallmadge Amendment of 1819 (led to Missouri Compromise)

Wilmot Proviso of 1846 (forbidding slavery in any lands taken from Mexico in the Mexican War)

Ostend Manifesto (said the United States would be justified in taking Cuba from Spain, interpreted as a way to extend slavery)

The above are the items from the mainstream of U.S. history that should be included in your answer. What is clear is that none of these had a positive effect on the life of the African American. All related to slavery and its possible expansion westward. They reflect the great division in the nation over the future of slavery. During the time period, agitation in the North over the horrors of slavery gradually grew, but the federal government did not even consider abolishing slavery. A good to excellent answer would address this matter, and include information to illustrate that there was concern over slavery and slave conditions. Among the items you might refer to make this point are the following:

Concern over the slave trade

Cotton gin and resulting expansion of the growth of cotton and the westward movement of slavery

The Vesey Conspiracy and reaction to it in South Carolina in 1822

The growing split between Northern and Southern values and society, reflected in Virginia's vote against gradual abolishment of slavery in 1832 and the tariff crisis of 1832–1833

Nat Turner's Rebellion in 1831

Growth of abolitionist sentiment as seen in publication of William Lloyd Garrison's *The Liberator* and founding of the American Anti-Slavery Society, 1833

Publication of *Uncle Tom's Cabin,* 1852

"Bleeding Kansas" and John Brown's activities leading to the raid on Harper's Ferry

These events all illustrate the temper of the nation in the years 1787 to 1860. It would be difficult to include all of these in an answer written in 35 minutes, but the idea they illustrate should be mentioned to provide the context in which the federal government failed to act.

Comments on Question 3 of Section II—Part B

The question combines a compare and a *To what extent . . .* question. It is on a mainstream topic—the comparison of the presidencies of Jefferson and Jackson. Both elections have been referred to as revolutionary. In fact, Jefferson used the phrase to describe the replacement of the Federalist Party by his own Jeffersonians. Today some historians see Jefferson's election as less than revolutionary. Some interpret Jackson and his administration as more revolutionary. As the student, you will have investigated both men and should have several ideas to call upon as you decide on the revolutionary nature of these two presidencies.

Jefferson spoke in states' rights terms in the Kentucky Resolutions in opposition to the Federalists' actions in the 1790s, but he acted as a nationalist in buying Louisiana, sending out Lewis and Clark, and in maintaining the navy. He also continued the Federalists' policy of negotiating to avoid involvement in the European conflict. Thus, to what extent did he continue to act like a Federalist? Were his actions truly revolutionary?

Jackson's presidency is known as the time of Jacksonian Democracy—a term that should bring many items to mind. His battles over the Bank of the United States and the Tariff Controversy with South Carolina, his handling of the Cherokee Indians and the Trail of Tears, his use of the "spoils system," and his western, "frontier" roots all provide important material for judging the revolutionary nature of his administration. The social changes that were going on during his presidency—extension of voting rights to all white males, extension of free education and growth of libraries, the beginnings of the abolitionist movement—are often cited as examples of revolutionary changes in the nation, and they form the heart of the movement of Jacksonian Democracy.

Recalling this information, it should not be difficult to form a thesis for this question and to develop an answer. One approach, and the simplest, would be to discuss Jefferson and then Jackson and conclude with a judgment on the revolutionary nature of the two presidencies. Another approach would be to consider issues such as foreign policy, domestic policy, and nationalism in separate paragraphs, discuss the actions of both men in a paragraph, and conclude with a paragraph on the revolutionary nature of the presidencies.

Comments on Question 4 of Section II—Part C

This is the familiar type of question with a quote followed by the direction to *Assess the validity* of the quote. The quote requires that you know the proposals of the Populist Party in the 1890s and the New Deal in the 1930s to handle the economic conditions of the time. To answer the question, you should recall the Peoples (Populist) Party Platform of 1892 (see p. 337) that was adopted at the party convention in Omaha to address issues of restricted monetary supply and agrarian (farmer) discontent. If you do not recall the platform, but have an idea of the economic conditions of the 1890s and such matters as William Jennings Bryan's Cross of Gold speech in 1896, you still could answer the question.

You must also be familiar with the main acts of the New Deal. These are often grouped under relief, recovery, and reform (see p. 244). However, for this question you will want to focus on issues of monetary and banking reform and agricultural issues, both of which were addressed by the Populists and the New Deal. Whether there is a link and the former provided the "framework" for the latter is for you to decide and express in your thesis. You'll discover that several Populist proposals, such as the direct election of senators, were achieved before the New Deal. This is an interesting question and one that requires your analytical skills as a historian.

Comments on Question 5 of Section II—Part C

You are asked in the question to discuss three of five choices. It is important to pick three that you can recall specific information on, but also three that you can relate to the issue of the question—the "establishment of the United States as a leader in international affairs."

The first four choices are often referred to in a discussion of the emergence of the United States as a world leader. Which three you pick will determine your thesis that must be based on an evaluation of the item as a factor in the emergence of the United States. The Spanish-American War in 1898 is often mentioned as the time the United States became an international force, defeating Spain quickly and acquiring an overseas "empire." However, the United States had been active in the Pacific since the clipper-ship trade with China. After the Spanish-American War, the United States could not be ignored, and President Teddy Roosevelt used that position to negotiate the Treaty of Portsmouth, ending the Russo-Japanese War, to become involved in the Algeciras Conference in 1905 that defused an international crisis in Morocco, and to send the U.S. Navy around the world. He also began the building of the Panama Canal.

The opening of the Panama Canal meant the United States could act quickly in both the Atlantic and Pacific, moving its navy from ocean to ocean, thus exercising great power. The United States also benefited from increased and easier trade between both coasts and internationally. The fact that the canal was U.S. owned and built enhanced U.S. prestige. Do you think that is enough information to make the canal a factor in establishing U.S. leadership?

The defeat of the Treaty of Versailles by the U.S. Senate was a blow for internationalists. However, it did not mean the United States would not act on the international stage. Instead it freed the United States to act where it wished without complying with League mandates. The U.S.-led disarmament talks in Washington, negotiated under the Kellogg-Briand Peace Pact, readjusted the postwar reparations in the Dawes Plan, and acted as a leader in international affairs when it suited the nation. Many interpret the defeat of the treaty as a retreat from world leadership and a return to isolation. How do you see it, based on your knowledge and interpretation of the evidence?

The outbreak of World War II led the United States to reaffirm neutrality and isolation. The entire 1930s is seen by some as an abandonment of world leadership, as the United States might have been able to lead a coalition to defeat the Nazis as was done after the United States was attacked at Pearl Harbor. Thus the start of World War II was not "a factor in establishing the United States as a leader in international affairs." The opposing view would point to the position of the United States at the end of the war, when it was the dominant victor and led one side in the Cold War for fifty years. How you will argue will, as in every essay question, depend on your personal knowledge and interpretation of evidence.

For instance, the Vietnam War came in the midst of the Cold War when most people would see the United States as already a leader in international affairs. However, you might argue that the position of the United States in 2003 as the single world power is a result of Reagan's military buildup and the first Gulf War, both of which can be interpreted as reactions to the national mood created by the Vietnam War. Thus you could say the Vietnam War was a factor in creating the United States as the dominant world power. On the other hand, you can always argue the negative and indicate the Vietnam War was not a factor in establishing U.S. leadership.

This is an excellent question with which to end this preparation for the Advanced Placement Examination in United States History. It requires you to do what you must do on every free-response question on the exam: analyze the question, sort and evaluate your information, develop a thesis, and write a coherent essay. Remember this when you take the examination, and good luck.

PART FIVE

Section A

Chronological Summary of Major Events and Developments in United States History

Introduction for the Student

This summary of major events in United States history is arranged according to the time divisions of the chapters in the book.

Included in each section are the names of leaders of each era. Their importance is usually not identified. You should look up information about those you don't know. Certain events are described briefly while others are merely listed. Again you should look up those with which you are not familiar, and you can add other events that you feel are important.

This summary can serve as a quick review of United States history or as an introduction to its study. It illustrates the basic factual material from the mainstream of United States history one needs, but under no circumstances should it be considered a substitute for the skills developed when reading different authors with conflicting opinions of our past. You are urged to add dates, people, and events to this summary as you study. The margins of this section provide space to do this.

At the end of this chronological summary is a chronological listing of events. These two chronologies provide an important introduction to or review of your study.

Introduction for the Teacher

This summary can be used effectively by the classroom teacher. Since it parallels the chapters in Part III, assignments can be given to students to look up further information on people, places, or events mentioned. Reports could be oral or written or incorporated into essays. Projects for small groups within the class can be designed around information in this section. Questions such as "What further information should be included?" or "What information could be eliminated?" would lead to an excellent review of United States history and would involve the student in analyzing the significance of various events, a skill that will be tested on the examination. Students using this book outside of class could also profit from such an analysis conducted on their own.

CHAPTER 1—Colonial America Before 1763

REASONS FOR EXPLORATION
Search for a sea route to the Far East
Desire for glory and wealth
Quest for new lands
Adventure

FACTORS FAVORABLE TO SUCCESSFUL EXPLORATION
Invention of the astrolabe and compass
Invention of the printing press
Growth of national states in western Europe
Increase of monetary resources and the use of the joint stock company as an economic organization
The Renaissance and revival of intellectual curiosity
Invention of gunpowder

EXPLORERS AND FOUNDERS OF COLONIES

SPAIN

Columbus: First visit to America, given publicity	1492
Balboa: First Spaniard to see the Pacific Ocean from Central America	1513
Magellan: First recorded circumnavigation of the globe	1519–1522
Cortez: Conquered and claimed Mexico	1519
Pizarro: Conquered and claimed Peru	1531
De Soto: First European to explore the Mississippi River	1541

PORTUGAL

Da Gama: Reached India by sailing around Africa	1498
Vespucci: Explored the coast of South America. America is named after him.	1501

FRANCE

De Champlain: Founded Quebec, the Father of New France; discovered Lakes Champlain and Huron	1608
Father Marquette and Joliet: Explored upper Mississippi River	1673
La Salle: Explored the Mississippi River to its mouth	1682

ENGLAND

Cabot: Explored the Labrador coast	1497
Frobisher: Explored the Labrador coast	1576
Drake: First Englishman to circumnavigate the globe	1577–1580
Raleigh: Attempted to found a colony off the coast of North Carolina	1584
Smith: Founder and leader of Jamestown	1607
Bradford: Leader of Plymouth Colony	1620
Lord Baltimore: Founder of Maryland	1634
Penn: Founder of Pennsylvania	1681

HOLLAND

Minuit: Founder of New Amsterdam (later New York)	1626

REASONS FOR COLONIZATION OF THE NEW WORLD

Religious freedom   Farming land
Economic opportunity   Social change
Political freedom   Spreading Christianity
Empire building

TERRITORY CLAIMED BY EUROPEAN NATIONS IN THE NEW WORLD

Spain: All of South America except Brazil, plus Central America, Mexico, Florida, California

Portugal: Brazil

France: All of Canada except the Hudson Bay region, plus the Great Lakes region, the Mississippi Basin, the French West Indies

Holland: The Hudson River Valley in New York

England: The eastern coast from New England to Georgia, west to the Appalachian Mountains

ENGLAND ACHIEVES DOMINATION OF EASTERN HALF OF NORTH AMERICA

English navy defeated the Spanish Armada, gaining control of the seas	1588
English drove the Dutch out of New York	1664

England defeated France at Quebec in the French and Indian War,
gaining control of Canada and the lands east of the Mississippi River   1763

GEOGRAPHY AND ITS EFFECT ON SETTLEMENTS
The physical nature of the settled land usually determined the occupation and manner
of life of the period.

New England: Rocky soil and long winters prevented extensive farming; wheat, corn,
hay, and flax were the main agricultural products; colonists lumbered vast forests and
fished off the coast; because of excellent harbors and rivers they developed trade as their
chief source of income.

Middle Colonies: Level, fertile, rich land and good rainfall made for abundant farming;
wheat, oats, and barley were grown in such quantity that these states were called "bread
colonies."

Southern Colonies: Warm climate, long growing season, and fertile lands produced rich
crops of cotton, tobacco, rice, and indigo; a good river system provided easy transportation inland; the produce was shipped to England and brought plantation owners large
profits and manufactured goods in return.

Southwestern Colonies: Warm climate, dry; limited agriculture and settlement; horse
and Christianity introduced to pueblo-dwelling Native Americans, which changed their
lifestyle.

EARLY SETTLEMENTS IN FUTURE UNITED STATES AND CANADA
St. Augustine, Florida (Spain)   1565
Jamestown, Virginia (England)   1607
Quebec, Canada (France)   1608
Santa Fe, New Mexico (Spain)   1609
Plymouth, Massachusetts (England)   1620
New York, New York (Holland)   1626

SOME CONTRIBUTIONS OF MOTHER COUNTRIES TO NORTH AMERICA
England: Democratic forms of local government; tradition of hard-working, zealous individuals; English language; Protestant (Puritan) religion.

France: Language, culture, and religion (Roman Catholicism) of France introduced to
Canada and Louisiana and to many Native Americans west of Appalachians.

Spain: Schools, hospitals, and printing presses established by missionaries; Spanish language in Southwest; teaching of Christianity (Roman Catholicism) and handicrafts to
Native Americans.

EVENTS THAT FOSTERED THE DEMOCRATIC IDEAL
IN THE ENGLISH COLONIES
Formation of Virginia House of Burgesses: First representative assembly
in America; the beginning of representative government in America.   1619

Signing of the Mayflower Compact: First agreement for self-government;
bound the freemen to obey "just and equal laws."   1620

New England Town Meeting: Taught people to express themselves
openly and helped further self-government.   after 1629

Petition of Rights and Bill of Rights: Established certain rights of
English subjects in relation to the Royal Power in England. The
colonists later claimed these rights also.   1628, 1689

Colonial Government: The governor of each colony, whether a royal or
charter colony, had to consult advisors before taking action.

Control of Purse: The settlers of most colonies voted for members of a
legislature, which in turn determined the governor's salary. When this
control was threatened, the colonists felt threatened.

Fundamental Orders of Connecticut: The first written constitution in America.	1639
Formation of New England Confederation: Connecticut, New Haven, Plymouth, and Massachusetts formed a league of friendship for defense, offense, and advice. This was a first step toward the later union of states.	1643
Passing of Maryland Toleration Act: Guaranteed religious freedom to all Christians.	1649
Bacon's Rebellion: Virginia farmers revolted against corrupt and oppressive government.	1676
Formation of New York Chapter of Liberties: This document granted freedom of religion to all Christians and gave all freeholders the right to vote.	1683
Zenger Case: Set a precedent that led to the establishment of freedom of the press.	1734

SOME IMPORTANT INDIVIDUALS OF THE PERIOD OF EXPLORATION AND COLONIZATION

Jeffrey Amherst	Anne Hutchinson	Mary White Rowlandson
Edmund Andros	Thomas Hutchinson	William Shirley
Nathaniel Bacon	Cotton Mather	Miles Standish
Edward Braddock	Montezuma	George Washington
Charles II	King Philip	William and Mary of England
John Cotton	Pocahontas	Roger Williams
Jonathan Edwards	Queen Elizabeth I of England	John Winthrop
Thomas Fairfax	Queen Isabella of Spain	John Witherspoon

**CHAPTER 2—
The Era of the
American
Revolution—
1763–1789**

CAUSES OF THE AMERICAN REVOLUTION

Mercantilism: Colonies existed only for the profit of the mother country; caused discontent among American businessmen and traders.

Navigation Acts: Controlled commerce with England and other countries.   1660, 1663, 1673

Concept of the Rights of English subjects: Colonists believed their rights, such as those in the Petition of Rights and English Bill of Rights, were being denied by Parliament.

Aftermath of the French and Indian War: British had acquired a large debt they felt the colonists should help pay; also, they acquired all of Canada, which they had to rule.   1763

The Proclamation of 1763: Tried to stop colonization of the West by closing the land between the Alleghenies and the Mississippi to protect the Native Americans from exploitation by the settlers until treaties could be negotiated.   1763

The Sugar Act: Taxed sugar to raise revenue, which threatened to destroy the profitable triangular trade between Britain, the colonies, and the West Indies.   1764

The Stamp Act: The colonists were forced to pay a tax on all papers—pamphlets, calendars, almanacs, etc.—for the purpose of raising money to support the British army in the colonies. It was during this controversy that Patrick Henry said, ". . . Give me liberty or give me death!"   1764

The Quartering Act: Required the colonists to quarter (house) British troops while they enforced unfavorable acts.   1766

Writs of Assistance: Allowed British officials to enter any home to search for smuggled goods, which contradicted the traditional right of English subjects to protection of their homes.   . . .

The Townshend Acts: Placed a tax on imported paper, lead, glass, tea, and painter's colors in order to pay the salaries of the governors and judges in the colonies, which would eliminate colonists' control of the purse.   1767

The House of Burgesses: Dissolved by the governor of Virginia.   1769

The Boston Massacre: Some Boston townspeople were fired upon by a group of British soldiers. Several people were killed.   1770

The Boston Tea Party: Enraged by the monopoly of the tea trade held by the East India Company and by the English refusal to rescind the tax on tea, about 50 men disguised as Indians boarded the tea ships at the wharf and emptied the tea into the harbor.   1773

The Intolerable Acts: The British government, in retaliation for the Boston Tea Party, closed the port of Boston until the tea was paid for, revised the charter of Massachusetts so that the Council would be appointed by the king, and forced the colonists of Massachusetts to house British soldiers. British officers were allowed to be tried in England for crimes of violence.   1774

Summary View of the Rights of British America: Expressed views of the colonists in opposition to England and called for the ending of slavery—written by T. Jefferson.   1774

SOCIAL CONDITIONS AT THE TIME OF THE REVOLUTION
Differences in the colonies continued up to and after the Revolution. These were often rooted in geography and the reasons for settlement. Class structures had developed in all the colonies by the time of the Revolution and there were tensions between settlers on the frontier and those in the more settled regions. In spite of the class divisions, there was no agreement within classes over their attitudes toward the mother country. For instance, prosperous merchants in Portsmouth, New Hampshire, both supported and organized against England. Similar divisions could be found throughout the colonies and the classes.

IMPORTANT EVENTS OF THE REVOLUTIONARY PERIOD
First Continental Congress: All colonies except Georgia were represented; they pledged to boycott all English goods if England did not settle existing disagreements.   Sept., 1774

Battle of Concord and Lexington: Minutemen and Massachusetts militia, forewarned by Paul Revere and William Dawes, routed English in the first battle of the Revolution.   April, 1775

Second Continental Congress: Met in Philadelphia, attended by all 13 colonies; made provisions for raising a colonial army, issuing and borrowing money; appointed George Washington as commander-in-chief of the army; drafted the *Articles of Confederation*, an agreement among the states outlining the operation of the united government.   1775

Declaration of Independence: Signed by John Hancock, president of the Second Continental Congress, and all the members present, stated the equality of all people, declared the right of the people to rebel when denied life, liberty, and the pursuit of happiness by their governments. July 4, 1776

Treaty of Paris: England recognized the independence of the colonies and ceded land from Canada to Florida.   1783

IMPORTANT BATTLES OF THE REVOLUTION
Battle of Trenton and Princeton: After New York was captured, Washington had fled to Pennsylvania. He recrossed the Delaware River and won these two victories, which made it clear the war would continue.   1776–1777

Battle of Saratoga: Considered the turning point of the war when Americans proved they could defeat the best soldiers in the world.   1778

Battle of Yorktown: Washington cornered a British army on land, while Admiral de Grasse, a French ally, prevented British reinforcements from landing by sea. As a result, Lord Cornwallis surrendered the British Army, bringing the war to an end.   1781

DEVELOPMENT OF THE CONSTITUTION

The Articles of Confederation: America's first Constitution, written by the Continental Congress and adopted by the states, had the following weaknesses:

Each state, regardless of size, had only one vote.

Congress could make laws, but there was no executive to enforce them.

Amendments could be adopted only by unanimous vote.

There was no national court to settle arguments between states.

Congress could not regulate commerce between states, collect taxes, or force states to contribute to government needs.

Congress could only ask states for troops, but could not raise an army.   1781

Annapolis Convention: Several states met at Annapolis, Maryland to consider ways of improving trade and making changes in the Articles. They issued a call for a meeting that became the Constitutional Convention.   1786

Constitutional Convention: Convened at Independence Hall, Philadelphia, to revise *Articles of Confederation* but decided to draw up a completely new document.   May, 1787

COMPROMISES REACHED IN FORMING THE CONSTITUTION

The Great Compromise: Resolved the conflict between large and small states by providing equal representation in the Senate and representation based on population in the House of Representatives.

Three-fifths Compromise: Resolved the conflict between slave and free states by counting five slaves as three people in determining each state's representation in the House of Representatives.

Commerce Compromise: Resolved the conflict between agricultural and manufacturing states by permitting Congress to tax goods entering but not leaving the country.

Indirect Vote for President: Resolved the conflict between aristocrats and democrats by having the president elected by electoral college.

THE GREAT ARCHITECTS OF THE CONSTITUTION

Known as *The Founding Fathers*, the men most responsible for its adoption were George Washington, James Madison, Alexander Hamilton, Gouverneur Morris, Robert Morris, Benjamin Franklin, and George Mason.

BRANCHES OF THE GOVERNMENT

Authority was vested in three branches that acted as a check on each other:

Legislative: The House of Representatives and the Senate make laws according to the power granted in Article I Section 8. These powers include making laws concerning such items as money, commerce, courts, war, the armed forces, immigration, and taxation. The Congress may override a presidential veto of passed legislation by a two-thirds vote. The Senate confirms presidential appointments and treaties.

Executive: The president, who heads the executive branch, enforces the laws, conducts foreign policy, and negotiates treaties with the "advice and consent" of the Senate. The president is commander-in-chief of the army and makes appointments of judges and members of the executive branch.

Judicial: Supreme Court, and such lesser federal courts as Congress establishes, determine the constitutionality of laws and the interpretation of the Constitution. Federal judges are appointed by the president and confirmed by the Senate.

THE BILL OF RIGHTS

A written guarantee of the people's liberties, these were added to the Constitution as the first ten amendments in 1791. Several states refused to ratify the Constitution unless a Bill of Rights was added immediately. The Bill of Rights guaranteed:

1. Freedom of speech, press, religion.

2. The need for a militia and thus the right to bear arms.

3. That people would not be forced to quarter soldiers.

4. Protection against illegal search.

5. The right to know reasons for arrest.

6. The right to a quick trial by a jury of peers.

7. The right to trial by jury in civil cases involving more than $20.

8. Protection against cruel and unusual punishment and excessive bail.

9. That no rights not listed in Constitution should be therefore denied.

10. That the people and states would retain powers not assigned to the federal government.

SOME IMPORTANT INDIVIDUALS OF THE REVOLUTIONARY PERIOD: 1763–1789

Abigail Adams	Nathan Hale	Gouverneur Morris
John Adams	Alexander Hamilton	Robert Morris
Samuel Adams	John Hancock	James Otis
Ethan Allen	Patrick Henry	Thomas Paine
Crispus Attucks	Sir William Howe	William Paterson
Daniel Boone	Thomas Hutchinson	Charles C. Pinckney
General Edward Braddock	John Jay	William Pitt
John Burgoyne	Thomas Jefferson	Edmund Randolph
George Rogers Clark	Sir William Johnson	Paul Revere
George Clinton	John Paul Jones	Daniel Shays
John Singleton Copley	Rufus King	Roger Sherman
Lord Cornwallis	John Lansing	John Trumbull
Benjamin Franklin	Ann Lee	George Washington
Joseph Galloway	Richard Henry Lee	Martha Washington
Elbridge Gerry	James Madison	Anthony Wayne
	George Mason	James Wilson

**CHAPTER 3—
The New
Nation—
1789–1824**

THE GROWTH OF POLITICAL PARTIES

Bank of the United States: Hamilton and Jefferson submitted papers to President Washington explaining their position on a National Bank. This involved their interpretation of the Constitution—strictly for Jefferson, loosely for Hamilton—since there was no mention of a bank in the Constitution. Gradually, others expressed opinions on the Constitution, and out of this discussion came the first two political parties in the nation.

The Federalists: Led by Alexander Hamilton, they became the political party representing investors, merchants, and manufacturers. It is viewed as the more conservative of the two parties. The Federalists were in power until 1800.

The Anti-Federalists, or Republicans: Led by Thomas Jefferson, the party represented the farming population, small business people, and some city workers. At the time it was the more liberal of the two parties and was dominant from 1800 to 1824. The leaders of the Republican Party grew increasingly conservative and finally it was absorbed by the Whig Party.

Disappearance of Federalist Party: It passed from the political scene in 1816. The Federalists lost credibility after the Hartford Convention and they opposed the War of 1812, which lost them support outside of New England.

The Democratic Party: It emerged with the election of Andrew Jackson in 1828; it represented the Western and Southern farmers and workers of the East; it became the more liberal party.

The Whig Party: It was formed after the Federalist and the Republican parties disappeared; Henry Clay, former Federalists, and some conservative Republicans organized the opposition to the Democratic Party in the form of the newly created Whig Party.

THE ESTABLISHMENT OF THE FEDERAL GOVERNMENT

President Washington developed the concept of a *cabinet* to advise him. Alexander Hamilton, Secretary of the Treasury, supported a *loose interpretation* of the Constitution to give power to the government in Washington. Thomas Jefferson, Secretary of State, supported a *strict interpretation* of the Constitution to give more power to the people and the state governments. These interpretations continue to divide people today. Congress passed laws establishing the framework of the government, including the *Judiciary Act of 1789*, which established the federal court system.

Whiskey Rebellion 1794: Washington used state and federal troops to crush a farmers' rebellion in Pennsylvania, giving strength to the federal government.

Washington's Farewell Address 1797: In it Washington called for no foreign alliances, two terms for the president, and no factions (parties) in political life.

Chief Justice John Marshall: Appointed to the Supreme Court, Marshall led the Court in interpreting the Constitution to give power to the federal government.

SOME IMPORTANT SUPREME COURT DECISIONS

Marbury v. Madison (1803) established that the Supreme Court had the power of judicial review.

Dartmouth College v. Woodward (1819) established the point that the charter of a private corporation is protected by the Constitution.

McCullough v. Maryland (1819) interpreted the elastic clause giving the federal government power to do those things not denied it in order to achieve legitimate goals. Also established the idea that the elastic clause applied to federal-state relations, thus extending the power of the federal government.

Gibbons v. Ogden (1824) established the concept of federal control over interstate commerce.

THE WAR OF 1812
Causes

Election to Congress of War Hawks from western states (example: Henry Clay from Kentucky) who wanted war with England to gain control of western lands and defeat the Native American tribes.

In the Northwest Territory and on the frontier, British furnished Native Americans with arms and encouraged them to attack settlers who were encroaching on tribal lands and breaking treaty agreements.

Economic warfare of the British and French symbolized in such acts as the British Orders in Council, Jefferson's Embargo of 1807, and the Non-intercourse Act of 1809.

British attacked U.S. ships and impressed American sailors into service in their crews.

British seized American ships.

British fired on frigate *Chesapeake,* killing three American sailors.

Important Events of the War

Captain Perry's naval victory on Lake Erie, reported with the famous words, "We have met the enemy and they are ours." Victories of the *USS Constitution* (*Old Ironsides*) at sea.

The capture of Washington, D.C., and the burning of the White House by the British.

The writing of the *Star-Spangled Banner* by Francis Scott Key as the British bombarded Fort McHenry in Baltimore, Maryland.

Battle of New Orleans, won by General Andrew Jackson ("Old Hickory") after the treaty ending the war had been signed.

Results of the War of 1812

The United States Merchant Marine was almost destroyed.

Development of national pride and increase of national unity (although the *Treaty of Ghent* [1814], did not reflect a victory, it established clearly our complete independence from Britain).

Increased western migration when unemployment spread in the East as a result of the destruction of United States commerce.

Manufacturing developed in different areas of the United States since Britain's wartime embargo prevented imports.

THE MONROE DOCTRINE

After Napoleon's defeat in 1815, *Russia, Prussia,* and *Austria* formed the Holy Alliance, to crush rebellions against monarchy wherever they might arise. Spain sought their help to regain its South American possessions lost due to popular revolts of the people led by Simón Bolivar and José de San Martín.

Russia was claiming the Oregon Territory, which both the United States and Britain were also claiming.

The British, in order to protect their trade, suggested joint action with the United States against European encroachment in the Americas, but this was rejected by the United States. Instead, to prevent European expansion in the Americas, President James Monroe, in an address to Congress in 1823, stated what became known as the Monroe Doctrine. The Doctrine, which became a cornerstone of American foreign policy, stated:

1. No part of North or South America was open to further European colonization.
2. European attempts to interfere with any existing American (North or South) governments would be considered unfriendly acts.
3. The United States would not interfere with existing European colonies.
4. The United States would not interfere in the affairs of Europe.

THE ERA OF GOOD FEELING

The Federalists disappeared as a result of not fully supporting the War of 1812. After the war the Republicans were in control of the nation. Henry Clay from Kentucky and John C. Calhoun from South Carolina soon emerged as national leaders. Clay, the "Great Compromiser," tried to reconcile the sectional differences with his "American System"—a protective tariff to aid manufacturers and better transportation (internal improvements), paid for with money from the tariffs, to aid farmers. Presidents Monroe and J. Q. Adams vetoed all bills for such improvements. Henry Clay offered the Missouri Compromise in 1820 to admit Maine (free) and Missouri (slave) as states, thus reconciling differences between the North and the South.

SOME IMPORTANT INDIVIDUALS OF THE PERIOD 1789–1824

John Adams	Samuel Chase	Citizen Genet
John Q. Adams	William Clark	Alexander Hamilton
Abigail Adams	Henry Clay	William H. Harrison
Aaron Burr	George Clinton	Washington Irving
John C. Calhoun	Albert Gallatin	John Jay

Thomas Jefferson	John Marshall	Haym Salomon
Rufus King	James Monroe	Winfield Scott
Henry Knox	Charles Wilson Peale	Tecumseh
Benjamin H. Latrobe	Charles C. Pinckney	Mersey Warren
Meriwether Lewis	John Randolph	George Washington
Dolley Madison	Susanna Rowson	Daniel Webster
James Madison	Sacajawea	Eli Whitney

CHAPTER 4—
Jackson and the
West—
1824–1850

THE GROWTH OF SECTIONALISM

The Industrial North: As trade and manufacturing became the most important activities of the northern section of the United States, the North developed the following political and economic needs:

A national bank that would guarantee uniform and stable currency.

The end of the sale of cheap lands in the West to workers needed for northern industry.

A high protective tariff to protect native manufactured products against foreign competition.

Internal improvements (roads and canals) to link the markets and raw materials of the West to the markets and manufacturing of the Northeast.

The prevention of the spread of slavery and the slave-based economic system to new western territories where it would compete with wage labor and provide less of a market.

The Slave South: With the invention of Eli Whitney's cotton gin in 1793, unskilled slave labor became increasingly important to plantation owners whose main crop, cotton, produced almost all of southern wealth. The economic and political needs of the South were:

Cheap western lands in which more cotton could be grown.

The extension of slavery to these lands.

No internal improvements (roads and canals) because they benefited only the Northeast and West and were to be paid for by tariffs.

No high tariffs since they raised the price of manufactured goods, which the South imported from Britain, to whom cotton was sold in payment.

The Farming West: Since agriculture was the principal activity and chief source of wealth in the West, its needs were:

Access to cheap land for expansion.

Cheap money (much money in circulation even though, as a result, the value of that money in terms of purchasing power is lessened), which meant opposition to the national bank that was controlled by eastern business interests.

Extension of voting rights to all, regardless of property holdings.

Internal improvements (roads and canals) to transport produce to the market.

JACKSONIAN DEMOCRACY

While the issue of slavery dominated the social issues in the pre-Civil War era, there were many other issues, many of which had important consequences for the United States. Many of these issues have been grouped under the term Jacksonian Democracy, but they were not confined to the years of his presidency.

The election of Jackson, first president from the frontier region, marked a revolution in thought. Life on the frontier was dangerous and difficult. Clearing land, creating farms, forming communities, dealing with the Native Americans—all these factors required self-reliance, initiative, and a will to work. Ancestry and education alone counted for little. These qualities placed an emphasis on the individual's abilities and, according to the later historian, Frederick Jackson Turner, created the American character. These qualities led to the political idea of the "spoils system," which Jackson employed. The spoils system held that every individual had the ability to run the government. It emphasized the equality of all but was limited in those days to white males.

This emphasis on the individual is the root of democracy and provided the philosophical base for Jackson's Democratic Party and the social relations of the era.

Issues of the pre-Civil War period grouped under Jacksonian Democracy were:

Education: Horace Mann in Massachusetts introduced from 1837 to 1848 many curriculum changes emphasizing useful skills and the first requirement for a minimum school year—six months. Emma Willard established the first high school for women in Troy, New York, in 1821.

Mental Health: Dorothea Dix was a leader in reform of prisons and insane asylums. In 1843 she published the *Memorial to the Legislature of Massachusetts* which was an indictment of the living conditions and treatment of insane in institutions in Massachusetts. She later published similar reports on conditions in several other states. Her actions led to changes in treatment of the insane as well as of prisoners and to the enlargement or establishment of state supported hospitals for the insane in 15 states and Canada.

Voting Rights: During the Jackson period, white males throughout the nation were able to vote as property requirements were dropped. A women's movement calling for the right to vote (women's suffrage) and giving them the legal rights of men developed. Leaders included Angelina and Sarah Grimke and Elizabeth Cady Stanton and Lucretia Mott. The latter two organized the Seneca Falls Convention in 1848, which issued a Declaration of Independence for women modeled on the U.S. Declaration.

Temperance: Susan B. Anthony became a leader of the movement to abolish the use of alcohol. According to the temperance leaders, drinking hurt families and limited the potential of the individual.

Religious Revival—the Second Great Awakening: Underlying many of the reform movements was a revival of interest in religion. This interest focused on the Bible and the need for every individual to read and interpret it. Revivals have been an important aspect of religion, especially Protestantism, throughout United States history.

SECTIONAL COMPROMISES

As each section tried to gain control of the federal government to pass bills advantageous to itself, bitterness between the sections increased and problems could be settled only by compromise. Some of the more important compromises were:

Missouri Compromise (1820): Since, if there were more free states than slave states, the North would gain political control of Congress, the South opposed the admission of free states unless they were balanced by the admission of an equal number of slave states. Likewise, the North opposed the admission of slave states. When Missouri requested admission to the Union in 1818 as a slave state, Henry Clay, (the "Great Compromiser") proposed the Missouri Compromise, which states that:

Missouri would be admitted as a slave state, Maine as a free state.

Slavery would be prohibited in the Louisiana Territory north of the 36° 30′ parallel. (Missouri was to be the one exception.)

Compromise Tariff of 1833: When the North pushed a high tariff through Congress in 1828, the South was angry. When the tariff was slightly modified and general duties lowered only a little in 1832, South Carolina, led by John Calhoun, threatened secession and refused to obey the law. After negotiating a new tariff acceptable to the South, Clay saw it pushed through Congress as well as a bill (Force Act) that would allow the president to use troops to collect the tariff. The compromise avoided civil war in 1832–1833.

Compromise of 1850: When California asked for admission in 1850, the balance between the North and South was once again endangered. The Compromise of 1850, called the Omnibus Bill, and also written by Henry Clay, provided that:

The people of Utah and New Mexico would vote to determine whether they should be free or slave states (this idea became known as popular or "squatter" sovereignty).

California would be admitted as a free state.

The Fugitive Slave Law would be strengthened.

Slave trading would be prohibited in the District of Columbia.

IMPORTANT MILESTONES IN EXPANSION 1787–1853

Northwest Ordinance of 1787: Adopted by the government under the Articles of Confederation, it made provision for lands north of the Ohio River and east of the Mississippi conquered by George Rogers Clark in the Revolution. It stated that

No more than five and no less than three states were to be formed from this Northwest Territory.

Inhabitants of a territory would be admitted as a state on equal terms when its population reached 60,000.

Slavery was prohibited in the territory.

Louisiana Purchase: Extending from the Mississippi River to the Rocky Mountains and from Canada to the Gulf of Mexico, this vast territory was purchased from Napoleon for $15 million during Jefferson's administration in 1803.

Florida Purchase: American settlers in western Florida revolted against Spain in 1810, and the land was annexed in 1812 and added to the state of Louisiana. In 1819 the United States purchased the eastern part of Florida from Spain for $5 million.

The Oregon Territory: Originally claimed by Britain, United States, Spain, and Russia; by 1818 the other two countries ceded rights to the United States and Britain, which occupied it jointly.

Marcus Whitman led American settlers into the area in 1840. A dispute developed over the territory as American settlers moved in. In 1844 the slogan "fifty-four forty or fight," which meant the United States would take over all the Oregon territory, helped elect James Polk president.

In 1846 a compromise was worked out with Britain and a treaty signed that gave the United States rights to the land south of the 49th parallel and Britain the land north of it.

Gadsden Purchase: A small strip of land, now incorporated in Arizona and New Mexico, was purchased from Mexico in 1853 to provide a good southern railroad route to the West. Its purchase completed the territory of what became the 48 contiguous United States (the lower 48).

Manifest Destiny: Many Americans hoped that war with Mexico (1846) would unite the nation and prevent the sectional conflicts from breaking up the Union. Many also believed that it was our *Manifest Destiny* to expand the borders of the nation to include all of North America. They held that this expansion would bring benefits to all peoples. Unfortunately, the war added to sectional divisions as New Englanders did not support it. The peace treaty added new territory that had to be organized as states. This created both economic tensions and problems over the spread of slavery to the new areas.

MEXICAN WAR

Annexation of Texas: General Sam Houston defeated the Mexican leader, Santa Anna, in 1836, and Texas was granted its independence from Mexico and established as a republic. In the following nine years there were various attempts to have Texas join the Union or ally with Britain. Finally, in 1845 Texas was admitted as the 28th state of the United States.

Outbreak of War: In 1846 war broke out between the United States and Mexico—Mexico being angered by American annexation of Texas and claims to all land north of the Rio Grande River. The United States, under the generalship of Winfield Scott and Zachary Taylor, won a series of battles in Mexico. California was captured under the combined efforts of Stephen Kearny, John Sloat, and John Fremont.

The Treaty of Guadalupe-Hidalgo: Signed in 1848 it provided that the Mexican areas of New Mexico (present Utah, New Mexico, Colorado, and Arizona) and Upper California (present California) were ceded to the United States.

The Rio Grande was fixed as the southern boundary of Texas.

The United States agreed to a payment of $15 million for the territory.

SOME IMPORTANT INDIVIDUALS OF THE PERIOD 1824–1850

John Q. Adams	Peggy Eaton	Samuel F. B. Morse
John Jacob Astor	Ralph Waldo Emerson	Lucretia Mott
John James Audubon	John C. Fremont	William S. Mount
Stephen Austin	Margaret Fuller	Edgar Allan Poe
Thomas Hart Benton	William Lloyd Garrison	James K. Polk
James Beckwith	Charles Goodyear	Winfield Scott
Nicholas Biddle	Angelina Grimké	John Slidell
James G. Birney	Sarah Grimké	Elizabeth Cady Stanton
John C. Calhoun	William H. Harrison	Zachary Taylor
Kit Carson	Robert Y. Hayne	Henry David Thoreau
Henry Clay	Sam Houston	Nat Turner
Samuel Colt	Andrew Jackson	John Tyler
James Fenimore Cooper	Hannah Farsham Lee	Martin Van Buren
Charlotte Cushman	Henry Wadsworth Longfellow	Daniel Webster
Dorothea Dix	Mary Lyon	Marcus Whitman
Frederick Douglass	Horace Mann	Brigham Young
Neal S. Dow		

CHAPTER 5—
The Coming of the
Civil War, Civil War
and Reconstruction—
1850–1877

EVENTS LEADING TO THE CIVIL WAR

North-South Hostility over Regional Differences: Disagreement over tariffs and the economic systems of the two areas was a basic cause of the hostility. As new territory was added to the Union, the question of the extension of slavery became crucial to the South for both economic and political reasons.

The Abolitionists: Led by William Lloyd Garrison, publisher of *The Liberator,* Frederick Douglass, and many others, the Abolitionists argued for an end to slavery.

Slave Rebellions: There were many rebellions in the South. Those led by Denmark Vesey and Nat Turner terrified slave owners and alerted Northerners to the many horrors of slavery.

National Fugitive Slave Law: This law, which the South demanded, pointed out vividly to Northerners some of the evils of the slave system as they saw slaves who had escaped being taken back, often in chains, to their owners.

Uncle Tom's Cabin: The famous novel (1852) by Harriet Beecher Stowe awakened Northern sympathy for the slaves.

The Underground Railroad: Organized largely by Abolitionists, it helped slaves escape to the North. Harriet Tubman was one of the famous and effective operators of the railroad.

Kansas-Nebraska Act: In 1854 this act repealed the Missouri Compromise and stated that each new state created from the territory of the Louisiana Purchase would decide whether to be free or slave. Both Northerners and Southerners financed settlers in both the Kansas and Nebraska territories to support their positions on slavery. Small-scale civil war broke out in both areas as they struggled to decide on a slave or a free status.

Dred Scott Case: In 1857, when a slave named Dred Scott demanded freedom because his master had moved from a slave state (Missouri) to a free state (Illinois), the case was taken all the way to the Supreme Court. The Court in *Dred Scott v. Sandford* decided that slaves were property that could be taken anywhere and that the Missouri Compromise was unconstitutional.

John Brown's Raid: In 1859 an Abolitionist, John Brown, led a raid on an arsenal at Harper's Ferry in Virginia. He planned to seize arms, distribute them to slaves, and lead them in a revolt for freedom. He was captured, tried, and hanged.

The Election of 1860: The Democratic Party split into two parts over the slavery issue. These were:

The northern wing, which ran Stephen Douglas on a platform of popular sovereignty to determine free or slave status.

The southern wing, which ran John C. Breckenridge on a policy based on the Dred Scott decision that slaves were property protected everywhere by the Constitution.

The remnants of the Whig and American parties nominated John Bell on a platform that condemned sectional parties and called for upholding the Constitution and the laws of the land.

The recently formed Republican Party nominated Abraham Lincoln on a platform that stated:

Kansas was to be admitted as a free state.

Slavery was not to be extended to the territories.

Free farming land was to be given to those settling in the West.

A high protective tariff was to be maintained.

In the four-party race no one won a majority. Lincoln was elected by the electoral college system, even though he received no more than 40 percent of the votes cast.

Southern Secession: With Lincoln's election, seven states (South Carolina, Texas, Louisiana, Mississippi, Alabama, Florida, and Georgia) seceded from the Union. They created The Confederate States of America with Jefferson Davis as president. Their constitution stated that:

There would be no Supreme Court.

States would have more rights than the central government.

Slavery was lawful.

Lincoln's Inaugural Address (1861): Lincoln refused to accept the dissolution of the Union, and stated that war or peace was in the hands of the South.

Fort Sumter: On April 12, 1861, Southern forces fired on Fort Sumter in the harbor of Charleston, South Carolina. The federal fort had been built years before to guard the harbor and was occupied by federal troops. Lincoln was determined to hold onto federal property in the seceded states and would not acknowledge the secession. Civil war therefore began. Virginia, Tennessee, Arkansas, and North Carolina seceded and joined the Confederacy.

BASIC CAUSES OF THE WAR

Economic: The northern manufacturers needed a high tariff, skilled labor, internal improvements, and a national bank. The southern planters needed low tariffs, slave labor, state banks, and opposed internal improvements.

Political: Northerners opposed the extension of slavery to new states because they wanted political control of Congress, which made laws. Most Southerners favored the extension of slavery because they, too, wanted to control Congress. Many Northerners believed the Constitution had created a Union—"one nation, indivisible"—that could not be dissolved. Southerners believed the states that made the Union could unmake it and secede.

Moral: Abolitionists and others felt that slavery was an evil and must be eliminated. The South defended slavery by claiming it was established by God and quoted Bible passages to prove it.

MAIN EVENTS OF THE CIVIL WAR

Blockade of the South: In order to cut the South off from supplies, the North blockaded the coast from Virginia to Texas. The blockade also succeeded in preventing the Confederacy from exporting cotton and tobacco. The iron-clad Confederate ship *Merrimac* attempted to break the blockade, but was prevented from doing so by the iron-clad Union ship, *Monitor.*

Capture of Vicksburg: Union forces captured Forts Henry (Kentucky) and Donelson (Tennessee) in 1862, which opened up the Mississippi River valley to invasion by the North. General Grant captured Vicksburg (Mississippi) in 1863, cutting off the West from the rest of the Confederacy since New Orleans (Louisiana) had been captured by the Union in 1812.

Emancipation Proclamation (effective January 1 1863): Lincoln's famous proclamation freed all slaves residing in states that had rebelled against the Union. This was a military move to help win the war. Lincoln offered other plans for dealing with the problems of slavery after the war.

The Battle of Gettysburg (1863): After defeating invading northern armies, General Robert E. Lee invaded the North and was himself defeated at Gettysburg (Pennsylvania) in the crucial battle of the war.

Capture of Atlanta (1864): General Sherman captured Atlanta (Georgia), and, in a famous march through Georgia, destroyed everything in his path that might help the enemy. This action, plus the capture of Vicksburg, cut the South into three sections.

Surrender at Appomattox (April 1865): Lee surrendered after steadily losing ground and after finding himself unable to lift the siege of Petersburg (Virginia). Petersburg fell to Grant on April 2. Lee then abandoned Richmond (Virginia), the Confederate capital, and fled west only to surrender a week later on April 9. This essentially ended the war, although some fighting continued until the end of May.

RESULTS OF THE CIVIL WAR

Northern Business and Industry: It grew and prospered during the war, and replaced Southern agriculture as the principal activity of this country.

Homestead Act (1862): The act provided free land in the West for those who settled on it and developed it. The South had not supported such legislation before the war.

Pacific Railroad Acts (1862 and 1864): Prior to the war southern routes for a transcontinental railroad were considered. The route approved after secession went from St. Louis to San Francisco. It would tie the industry of the East to raw materials and farm products of the West. The acts granted rights of way and land to the builders, thus providing government subsidies for the road's construction.

Constitutional: The federal government was proven more powerful than any state government. No state could secede from the Union. Three amendments to the Constitution (Thirteen, Fourteen, and Fifteen) ended slavery and gave equal protection of the laws and the vote to all males.

Destruction of the Southern Plantation Economy: Based on slavery, it was destroyed forever. It was replaced by sharecropping.

Wartime Rights of Civilians: The Supreme Court in *ex parte Milligan* upheld the Constitutional rights of a civilian during wartime. The case established civilian rule as primary over military government even in times of war.

RECONSTRUCTION

Issue I: Readmission of rebel states to the Union.

Solution: Lincoln's plan was to readmit states when 10 percent of the voters pledged loyalty to the United States and agreed to the abolition of slavery. After his assassination, northern members of Congress, called Radical Republicans, became harsher, passed the *Reconstruction Acts of 1867*, which treated the South as a conquered province. To gain admittance the seceded states had to ratify the Fourteenth Amendment and meet other requirements. Northern troops occupied the Southern states until a state met all conditions of readmission. The last occupation troops were withdrawn in 1877.

Issue II: Guarantee of civil rights to African Americans.

Solution: *The Civil Rights Bill of 1866* was aimed at undoing the effects of Black Codes established by southern governments. The Fourteenth and Fifteenth amendments were to guarantee the civil rights of the former slaves. None of these actions were successful in protecting civil rights. The Supreme Court limited the application of the Civil Rights Bill to national issues. Southern legislators maintained some Black Codes and found other ways, including the later Jim Crow laws, to restrict the rights of the freed slaves.

Issue III: Government of rebel states.

Solution: Former slaves, but not Confederate leaders, were allowed to vote at state party conventions and in elections until states were readmitted, after which the states again set their own rules as to who could vote. Immediately after the war many of the state governments passed important social legislation dealing with schooling and other issues.

RESULTS OF RECONSTRUCTION

Reconstruction problems focused on the issue of whether the southern states were ever out of the Union. The Radical Republicans held that they were, and so developed plans to readmit the states that differed from Lincoln's plan, as he believed the states had always been part of the Union, even if in rebellion. The freed slaves were often treated as pawns in the game of power politics, especially by northerners who came south (Carpetbaggers). In many southern states ex-slaves held important political offices and helped to write new enlightened state constitutions.

Formation of the Solid South: The federal occupation troops were recalled from the South by President Hayes (1877) after he was declared the winner of the disputed presidential election of 1876. After 1877, and the withdrawal of all federal troops from the South, for many years the southern states voted for the Democratic Party on almost all occasions, as a result of the whites' dislike of Radical Republicans. This concept of the Solid South was still a consideration in elections in the post-World War II period.

Thirteenth Amendment: 1865—Abolished slavery in the United States.

Fourteenth Amendment: 1868—African Americans were made citizens of the United States. It guaranteed that no state could deny life, liberty, or property without due process of law.

Fifteenth Amendment: 1870—Stated that no state can deny the right to vote on account of race, color, or previous condition of servitude.

Ku Klux Klan: It was formed to control ex-slaves and to "keep them in their place" and not allow them to change the basic political and social structure of the South. The Klan grew, especially after 1877.

New Constitutions of Southern States: Established free public schools for all children, abolished imprisonment for debt, abolished property qualifications for voting and jury duty.

Railways, Highways, and National Banking System strengthened the federal government.

Prevention of Voting (after 1877): To counteract the influence of ex-slaves, the South tried to deny them political rights by state measures that limited voting privileges to those:

Who could pass literacy tests

Who could pay a poll tax

Who owned property

Whose grandfather had voted

SOME IMPORTANT INDIVIDUALS OF THE PERIOD 1850–1877

Louisa May Alcott	Jefferson Davis	Jay Gould
Horatio Alger	Ignatius Donnelly	Ulysses S. Grant
Clara Barton	Stephen Douglas	Horace Greeley
John Brown	Mary Baker Eddy	Rutherford B. Hayes
Blanche K. Bruce	Millard Fillmore	Julia Ward Howe
Jay Cooke	William Lloyd Garrison	"Stonewall" Jackson

Andrew Johnson	Hiram R. Revels	James E. B. Stuart
Robert E. Lee	Dred Scott	Charles Sumner
Abraham Lincoln	Horatio Seymour	Roger B. Taney
George McClellan	William T. Sherman	Samuel Tilden
Herman Melville	Thaddeus Stevens	Sojourner Truth
Francis Parkman	Lucy Stone	Harriet Tubman
Matthew C. Perry	Harriet Beecher Stowe	William "Boss" Tweed
Franklin Pierce	Carl Schurz	Walt Whitman

**CHAPTER 6—
Industrial Growth of
America, Populists,
and Progressives—
1877–1916**

THE INDUSTRIAL REVOLUTION

The Industrial Revolution was a change from hand manufacturing, which was done in homes, to machine manufacturing done in a factory. The Revolution was stimulated in the United States by:

Growing trade, especially after the Revolutionary War removed British restrictions on American industry. Markets for exported goods were soon found. The United States was also free to import under our own tariff regulations.

Invention of the cotton gin by Eli Whitney in 1793 provided northern textile workers with an abundance of raw material. It also established the idea of interchangeable parts in manufacturing, which standardized products.

Power from swift-running rivers was easily available, especially in New England and along the Fall Line of the Appalachian Mountains.

Coal, iron ore, and lumber in abundance and near population centers.

Napoleonic Wars, War of 1812, and British blockade all forced American manufacture to grow, since we could not rely on imports.

Westward expansion throughout the 19th century opened new markets and created new demands.

Labor shortage and wartime needs during the Civil War led to increased use of machinery.

Building of roads, railroads, and canals made transportation of raw materials and finished products easier and stimulated manufacturing in industrial centers.

INFLUENCE OF GEOGRAPHIC FACTORS ON INDUSTRIAL AND AGRICULTURAL DEVELOPMENT

The United States can be divided into four major geographic areas: the Atlantic coastal plain, the Appalachian highlands, the great central plain, the Cordilleran highlands.

Atlantic Coastal Plain: East of the Appalachian Mountains.
First area settled by English colonists.
Suitable for growth of manufacturing cities because of:
  Power available from rivers flowing down from Appalachian Mountains.
  Rivers that also allow for some transportation inland (such as the Hudson River).
  Excellent harbors.
Long, narrow plainland between mountains and the Atlantic provides excellent areas for farming to supply food to large population centers.

Appalachian Highlands: From Adirondack Mountains through Allegheny and Cumberland plateaus to central Alabama in the South.
Mountain area, originally dense forest, provided protection for colonists during the Revolutionary War.
Rich mining areas—coal and iron—in mountainous parts of Pennsylvania, West Virginia, and Alabama.
Valley areas are suitable for farming.

The Great Central Plain: From the Appalachians to the Rockies, and from Canada to Mexico, this is the largest region, comprising almost half of the land in the United States. Richest agricultural region in the world because of great fertile plains.

Lush land for stock grazing from North Dakota to Texas.
Mississippi River, great North-South waterway, drains the area and supplies excellent transportation, along with its tributaries such as the Ohio and Missouri Rivers.

Cordilleran Highlands: From Rocky Mountains to the Pacific Ocean.
Mountainous area rich in lumber and mineral resources.
Fertile valley and lowland area near the Pacific is suitable for fruit orchards and farming.

18TH-CENTURY INVENTIONS THAT SPURRED INDUSTRIAL REVOLUTION

Flying Shuttle: John Kay (English), increased speed of weaving.   1733

Spinning Jenny: James Hargreaves (English), spun several threads at one time.   1765

Water Frame: Richard Arkwright (English), machine operated by water power spun thread very fast.   1769

Steam Engine: Invented by Thomas Newcomen (English) in 1703, and improved by James Watt (English) in 1769, ushered in the Age of Steam. The use of steam power transformed:

Transportation because of application to water and land travel.

Factories, which were no longer dependent on water power, and so could produce at much greater rates of speed and could be located in different areas nearer to raw materials and away from waterfalls.

IMPORTANT 19TH- and 20TH-CENTURY INVENTIONS

Industry: Many inventions transformed the American way of life. Among them were:

Colt Revolver: Samuel Colt   1831

Electric Dynamo: Michael Faraday   1831

Rubber: Charles Goodyear   1837

Kerosene: Abraham Gesner   1850s

Electric Light Bulb: Thomas A. Edison   1879

Zipper: Whitcomb L. Judson   1893

X-Ray: Wilhelm Roentgen   1895

Radio Vacuum Tube: Lee De Forest   1907

Bakelite (Plastic begins synthetics revolution): Leo Backeland   1909

Cellophane: Jacques Brandenberger   1912

Liquid Fuel Rocket: Robert Goddard   1926

Synthetic Superpolymer (Nylon): Wallace Carothers   1937

Mark I (computer): Howard Aiken   1937

Controlled Nuclear Fission: Enrico Fermi   1942

Power-Producing Nuclear Fission: United States Atomic Energy Commission   1951

Double Helix: Francis Crick and James Watson   1953

Solar Battery: Bell Telephone and Air Research Development   1954

Microwave (Radar) Oven: Raytheon   1955

Velcro: Georges de Mestral   1956

Demonstration of Laser Action: Theodore Maiman   1960

Astroturf: Monsanto Chemical Company   1965

Calculator (pocket): Jack Kilby, Jerry Merryman, James Van Tassel	1967
Kevlar (Bullet Proof Vest): Stephanie Kwolek (Dupont)	1976

Agriculture: Until 1800, all farm work was done by hand with the help of draft animals and using primitive tools that had changed very little over the centuries. The following inventions revolutionized farming in the 19th century:

Cotton Gin: Eli Whitney	1793
Iron Plow: Charles Newbold	1797
Reaper: Cyrus McCormick	1834
Modern Steel Plow: James Oliver	1868

Transportation and Communication: Inventions also drastically changed the speed of travel and communication. Outstanding ones were:

Steamboat: Robert Fulton	1807
Locomotive: George Stevenson	1830
Screw Propellor: John Ericsson	1831
Telegraph: Samuel Morse	1844
Sleeping Car: George Pullman	1867
Air Brake: George Westinghouse	1872
Telephone: Alexander Graham Bell	1876
Automobile: developed by Henry Ford and others	1895
Motion Pictures: C. F. Jenkins	1896
Airplane: Wright Brothers	1903
Radio: R. A. Fressenden	1906
First Rocket: Robert Goddard	1926
Diesel tractors and trains	1930s
Helicopter: I. Sikorsky	1939
Electric Computer: American Industry	1940s
Television: Philo Farnsworth (1921), C. F. Jenkins, V. Zworykin, RCA, and CBS	1941
Jet Planes: Lockheed Company	1942
Transistor: William Shockley and Bell Telephone Team	1948
UNIVAC (Universal Automatic Computer): Eckert-Mauchly Corp.	1951
Duplicating Machine (Xerox)	1959
Microchip (I. C. Chips): Robert Noyce (Fairchild Co.), Jack Kilby (Texas Instruments, Inc.)	
Manned Space Flight (NASA)	1961
Facsimile Machine (fax)	1970
Microsoft Basic: William Gates, Paul Allen	1974
Personal Computer—Floppy disk: Steve Wozniak	1978
First Space Shuttle	1981
Compact Disk: Sony and Phillips Companies	1983
Cellular Telephone: Bell's AmeriTech Mobile Communications Lab	
Start of assembly of international space station: U.S. (NASA) and Russia (organizers)	1998

Mining and Smelting: As steel became increasingly important in manufacturing, the following processes developed:

New method of making steel from iron: William Kelly	1851
Bessemer Process: Henry Bessemer, used blast of hot air to remove impurities from molten iron.	1856
Open Hearth Method used more of the iron effectively.	1868

New steel alloys with special strengths were developed to aid the growing industrial demands of car, plane, and rocket industries.

CONTRIBUTION OF IMMIGRANTS TO THE UNITED STATES

Immigration: All Americans are immigrants. Even the ancestors of the Native Americans came as immigrants from Siberia across the Bering Sea. All immigrants both as groups and as individuals have contributed to the development of the nation. The Native Americans cultivated plants, developed a special understanding of their relationship with the environment, and aided the first white settlers. The first settlers on the coast carved cities and farms out of forests. The slaves gave their labor to produce much wealth and capital for the later industrial development of the nation. Chinese laborers built the great railroads through the Rockies. Later immigrants from Europe supplied labor in the early factories and mines of the Northeast, working under poor conditions to build the wealth of America. After the Civil War, immigration increased greatly and America was considered the melting pot of peoples. How closely this idea was achieved is debatable, but for generations it was the stated goal of the nation—*e pluribus unum*—from many, one. In more recent years the concept of pluralism has replaced the melting pot image. Pluralism suggests greater emphasis on the many, the *pluribus,* but pluralism still holds that the many peoples make one nation. Some individual contributions by immigrants to the United States illustrate how beneficial this immigration has been to the nation and how diversified the peoples have been.

SOME WELL-KNOWN IMMIGRANTS

British West Indies:	Alexander Hamilton (politics)
Canada:	James J. Hill (railroads)
China:	Yung Wing (diplomacy)
	Poon Chew Ng (publishing)
Denmark:	Jacob Riis (social reform and literature)
England:	Alexander Graham Bell (invention)
Germany:	Walter Damrosch (music)
	Albert Einstein (science)
	Carl Schurz (politics)
Greece:	Dimitri Metropoulos (music)
India:	Ananda Keutish Coomaraswamy (philosophy)
Ireland:	Augustus St. Gaudens (sculpture)
Italy:	Arturo Toscanini (music)
	Amadeo P. Giannini (banking)
Jamaica:	Marcus Garvey (civil rights)
Japan:	Hideyo Noguchi (medicine)
	Yamasaki (architecture)
	Jokicho Takamine (medicine)
Lithuania:	Sydney Hillman (labor)
Mexico:	José Limón (dance)
Russia:	David Sarnoff (television)
	Mark Rothko (painting)
	Al Jolson (entertainment)
Santo Domingo:	John James Audubon (ornithology)
Scotland:	Andrew Carnegie (industry)
Switzerland:	Louis Agassiz (zoology)
Yugoslavia:	Michael Papin (X-ray)

OTHER FACTORS

Resources: America has been blessed with rich deposits of oil, coal, iron, and other minerals needed for industry. Farmlands are rich and can produce almost every type of product needed for manufacture, except natural rubber. There have been abundant water resources and the nation is blessed with a variety of climates, none of which is truly oppressive.

Psychological Factors: Open lands, political freedom, inventiveness, and individualism were factors that created a climate of opinion that encouraged industrial growth.

RESULTS OF EARLY INDUSTRIAL REVOLUTION

Growth of great cities, as people changed their occupation from farming to manufacturing.

Rapid growth of city population, causing slums and increased crime rate.

Bad working conditions shared by many people, leading to development and growth of trade unions.

Trade unions that organized laborers to demand such items as shorter working days, safer working conditions and insurance to cover injuries.

Greater interest in social reforms and politics to provide solutions to problems.

Demand for political parties to change programs to meet new problems created by industrial change.

Increase of America's productivity and power.

Imperialism, as leaders and the people perceived a need for colonies as sources of raw materials and markets for finished products in competition with other industrializing nations.

Increased militarism, as international competition grew.

Speeding up of transportation, bringing people closer together.

Increased need for education.

More foods and materials available to a greater number of people.

New giant industries (railroad, oil, steel, sugar, aerospace, computers).

Transformation in farming techniques.

Increased standard of living of most people in industrialized societies.

Rising expectations of most people to share in the "good life" produced by material plenty.

EFFECTS OF INDUSTRIAL REVOLUTION ON AMERICAN LIFE

New Production Methods: Large-scale production in factories produced new techniques of organizing work. These were:

Division of labor: Each worker performs one small task over and over again.

Assembly line: Each worker adds one part to the product being made as it moves along from worker to worker.

Standardization of parts: Many parts of each machine and the same part in different machines are made the same in shape and size so that, when defective or worn out, individual parts can be easily changed and replaced with new parts or parts from another similar machine. The parts are thus interchangeable.

Business Combines: Until the Civil War, most factories were small but afterward they began growing larger and larger; railroads opened up new markets; the heavy flow of immigrants provided cheap labor, and discovery of new mineral resources increased tremendously the supply of raw materials. As a result, factories increased in size, hiring many more workers and buying more machinery. Individual capitalists were unable to finance these huge projects, and new business forms were created. They were:

The Corporation: A company sells shares of stocks; shareholders elect the management (the Board of Directors), casting one vote, usually, for each share of stock owned; the management then selects the officers of the company who run the business on a day-to-day basis but who are responsible to the Board of Directors and ultimately to the shareholders.

The Trust: As industries grew, many related corporations such as sugar refineries merged into one large combination, run by a Board of Trustees.

Shareholders assigned their share in the corporation to trustees who managed the new trusts as Boards of Directors did for the corporation. The trustees were often members of the Board of Directors of the corporations. Often the creating of a trust was the work of an individual such as John D. Rockefeller who created the Standard Oil Trust to control the industry.

Advantages of the trust: Huge amounts of raw materials can be purchased more economically.

Large-scale manufacture creates more efficient production and distribution. The industry can make gainful use of by-products.

Disadvantages of the trust: Drives out small business and destroys competition. Regulates prices often unfairly through price cutting wars.

Concentrates great wealth and power in the hands of a few.

May control an industry by achieving a vertical or horizontal control. A *vertical trust* or organization is one where the trust owns or controls everything—raw materials, manufacturing, distribution facilities—needed by the company. A *horizontal trust* or organization is one where the trust owns either all the raw materials or all the manufacturing or all the distribution facilities of an industry.

Other related forms of business organization were the pools and holding companies. Pools were combinations of businesses that agreed to control prices; *holding companies* were arrangements in which a company controlled a portion of the stock in other corporations (for example, U.S. Steel Corporation).

Development of Trade Unions: The early factory system was responsible for many evils such as:

Use of child labor.

Low pay and a long working day.

Unsanitary working conditions.

Forced purchase at company stores.

There were no laws to restrain abuses by employers or to protect workers. Workers in America had found as early as 1793 that they could best achieve their demands and changes in working conditions by uniting. Gradually, large unions grew. The most important were:

Knights of Labor: Organized in Philadelphia, 1879, by garment workers, it aimed at organizing all workers into one large union. Although it reached a membership of 700,000, poor leadership and internal disputes caused its gradual collapse.

American Federation of Labor (AFL): Founded in 1886, it soon replaced the Knights of Labor; it organized skilled workers according to their trade, or craft. Craft unions in different cities united to form national craft unions in different fields (carpenters, painters, and so on). Thus the AFL is an organization of many craft unions united under a single leadership. Noted early leaders of the AFL: Samuel Gompers, one of the founders; William Green, who succeeded on Gompers's death and remained in charge from 1924 to 1952; George Meany.

Congress of Industrial Organization (CIO): In the early 1930s the AFL formed a Committee of Industrial Organization to consider the establishment of industry-wide—rather than craft—unions. It met with limited success and there were internal disagreements. In 1936 the Committee broke away from the AFL to create a union (CIO) based on all the workers in a particular industry—for example, all workers in the steel industry became members of the Steel Workers Union. The CIO gained recognition for its new unions through a series of sit-in strikes in the late 1930s. The AFL and CIO reunited as one union in 1955.

THE POPULIST MOVEMENT

With the disputed election of 1877 settled in favor of Hayes, the Reconstruction Era ended. The nation's interests turned to issues of economics. As business grew, wealth accumulated in the hands of businesspeople and bankers. Agricultural prices began a decline in 1884, which again intensified farm protests. Sectional antagonism intensified. A number of previous attempts to help the farmer's cause were revitalized, such as the Granger Movement, with little impact. Finally in 1892, several years of efforts to unite labor and farmers led to the formation of a third political party—the People's or Populist Party. Holding its first national convention in Omaha, the Populist Party produced a platform (Omaha Platform) that proposed significant reforms. To address the farmer's need for inflation and cheap money the Populists called for the coinage of silver at a 16 : 1 ratio with gold. The Platform also called for a graduated income tax, direct election of senators, a shorter work day and restrictions on immigration. In the presidential election James B. Weaver came in third behind Cleveland (Dem.) and Harrison (Rep.). Eventually the major features of the Omaha Platform were adopted by the federal government.

In 1896 the Populists nominated William Jennings Bryan for president. He was also the nominee of the Democrats who were won over to the 16 : 1 ratio for the coinage of silver by Bryan's stirring *Cross of Gold Speech,* one of the most famous speeches in American history. His campaign, while extensive, focused on the issue of the coinage of silver, which was considered the best way to help the farmers and workers as it would create an inflationary pattern. Bryan lost to William McKinley (Rep.) and with the return of better economic conditions and the start of the Spanish-American War the Populist Party declined and eventually died.

THE PROGRESSIVE MOVEMENT

The Progressive movement developed at the turn of the century, largely as a response to problems created in urban areas by industrial growth. The Progressives worked within the established party framework, with the exception of Theodore Roosevelt's "Bull Moose" party in 1912. They achieved a variety of reforms ranging from the Pure Food and Drug Laws (1906) under Theodore Roosevelt (Rep.) to the establishment of the Federal Reserve System (1913) under Woodrow Wilson (Dem.). Theodore Roosevelt and Woodrow Wilson were both leaders of the Progressive movement as was Robert La Follette of Wisconsin. They illustrate the range of participation in the movement.

Others involved in the movement were writers and publicists such as Lincoln Steffens (*Shame of the Cities*), Ida Tarbell (*History of the Standard Oil Company*), and Upton Sinclair (*The Jungle*).

The movement died with the U.S. entry into World War I but not before it had made profound changes in America's business and political life. The Progressive Movement is one example of a period of reform. They occur periodically throughout United States history. Other examples are Jacksonian Democracy, the New Deal, and the Great Society.

LEGISLATION AND SUPREME COURT DECISIONS RELATED TO INDUSTRIAL GROWTH AND THE PROGRESSIVE MOVEMENT: 1877–1916

Munn v. Illinois: In this Supreme Court case the Court declared that the state, not the federal government, had the right to regulate business. Therefore, citizens had to resort to the polls and control of state government rather than to the federal courts for redress in cases involving control and regulation of business. The case has been grouped with several other cases as the Granger Cases; cases that worked against the interests of the people and in favor of business. These attitudes eventually led to the Populist movement.

1877

Civil Rights Cases: In these cases the Supreme Court declared that the Fourteenth Amendment applied only to state actions involving infringement of civil rights. If one individual infringed on another's rights as guaranteed by the Fourteenth Amendment, it was an individual offense and redress had to be found in the state courts. Federal law and the Fourteenth Amendment did not apply. The reaction of Congress to this interpretation of its limited powers was to pass no further civil rights legislation until the 1950s.   1883

Wabash, St. Louis and Pacific Railroad Company v. Illinois: In this famous case the Supreme Court declared that the state of Illinois could not regulate interstate commerce. A state could only regulate intrastate commerce. This created a great need for federal legislation, which came in the Interstate Commerce Act.   1886

Interstate Commerce Act: This act set up fair rate schedules for railway freight, prohibiting special rates to trusts and the charging of higher rates for short hauls than for long hauls. It also established the Interstate Commerce Commission (ICC) to enforce the act.   1887

Sherman Antitrust Act: Aimed at breaking huge trusts into smaller units, it failed because it was not enforced and because some administrations favored big business.   1890

Plessy v. Ferguson: In this Supreme Court decision the court validated the principle of separate but equal facilities for African Americans established by the Jim Crow laws. These laws created a two-tier system of rights for African Americans and whites. The Jim Crow laws created a subservient class who had poor educational opportunities. The civil rights system of America was based on the concept of separate but equal until the 1950s.   1896

Pure Food and Drug Act: This act prohibited the sale of impure food and medicine; four years later the act was amended to include the prohibition of false advertising.   1906

Department of Labor: This was created to give labor representation in the cabinet.   1913

Federal Reserve Act: This act set up a system of Federal Reserve banks under the joint control of the people, government, and the banking industry to regulate and control credit.   1913

Clayton Antitrust Act: This act prohibited unfair agreements that might diminish competition; established a Federal Trade Commission (FTC) to investigate charges of unfair competition and prosecute such cases; prohibited competing businesses from having the same men on Boards of Directors.   1914

Conservation of Resources: Greedy lumber cutting depleted woods without replanting; unintelligent farming ruined soil; inefficient mining methods wasted oil and gas; indiscriminate hunting and fishing decimated wildlife. Under President Theodore Roosevelt, a conservation program to end these abuses was begun. The following measures were aimed at conserving our national resources:

   National forests: Under Roosevelt, millions of acres were set aside as forests; timber cutting was regulated so that there would be a continuous supply.

   Hunting licenses: In order to regulate killing of game, laws were passed by states requiring hunters and fishermen to purchase licenses.

Reclamation Law of 1902 known as the Newlands Act: Irrigation projects were made possible by the act. Projects were initiated aimed at controlling floods (which washed away valuable topsoil and caused much other damage), improving navigation and producing electric power for outlying areas, and reclaiming wastelands. The most important projects were: Boulder Dam in Arizona and Nevada, Grand Coulee Dam and Roosevelt Dam in Washington, Shasta Dam in California, Fort Peck Dam in Montana, Garrison Dam in North Dakota.

AMERICAN EXPANSION IN THE POST-CIVIL WAR PERIOD

In the post-Civil War period, Americans continued to move westward and settle the frontier. The railroad made settlement easier and opened new markets for eastern products and western raw materials and food. The movement led to warfare with the Native Americans and fighting on the plains continued until late in the century. The Dawes Act (1887) was an attempt to replace the tribal organization of the Native Americans by eventually making them citizens of the United States. In 1890 the Census Bureau reported there was no longer a definable frontier line as the country was settled coast to coast, although there were large areas with very few white settlers. The historian, Frederick Jackson Turner, developed an important thesis on what the "closing of the frontier" meant, stating that the formative years of American history were over. However, the nation continued to grow and expand. The growth of cities became the chief focus of domestic growth while expansion overseas became very important, especially after 1890.

THE GROWTH OF GREAT CITIES IN THE 19TH CENTURY

Cities were founded by the earliest colonists. Transportation facilities—harbors, rivers, river fords, and later canal and railroad lines—were important in determining the location of many cities. The nearness of raw material and a power supply, the availability of a labor supply, and the convenience of cheap transportation also were important factors in city location and growth.

Some Major U.S. Cities
BOSTON
Became an early shipping center because of Massachusetts Bay, proximity to the mouths of the Mystic and Charles rivers

CHICAGO
Railroad center; chief market for agricultural products of the central plains; approximate geographic center of great coal mining and steel manufacturing areas; harbor on Lake Michigan

DENVER
Junction of South Platte River and Cherry Creek; center of the Rocky Mountain states; access to mineral resources and oil

DETROIT
Center of a network of waterways made it a terminal for shipping on the Detroit River, River Rouge, St. Clair, Lake Erie, and Lake Huron; easy access to coal and steel by river and rail transport made it the birthplace of the automobile industry in the late 19th century

NEW ORLEANS
Located near the mouth of the Mississippi River and close to the Gulf of Mexico; proximity to external shipping (Gulf of Mexico) and internal transportation facilities (Mississippi River) made it the center of cotton and later oil industries

NEW YORK
Great natural harbor; juncture of Hudson River with Atlantic Ocean; waterway to the Midwest created by linking Hudson River to the Great Lakes via the Erie Canal

PHILADELPHIA
Junction of Schuylkill and Delaware rivers; proximity to coal fields; Pennsylvania Railroad gave it a link to the West

PITTSBURGH
Junction of Ohio, Allegheny, and Monongahela rivers; proximity to both coal and iron ore, making it convenient for growth of the smelting industry; oil and natural gas fields nearby

SAN FRANCISCO
Proximity to Sacramento and San Joaquin rivers; located on the Pacific Ocean, with one of the world's finest harbors; near great gold fields

SEATTLE
Located on Puget Sound and Lake Washington; the gateway to Alaskan gold fields; great shipping center for the Pacific; the center for the lumber and salmon fishing industries

OVERSEAS EXPANSION 1867–1917

The Alaska Purchase: Called "Seward's Folly," Alaska was purchased from Russia upon the urging of Secretary of State Seward in 1867 for $7.2 million.

Annexation of Hawaii: Discovered by an Englishman, Captain James Cook, in 1778, Hawaii first attracted the interest of the United States in 1820 when missionaries went there. In 1884 the United States leased Pearl Harbor as a naval station. In 1889 the native queen was overthrown by a rebellion, and the new government petitioned the United States to annex the islands. In 1898 Congress approved annexation.

Pacific Islands: In 1867 the United States annexed uninhabited Midway Island as a coaling station.

In 1889, by negotiation with European nations, the United States acquired Tutuila, Pago Pago for its valuable harbor.

The Panama Canal Zone: With possessions in the Atlantic and Pacific, the United States needed a way to get its navy from ocean to ocean without sailing around South America or Africa. A canal providing a short water passage between the two oceans was the ideal solution. Such a canal was first attempted by a French company, but it failed.

The United States under President Theodore Roosevelt in 1903 offered $10 million and a yearly rental of $250,000 to Colombia for use of land in the province of Panama where a canal could be built. The Colombian government refused the offer.

In November 1903 the Panamanian people rebelled, and with United States support, set up an independent government. Fifteen days later the new republic of Panama accepted the same terms offered to Colombia and gave the United States the right to build a canal and exclusive control of a Canal Zone in perpetuity. The United States paid Colombia $20 million as redress for the loss of her Province of Panama and Colombia recognized the independence of the Republic of Panama.

Virgin Islands: These islands, purchased from Denmark in 1917, provided a defense for the Panama Canal. They provided naval bases on the perimeter of the Caribbean Sea.

SPANISH-AMERICAN WAR

Steps Leading to War: In 1895 Cuban patriots revolted against harsh Spanish rule and were severely punished. Sensational American newspaper stories demanded intervention, as did American business owners who had considerable investments in Cuban sugar and tobacco.

In February 1898 the American battleship *Maine* was mysteriously blown up while in the harbor of Havana. The slogan "Remember the Maine" aroused the American public as did articles in the "yellow press."

The War: In April 1898 Congress declared war on Spain. An American army landed in Cuba and soon destroyed Spanish resistance. Meanwhile, the Spanish fleet bottled up in the harbor of Santiago, was thoroughly beaten while trying to escape. The Under Secretary of the Navy Theodore Roosevelt, before leaving to lead a contingent of the Army in Cuba at the Battle of San Juan Hill, arranged for the U.S. Navy in the Pacific to be ready to attack the Philippines in case of war with Spain. When war came, the fleet attacked the Spanish Fleet in the Philippines and occupied Manila. Spain then sought peace.

The Treaty of Paris: Signed in December 1898, it ended the war. It contained the following provisions:

Puerto Rico, Guam, and the Philippines were ceded to the United States.

Cuba was granted independence. The United States was to supervise this independence.

The United States paid $20 million to Spain for the Philippines.

SOME IMPORTANT INDIVIDUALS OF THE PERIOD 1877–1916

Jane Addams	James A. Garfield	Terrence V. Powderly
John P. Altgeld	Charlotte Perkins Gilman	Joseph Pulitzer
Susan B. Anthony	Samuel Gompers	Thomas B. Reed
Chester Arthur	Mark Hanna	Walter Reed
Ethel Barrymore	Benjamin Harrison	Jacob Riis
Edward Bellamy	John Hay	John D. Rockefeller
James G. Blaine	Rutherford B. Hayes	Theodore Roosevelt
William Jennings Bryan	William Randolph Hearst	Augustus Saint-Gaudens
Andrew Carnegie	Oliver W. Holmes	Margaret Sanger
George Washington Carver	Winslow Homer	Louis H. Sullivan
Mary Cassatt	William Dean Howells	William H. Taft
Willa Cather	Charles E. Hughes	Ida Tarbell
Tennessee Claflin	Helen Hunt Jackson	Samuel Tilden
Grover Cleveland	Sarah Orne Jewett	Mark Twain (Samuel
Roscoe Conkling	Oliver Kelley	Clemens)
Eugene Debs	Robert La Follette	Cornelius Vanderbilt
Emily Dickinson	Sidney Lanier	Booker T. Washington
Dorothea Dix	Mary Elizabeth Lease	Tom Watson
W. E. B. DuBois	Alfred T. Mahan	James B. Weaver
Isadora Duncan	Margaret Mead	Frances Willard
Thomas Eakins	Frank Norris	Woodrow Wilson
Enrico Fermi	Frederick Olmstead	Pearl White
Jim Fisk	John J. Pershing	Victoria Claflin Woodhull
Henry Ford	Gifford Pinchot	

**CHAPTER 7—
World War I, the
Interwar Period, and
World War II—
1916–1945**

HIGHLIGHTS OF AMERICAN FOREIGN POLICY TO WORLD WAR I

Throughout its history the United States has had contact and involvements with foreign nations. Our interest in South America stems from the founding of the nation. Interest in the Pacific was officially acknowledged as early as 1785, when still governed under the Articles of Confederation, Americans began trading with China, and, of course, the United States introduced Japan to modern times with the "opening" of Japan by Perry in 1853. There have always been foreign policy relations with Europe, but many have suggested the United States followed a policy of isolation from Europe during most of the 19th century. The War of 1812, efforts to keep England and France out of the Civil War, and the Spanish-American War are three among many possible indications that U.S. isolation from Europe was only a theory in the 19th century, and in fact, the United States interacted with other nations in pursuit of her national interests.

During the first 35 years of the nation's history several actions were taken that provided a foundation and attitude for much of United States foreign policy.

Proclamation of Neutrality by President Washington stated that the United States would be neutral in the war between England and France. This established the tradition of U.S. neutrality in European affairs.   1793

Washington's *Farewell Address* urged America not to sign an alliance with any nation.   1796

Jefferson's Inaugural Address promised that the United States would seek peace, commerce, and friendship with all nations, but would enter into entangling alliances with none. This became the basis of U.S. foreign policy until after World War II when the NATO alliance was established. Since then, the United States has signed many treaties allying itself with foreign nations, establishing a multilateral approach to international affairs.   1801

The *Monroe Doctrine* states an idea that guided U.S. policy toward the Americas. President Monroe promised that America would stay out of European affairs, and demanded that European countries stay out of the affairs of North and South America. Later presidents added their own interpretations to this basic policy as it applied to South America.

1823

INVOLVEMENT IN THE AMERICAS AND THE PACIFIC

Involvement in the Americas even preceded the Monroe Doctrine. In the post-Civil War period U.S. interest in the Americas became focused on Central America and new markets. Concern over Cuba culminated in the Spanish-American War. Desire to maintain "order" and keep European powers out of the area led to the sending of U.S. Marines to several nations. A highlight of U.S. involvement was the support of Panama's revolution and the building of the *Panama Canal* (completed in 1914). Involvement in the Mexican Civil War after 1911 almost led to a second war with Mexico.

Involvement in the Pacific became important for the United States after the Civil War with the rapid industrial growth that followed. Acquisition of islands as coaling stations (Samoa) and interest in new markets (Hawaii) illustrate this early involvement. Later the proclaiming of the *Open Door Policy* in China in 1899, U.S. involvement in the *Boxer Rebellion* in China in 1900, and the fact that President T. Roosevelt arbitrated the Russo-Japanese War in 1905 (for which he won the Nobel Peace Prize) showed continued concern for the U.S. position in Asia and the free access to markets. The *Spanish-American War* marked the emergence of the United States as a great power on the international scene. U.S. interest in Asia was seen by the acquisition of the Philippines at the end of that war.

WORLD WAR I

Causes: Sparked by the assassination of Archduke Ferdinand of Austria-Hungary on June 28, 1914, World War I was really caused by imperialistic and economic rivalries.

Why America Joined: Although President Wilson urged a policy of neutrality, Americans sold arms to the Allies, and in 1917 the United States abandoned its neutral position. The following events caused the United States to enter the war:

Sinking of the *Lusitania* by German submarines aroused public opinion.

The use of unrestricted submarine warfare (sinking ships without warning) by Germany. Such warfare was stopped temporarily after U.S. protest.

Arms sales and loans to the Allies led business to support them.

Anti-German propaganda by the Allies was effective.

Discovery of the Zimmermann Note, which demonstrated that Germany planned to urge Mexico to attack the United States.

On April 5, 1917, after Germany resumed unrestricted submarine warfare, sinking U.S. ships and those of other neutral nations despite a U.S. note of warning, Congress declared war.

The War: An army of 4 million troops was raised by a draft (Selective Service). Many volunteered. Bond drives helped to pay the huge expense of financing the war. These bonds were called Liberty Bonds.

The nation was mobilized for a total war effort including a *War Industries Board* and a *Committee for Public Information*.

American naval power broke Germany's blockade of England and helped destroy its fleet of submarines.

Two million American soldiers in the *American Expeditionary Force* (AEF), added to the forces of the Allies, crushed Germany on land under General John J. Pershing participated in battles at *Belleau Wood, Chateau-Thierry, St. Mihiel,* and the *Argonne Forest*.

An armistice was signed on November 11, 1918.

Wilson's Fourteen Points: Wilson's plan for a peace treaty included fourteen points that he hoped would prevent future wars. Some important points were:

Reduction of armaments.

An end to secret treaties.

Freedom of the seas.

An equitable solution to the colonial problem.

Self-determination of peoples.

Establishment of a League of Nations to arbitrate problems among nations peacefully.

Treaty of Versailles: Largely ignoring the Fourteen Points and intending to make Germany powerless to wage war forever, the Allies formulated a treaty that was signed June 28, 1919. Some of its important provisions were:

Surrender of German Territory: Cession of Alsace-Lorraine on the border of France and Germany to France; cession of other territories and colonies to other European allies and Japan. The colonies were to be administered by the various victorious nations under *mandates* of the League of Nations.

Reparations: Germany was forced to compensate the Allies for war damages.

Allied Occupation: The Allies occupied the Rhineland region in Germany, between the Rhine River and the French and Belgian borders.

War Guilt: Germany was forced to admit guilt for starting the war.

A League of Nations: Designed to provide a forum for the nations to discuss issues of conflict and prevent war, the League failed to act effectively in disputes and proved to be ineffective in preventing the outbreak of World War II. Although the League was Wilson's idea, the U.S. Senate voted not to accept the treaty. The failure of the United States to join is considered one reason for the League's failure.

THE 1920s

The Roaring Twenties: In the immediate postwar period there were many problems of adjustment to peace. Jobs were hard to find for many returning veterans. Farm prices were depressed and remained so during the entire period until the New Deal. Industry slowly recovered, prosperity returned, and there was an economic boom but it is now clear that the prosperity was not evenly distributed. There was a great land boom in Florida in which many people lost money and heavy speculation on the stock market culminated in the crash of October 1929.

Prohibition was instituted and led to the growth of crime as criminal leaders like Al Capone organized others to supply illegal alcohol. New attitudes towards sex and morality, the growth of "speakeasies" (bars), and the development of jazz and the blues have led scholars to refer to the period as the "roaring twenties."

The Red Scare of the early 1920s was a reaction to communism, which Americans came to fear after a Communist government was established in the Soviet Union and a Communist-led uprising occurred in Germany. Attorney General Palmer and J. Edgar Hoover made reputations for themselves, but the actual threat to the nation was exaggerated.

Return to normalcy was the slogan of the Harding Administration (Republican) elected in 1920. It supported a return to prewar attitudes and foreign policy positions. The United States Senate had turned down the Treaty of Versailles with its League of Nations. The Republicans returned to *isolationism,* as the policy of ignoring Europe was called. The administration ended with several scandals, such as Teapot Dome, and this discredited the federal government. Harding died in office. His successors, Coolidge and Hoover, basically followed the pattern of support of business and little government regulation begun by Harding. In foreign policy, although they professed a policy of isolationism, they supported negotiations over reparations from Germany and sent military forces to Central American nations on several occasions to protect the status quo and American business interests.

THE GREAT DEPRESSION AND THE NEW DEAL

Although a decade of good times and prosperity for some followed World War I, the United States was engulfed in a major depression at the end of the 1920s. Causes of the depression included:

High tariffs aimed at eliminating European competition from American markets but the reduced trade made it impossible to sell U.S. goods abroad.

Speculation in real estate and stocks caused artificial rises in prices.

Overproduction and unemployment caused in part by replacement of workers with machines.

War debts absorbed European purchasing power, lessening foreign trade.

Too much credit on easy terms caused financial collapses when borrowers were unable to pay back their loans.

The stock market crash of October 1929 is considered the starting point of the Great Depression. The federal government under President Hoover took little action to correct the economic problems believing the economy would adjust naturally without interference and that the states or local charity should help the jobless until the economy again was operating fully. It reflected the laissez-faire attitudes and Social Darwinist philosophy that had prevailed in the Republican Party in the 1920s. After two years with no economic improvement, Hoover did support some federal help (Reconstruction Finance Corporation).

In the *election of 1932* Franklin D. Roosevelt, a Democrat, defeated Herbert Hoover. As a candidate, Franklin D. Roosevelt promised action to combat the depression. The actions became incorporated in what is known as the *New Deal*—another period of major reforms. The various measures of the New Deal taken to combat the depression have been grouped by some historians in the general categories of the "3 Rs"—relief, recovery, reform. Some historians reject this classification as some acts fit in more than one category. However, the "3 Rs" provide one organizational scheme for categorizing the many New Deal measures. Examples of each type of legislation are:

1. *Relief*—direct giving of goods, clothing, shelter, and jobs to the unemployed. *Works Progress Administration (WPA)*: The federal government gave employment to men on work projects it initiated.

2. *Recovery*—laws aimed at curing the poor state of the economy at that moment. *Home Owners Loan Corporation (HOLC)*: Government made loans available to homeowners to prevent loss of their homes to mortgagees.

   Agricultural Adjustment Act (AAA): Reduced amount of crops planted to create artificial shortages and stimulate prices.

3. *Reform*—long-term changes in the economy designed to prevent future depressions.

   Tennessee Valley Authority (TVA): Comprehensive development of the production of electricity and the control of flooding in the Tennessee River valley. Opposed by many as socialism—government involvement, development, and ownership of industry—the TVA was approved by the Supreme Court. The electricity produced proved vital to the development of the atomic bomb by the United States in World War II.

   Reciprocal Tariff Act: Removed barriers to trade by lowering tariffs through negotiation.

   National Industrial Recovery Act (NIRA): Codes of fair practices including rights of workers were drawn up by each industry involved in interstate commerce. The codes were administered by the National Recovery Administration (NRA). The Supreme Court, interpreting the Constitution very strictly, declared this and some other early New Deal legislation unconstitutional.

Supreme Court Controversy: Roosevelt attempted in 1937, after his overwhelming reelection, to change the composition of the Supreme Court. Roosevelt was upset by the failure of the Court to approve much of his legislation. Congress refused to support his "court packing" plan. With the death of several judges, Roosevelt was able to appoint new judges who supported his legislation and interpreted the Constitution more loosely.

Recession of 1937: In the first few years of the New Deal economic conditions improved in the nation. In 1937 recovery staggered and there was a little recession. With the coming of World War II the American economy improved rapidly and the Great Depression quickly receded from view.

Organized Labor: The American Federation of Labor (AFL) had organized only skilled workers. In 1935 the AFL created a Committee for Industrial Organization, headed by John L. Lewis, to organize unskilled and semiskilled workers. The committee left the AFL in 1936, and in 1938 formed its own labor organization, the Congress of Industrial Organization (CIO). Instead of dividing workers by craft, the CIO divided them by industry. For example, all workers in the automobile industry, whether skilled or unskilled, became members of the United Automobile Workers. The CIO made quick progress in organizing previously unaffiliated industrial workers in such fields as steel, textile, shipbuilding, and rubber. The CIO used "sit-in" strikes as a tool to gain recognition from industry.

IMPORTANT LEGISLATION AND SUPREME COURT DECISIONS 1916–1945

Adamson Act: Provided for eight-hour day for railroad workers.   1916

Norris-LaGuardia Anti-Injunction Act: Limited power of courts to issue injunctions and curtail workers' rights to strike and picket.   1932

New Deal Legislation: (See acts mentioned above). Acts were passed dealing with many issues from agricultural reform to workman's compensation; they changed the American economy. A number of the programs were reversed during President Reagan's terms in office.   1933

Federal Communications Commission (FCC): Regulates communication by telephone, telegraph, radio, and television.   1934

Securities and Exchange Commission (SEC): Protects investors by establishing fair procedures in sale of stocks; in 1935 the SEC was given power to regulate financial practices of public utilities involved in interstate commerce.   1935

Schechter Poultry Corp. v. U.S.: The Court declared the National Industrial Recovery Act unconstitutional.   1935

National Labor Relations Act (called Wagner Act): Safeguarded labor's rights to organize and bargain through unions.   1935

Social Security Act: Established a federal-state system of unemployment compensation and old age pensions paid for by a federal tax on employee's income and employer's total payroll.   1935

U.S. v. Butler: The first Agricultural Adjustment Act was declared unconstitutional.   1936

NLRB v. Jones and Laughlin Steel Corp.: The Court, in a 5-4 decision upheld the National Labor Relations Act.   1937

Fair Labor Standards Act: Established minimum wage and work week of 40 hours with time and a half for overtime.   1938

Serviceman's Readjustment Act (GI Bill): Addressed the issue of demobilizing the 12,000,000 servicemen who had fought in World War II by providing loans to veterans for housing and education.   1944

WORLD WAR II
Background: Many interrelated incidents and complex problems led to the outbreak of World War II.

Rise of Fascism: In 1922 Mussolini, leader of the Italian Fascists, took power. Pursuing a militaristic policy as a solution to Italy's economic problems, he attacked Ethiopia in 1935. The League of Nations failed to intervene and Italy annexed Ethiopia and later Albania.

In 1931 Japan, led by a military dictatorship, attacked China and annexed Manchuria. In 1937 Japan invaded China. China lost Shanghai and coastal areas to the Japanese but continued fighting.

Germany, under Hitler, who took power in 1933, also embarked on a militaristic program to address economic problems. The three Fascist powers—Germany, Italy, and Japan—formed an alliance known as the Axis. Hitler denounced the Treaty of Versailles. He seized the industrialized Ruhr in 1936 and annexed Austria in 1938. Hitler and his Nazi Party made vicious attacks on Catholics and Jews and suppressed all who did not agree with his policies. Yet the League of Nations and the World War I Allies did not join together to stop any of the aggressive moves of the Axis powers. In 1938 England and France negotiated the Munich Agreement with Hitler hoping to bring "peace in our time" by allowing Hitler to take the Sudetenland from Czechoslovakia but Hitler soon broke the agreement. Hitler invaded Poland in September 1939.

The War before the Entry of the United States: France and Britain declared war on Germany to help Poland resist the attack, but they failed. Germany speedily conquered Norway, Denmark, the Netherlands, Belgium, and then France. Great Britain and the British Commonwealth together with governments in exile from the conquered countries and the colonies of these countries continued the war. England withstood a massive air onslaught by the Germans in 1940. Finally in June, 1941, Hitler broke a treaty with the Soviet Union and attacked, bringing the Soviets into the war on the side of the Allies—those fighting against Germany and Italy and later Japan. In spite of severe losses China continued to resist the Japanese forces. The feuding Chinese Communist and Nationalist forces joined in the resistance.

American Involvement in the War: On the outbreak of war in Europe in 1939, a policy of neutrality was declared by President Roosevelt. It was later repealed and replaced by the Lend-Lease Act, which gave the president power to sell or lease war equipment to any country whose defense he deemed important to the preservation of American safety. America became "the arsenal of democracy," and supplied Great Britain with arms after the fall of France in 1940.

America Enters: Relations between the United States and Japan became very strained in the 1930s. Negotiations were undertaken in Washington to address these differences. Then, on December 7, 1941, the Japanese air force and navy, in a surprise attack on Pearl Harbor, destroyed a large part of the American fleet that was stationed there. The United States became a participant in World War II when, the next day, Congress declared war on Japan, and three days later, Germany and Italy declared war on the United States.

Wartime Government Agencies: The government quickly organized for full-scale war while military forces were rapidly built up. A number of agencies were established to run the war. Among them were:

War Production Board (WPB): Organized industry so that war materials could be produced at the highest level of efficiency.

Office of Price Administration (OPA): To prevent inflation and a black market, the OPA set prices and rationed goods such as oil and food. This assured a fair distribution of the limited consumer supplies and assured the needs of the military would be met.

War Labor Board (WLB): Settled disputes between business and labor without strikes so that production would not be interrupted and morale would be high.

Fair Employment Practices Committee (FEPC): Aimed at insuring morale and maximum use of the labor force by preventing employer discrimination against workers because of race or religion. The efforts of this committee laid the foundation for the Civil Rghts Movement of the 1950s.

Office of War Information (OWI): Issued patriotic material and served as the propaganda branch of the government. Its goal was to maintain morale by warning people against defeatist and harmful propaganda.

Allied Wartime Cooperation: During the war the allied leaders, Churchill (England), Stalin (Soviet Union), De Gaulle (Free France), Jiang Jieshi (China), and Roosevelt (United States) held a series of conferences (Casablanca, Cairo, Teheran) to plan war strategy, and at Yalta (1945) to plan for the postwar world. Different combinations of these Big Five leaders attended these meetings, which made it possible for the war effort to be unified. These wartime conferences set the precedent for postwar summit meetings.

The War in Europe: In November, 1942, General Eisenhower, Commander of Allied Forces, landed with Allied armies in French West Africa and captured Morocco and Algeria. In 1943 Sicily and then Italy were invaded.

The final phase of the war began on June 6, 1944, with the Allied invasion of the Normandy peninsula in France. Caught between an attack by Soviet troops on the east and Allied troops on the west, German resistance crumbled after a final attempt to stop the invasion in the Battle of the Bulge in December, 1944. On May 1 it was announced that Hitler had committed suicide, and on May 7, 1945, the Germans surrendered unconditionally.

The War in Asia: Japan quickly captured the Philippines, Guam, Wake, Hong Kong, and Singapore. The crippled U.S. fleet was unable to stop the occupation of these and other islands. By the spring of 1942, the tide began to turn with aid from Australia and New Zealand.

Important naval victories in the Coral Sea and at Midway (the "turning point of the war") shattered most of the Japanese fleet. This was followed by a series of American victories in hotly fought battles on Pacific islands. Guadalcanal, the Aleutians, and Bougainville fell in 1943; the Marshalls, Saipan, the Philippines, Corregidor, and Iwo Jima in 1944 and 1945.

Meanwhile, China continued to fight Japan on the mainland, and following the agreement signed at Yalta, Russia invaded Japanese-held lands in Manchuria on August 8, 1945. On August 6 and 9, 1945, atomic bombs were dropped on the Japanese cities of Hiroshima and Nagasaki. On the 14th of that month, the Japanese agreed to unconditional surrender. The official surrender document was signed on board the U.S.S. *Missouri* on September 2, 1945, ending World War II. The fighting in Europe had already ended.

SOME IMPORTANT INDIVIDUALS OF THE PERIOD 1918–1945

Marian Anderson	Marcus Garvey	Douglas MacArthur
Stephen V. Benet	Warren Harding	George Marshall
David Ben-Gurion	Ernest Hemingway	Benito Mussolini
Mary Bethune	Adolf Hitler	Georgia O'Keeffe
Louis D. Brandeis	Herbert Hoover	A. Mitchell Palmer
Willa Cather	Harry Hopkins	George Patton
Charles Chaplin	Charles E. Hughes	Frances Perkins
Winston Churchill	Cordell Hull	John Pershing
Calvin Coolidge	Harold Ickes	Mary Pickford
Charles De Gaulle	Jiang Jieshi	A. Philip Randolph
T. S. Eliot	Al Jolson	Paul Robeson
Albert Einstein	Frank Kellogg	Eleanor Roosevelt
Dwight Eisenhower	Robert LaFollette	Franklin Roosevelt
Albert B. Fall	Fiorello LaGuardia	George H. "Babe" Ruth
F. Scott Fitzgerald	Vladimir I. Lenin	Nicola Sacco
Daniel C. French	John L. Lewis	Carl Sandburg
Clark Gable	Charles Lindbergh	Alfred E. Smith
Mahatma Gandhi	Henry Cabot Lodge	Joseph Stalin
Greta Garbo	Joe Louis	Gertrude Stein

John Steinbeck	Orson Welles	Frank Lloyd Wright
Norman Thomas	Edith Wharton	Richard Wright
Jim Thorpe	Wendell Willkie	Minoru Yamasaki
Bartolomeo Vanzetti	Woodrow Wilson	Mao Zedong

CHAPTER 8—
The Postwar Period,
the Cold War, and
After—1945–2003

THE IMMEDIATE POSTWAR PERIOD

The problem of demobilizing 12 million servicemen and women and returning them to civilian life was addressed by the *Serviceman's Readjustment Act of 1944*, commonly known as the G.I. Bill of Rights. Among its provisions were:

Government-financed job training and education for discharged servicemen and women.

Unemployment payments for veterans.

Loans to veterans for business, farm, and home construction.

With the end of rationing and price control, prices rose rapidly. There was a period of inflation, but a postwar depression, which many people had feared, was avoided. No truly satisfactory solution for the problem of inflation was found, and inflationary pressure continued to affect the nation for many years.

FOREIGN POLICY ISSUES
The United Nations
Meetings at Bretton Woods in 1943 and at Dumbarton Oaks in 1944 laid the basis for a worldwide organization dedicated to finding peaceful solutions to international problems. On April 25, 1945, delegates from 50 nations met in San Francisco to draw up the charter for a new organization, the United Nations, to replace the League of Nations. The main provisions of the charter were:

Member nations would not help an aggressor nation.

Member nations would settle disputes peacefully.

Member nations would use neither force nor the threat of force to settle disputes.

Member nations would use the armed might of an international police force to fight against aggressors.

The Charter of the United Nations created the following governing bodies:

General Assembly: Composed of delegates from each member nation, it discusses and recommends solutions to international problems, but must refer all solutions regarding the use of force to the Security Council. Each nation has one vote.

Security Council: Consists of 15 members, five permanent members—the Big Five: (the victors in World War II over Germany and Japan) the United States, Great Britain, France, China (the government of Jiang Jieshi on Taiwan held the seat until 1972 when the People's Republic was given the seat), the Soviet Union (replaced by Russia in 1991)—and ten nonpermanent members elected for a two-year term by the General Assembly. Decisions may be passed by the vote of nine members, but must include all of the Big Five. That gives any one of the great powers veto power over the Council's decisions.

The Council bears primary responsibility under the UN Charter for the maintenance of international peace and security. Situations may be brought to its attention by any nation and the Council can investigate it or initiate action. Peacekeeping missions are voted on by the Security Council.

The Economic and Social Council: Studies and makes suggestions for economic and social betterment of countries.

The Secretariat: The UN's administrative arm, headed by the Secretary General, who is elected by the General Assembly. Its task is to carry out those policies adopted by the Assembly and Council. It oversees peacekeeping forces. The headquarters is in New York City. Other offices are in Geneva, Switzerland, former headquarters of the

League of Nations, the Hague, the Netherlands, seat of the International Court of Justice, and other cities.

There are many other important organizations and committees connected with the United Nations. Among the more important are:

Trusteeship Council, International Court of Justice, International Labor Organization, and World Health Organization.

THE COLD WAR

At the end of World War II, previously amicable relations between the United States and the Soviet Union deteriorated. President Truman, who had become president after the death of Roosevelt in April 1945, reacted quickly, and the basis of the U.S. post-World War II foreign policy was set by the end of 1947. The focus was a struggle with the Soviet Union to block their expansion while protecting the interests of the United States and its allies. Nuclear weapons held by both sides after 1948 deterred a "hot war" between the superpowers. The antagonisms remained between the two superpowers until the mid-1980s although there were times of improved relations such as the period of *détente* under President Nixon. With the introduction of the policy of glasnost by President Gorbachev in 1985, relations between the two powers changed rapidly. Presidents Reagan and Gorbachev held several summit meetings and negotiated arms reductions. With the fall of the Berlin Wall in 1989 and the subsequent breakup in 1991 of the Soviet Union into the *Union of Independent States*, the Cold War was declared ended.

MAJOR COLD WAR EVENTS

Truman Doctrine: Truman announced a pledge of aid to the governments of Greece and Turkey, which he believed were being threatened by Soviet-led Communist interests. The doctrine was later interpreted to mean the United States would oppose the overthrow of any democratic government.   1947

"X" Article: George Kennan of the State Department published an article in the magazine *Foreign Affairs* that outlined as the goal of U.S. policy the containment of the Soviet Union to prevent its expansion and spreading doctrines of communism. Known as the *Containment Policy,* it was adopted as the basis of U.S. Cold War policy and underlay many of the events of the Cold War.   1947

National Security Act: This act established the National Security Council as an advisory body to the president and the CIA as an information-gathering/spying organization.   1947

Marshall Plan: Secretary of State Marshall's European Recovery Program, known as the Marshall Plan, made provision for United States' financial assistance to European countries whose economies had not recovered from World War II. Offered to all European nations, the plan was rejected by Communist countries.   1947

Berlin Blockade: The Soviet Union blocked land access to Berlin and the United States responded with an airlift of supplies.   1948

North Atlantic Treaty Organization (NATO): NATO, the first U.S. peacetime military alliance, reversed George Washington's advice of 1797 to avoid permanent alliances. NATO was designed to block or contain Communist, especially Soviet, expansion in Europe.   1949

Communist Victory in China: After a struggle dating back to the 1920s, the Chinese Communists under Mao Zedong defeated the Nationalist forces of Jiang Jieshi. The Nationalists fled to Taiwan, establishing a government there that was recognized as the government of China by the United States and the UN until the Nixon administration reversed the policy and officially recognized the mainland government of Mao Zedong. In the early 1950s this "loss of China" was a divisive issue in U.S. domestic politics.   1949

Korean War: Communist North Korea attacked South Korea; the United States and other nations under the United Nations flag fought for three years to block the aggression. The armistice terms essentially restored the status quo. Communist North Korea continues as a threat to international security, having announced in 2003 that it had developed nuclear bombs.

1950–53

Southeast Asia Treaty Organization (SEATO): Designed to contain Communist, especially Chinese, expansion in Asia.

1954

Fall of Dien Bien Phu and *Geneva Conference on Vietnam*: After the French lost their important base at Dien Bien Phu to the Vietnamese Communists, at Geneva, a peace plan was developed for the region. It was rejected by Ngo Dinh Diem, premier of South Vietnam.

1954

Involvement in Vietnam: The United States became more and more involved in Vietnam as U.S. foreign policy focused on the containment of Communism in Southeast Asia (see Vietnam War on pp. 353–354).

1955

Hungarian Revolt: Hungary's attempt to throw off Soviet domination was crushed by Soviet military intervention.

1956

Aswan Dam: Foreign aid became a tool of the Cold War. The United States and Great Britain offered to help Egypt build a high dam at Aswan to aid economic development of the nation. They later withdrew the offer and Egypt received funding from the Soviet Union.

1956

Suez Canal Seized: Responding to Egypt's seizure of the Canal in an attempt to raise money for development, France, England, and Israel invaded Egypt and were stopped by the United States and the USSR. This provided a rare example of superpower Cold War cooperation.

1956

Eisenhower Doctrine: Approved by Congress, this permitted the United States to extend economic and military aid to Middle Eastern countries that wanted it because they believed they were threatened by Communists.

1957

Lebanon: United States sent troops to keep Communists from seizing power.

1958

U-2 Spy Plane: The Soviets shot down a U.S. spy plane over Soviet territory, which ended a move toward rapprochement at the end of Eisenhower's presidency.

1960

Independence of African Nations: The United Nations admitted 13 new African nations to membership. Civil War broke out in the Republic of the Congo and the United Nations intervened. Many of the nations were caught in the Cold War seeking financial and military aid from both sides.

1960

Cuban Revolution: Castro's guerrilla troops seized control of Cuba. Relations with the United States rapidly deteriorated as Castro established a Communist state in Cuba. Many Cubans fled to the United States and finally the United States broke diplomatic relations with Cuba.

1961

Bay of Pigs: Unsuccessful attempt by Cuban refugees backed by United States to invade and overthrow Castro's Communist regime in Cuba.

1961

Berlin Wall: East Germans sealed off their part of Berlin from the West. The wall became the symbol of the Cold War.

1961

Cuban Missile Crisis: Soviet attempt to set up intermediate range missiles in Cuba was blocked by a U.S. blockade and political maneuvering. Nuclear war was narrowly avoided.

1962

Hot Line Agreement: Established direct rapid communication between Moscow and Washington, suggesting cooperation was possible between the superpowers. First used during the Six-Day War of 1967 between Israel and its Arab neighbors.

1963

Limited Nuclear Test Ban Treaty: After many years of bomb testing and unilateral stopping of tests, a treaty was signed banning the testing of nuclear weapons in the atmosphere, in outer space, or underwater. Underground tests were permitted.

1963

Dominican Republic Intervention: President Johnson sent U.S. troops into the Dominican Republic to crush a "band of Communist conspirators" who the president claimed had gained control of a revolution against an authoritarian president.

1965

Outer Space Treaty: Banned military bases, weapons, and weapons tests in space and established principles for peaceful development of space.

1967

Pueblo Seized: A U.S. intelligence-gathering ship was seized off Korea. After a U.S. officer signed a statement accepting guilt for spying, the ship was released by the North Korean government.

1968

Nuclear Nonproliferation Treaty: The treaty banned the spread of nuclear weapons among signatory nations. It approved of access to nuclear energy for peaceful uses.

1969

Nixon's Visit to China: A new era in relations was confirmed with President Nixon's visit to the People's Republic of China. The U.S. accepted the People's Republic, not Taiwan, as the holder of the Security Council seat.

1972

Moscow Summit: President Nixon visited Moscow and signed several agreements including the ABM (Anti-Ballistic Missile) Treaty. An easing of Cold War tensions was obvious and was given the name *détente* by the press.

1972

Yom Kippur War and Shuttle Diplomacy: After the overwhelming Israeli victory in the Six-Day War of 1967 an uneasy truce settled in the Middle East. War erupted again in October 1973, which resulted in a costly Israeli victory. Secretary of State Kissinger undertook a series of visits to the Middle East ("Shuttle Diplomacy"), which resulted in cease-fire agreements between Israel and Syria. The Soviet Union sought influence in the Middle East to balance that of the United States and Israel. Arms were sold to both Arab nations and Israel by the United States and to the Arab nations by the Soviet Union, which led to further Cold War tensions.

1974

SALT II Agreement: The agreement limited the number of missiles and long-range bombers held by the United States and Soviet Union. President Carter asked the Senate to delay ratification after the Soviet Union invaded Afghanistan.

1979

Afghanistan Invasion: The Soviet Union sent troops into Afghanistan to maintain Soviet influence over the government. President Carter responded with a grain embargo, cutting off Soviet food supplies from the United States. With the advent of *glasnost*, an agreement involving the Soviet Union, the United States, and various Afghan factions was negotiated and Soviet troops were withdrawn. The United States ignored Afghanistan until September 11, 2001, and the start of the war on terrorism when an invasion was launched to drive out the Taliban and destroy the bases of al-Qaida.

1979

Iran-Iraq War: War broke out between these two oil-producing Muslim nations on the Persian Gulf. Both the United States and the Soviet Union had important interests in the region and the conflict added tensions to relations between the superpowers. The war became a stalemate with neither side able to win. With the change in U.S.-Soviet relations after 1985, a cease-fire was finally negotiated in 1988.

1980

The "Evil Empire": In a speech President Reagan declared his view of the Soviet Union as the "evil empire" responsible for the evils of the world. The policy dominated his administration's foreign policy in the first five years and led to such policies as the Anti-Soviet trade boycott that followed Reagan's declaration that the Soviet Union was responsible for repression in Poland.

1981

El Salvador/Nicaragua: Early in the Reagan years guerrilla movements in El Salvador and their relationship to the Sandinista-controlled government of Nicaragua became a major foreign policy concern of the Reagan administration with many Cold War ramifications. The administration established a guerrilla organization, the Contras, in Nicaragua to oppose the Sandinista government (considered communist) and asked Congress for funding, which was alternately given and denied.

1981

Invasion of Grenada: The Cubans and Soviets appeared to be building a major airstrip on the island of Grenada. Reagan ordered an invasion "to protect" Americans there. A new anti-communist government was then established.

1983

Iran-Contra Affair: Denied funding for the Contras, the Reagan administration developed a complex plan to free the American hostages held in Lebanon by selling arms to Iran thus getting Iran's support and then using the monetary profits to fund the Contras fighting against the Sandinista government of Nicaragua. The plan was developed secretly and lacked congressional approval. Several individuals involved in the plan, including President Reagan's National Security Advisor, Admiral Poindexter, and White House Aide Marine Lt. Col. Oliver North, were indicted on several counts of lawbreaking. Found guilty, on appeal the judge dismissed charges because testimony freely given before Congress by North and Poindexter was used to convict them thus encroaching on their Constitutional rights. The investigation ended inconclusively

1987

END OF THE COLD WAR

Glasnost and Peristroika: Mikhail Gorbachev emerged as the leader of the Soviet Union after several older Communist leaders died having served brief terms as head of the Soviet government. As a member of the younger generation, Gorbachev addressed domestic reform (peristroika) and changes in foreign policy (glasnost). His goal was to create limited reforms while maintaining Communism, but changes came rapidly in foreign affairs yet too slowly for many within the Union. The reform movements led to the collapse of the Soviet Union and the fall of Communism in Eastern Europe.

1985

Fall of the Berlin Wall: President Gorbachev refused to suppress reforms and changes in Eastern European nations militarily as had been done during the Cold War. Changes in Poland led by *Solidarity*, a nationalist, anti-communist labor union, and the *"Velvet Revolution"* in Czechoslovakia are examples of the changes. Finally, the East German government announced in November that the Berlin Wall, symbol of the Cold War, would be torn down and Germans could travel freely between East and West. Within a year the two Germanies voted for reunification, thus ending the division created by the "Iron Curtain" after World War II.

1989

Persian Gulf War: Iraq invaded Kuwait and the United States led a united effort through the United Nations to reverse the aggression. While not supplying troops, the Soviet Union and China supported the move in the Security Council. After considerable debate in the country, on January 12 the Senate narrowly passed (52-47) the *Resolution on Use of Force Against Iraq*, which authorized the use of U.S. military force. Operation Desert Shield, designed immediately after Iraq's attack to protect the Gulf states, became Operation Desert Storm. On January 15, 1991, President Bush ordered air attacks on Iraq. A ground attack followed on February 22, which ended with a cease-fire on February 27. The cease-fire called for the destruction of Iraq's nuclear, biological, and chemical weapons. A UN team was to oversee the destruction of weapons but over the years Iraq refused full cooperation, which led to the bombing of Iraq. Finally, Iraq forced the UN team to leave Iraq in 1998. The British and Americans, with limited UN support, mounted heavy bombing raids on Iraqi bases in late 1998.   1990

United Nations Negotiated End to Military Conflicts: With the Cold War ending, an end to several international conflicts with roots in the Cold War were negotiated including an end to the war in Afghanistan and an agreement ending the conflicts in Cambodia and El Salvador. The El Salvador accord has lasted. In Cambodia there was a UN-supervised election. When the Soviet Union withdrew its troops from Afghanistan, civil war broke out. The Taliban (Muslim Fundamentalists) forces gained control of most of the country by 2000. Russian–U.S. cooperation within the United Nations continued until the lead up to the war in Iraq in 2003.   1990

Coup Against Gorbachev: Communist conservatives led a coup against Gorbachev in August. It failed and Boris Yeltsin was elected president of Russia. The Soviet Union broke up into its separate states. Russia under Yeltsin was the strongest, although beset by many economic problems.   1991

Commonwealth of Independent States: A loose confederation, the Commonwealth of Independent States was formed. The Communist Party was declared unconstitutional in Russia and other states, thus ending the 74 years of Communist rule.   1991

Nuclear Arms Negotiations: With the breakup of the Soviet Union, four successor states held nuclear weapons. Tentative agreements were reached that would reduce arms by half. Russia was identified as the sole successor nuclear power. In spite of negotiations and agreements the future of Soviet nuclear weapons still remains unclear. Russia was allotted the Soviet Union's seat in the Security Council.   1991

Rising Nationalism and Continued Economic Instability: Russia and most of the other successor states to the Soviet Union struggled with economic reform made more difficult by high inflation, a rising crime rate, and intense nationalistic sentiments. Russia's invasion of the Muslim region of Chechnya provoked a continuing conflict that became involved with the war on terrorism.   1994

VIETNAM WAR

Background: Starting in 1945, the United States showed an interest in a non-communist Vietnam. The area soon became a battleground in the U.S. effort to contain Communism. The United States encouraged and gave limited support to the French in their fight against the Communist Viet Minh. When the French were defeated at Dien Bien Phu in 1954, their withdrawal was negotiated in the Geneva Accords and the nation was split into North and South. The United States secretly aided South Vietnam in a small way under Eisenhower. As war between the Communist North Vietnamese and their Viet Cong allies and the South Vietnamese intensified, the United States continued to expand its involvement to block Communism's spread. The "*domino theory*"—if one nation in Southeast Asia goes Communist, the others will also—was followed in establishing U.S. policy.

United States Involvement: President Kennedy insisted it was the Vietnamese's war to "win or lose" but he increased U.S. aid and sent in more troops. President Johnson continued the policy and after a confusing incident in the Gulf of Tonkin involving U.S. naval vessels, he obtained support from Congress for the *Gulf of Tonkin Resolution,* which gave the president full power to protect South Vietnam from further aggression and to protect U.S. forces. Johnson used the Resolution as a declaration of war.

Fighting the War: Lyndon Johnson's support for the war put strain on his Great Society program. Protest against U.S. involvement grew steadily and led to Johnson receiving less than a majority of the votes in the New Hampshire primary in 1968. He then withdrew from the presidential race. Hubert Humphrey, Johnson's vice president, was unable to extricate himself from the taint of war support. Nixon won the election and sought ways to end U.S. involvement in the Vietnam War. The massacre of civilians by U.S. troops at My Lai in 1969 and the shooting of student demonstrators by the National Guard at Kent State intensified U.S. protests against the war.

End of the War: Nixon desired to end the war but "with honor." Negotiations were begun. He authorized the invasion of Cambodia in 1970, and in 1972 he ordered the bombing of North Vietnam to put pressure on North Vietnam to negotiate. A reduction of U.S. forces was begun with the South Vietnamese gradually taking over responsibility for defending their nation. After lengthy negotiations that began in 1969 a settlement was reached in 1973, and U.S. forces were completely withdrawn. In 1975 the governments of South Vietnam, Cambodia, and Laos all fell to the Communists. In 1974 President Ford offered clemency to Vietnam War draft dodgers and in 1977 President Carter granted a full pardon to Americans who fled to Canada rather than be drafted to fight.

Effect of the War on the United States: This war, which some Americans see as the first war the United States "lost," continues to have a profound effect on the nation. Many refugees, including the so-called "boat people," fled Vietnam and some have found asylum in the United States. Many veterans, seeing the lack of support from the nation, felt alienated. During the Reagan and Bush administrations contacts with the Communist government of Vietnam gradually increased but relations remained strained over the issue of missing American soldiers. The "lessons of Vietnam" were referred to in debates over policy for Central America in the 1980s, but there was often disagreement as to what these lessons were—to interfere or not to interfere in foreign civil wars, to fight against native Communist movements or not, to subsidize guerrilla warfare in other nations or not, the validity of the "domino theory." President Bush seized the victory in the Persian Gulf War as a way of "putting Vietnam behind us." He claimed the successful United States intervention in the Middle East to stop aggression proved that the United States could pull together as a nation in support of a cause and be successful in a war. Immediately after the Persian Gulf War the president received the strong support of the American people and he announced the tragedy of Vietnam had been replaced by a new sense of American spirit and nationalism. In the 1992 presidential election campaign Bill Clinton's failure to serve in Vietnam was made a major issue by the Republican Party. After his election in 1993 Clinton stopped the government policy of blocking Vietnam's access to international trade loans and in 1994 ended the embargo on trade with Vietnam. There was progress on the issue of missing servicemen (MIAs) as Vietnam joined the search for remains. Finally, in 1995, following an agreement on seized property and the opening of liaison offices in Hanoi and Washington, Clinton recognized the government of Vietnam. Some Republicans opposed the move but the majority of business and political leaders supported normal relations with Vietnam.

MIDDLE EAST

Israeli-Palestinian Wars: The nation of Israel was established by U.N. vote in 1948. The first of six wars between the Palestinians and Israelis immediately began. The conflict in the Middle East continues to the present, with U.S. involvement a continuing factor. The United States has been a strong ally of Israel while trying to negotiate a resolution to the conflict.

U.S. Involvement: Beginning with the Eisenhower Doctrine (1957) the United States sent troops to the Middle East on several occasions. In 1957 troops helped crush a rebellion in Lebanon. Reagan sent marines to pacify Lebanon but withdrew (1983) them after 241 marines were killed in a terrorist attack on their barracks. The U.S. has bases in Saudi Arabia and other Gulf states.

Camp David Accords: (1978) President Jimmy Carter invited President Anwar Sadat of Egypt and Prime Minister Menachem Begin of Israel to Camp David, where agreements were reached. Egypt and Israel signed a peace treaty—the first Arab nation to recognize Israel.

Iran-Iraq War: (1978) The U.S. backed Saddam Hussein of Iraq in this long war, which included the use of poison gas by Iraq. Iran was led by Khomeini, who established the first Islamic fundamentalist state and supplied support for the Palestinians and terrorists in Lebanon.

Palestine Liberation Organization (PLO) and Israel's Invasion of Lebanon: (1982) Failing in war, the PLO mounted terror attacks on Israel with support from Iran and Lebanon. Israel invaded Lebanon but was forced to withdraw after years of fighting. The Palestinians began sustained attacks (the Intifada) on the Israeli forces occupying the West Bank. In 1988 President Reagan opened a limited dialogue with the PLO.

Persian Gulf War: (1990–1991) Iraq invaded Kuwait to control her oil production. President George H. W. Bush organized a coalition through the United Nations to drive Iraq out of Kuwait in Operation Desert Storm. An armistice called for the disarmament of Iraq's weapons of mass destruction, supervised by U.N. weapons inspectors. Saddam Hussein failed to cooperate; inspectors were withdrawn in 1998; Britain and the United States bombed military targets. George W. Bush reopened the issue in 2002 as part of his war on terrorism.

Oslo Accords: (1993) This agreement reached between Israel and the Palestinians outlined negotiating steps to achieve peace. First step was a peace treaty between Jordan and Israel (1994). Negotiations continued throughout Clinton's presidency with limited success and ended when President Arafat rejected an Israeli offer (1999).

Second Intifada: (2000–) Palestinians attacked Israeli forces in the West Bank. Israel reoccupied the area. Fighting and suicide bombings continue. Bush, unlike Clinton, ignored the situation as it worsened, finally linking a solution to the Israeli-Palestinian issue with the war in Iraq.

War in Iraq: (2003) Responding to the September 11, 2001 attack on the United States, war was first fought against al-Qaida and the Taliban in Afghanistan. Then President Bush turned attention to Iraq, seeking first a regime change, then the destruction of weapons of mass destruction, and finally arguing for a democratic Iraq as a model for a new Middle East that would include peace between Israel and Palestine and the recognition of two separate states. Bush had announced this as the administration's goal previously but had not become involved in negotiations. In mid-2003 a new negotiation timetable was introduced by several groups, including the E.U. (European Union), Russia, and the United States. As this is written in April 2003, the war in Iraq continues and the future of the Middle East and the role of the United States in the area is uncertain.

DOMESTIC ISSUES

MAJOR LEGISLATION AND SUPREME COURT DECISIONS—1945–2003

Taft-Hartley Law: Aimed at making unions more responsible in relations with management, it prohibited unfair labor practices.   1947

Presidential Succession Act: Revised the 1886 law and made the speaker of the house and then the president pro tempore of the Senate successors after the vice president.   1947

National Security Act: Reorganized the army, navy, and air force and established the cabinet-level Department of Defense, the National Security Council, and the CIA.   1947

Internal Security Act (McCarran Act): Required registration of Communists and all Communist front organizations.   1950

Department of Health, Education and Welfare: Created new cabinet-level department to handle these areas of social concern.   1953

Atomic Energy Act: Permitted private power companies to own reactors for the production of electric power.   1954

Brown v. Board of Education: Supreme Court decision reversed the concept of separate but equal in race relations and ordered the integration of schools to provide equal educational opportunities for blacks and whites.   1954

Highway Act: Established the federal interstate highway system.   1956

Civil Rights Act: First act dealing with civil rights and their guarantee passed by Congress since Reconstruction. Established a six-person Commission on Civil Rights to investigate civil rights violations.   1957

Landrum-Griffin Act: Included provisions to curb labor racketeers.   1959

Peace Corps: Program to aid economically undeveloped countries by sending volunteers to help in the development of their economy by doing many things from teaching farming techniques to building schools.   1961

Gideon v. Wainwright: The Supreme Court determined that a lawyer must be provided by the state for all those charged with committing a felony.   1963

Escobedo v. Illinois: The Supreme Court ruled that if requested, a lawyer had to be present during police interrogration before an indictment is made.   1964

Voting Rights Act: Act guaranteeing to all the right to vote in federal elections—directed toward southern blacks who flocked to register supported by federal marshals.   1965

Medicare Act: Provides medical service to those over 65 under the administration of the Social Security System.   1965

Office of Economic Opportunity (OEO): Catchall office set up to operate Job Corps, Operation Head Start, and other parts of Johnson's Great Society program to benefit depressed areas and underprivileged persons.   1965

Elementary and Secondary Education Act: Provided federal money for certain programs in public and parochial schools to improve the quality of education in the United States.   1965

Water Quality Act: Allowed federal government to set water purity standards for states to force industry to clean up the lakes and rivers of the nation.   1965

National Traffic and Motor Vehicle Safety Act: Set some federal safety standards for the auto industry.   1966

Freedom of Information Act: Made certain documents and records available to citizens who asked to see them, including some secret documents.   1966

National Committee on Product Safety: Commission to study potentially hazardous products and evaluate laws to protect consumers.   1967

Civil Rights Act: Directed toward eliminating racial barriers in most of the nation's housing.   1968

Consumer Credit Protection Act (Truth in Lending): Requires lenders and retailers selling merchandise on credit to make full disclosures of the total cost of such credit to the consumer.   1968

Washington Omnibus Anti-Crime Law (No-Knock Law): Designed to give more authority to police enforcement officials in the District of Columbia and to serve as a model of tough reform police laws for the nation.

1970

Environmental Policy Act: Established a commission in the White House to report on environmental quality and to oversee the enforcement of environmental legislation.

1970

Furman v. Georgia: The death penalty was held unconstitutional. Later decisions modified this opinion to make it permissible in some circumstances if applied fairly.

1973

Roe v. Wade: Declared state laws denying abortion during the first trimester of pregnancy unconstitutional as a violation of a woman's privacy to determine to end a pregnancy.

1973

Energy Policy and Conservation Act: Set control limits on car exhaust and gave the president more control over energy policy.

1973

Department of Energy: In response to the OPEC energy crisis of the 1970s, the Department of Energy was created, taxes on oil increased, and conservation measures were instituted.

1977

Civil Service Reform Act: These measures were part of President Carter's attempts to streamline and increase the efficiency of the government's bureaucracy. The act reduced the Civil Service.

1978

Air Transport Deregulation Act: Airline fares and routes were no longer to be controlled by government regulation.

1978

Bakke v. Board of Regents: The Supreme Court held that Bakke, a white who had been denied admission to medical school in California, had been discriminated against since his scores were higher than those of persons admitted to positions at the school reserved to minorities. The Court also upheld the University of California's use of race as a criterion for admission to achieve a mixed student body.

1978

Department of Education: As part of the streamlining efforts of President Carter, the various government offices dealing with education were consolidated in one department.

1979

Peacetime Draft Registration: Draft registration was required of 18-year-olds to have the country prepared for any international emergency. No one, however, was actually drafted into the armed services.

1980

Toxic Waste Superfund: Established to treat quickly dangerous spills of toxic wastes and to clean up toxic waste dumps.

1981

Economic Recovery Tax Act (ERTA): A supply-side tax program that reduced taxes and cut the budget, changing the long-standing taxing policies of the government.

1981

Anti-Drug Legislation: Each session of Congress from 1982–1989 passed drug legislation reflecting the continuing concern with drug use and traffic. The 1989 law established a cabinet-level position of *Director of National Drug Policy* (Anti-Drug "Tsar") to coordinate President Bush's war on drugs. The 1989 legislation included the death penalty for major drug trafficking and the 1988 law required schools to implement programs aimed at preventing illegal substance use and provided assistance to Colombia, Peru, and Bolivia to fight drug traffickers.

1982

Clean Water Act: Authorized a 10-year extension of the federal program for subsidizing building of sewer plants. It was passed over President Reagan's veto.

1987

Savings and Loans (S & L's) Bailout Legislation: Congress provided funds and approved a program to buy or shore up financially failing S & L's.   1987

Repeal of the Catastrophic Health Care Act of 1988: In a major change of policy and under heavy pressure from AARP (American Association of Retired Persons), Congress repealed the expansion of the Medicare program that it had passed the previous year. This was the first time Congress had repealed a major social benefit it had enacted. The act had extended Medicare to cases of long-term hospital care and catastrophic illness to be paid for by a surtax on Medicare enrollees. Their objection to this tax led to the repeal of the law.   1989

Crime Control Bill: In this compromise bill Congress continued to reject tight gun control provisions. The law increased support of police training.   1990

Board of Education of Oklahoma City v. Dowell: Supreme Court held that a school district could end busing to achieve integration if it had done "everything practical" and the schools were single race because of local housing patterns. The case illustrated the continuing importance of the courts in the struggle for civil rights.   1990

Americans with Disabilities Act: The act prohibits discrimination against disabled persons in employment, public services, and accommodations, and requires that telecommunication be made accessible to those with speech and hearing impairments. Employers are required to make reasonable accommodations for disabled workers.   1990

Immigration Bill: The first major revision of immigration policy in 25 years changed visa requirements, allowed for more immigrants, especially those with education and skills needed in the United States, and made it harder to exclude foreigners because of their sexual persuasion.   1990

Clean Air Act: After 10 years of inaction the 1977 Clean Air Act was revised and updated with support from President Bush. Deadlines for control of harmful emissions by cities and motor vehicles were revised. Provisions to control acid rain and chlorofluorocarbons, which harm the earth's ozone layer, were also made.   1990

Rust v. Sullivan: The Supreme Court by a 5-4 vote upheld regulations issued in 1988 by the Department of Health and Human Services that barred federally funded health and family planning clinics from providing information on abortion. It was one more case in the ongoing struggle over abortion rights fought out in the courts.   1991

Civil Rights Act (Job Bias Bill): After several years of debate and struggle between Congress and President Bush, the president signed a bill that reversed several recent Supreme Court decisions that had made it more difficult to achieve redress in cases of job discrimination in employment.   1991

Planned Parenthood v. Casey: The Supreme Court by a 5-4 vote upheld several Pennsylvania laws restricting a woman's access to abortion, but the Court affirmed the basic right to abortion established in *Roe v. Wade.*   1992

Family and Medical Leave Act: The act provides up to 12 weeks of unpaid leave in any 12-month period for workers giving birth or adopting a child, to care for a seriously sick child, spouse, or parent, or in case of workers' illness. It applied only to companies employing 50 or more people.   1993

National Service Trust Act (Americorps): A federal program was established to allow students to receive financing for college or technical training in return for one or two years of public service in education, environment, public safety, or other areas of need. Students receive $5,000 per year of service. After their victory in 1994, Republicans moved to abolish the program. Under George W. Bush they reversed their position and supported the idea of service, although they found it difficult to increase the funding because of tax cuts and the war on terrorism.   1993

NAFTA (North American Free Trade Agreement): The pact between the United States, Canada, and Mexico was to eliminate or reduce tariffs and other restrictions on investment and trade over a 15-year period beginning on January 1, 1994.   1993

Brady Handgun Violence Prevention Act: The so-called Brady Bill imposes a five-day waiting period for the purchase of a handgun. The act was the result of twelve years of lobbying by Reagan's press secretary, who was disabled in the 1981 attempted assassination of President Reagan.   1993

Education Act (Goals 2000): Following an initiative begun under President Bush, the act set goals for the nation to reach voluntarily by the year 2000. A National Education Standards and Improvement Council was established to develop national education standards.   1994

Anti-Crime Act: The bill, the first passed in six years, called for spending $30 billion over six years divided among enforcement (100,000 more police), prison construction, and prevention measures. The bill also extended the death penalty to more than 50 crimes and required that released sex offenders had to notify authorities of their address and communities were to be notified of it.   1994

GATT (General Agreement of Tariffs and Trade): The agreement, negotiated over several years and known as the Uruguay Round, was designed to liberalize existing national and international trade regulations, eliminate quotas and tariffs, and introduce measures to increase trade. GATT established the WTO (World Trade Organization), a new organization responsible for implementing the agreement.   1994

Clinton Vetoes Stopgap Spending Measures: Budget disagreements between Democratic President Clinton and the Republican-controlled Congress led to two government shutdowns and a standstill in legislation.   1995

Telecommunications Act: This act expanded competition in telephone long-distance service and allowed cable companies to compete for regional calling; relaxed restrictions on TV station ownership; deregulated cable rates.   1996

Antiterrorism Act: This act appropriated $1 billion to fight terrorism over four years; denied entry into the United States to members of any terrorist groups, and permitted prosecution of anyone making donations to such groups; required an ID to purchase any plastic explosives.   1996

Welfare Reform Act: This act "ended welfare as we know it." Block grants for welfare were given to states; five-year limit on grants to individuals; welfare participants to be cut 50 percent by 2000.   1996

Health Insurance Portability Act: This act permits individuals changing jobs to keep their health insurance.   1996

Illegal Immigration Bill: This bill has penalties for smuggling or providing false documents; it expanded the border patrol and fence in San Diego.   1996

Balanced Budget Agreement: Democrats and Republicans finally agreed on the plan to create a balanced budget by 2002. (The goal was achieved by 1998 due to the booming economy.)   1997

NATO Expansion Act: With this act, admission of Poland, Hungary, and the Czech Republic to NATO was approved.

1997

Transportation Equity Act: With this act, $173 billion was approved for highways, $41 billion for mass transit plans, and $2 billion for highway safety.

1998

Internal Revenue Service Reform Bill: This bill established an oversight board for IRS operations; included a taxpayers' "Bill of Rights," an attempt to make the IRS both more efficient and more helpful to taxpayers.

1998

Impeachment: House voted to impeach President Clinton on two charges—perjury and obstruction of justice.

1998

President Clinton Acquitted: The Senate, acting as the jury in the impeachment trial of President Clinton, found him "not guilty" on all counts. House members acting as prosecutors obtained only 45 votes on the first charge (perjury) and 50 on the second (obstruction of justice), thus failing to win the necessary two-thirds (67) votes of the Senate.

1999

Bush v. Gore: The Supreme Court's 5–4 decision gives Florida's electoral votes to George W. Bush, thus giving him the presidency. Gore wins the popular vote but Bush wins in the Electoral College by four votes.

2000

Tax Reform Act: Republican idea of returning the surplus to the people incorporated in $1.35 trillion 10-year tax cut reducing projected surplus by nearly a half.

2001

September 11 Attacks on World Trade Center (New York City) and Pentagon (Washington) by terrorists: Four hijacked planes crash, killing more than 2,800 people. President proclaims war on international terror. Taliban rulers of Afghanistan attacked in attempt to destroy al-Qaida terrorist network.

2001

Airline Bailout Act; Airline Security Act; U.S. Patriot Act: Congress's first responses to September 11 aid airlines and victims, protect air travelers, and give powers to Department of Justice to limit civil rights in war on terrorism.

2001

"Axis of Evil": In State of the Union Address Bush labels Iraq, Iran, and North Korea an "axis of evil."

2002

Education Reform Bill: Labeled "No Child Left Behind," the measure calls for extensive testing of students to hold schools "accountable" in assuring each child can read and do math.

2002

Campaign Finance Reform: Led by Republican John McCain a bill restructuring how campaign contributions can be made by business and individuals was finally passed and signed.

2002

Vote on Iraq: Responding to the president's request, the Senate overwhelmingly supported a measure giving the president the power to use whatever force was necessary to destroy any weapons of mass destruction held by Iraq. The measure encouraged consultation with the United Nations.

2002

Security Council Vote: Introduced by the United States, the U.N. Security Council unanimously approved a resolution to send weapons inspectors back to Iraq in one last attempt to remove weapons of mass destruction.

2002

Homeland Security Bill: The largest government reorganization in fifty years brought together many departments dealing with immigration and terrorism in a new cabinet-level department. The bill excluded the CIA and FBI from the department.

2002

Atkins v. Virginia; Ring v. Arizona: (Death penalty decisions).   2002

War in Iraq: Failing to gain U.N. approval, the U.S. unilaterally attacked Iraq, stating the Senate's approval in 2002 was sufficient to permit the action. Victory was declared after six weeks but then guerilla warfare broke out, creating uncertainty for the future.   2003

Supreme Court Decisions: In *Lawrence v. Texas* the Court declared unconstitutional a Texas law making sodomy a crime; in *Gratz v. Bollinger* the use of race as a factor in admission to the University of Michigan was declared unconstitutional but in *Grutter v. Bollinger* a different use of race was accepted in admission to the University of Michigan Law School.   2003

PRESIDENTIAL ADMINISTRATIONS 1945–2003

Harry Truman: (Democrat) Truman became president upon the death of Franklin Roosevelt in April 1945. Not well informed by Roosevelt on issues, he quickly took control supporting the establishment of the United Nations at the San Francisco Conference, making the decision to drop atomic bombs on Japan, and presiding over the end of World War II. His foreign policy focused on containing the perceived Communist threat, which became the key element of the Cold War. He announced the Truman Doctrine of containment, supported Foreign Aid (the Point Four Plan) and the Marshall Plan, and responded to Communist North Korea's invasion of South Korea by sending troops and appealing to the United Nations. In a very close election, he won a second term, defeating Governor Thomas Dewey of New York. His stance on the Communist threat and his support of labor in vetoing the Taft-Hartley law (passed over his veto) gained him support.

Dwight D. Eisenhower: (Republican) Eisenhower defeated Adlai Stevenson in the 1952 election. The Korean War was a major issue in the campaign. Eisenhower's foreign policy was one of Cold War confrontation and brinkmanship. John Foster Dulles served as a forceful secretary of state. Domestically, after Joseph McCarthy's "witch hunts" against the domestic threat of Communism ended and he was censured by the Senate, the Eisenhower years were quite peaceful. The Civil Rights Movement was stimulated by the *Brown v. Board of Education* Supreme Court decision on school integration. Eisenhower gave only moderate support to the movement but did finally send federal troops to support the integration of the high school in Little Rock, Arkansas. His administration held to a high standard of honesty in government. Sherman Adams, his White House Chief of Staff, was asked to resign after it was revealed he had accepted a vicuna coat as a gift. The most far-reaching domestic legislation of his presidency was the National Highway Act, which set up the interstate highway network.

John F. Kennedy: (Democrat) Kennedy was elected president in 1960 by a narrow margin over Richard M. Nixon. He was the first Catholic to win the office and the youngest ruler of a major world power. His administration supplied much polish and glitter, but little substantial domestic legislation. Kennedy's administration is most noted for foreign policy developments, among them the Alliance for Progress, the Peace Corps, the Bay of Pigs, the Cuban Missile Crisis, the start of the Space Race, and the extension of the U.S. commitment to Vietnam. Kennedy was assassinated on November 22, 1963 in Dallas, Texas and Vice President Lyndon Johnson became president.

Lyndon Johnson: (Democrat) In the aftermath of Kennedy's tragic death, Johnson initiated a number of domestic reforms including a Civil Rights Act.

   The Civil Rights movement was an important aspect of the Kennedy/Johnson years. Supreme Court decisions, congressional legislation, and the efforts of many workers and leaders led to a great breakthrough in the extension of rights to African Americans. However, the assassination in 1968 of Martin Luther King, Jr., a believer in nonviolent protest, was followed by outbreaks of violence, and the movement lost momentum. More militant leaders called for Black Power. The eventual success of the movement inspired many other minority groups to seek power, with the result that Mexican-Americans (Chicanos), Native Americans, homosexuals (Gay Power), and women organized to have an impact on political affairs.

Johnson initiated a *War on Poverty* in an attempt to eradicate poverty in America and create a Great Society. In many ways it was an updating and extension of Franklin Roosevelt's New Deal. It began well and included such diverse programs as Head Start and Medicare, but implementation of the Great Society was hampered by increased involvement in the war in Vietnam.

The Vietnam War came to dominate Johnson's presidency. Student unrest in the mid-1960s reflected a change in attitude among some young people and culminated in antiwar protests. President Johnson announced he would not run for a second term. Unrest took many forms, including the "hippie" movement, greater use of illegal drugs, establishment of communes, antiwar demonstrations, and violence at the Democratic Convention in Chicago in 1968. One hero of the movement, Robert Kennedy, was assassinated in Los Angeles in 1968 while campaigning for the Democratic presidential nomination, removing an important political leader of the protest.

Richard M. Nixon: (Republican) Elected president in 1968, Nixon promised to "bring the nation together." Antiwar protests increased and there were periodic outbursts of antiwar violence, such as Kent State, 1970, during his presidency that led his administration to seek ways to prevent it. He negotiated an end to the war in Vietnam.

As the Vietnam War was winding down, the Nixon administration made moves to reverse the policies of the previous 25 years. His actions collectively have been referred to as *détente*. Some observers saw this as the beginning of the end to the Cold War. Nixon's negotiations with the Soviet Union and recognition of the People's Republic of China were the most important developments in foreign policy during his administration.

Domestically, Nixon pursued a conservative political agenda, trying to cut federal programs under a program of *New Federalism*. *Watergate* was the most memorable event of his presidency domestically. Nixon was concerned by the antiwar protests and the possibility of a Democratic victory in 1972. He approved of "dirty tricks" including a break in at the Democratic Headquarters in the Watergate apartment complex in Washington. A cover-up unraveled through newspaper exposés, the appointment of a special prosecutor, and grand jury inquiries. Meanwhile Vice President Spiro Agnew was forced to resign as a result of illegal acts involving his personal taxes. Finally, tape recordings of White House meetings revealed that Nixon was aware of the break in and cover-ups of illegal acts. Congress began impeachment proceedings and President Nixon resigned in August 1974. He was the first president to be forced from office. He was succeeded by Gerald Ford, who had been chosen to succeed Agnew as vice president, following the procedure set forth in the Twenty-fifth Amendment, which was ratified in 1967. Nelson Rockefeller, four-term governor of New York, was chosen as vice president following the same procedure.

Gerald R. Ford: (Republican) President Ford, the first man to come to the presidency by appointment rather than election, served the remaining years of Nixon's term. Ford continued the policy of *détente,* holding a summit conference in Vladivostok in 1974 and visiting China in 1975. The aftermath of Watergate, including Ford's pardon of Nixon, colored his administration. There was high inflation and Ford introduced his WIN (Whip Inflation Now) policy to combat it with limited success. OPEC (Organization of Petroleum Exporting Countries) and its oil pricing policies affected domestic affairs and led to large increases in oil costs. Ford was defeated in his reelection campaign by Governor Jimmy Carter of Georgia.

James E. Carter: (Democrat) Jimmy Carter considered himself a "born again" Christian. Elected in 1976 as an "outsider," President Carter found it difficult to be effective in dealing with the established bureaucracy of Congress and government. He wanted to streamline the government and make it more efficient. He began the deregulation of business (Air Transport Deregulation Act), which intensified under Reagan. Domestic issues of inflation and energy crises, together with the international crisis of the Iranian Revolution and the seizure of American hostages, clouded his administration. His foreign policy focused on the issue of human rights. The highlight of the administration of Jimmy Carter was the establishment of the *Camp David Peace Accord*, which finally brought peace in the Middle East between Israel and Egypt, although it did not solve all of the outstanding issues in the area. He also negotiated a new treaty with Panama, which gave that nation control over the Panama Canal.

Ronald Reagan: (Republican) Viewed by many as an extreme conservative Republican, Ronald Reagan overwhelmed Jimmy Carter in the election of 1980. The Republicans gained control of the Senate; Reagan's goals were to reduce inflation, reform the tax structure, reduce taxes, deregulate business and industry, cut social welfare programs, and build up the military. A major debate developed about the need for a balanced budget and military versus social welfare expenditures. *Supply-side economics*, the philosophical position behind the Reagan economic reforms, did not operate as expected and a huge government budget deficit and a large trade deficit developed, although the inflation rate slowed dramatically. Reagan appointed Conservatives to the Supreme Court and the Court's views on privacy, especially the right to abortion, began to shift.

Reagan's foreign policy centered on the concept of the Soviet Union as an "evil empire" responsible for the Cold War and world unrest. This view guided Reagan's foreign policy in such matters as his support of the Contras against the Sandinista government of Nicaragua and his policy of peace through strength. He introduced SDI—*Strategic Defense Initiative*, commonly known as Star Wars—which antagonized the Soviets but led to negotiation with them for a disarmament agreement. When Mikhail Gorbachev came to power, his policies of glasnost improved relations. Negotiations led to summit meetings at Geneva, Reykjavik (Iceland), and Washington, where in 1987 an Intermediate Range Missile Treaty (INF) was signed marking the beginning of a new phase of the Cold War.

The release of the American hostages by Iran on Reagan's inauguration day led Democrats to investigate an "arrangement," but nothing was proven. The Israeli invasion of Lebanon, which left that country divided, led Reagan to send in marines, who were later withdrawn after 237 were killed in a terrorist bombing of their barracks. The Iran-Iraq War led to unrest in the Persian Gulf and caused Reagan to put the American flag on Kuwaiti oil tankers and escort them through the Gulf with U.S. Navy ships in order to assure the flow of oil to Europe and Japan.

George H. W. Bush: (Republican) [Bush 41—i.e., the first president Bush, George H. W. Bush, was the forty-first President of the United States, and so some have referred to him in this way since the election of his son, George W. Bush or Bush 43—the forty-third president of the United States.] In 1988 Reagan's vice president, George Bush, overwhelmingly defeated Democrat Michael Dukakis, governor of Massachusetts, in a negative campaign that addressed such issues as the environment, crime, patriotism, and family values. The public's alienation from politics grew during Bush's term reinforced by the deadlock between the Democratic Congress and the Republican president, the battle over conservative Supreme Court appointments such as Judge Clarence Thomas, the S & L bailout, continued investigations of the Iran-Contra Affair, and several scandals involving Congress (Keating Five, House of Representatives Post Office and Bank Scandals).

The administration, led by Vice President Quayle, supported the conservative agenda of pushing family values and overturning *Roe v. Wade*. Bush supported a Clean Air Act but did not support the UN. Conference on the Environment and Development (Rio Conference). What began as a mild recession continued to worsen and was seen as a depression by 1992. Differences between Congress and the president led to near deadlock in response to the economy, and the trade and budget deficits continued to grow. Bush was unable to present a balanced budget to the Congress.

President Bush had extensive foreign policy experience and used it to deal directly with world leaders. His great success was the *Persian Gulf War*. After Iraq, led by its president, Saddam Hussein, had seized the country of Kuwait Bush organized Operation Desert Shield through the United Nations. Then Operation Desert Storm forced Iraq's withdrawal from Kuwait. Bush gained strong public support for his war actions, but it quickly evaporated as the recession developed.

Bush developed a close relationship with Gorbachev and his successors as the Soviet Union collapsed. The end of the Cold War heightened the domestic argument over military defense vs. social welfare spending. Outbreaks of fighting in former states of the Soviet Union and in Yugoslavia based on nationalistic interests indicated the "New World Order" proclaimed by President Bush after the success in the Persian Gulf War would not be peaceful. Other foreign policy events included the invasion of Panama to seize accused drug dealer General Manuel Noriega and the opening of Arab-Israeli peace talks.

The election of 1992 saw third-party candidate, unknown businessman H. Ross Perot win 20 percent of the vote in many states. Bill Clinton and Al Gore (Democrats) won with 43 percent of the vote, defeating Bush and Quayle.

William Jefferson Clinton: (Democrat) Clinton focused his campaign on the saying "It's the economy, stupid," but Congress failed to enact his major economic proposals. However, the economy boomed during his eight years, led by the computer industry. A budget crisis in 1995 led Clinton to shut down government operations that led to budget agreements and the first budget surplus in thirty years. Legislation passed under Clinton included Welfare Reform that reduced time on welfare; an education bill, Goals 2000, that set standards for subject areas; an anti-crime bill that increased the number of police; a family and medical leave bill; a reform of the IRS; and the Brady Bill, which restricted the sale of handguns.

Health care reform was a major legislative defeat. A committee headed by Hillary Rodham Clinton offered a plan for comprehensive health care, but the medical and insurance company opposition defeated the measure in 1994. Clinton was forced to compromise on his order to include gays in the military and a "don't ask, don't tell" policy was adopted. Republicans won control of both the House and Senate in 1994 with a specific campaign platform, the Contract with America. The victory established divided and confrontational government. However, Clinton and Gore won reelection in 1996, although the Republicans controlled Congress.

Investigation of possible scandals involving the Clintons and several members of his cabinet dominated the Clinton years, culminating in an impeachment proceeding in 1999 that found the president innocent. Early in Clinton's administration a special prosecutor, Kenneth Starr, was appointed to investigate the Clintons' involvement in a land development scheme on the Whitewater River in Arkansas. Other possible scandals involving the White House travel office and a White House intern, Monica Lewinsky, became part of the Whitewater investigation. Democratic fund raising in 1996 and the final presidential pardons were also investigated, as were several congressional scandals—one involving Newt Gingrich, Republican Speaker of the House. The "politics of personal destruction" appeared to dominate Washington during the 1990s.

Clinton pursued an active international foreign policy, seeking resolution to crises in the Balkans, examples being the Dayton Accords on Bosnia and cooperation with NATO in Kosovo, and bringing peace to Northern Ireland. Trade initiatives led to the passage of NAFTA (North American Free Trade Agreement), more trade with China, the passage of GATT, and increased globalization and use of the Internet. Clinton actively pursued peace in the Middle East following the Oslo Accords, but he failed as he had in Somalia, from which he withdrew U.S. troops.

George W. Bush: (Republican) [Bush 43—i.e., the second President Bush, the forty-third president] George W. Bush gained the presidency as a result of a Supreme Court 5–4 decision, *Bush v. Gore*, which ended a vote recount in Florida and gave him the state's electoral votes, assuring him of a four-vote victory in the Electoral College. Al Gore won the popular vote and had contested irregularities in the Florida voting. Bush chose several leaders of his father's administration for top positions, including Vice President Dick Cheney, Defense Secretary Donald Rumsfeld, Secretary of State Colin Powell, and National Security Advisor Condoleezza Rice. Several advisors, including Paul Wolfowitz and Paul Nitze, took a new view, termed *unilateralism,* of U.S. foreign policy, rejecting the multilateralism of the post-World War II period. These leaders believed the United States should use its power as the world's only superpower to achieve what the United States considered best for itself. Following this concept the administration withdrew from the Antiballistic Missile Treaty to develop SDI (an antimissile shield to protect the United States), refused to sign the Anti-Land Mines Treaty and the U.N. Convention on the Rights of Children, rejected the Kyoto Accords on Global Warming, as they were not in the economic interests of the United States, and refused to join the U.N. War Crimes Tribunal. The Israeli-Palestinian issue was ignored for more than two years until a proposal from the European Union and Russia was adopted as the war in Iraq began in 2003.

The defining event of the Bush administration was the terrorist attacks on the World Trade Center and Pentagon on September 11, 2001. Bush proclaimed a war on international terrorism and identified Osama bin Laden and his Al-Qaida network as behind the attack. The United States gained international sympathy and attacked Afghanistan's Taliban leaders, who supported bin Laden. The Taliban fell, but nation rebuilding in Afghanistan is ongoing. In January 2002 Bush defined Iraq, Iran, and North Korea as an "axis of evil" and shifted the focus of the war on terrorism to Iraq, its president, Saddam Hussein, and its possible weapons of mass destruction. Iraq accepted a U.N. resolution, number 1440, bringing back U.N. weapons inspectors in 2002. The United States sent troops to the Persian Gulf and, failing to gain U.N. support for a deadline for Iraq to disarm, attacked Iraq in March 2003. At this writing the war continues. The international community both protests and plans for future nation rebuilding in Iraq while the United States has developed, unilaterally, plans for the future of Iraq. Bush and his advisors foresee a democratic Iraq that will serve as a model for other Arab nations and a solution to the Israeli-Palestinian conflict. Islamic fundamentalists have other views. Meanwhile, Iran has indicated it has an advanced nuclear industry, and North Korea has developed nuclear weapons and missiles. Both nations sell weapons on the international market and could make them available to terrorist networks. What the future holds is not clear.

Congressional responses to September 11 included passage of the Patriot Act curtailing civil rights, the Airlines Security Act, the establishment of the Homeland Security Department, and the Senate's approval of the use of force against Iraq.

Before September 11, 2001, Congress passed a massive $1.35 trillion tax cut following the supply-side theory of the Reagan years and an education bill that focused on testing and accountability. Congress continues to debate a Bush energy policy. The cost of health care and prescription drugs and the future of Social Security were major issues facing Congress, controlled by Republicans again after 2002.

A recession began in 2001, ending the long bull market. The computer industry and e-commerce were hit hard. Compounding the problem were several business scandals, including the bankruptcy of Enron and Global Crossing. The recession, combined with the tax cuts and the cost of the war in Iraq, eliminated the projected budget surpluses in 2002.

SOME IMPORTANT INDIVIDUALS OF THE PERIOD 1945–1999

Madeline Albright	Eminem	Martin Luther King, Jr.
Muhammad Ali	Jerry Falwell	Henry Kissinger
Woody Allen	William Faulkner	John Lennon
Neil Armstrong	Geraldine Ferraro	Monica Lewinsky
John Ashcroft	Gerald Ford	Douglas MacArthur
Leonard Bernstein	Betty Friedan	Malcolm X
Tony Blair	William Fulbright	Nelson Mandela
Humphrey Bogart	Bill Gates	George Marshall
David Brinkley	Newt Gingrich	Thurgood Marshall
Edward Brooke	Ruth Bader Ginsburg	Eugene McCarthy
H. Rap Brown	Barry Goldwater	Joseph McCarthy
Pat Buchanan	Mikhail Gorbachev	George Meany
Ralph Bunche	Albert Gore	Arthur Miller
Warren Burger	Billy Graham	George Mitchell
George H. W. Bush	Martha Graham	Marilyn Monroe
George W. Bush	Alan Greenspan	Toni Morrison
Jimmy Carter	Joseph Heller	Ralph Nader
Rosalyn Carter	Hubert Humphrey	Richard M. Nixon
Cesar Chavez	Saddam Hussein	Oliver North
Dick Cheney	Daniel Ken Inouye	Sandra Day O'Connor
Bill Clinton	Jesse Jackson	Jacqueline Kennedy Onassis
Hillary Rodham Clinton	Lyndon B. Johnson	J. Robert Oppenheimer
Thomas Dewey	Helen Keller	Rosa Parks
Elizabeth Dole	Edward M. Kennedy	H. Ross Perot
Robert Dole	John F. Kennedy	Jackson Pollock
John Foster Dulles	Robert Kennedy	Nancy Pelosi
Dwight Eisenhower	Ayatollah Khomeini	Pope John Paul II
Ralph Ellison	Billy Jean King	Adam Clayton Powell

Colin Powell	Benjamin Spock	Arthur Vandenberg
Elvis Presley	Joseph Stalin	Kurt Vonnegut
Ronald Reagan	George Steinbrenner	Lech Walesa
William Rehnquist	Gloria Steinem	George Wallace
Walter Reuther	Edward Stettinius	Andy Warhol
Condoleezza Rice	Adlai Stevenson	Earl Warren
Nelson Rockefeller	Kenneth Starr	William Westmoreland
Donald Rumsfeld	Robert Taft	Tennessee Williams
Eleanor Roosevelt	Edward Teller	Wendell Willkie
Dean Rusk	Margaret Thatcher	Oprah Winfrey
Jonas Salk	Clarence Thomas	Richard Wright
Alan B. Shepard	Strom Thurmond	Boris Yeltsin
Frank Sinatra	Harry Truman	Andrew Young
B. F. Skinner	Donald Trump	
David Souter	Ted Turner	

Chronology of Important Dates

The following Time Line of United States History provides an overview that should prove useful in a quick review. You may wish to add your own dates to this Time Line as you study.

Time Line

about 50,000 years ago — First Native Americans cross land bridge from Siberia

about 500 A.D. — Pueblo culture develops in southwestern United States

1492 — Columbus's first voyage to America

1497–98 — Voyage of John Cabot

1519–21 — Magellan circumnavigates the globe

1565 — St. Augustine founded by Spanish

1580s — Failure to establish permanent colony at Roanoke by Sir Walter Raleigh

1607 — Colony founded at Jamestown by English

1608 — Santa Fe founded by Spanish

1609 — Quebec founded by French

1619 — House of Burgesses

1619 — First slaves brought to Virginia

1620 — Mayflower Compact — colony at Plymouth

1630 — Boston founded

1634 — Maryland founded

1638 — New Sweden founded by Swedes

1639 — Fundamental Orders of Connecticut

1664 — Dutch driven from New York

1675 — King Philip's war

1682 — Pennsylvania founded

1689–97 — King William's war

1692 — Salem witch trials

1696 — Navigation Acts restated

1702 — Cotton Mather publishes *The Ecclesiastical History of New England*

1702–13 — Queen Anne's War

1718 — San Antonio founded

1733 — Molasses Act

— Georgia, last of original 13 colonies, founded

1739–42 — War of Jenkin's Ear

1740–48 — King George's war

1754 — Albany Plan of Union proposed

— Fort Necessity (Pitt) built

— Jonathan Edwards, noted preacher and writer, dies

1754–63 — French and Indian War

1759 — Fort Ticonderoga captured

— Quebec captured

1763 — Treaty of Paris — France loses Canada and Northwest Territory

— Pontiac's Rebellion

1764 — Sugar Act

1765 — Quartering Act

— Stamp Act/Stamp Act Congress

1766 — Stamp Act repealed

— Declaratory Act passed

1767 — Townshend Acts passed

— New York Assembly suspended

— Nonimportation of British goods

1768 — Massachusetts Assembly dissolved
— Troops stationed in Boston
1769 — San Diego founded by the Spanish
— First California mission
1770 — Townshend Acts repealed
— Tea Tax maintained
— Boston Massacre
1772 — Massachusetts Committee of Correspondence
— *Gaspée* burned
1773 — Boston Tea Party
1774 — First Continental Congress
— Intolerable Acts
— Quebec Act
— Galloway's Plan of Union
1775 — Battles of Lexington and Concord
— Lord North's Conciliation Plan
1776 — Second Continental Congress
— Declaration of Independence
1778 — Battle of Saratoga
— France becomes U.S. ally
1781 — Battle of Yorktown
— Articles of Confederation ratified
1783 — Treaty of Paris
1785 — Basic Land Ordinance
1786 — Annapolis Convention
1786–87 — Shays' Rebellion
1787 — Constitutional Convention
— Northwest Ordinance
1788 — Nine states ratify Constitution
1789 — George Washington elected first president
— 13 states join federal union
1790 — Alexander Hamilton's financial program
1791 — Bill of Rights adopted
— Bank of the United States chartered
— Benjamin Franklin's *Autobiography* first published
1792 — Gilbert Stuart portrait of George Washington
1793 — Proclamation of Neutrality
— Citizen Genêt affair
1794 — Whiskey Rebellion
1795 — Jay's Treaty
— Pinckney's Treaty
1796 — John Adams elected second president
1797 — XYZ Affair
1798 — Alien and Sedition Acts
— Kentucky and Virginia Resolutions
1800 — Thomas Jefferson elected third president
1801 — John Marshall Chief Justice
1803 — Louisiana Purchase
— *Marbury v. Madison*
1804–07 — Lewis and Clark Expedition
1807 — Embargo
— Fulton invents the steamboat
— Aaron Burr conspiracy trial
1808 — James Madison elected fourth president
— Slave trade stopped by congressional law
1810 — Annexation of West Florida
— *Fletcher v. Peck*
1812–15 — War of 1812
1815 — Battle of New Orleans
— Hartford Convention

— Treaty of Ghent
1816 — James Monroe elected fifth president
— Second Bank of the United States chartered
1817 — Rush-Bagot agreement
1818 — Convention of 1818
1819 — Washington Irving's *Sketch Book* published (includes *Legend of Sleepy Hollow)*
— Knickerbocker School of New York writers
— *McCulloch v. Maryland* and *Dartmouth College v. Woodward*
1820 — Missouri Compromise
— Greek Revival architecture dominates
1821 — *Cohens v. Virginia*
1823 — Monroe Doctrine
1824 — John Quincy Adams elected sixth president
1825 — Erie Canal opened
— *Self Portrait in His Museum* painted by Charles Wilson Peale
1828 — Tariff Act
— Andrew Jackson elected seventh president
1830 — Webster-Hayne debate
1831 — Alexis de Tocqueville visits United States
— Peggy Eaton Affair
— Nat Turner slave rebellion
— Maysville Road bill vetoed
— William Lloyd Garrison publishes *The Liberator*
1832 — Tariff Act
— Nullification controversy
— Jackson vetoes bill to recharter Second Bank of the United States
— Telegraph invented
— Reaper invented
1834 — Whig Party formed
1836 — Texas Revolution
— Martin Van Buren elected eighth president
— Ralph Waldo Emerson's *Nature* published
— Transcendentalism
1837 — Panic of 1837
— Gag Rule in Congress
— Specie Circular
— *Charles River Bridge v. Warren Bridge*
1840 — William Henry Harrison elected ninth president
— Independent Treasury Act
1841 — Harrison dies; John Tyler becomes tenth president
1842 — Webster-Ashburton Treaty
1844 — James K. Polk elected eleventh president
— Oregon Dispute
1845 — Texas annexed
1846 — Oregon settlement
1846–48 — Mexican War
1848 — Treaty of Guadalupe Hidalgo
— Gold discovered in California
— Zachary Taylor elected twelfth president
— Seneca Falls Convention
1849 — California gold rush
1850 — Taylor dies; Millard Fillmore becomes thirteenth president
— Compromise of 1850
1851 — Melville's *Moby Dick* published
1852 — Harriet Beecher Stowe's *Uncle Tom's Cabin* published
— Franklin Pierce elected fourteenth president
1854 — Republican Party formed
— Kansas-Nebraska Act
— Japan reopened by Admiral Perry
1856 — Violence in Kansas
— James Buchanan elected fifteenth president

1857 — *Dred Scott v. Sandford*
1858 — First transatlantic cable
     — Lincoln-Douglas debates
1859 — John Brown's raid on Harper's Ferry
     — First oil well drilled
1860 — Abraham Lincoln elected sixteenth president
     — South Carolina secedes
1861 — Confederacy formed
     — Fort Sumter attacked
     — Morrill Tariff
1862 — Morrill Act
     — Pacific Railways Act
1863 — Emancipation Proclamation
     — Battle of Gettysburg
1864 — Homestead Act
     — Sherman's march through Georgia
1865 — Wade Davis Bill
     — Lee surrenders
     — Lincoln assassinated; Andrew Johnson becomes seventeenth president
     — Thirteenth Amendment (abolished slavery)
1866 — Civil Rights Act
     — *Ex parte Milligan*
1867 — First Reconstruction Act
1868 — President Johnson impeached
     — Fourteenth Amendment (equal protection of the laws)
     — Ulysses S. Grant elected eighteenth president
1870 — Ku Klux Klan formed
     — Fifteenth Amendment (no discrimination in voting)
1871 — Tweed Ring in New York
1873 — The "Crime of '73"
     — Slaughterhouse cases (first under Fourteenth Amendment)
1875 — Rutherford B. Hayes elected nineteenth president
1877 — Last federal troops removed from South
     — *Trinity Church Boston* designed by Henry Hobson Richardson
     — *Munn v. Illinois*
1878 — Bland-Allison Act
1880 — James A. Garfield elected twentieth president
1881 — James A. Garfield assassinated; Chester A. Arthur becomes twenty-first president
1883 — Pendleton Civil Service Act
     — Civil Rights cases
1884 — Grover Cleveland elected twenty-second president
1885 — Mark Twain's *Huckleberry Finn* published
1886 — American Federation of Labor formed
1887 — Interstate Commerce Act
     — Dawes Act
1888 — Benjamin Harrison elected twenty-third president
1889 — Oklahoma opened for settlement
1890 — Frontier "closes" according to Census Bureau
     — Sherman Antitrust Act
     — Sherman Silver Purchase Act
     — Battle of Wounded Knee
1892 — Bering Sea Dispute
     — Homestead Steel strike
     — Populist Party nominates James B. Weaver for presidency
     — Grover Cleveland elected twenty-fourth president
1893 — Panic of 1893
1894 — Eugene V. Debs leads Pullman strike
     — Carey Act passed (Reclamation)
     — *Chicago Stock Exchange* building designed by Louis Sullivan
1895 — Venezuela Boundary dispute
     — *U.S. v. E. C. Knight Co.*

1896 — William McKinley elected twenty-fifth president
— *Plessy v. Ferguson*
1897 — Diesel engine invented
1898 — Battleship *Maine* sunk
— Spanish-American War
— Edward Bellamy's *Looking Backward* published
1899 — Open Door Policy announced
1901 — President McKinley assassinated; Theodore Roosevelt becomes twenty-sixth president
1902 — Newland Act passes (conservation movement)
— Owen Wister's *The Virginian* published
1903 — Panama Revolt
1904 — Roosevelt Corollary to Monroe Doctrine
1905 — Russo-Japanese War ended by Treaty of Portsmouth
— *Lochner v. New York*
1906 — Pure Food and Drug Law passed
— Hepburn Act
1907 — Gentlemen's Agreement with Japan
1908 — William Howard Taft elected twenty-seventh president
— White House Conservation Conference
— *Muller v. Oregon*
1911 — U.S. Intervention in Nicaragua
1912 — Woodrow Wilson elected twenty-eighth president
1913 — Underwood Tariff passed, reducing tariff rates
— Federal Reserve Banking Act
— Sixteenth Amendment (income tax)
— Seventeenth Amendment (direct election of senators)
— *Cliff Dwellers* by George Bellows painted
1914 — Federal Trade Commission established
— Clayton Antitrust Act
— World War I begins in Europe
— Panama Canal opened
1915 — Sinking of the *Lusitania*
— Reelection of Woodrow Wilson in "He kept us out of war" campaign
1916 — Mexican border campaign by U.S. Army
— Keating-Owen Child Labor Act passed
— National Defense Act
1917 — United States enters World War I
— Virgin Islands purchased
— Law limiting European immigration passed
1918 — Wilson announces 14 Points
— World War I ends
— *Hammer v. Dagenhart*
1919 — U.S. Senate rejects Treaty of Versailles
— Eighteenth Amendment (Prohibition)
— Palmer raids
— *Schenck v. U.S.*
1920 — Warren G. Harding elected twenty-ninth president
— Nineteenth Amendment (vote for women)
— Prohibition begins
— Sinclair Lewis' *Main Street* published
1921 — Quota system for immigration introduced
— Washington Disarmament Congress
1923 — President Harding dies; Calvin Coolidge becomes thirtieth president
— Ku Klux Klan exposés
— *Adkins v. Children's Hospital*
1924 — National Origins Act passed
— Dawes plan on German reparations
— Harding administration scandals revealed
1925 — Scopes "Monkey" trial
— *The Great Gatsby* by F. Scott Fitzgerald published

1926 — *Eleven A.M.* by Edward Hopper painted
1927 — Geneva Disarmament Congress
— Sacco-Vanzetti case
— *The Jazz Singer* — first talking motion picture
1928 — Herbert Hoover elected thirty-first president
— *Strange Interlude* by Eugene O'Neill performed
1929 — Stock market crash, start of the Great Depression
— Ernest Hemingway's *A Farewell to Arms* published
1931 — Hoover debt moratorium
1932 — Franklin D. Roosevelt elected thirty-second president
— Reconstruction Finance Corporation established
— Glass-Steagall Act
1933 — New Deal Begins: First AAA, NIRA, TVA, FERA, HOLC, FDIC, CCC, SEC, FHA
— Twenty-first Amendment (ends Prohibition)
— Good Neighbor Policy announced
1934 — Philippine Independence Act passed
— Nye Committee munitions investigations
1935 — "Second New Deal"
— Social Security Act
— *Schechter v. U.S.*
1936 — *U.S. v. Butler*
1937 — Supreme Court "packing" plan
— *Falling Water* house designed by Frank Lloyd Wright
— *NLRB v. Jones and Laughlin Steel Corp.*
1938 — Second Agricultural Adjustment Act
1939 — Limited national emergency declared as World War II begins in Europe
— Neutrality Act
— New York World's Fair
1941 — Four Freedoms speech
— Lend-Lease Act
— Japanese attack Pearl Harbor
— United States enters World War II
— Film, *Citizen Kane,* produced by Orson Welles
1942 — Bataan and Corregidor captured by Japanese
— Battle of Midway
— U.S. forces invade North Africa
— Price control and rationing
1943 — Invasion of Philippines
— Invasion of Sicily and Italy
1944 — D-Day invasion of France
— Battle of the Bulge
— G.I. Bill
— *Korematsu v. U.S.*
1945 — End of World War II: Germany (May) and Japan (August) surrender
— President Franklin D. Roosevelt dies; Harry Truman becomes thirty-third president
— Atomic bombs dropped on Hiroshima and Nagasaki
— Yalta Conference
1946 — First meeting of General Assembly of United Nations
— Cold War begins
— Philippine independence
1947 — Truman Doctrine
— Marshall Plan
— Taft-Hartley Act
— *Cathedral* by Jackson Pollock painted
— Jackie Robinson becomes first African American player on major league baseball team
1948 — Berlin Blockade and airlift
— Organization of American States formed
— Hiss case

— *Sexual Behavior in the American Male* by Kinsey published
1949 — NATO formed
— Fall of mainland China to Chinese Communists
1950 — McCarran Internal Security Act
1950–53 — Korean War
1951 — Japanese Peace treaty
— West German Peace contract
— *Dennis* v. *U.S.*
— Internal Security Act (McCarran Act)
— Twenty-second Amendment (two terms for president) ratified
— J. D. Salinger's *Catcher in the Rye* published
1952 — United States explodes first H-Bomb
— Dwight D. Eisenhower elected thirty-fourth president
— Ralph Ellison's *Invisible Man* published
1953 — Execution of convicted spies Julius and Ethel Rosenberg
— Department of Health, Education, and Welfare created
1954 — *Brown v. Board of Education*
— Senator Joseph McCarthy censored by Senate
— SEATO formed
— Dien Bien Phu captured by Vietminh
— Atomic Energy Act
— Elvis Presley introduces his style of rock and roll
1955 — Summit conference at Geneva
— Austrian Peace Treaty
— AFL and CIO merge to form AFL-CIO
— Montgomery, Alabama, bus boycott; Martin Luther King, Jr. emerges as leader
1956 — Suez crisis
— Hungarian revolt
— Federal Aid Highway Act
— Allen Ginsberg's poem *Howl* introduces the "Beat Generation"
1957 — Eisenhower Doctrine
— *Sputnik* (first earth orbiting satellite) launched by Soviet Union
— Civil Rights Act
— Little Rock, Arkansas, school integration riots
— Defense Reorganization Act
— Jack Kerouac's *On the Road* published
— Postwar Baby Boom peaks
1959 — St. Lawrence seaway opened
— *Black on Maroon* by Mark Rothko painted
— Xerox machine available for public use
1960 — John F. Kennedy elected thirty-fifth president
— U-2 incident
— John Updike's *Rabbit Run* published
1961 — Berlin Crisis
— Bay of Pigs
— First man in space
— Advisory group sent to South Vietnam
— Peace Corps formed
— Twenty-third Amendment (District of Columbia voting rights)
— *Mapp v. Ohio*
1962 — Cuban Missile Crisis
— Trade Expansion Act
1963 — President Kennedy assassinated; Lyndon Johnson becomes thirty-sixth president
— Supreme Court (Warren Court) declares prayer in public schools unconstitutional and supports rights of criminal suspects
— Civil Rights March on Washington
— Betty Friedan's *The Feminine Mystique* published
1964 — Civil Rights Act passed
— War on Poverty begins; Economic Opportunity Act
— Warren Commission report on Kennedy assassination

- — Twenty-fourth Amendment (No Poll Tax)
- — *Escobedo v. New York*
- — The Beatles tour the United States
- 1965 — U.S. Troops engage in combat in South Vietnam
- — Voting Rights Act
- — Great Society programs: Elementary and Secondary School Act; Medicare; Water Quality Act: Omnibus Housing Act; Higher Education Act
- — Assassination of Malcolm X
- — Selma to Montgomery, Alabama, Civil Rights March
- — *Sixteen Jackies* by Andy Warhol painted
- 1966 — Department of Transportation
- — NOW (National Organization for Women) founded
- — Freedom of Information Act
- — *Miranda v. Arizona*
- 1967 — Urban riots (Detroit, Newark, Rochester, Milwaukee, Washington)
- — Twenty-fifth Amendment (presidential succession)
- 1968 — Dr. Martin Luther King, Jr., assassinated
- — Robert Kennedy assassinated
- — Riots at Democratic Convention in Chicago
- — Richard M. Nixon elected thirty-seventh president
- — Columbia University students seize the campus (SDS)
- — Non-Proliferation Nuclear Treaty passed by United Nations
- — Anti-Vietnam War protests
- — *U.S.S. Pueblo* seized by North Korea
- 1969 — Men land on the moon
- — My Lai massacre revealed
- — Nixon "Silent Majority" speech
- — Woodstock rock concert
- — *La Grande Vitesse* sculpture by Alexander Calder
- 1970 — U.S. troops invade Cambodia on orders of President Nixon
- — Independent U.S. Postal Service established
- 1971 — Twenty-sixth Amendment (voting age)
- — *Reed v. Reed*
- — Amtrak (train) service initiated
- — *Pentagon Papers* published
- — New Economic Program — price control
- 1972 — Watergate break-in by agents of the Republican White House; "cover-up" begins
- — Death penalty decisions (*Furman v. Georgia* and others) of the Supreme Court
- — President Nixon visits Communist China
- — Senate passes Equal Rights Amendment (ERA) but it is not ratified by states
- — SALT disarmament treaty signed
- 1973 — Vice President Agnew forced to resign; Gerald Ford chosen as vice president by Nixon with congressional approval
- — *Roe v. Wade*
- — Wounded Knee incident
- — Existence of White House tapes revealed as part of Watergate investigation
- — "Saturday Night Massacre"—Resignation of Attorney General Eliot Richardson and Special Prosecutor Archibald Cox over Watergate
- — United States negotiates withdrawal from Vietnam
- 1974 — Presidential impeachment hearings
- — *U.S. v. Nixon*
- — President Nixon resigns presidency; Gerald Ford becomes thirty-eighth president
- — Nelson Rockefeller confirmed as vice president
- — Ford pardons Nixon
- — Ford Vietnam War amnesty program
- — Oil shortages due to embargo and OPEC
- — Privacy Act
- 1975 — Oil price controls ended
- — President Ford visits mainland China

— Government of South Vietnam surrenders to the North Vietnamese
— Former Attorney General Mitchell and Nixon presidential aides Haldeman and Ehrlichman sentenced to prison for roles in Watergate scandals

1976 — Bicentennial Year
— 200-mile fishing limit proclaimed by United States
— Supreme Court upholds busing in Boston to achieve integration
— Copyright Revision Bill
— Jimmy Carter elected thirty-ninth president of the United States

1977 — Carter opens presidency by granting a pardon to draft evaders and proposing a large government spending program to reduce unemployment
— Trans-Alaska pipeline opens
— Clean Air Bill
— President Sadat of Egypt visits Israel
— Government Reorganization Bill
— Government Ethics Law (includes provision for Independent Council)

1978 — California tax cut (Proposition 13) approved by voters
— Air Transport Deregulation Act
— Civil Service Reform Act
— *Bakke v. University of California*
— Humphrey-Hawkins Employment Bill
— Camp David meetings (Israel-Egypt peace talks) and accord

1979 — U.S.-China diplomatic recognition finalized
— Egypt-Israel Peace Treaty
— Three-Mile Island nuclear plant accident
— Iranian students seize U.S. embassy in Teheran and take employees hostage
— Boat people leave Vietnam
— Government Ethics Law extended

1980 — Inflation continues as consumer prices rise 13.3 percent
— Attempt to rescue Iranian hostages fails
— John Anderson announces independent race for the presidency
— Peacetime draft registration is begun
— Ronald Reagan elected fortieth president

1981 — Inflation continues as consumer prices rise 12.4 percent
— Reagan supply-side economic plan reduces taxes, cuts welfare benefits, and increases spending for defense
— Soviet grain embargo lifted by President Reagan
— AIDS identified
— United States increases aid to El Salvador

1982 — Inflation rate slows as unemployment reaches post-World War II record
— Equal Rights Amendment to Constitution (ERA) defeated
— U.S. troops ordered to Lebanon due to civil war and fight between Israel and PLO
— Congress passes budget with a projected deficit of $100 billion
— START talks open
— Reagan introduces Strategic Defense Initiative (SDI or "Star Wars")

1983 — U.S. troops invade Grenada
— Terrorists bomb U.S. Marine barracks in Beirut, Lebanon, killing 237
— Congress passes bill to reform Social Security System
— Unemployment rate goes over 10 percent

1984 — Ronald Reagan and George Bush overwhelmingly reelected, defeating Walter Mondale and Geraldine Ferraro (Democrat, NY), first woman vice presidential candidate for a major party
— Record deficit in balance of trade payments

1985 — Gramm/Rudman Act (balanced budget)
— Mikhail Gorbachev becomes leader of Soviet Union and introduces reforms (glasnost and peristroika); summit meeting in Geneva between Mikhail Gorbachev and Ronald Reagan
— Supreme Court bars "moment of silence" in schools
— S & L (savings and loan) failures upset economy

1986 — *Challenger* space shuttle explodes
— Chernobyl nuclear power plant accident in Soviet Union
— Iran-Contra affair revealed
1987 — Iran-Contra congressional hearings
— Stock Market collapses with over 500-point loss on the Dow Jones in one day
— INF Treaty signed
— Congress approves S & L bailouts program
— Clean Water Act passed over Reagan's veto
— Toni Morrison's *Beloved* published
1988 — George H. W. Bush (Bush 41—Republican) elected forty-first president with Dan Quayle as vice president
— Anti-Drug Act passed (fourth act in six years)
— Peace accord signed in Nicaragua and Sandinistas are voted out of office
1989 — Fall of Berlin Wall
— United States invades Panama to seize accused drug dealer General Noriega
1990 — Second Earth Day celebration heightens environmental concerns
— Iraq invades Kuwait—Bush organizes anti-Iraq coalition in United Nations (Operation Desert Shield)
— Clean Air Act renewed
— Non-Communist governments established in all of Eastern Europe
— Cold War ends
— Americans with Disabilities Act
— Fox Network established
1991 — Kuwait freed and Iraq invaded by UN coalition led by United States (Operation Desert Storm); fighting ends with armistice and Saddam Hussein still in control
— Economic downturn continues and country goes into a major recession
— Soviet Union breaks up—replaced by Commonwealth of Independent States
— Slovenia and Croatia separate from Yugoslavia
— Clarence Thomas approved as judge of United States Supreme Court in spite of charges of sexual harassment
— Cambodian Peace Accords; El Salvador Peace Pact; Afghanistan Peace Agreement; Namibia Accord—all arranged through United Nations with U.S.-Russian cooperation
— Last U.S. hostages freed in Lebanon
— *Rust v. Sullivan* Supreme Court decision upholds *Roe v. Wade*
1992 — UN Conference on Environment and Development (Rio Conference)
— Legislative stalemate as President Bush continues to veto Democratic legislation; recession worsens
— Rodney King case followed by riots in Los Angeles
— Bill Clinton (Democrat) elected forty-second president of the United States with Al Gore as vice president, defeating George Bush and Dan Quayle (Republican) and H. Ross Perot and James Stockdale (Independent)
1993 — NAFTA (North American Free Trade Agreement) approved
— Bio-Diversity Treaty signed
— Israel–PLO Oslo Peace Accords signed
— Whitewater investigation begins
— Yugoslavia Civil War spreads to Bosnia
— South Africa ends apartheid and adopts a multiracial constitution
— Davidian cult attacked by FBI at Waco, Texas
— health care reform fails
1994 — GATT (General Agreement on Tariffs and Trade) approved
— Jordan–Israel sign peace treaty
— Brady Bill (arms registration) passed
— Republicans gain control of Senate and House of Representatives in mid-term election: Republican Contract with America
— Federal Reserve raises interest rates five times to curb inflation and slow economic recovery
— Civil war in Rwanda

1995 — Newt Gingrich elected Speaker of the House of Representatives
 — O. J. Simpson acquitted of murder of Nicole Simpson and Ronald Goldman
 — Oklahoma City Alfred P. Murrah Federal Building bombed; Timothy McVeigh
 and Terry Nichols later found guilty
 — Clinton and Congress approve closing of 79 military bases
 — Welfare Reform Bill "ends welfare as we know it"
 — Dayton Accords signed; commitment of U.S. troops to peacekeeping in Bosnia
 — Clinton and congressional disagreements over budget lead to government
 shutdowns in November and December; public supports Clinton stance;
 budget finally passed in January 1996
 — Beginning of Monica Lewinsky–Bill Clinton affair
1996 — Telecommunications Overhaul Bill
 — *Romer v. Evans* (gay rights)
 — Late Term Abortion Bill vetoed
 — Antiterrorism Bill
 — Health Insurance Portability Bill
 — Illegal Immigration Bill
 — Line Item Veto Bill
 — Clinton–Gore (Democrat) reelected with 49.2% of the vote over Bob Dole–Jack
 Kemp (Republican) and Ross Perot (Reform)
1997 — "Politics of self destruction" dominate political life in Washington
 — Balanced budget by 2002 plan approved
 — Arab-Israel talks at impasse; civil war in Zaire; Northern Ireland peace talks
 — U.S. refuses to sign Land Mine Treaty
 — Thailand currency devaluation precipitates Asian financial crisis
 — Dow Jones drops 554.26 points, largest one day drop, yet ends year up 22.6
 percent as U.S. economy continues to boom
1998 — House of Representatives impeaches President Clinton
 — First budget surplus in 30 years; Clinton calls for surplus to be used for
 Social Security; Republicans call for tax cuts
 — Dow Jones drops 20 percent in August but ends year up 16.1 percent
 — NATO expansion approved; Hungary, Czech Republic, Poland to join
 — Line Item Veto Act of 1996 declared unconstitutional
 — Internal Revenue Service Reform Bill
 — India and Pakistan explode atomic bombs
 — United States and Britain bomb Iraq; UN arms inspection teams withdraw
 — Many states settle with tobacco companies after national settlement fails to
 win congressional approval
1999 — Senate holds impeachment trial; Clinton cleared on all charges
 — NATO bombs Yugoslavia (Serbia and Kosovo); peace agreement reached;
 NATO sends in troops
 — Independent counsel section of 1979 Government Ethics Law expires
 — Possibility of Y2K computer crisis leads to law limiting Y2K lawsuits
 — *Alden v. Maine, College Savings Bank v. Florida* (interpretation of
 state sovereignty)
 — *Murphy v. U.P.S.* (limits Americans with Disabilities Act)
 — Senate rejects Nuclear Test Ban Treaty
2000 — Y2K arrives with few computer problems
 — Drunk Driving Bill
 — U.S.-China Trade Agreement
 — George W. Bush (Bush 43) (Republican) elected forty-third president of the
 United States with Dick Cheney as vice president, defeating Al Gore and
 Joseph Lieberman (Democrat) in closest election in U.S. history; Gore wins
 popular vote—Bush wins Electoral College vote
 — *Bush v. Gore* settles disputed Florida presidential vote
 — Dow Jones drops 6.2 percent as bull market ends
2001 — Tax Reform Act
 — Senator Jeffords of Vermont leaves Republican Party
 — United States withdraws from Antiballistic Missile (ABM) Treaty

— September 11 (9/11) terrorist attacks on World Trade Center and Pentagon
— War on terrorism proclaimed
— War in Afghanistan
— Antiterrorism Bill
— Airline Security Act
— Computer industry suffers major losses
— Enron bankruptcy reveals business scandals

2002 — Campaign Finance Reform Bill
— Education Reform Bill (No Child Left Behind)
— Bush 43 labels Iraq, Iran, and North Korea an "axis of evil"
— U.N. weapons inspectors return to Iraq; Security Council votes Resolution 1440—"one final chance for Iraq to disarm"; U.S. sends troops to Persian Gulf
— Rebuilding begins in Afghanistan
— Budget surplus disappears with tax cuts and recession

2003 — U.N. weapons inspectors report to Security Council some progress in Iraq
— United Nations rejects United States, Britain, and Spain's proposal for deadline for war in Iraq
— United States, Britain, and "coalition of the willing" attack Iraq to topple government of Saddam Hussein and destroy any weapons of mass destruction (WMDs); war begins March 19; Bush declares war over on May 1 after Baghdad falls
— Bounty out on Saddam Hussein as guerilla-type war breaks out in Iraq
— Tax cut passed by Congress increases deficit as war costs rise
— North Korea announces it has nuclear weapons; Bush refuses direct talks; Bush attempts to start negotiations to include China, Japan, South Korea, and Russia
— Supreme Court declares Texas sodomy laws unconstitutional (*Lawrence v. Texas*)
— Nine Democratic candidates seek party's 2004 nomination; Bush begins massive fund raising for his reelection campaign

Glossary

The words listed in this glossary are ones you should have encountered during your study of United States history. Read the list and see how many are familiar. It is important to know the vocabulary of history, so be certain you understand those words that are new to you.

Abolitionist — before the American Civil War, one who believed in the abolition of slavery

Abrogation — the terminating or voiding of a treaty or agreement

Absolutism — control of a people or nation with no checks on the authority of the ruler

Admiralty Court — a court that has jurisdiction over maritime cases

Aggression — attack on or invasion of territory of another country

AIDS — Acquired Immune Deficiency Syndrome — A fatal disease first diagnosed in 1981 that has become a worldwide epidemic and for which a cure is being sought

Alien — someone not a citizen of the country

Alliance — a formal temporary union of two or more countries

Amendment — a change or proposed change in a bill or in the Constitution

Amnesty — the act of forgiving a large group en masse

Anarchy — a government without law or order, or in which no central authority is obeyed; a state of society in which law and order are absent

Appeasement — the act of giving in to a potential enemy in the hope that the enemy's appetite for further plunder or aggression will be filled

Appropriation — setting aside funds for a particular use, especially as applied to government expenditures

Arbitration — settlement of a dispute by a hearing before one or more persons chosen by the conflicting parties

Aristocracy — the theory or practice of government rule by an elite considered to be the best. In common historical usage it implies an inherited nobility

Armistice — a cease-fire in anticipation of negotiations for a more durable peace

Assassination — the killing of a politically important individual by surprise attack

Autocracy — government by one person who exercises supreme authority

Automation — use of machines to take the place of labor

Autonomy — the right of self-government within a framework of a larger political unit

Axis — the alliance of Germany, Italy, and Japan in World War II

Baby Boom — the sudden precipitous rise in the birth rate after World War II that lasted through the 1950s

Balance of Payments — specie, credit, or exchange of goods needed by one nation to clear its accounts with another nation over a set trading period

Balance of Power — policy that attempts to balance a nation's power either by alliances or by national action against a combination of nations that might threaten the nation's national interests

Bear Market — a period of declining prices on the stock market or any market

Belligerent — a country that is at war or is openly supporting another country at war

Bicameral — a legislature that has two chambers or houses; for example, the American Congress is bicameral, having a House of Representatives and a Senate. Nebraska's legislature is unicameral, having but one legislative chamber

Bilateral — two-sided, as opposed to unilateral, one-sided, or as compared to a multilateral, many-sided action or treaty

Bimetallism — backing a nation's currency with use of both gold and silver

Black Code — a series of laws relating to the control and dehumanization of African Americans during the Reconstruction period and after, largely in Southern states

Black Power — a political and social concept that African Americans should exercise control over their destiny without pressure from members of the majority; assumes the group needs political and economic independence to achieve this goal. The concept can be applied to other groups, such as Chicano Power

Bloc — a group of politicians or political parties temporarily joined to work for the same goal

Blockade — use of ships or troops to prevent entrance to or exit from a country

Bloody Shirt — term used as a symbol of the rebellion of the Confederate states by the Republican Party to discredit the South in the years after 1865

Blue Laws — laws written to enforce moral behavior

Boondoggling — word invented during the New Deal period and used primarily by conservative forces to describe what they termed wasteful expenditure of public money

Bourbon — very conservative Southern Democrat

Bourgeoisie — the middle class — particularly merchants and industrialists in that period when nobility was the upper class; used by Marx in his analysis of the class struggle

Boycott — to refuse to have business dealings with a nation, firm, or person

Brinkmanship — a term coined in respect to the foreign policy approach of Secretary of State John Foster Dulles, and used since to describe a gambler's attitude in the management of foreign relations. Dulles said that one must be prepared to go to the "brink," presumably atomic war, if a nation were to be taken seriously in international affairs

Budget — a financial statement that estimates and limits future expenses

Bull Market — a period of increasing prices on the stock market or any market

Cabinet — advisory council of a president or other ruler; usually appointed

Capital — money that can be used for building factories, railroads, etc.

Capitalism — the economic system in which means of production and distribution are privately owned under competitive conditions

Carpetbagger — a northerner who traveled to the former Confederacy during the Reconstruction period to participate in the political reorganization of the South, often for profit

Cartel — a business monopoly that extends beyond national boundary lines

Catch-22 — a situation in which a decision is required and whatever decision is made will work against you because of regulations and circumstances. It came into common usage as a result of a war novel, *Catch-22*, by Joseph Heller in which the hero is caught in an impossible situation

Caucus — a private meeting of leaders of a political party to determine policy

Cavalier — a supporter of Charles I of England, particularly a soldier defending his reign; now someone of aristocratic leaning

Charisma — magnetic personality, charm, leadership, attractiveness; used in reference to political candidates

Charter — a document issued by a government or ruler granting rights and privileges to an individual or group

Charter Colony — a corporate colony operating under a charter obtained from the king by a company's stockholders

Chauvinism — extreme or exaggerated patriotism or commitment to a position; it comes from Nicolas Chauvin, who supported Napoleon in the extreme

Chicano — individuals of Mexican ancestry; Mexican Americans

Civil Rights — the liberties and privileges of citizens, especially those granted in the Bill of Rights

Closed Shop — a factory or place of business at which only union members may be employed

Coalition — a temporary union of individuals or political parties to attain some common aim

Cold War — a state of hostility between nations not involving physical contact. Applied specifically to U.S.–USSR relations between 1946 and 1990

Collective Bargaining — settlement of labor management disputes by discussion between representatives of the workers and the employer

Colony — an inhabited region politically dependent on and dominated by a more powerful nation

Collective Security — combining nations in an effort to provide greater protection from aggression

Communism — an economic system in which all means of production and distribution are owned and controlled by the government

Compact — an agreement, a contract

Computer — a machine that can solve problems very quickly because of its ability to do calculations fed into it by operators

Conscription — compulsory enrollment for military service; draft

Conservation — official care and protection of natural resources

Conservative — in politics, one who wishes to keep conditions basically as they are with little or no change

Continental — a soldier in the Revolutionary army; paper money issued by the Continental Congress, which continually depreciated in value

Contras — those forces opposing the Sandinista government of Nicaragua and funded and supported by the Reagan administration

Convention — a body of delegates meeting for a particular reason

Copperhead — a Northerner in sympathy with the South and active in its cause, or one in favor of a negotiated peace with the South

Corporation — a firm (usually in business) operating under a government charter that legally authorizes it to act as a single person with all the rights of a person under the law, but actually composed of two or more people who share ownership

Coup d'Etat — a sudden, forceful overthrow of government at the top

Culture — the way of living and ideas a people share

Delegate — a representative of a group to a meeting or convention

Democracy — government by the people, by majority vote

Depression — time of unemployment and financial collapse. The depression that began in 1929 was so long and severe that it is known as the Great Depression

Desegregation — ending of segregation, usually by integration

Despot — a ruler with absolute power, usually a tyrant

Detente — a relaxing and easing of tensions between nations used particularly in reference to the foreign policy of President Nixon in relation to the USSR

Deterrence — measures taken by one country to discourage attack by other nations

Dictator — a ruler who has supreme and absolute power; one who has usurped that power by force or legal trickery

Diplomacy — the conduct of negotiations to achieve agreements between countries; international contacts

Discrimination — a majority's denial of advantages to certain minority groups

Displaced Persons (DPs) — those uprooted from their native land by war and forced to move elsewhere

Divine Right — the belief—especially prevalent in the 16th and 17th centuries in Europe—that kings ruled and held power because of God's will

Dollar Diplomacy — a type of economic imperialism whereby the United States sought to insure its investment abroad, particularly in Latin America, by using military power or threat of military power

Due Process — traceable in English and American legal tradition to Magna Carta, due process has come to mean the procedure guaranteed to all citizens, that affords them their "day in court"

Duty — a tax, usually on imports

Ecology — the study of the relationship between individual organisms and their environment

Edict — an order issued by a governmental authority that has the same effect as a law

Electoral College — the procedure by which the president and vice president of the United States are elected. Every state has as many votes in the electoral college as it has senators and representatives combined, and the electors are voted for at the November presidential election every four years. The electors collectively (the college) then vote for president and vice president

Embargo — a government order preventing the movement of merchant ships and/or the prohibition of trade

Emigrants — those who leave their country to settle in another

Empire — many lands ruled by one ruler or nation

Entente — an agreement temporarily uniting two or more countries, usually informal and unsigned

Entitlements — programs such as Social Security to which the recipients believe they have a right

Environment — surroundings; all the conditions around us

Equality — everything being equal or everyone having the same rights

Ethnic Cleansing — the expulsion, imprisonment, or killing of ethnic minorities by a dominant majority group. It drew world-wide attention to Rwanda and Yugoslavia in the 1990s, but throughout history it has been used by dominant groups to establish their control over an area

Excise Tax — an internal tax on the manufacture, sale, or consumption of goods, such as tobacco, alcohol

Executive Agreement — an agreement between the president and the head of a foreign country

Expansion — as applied to countries, the acquisition of additional territory

Exports — goods sent out of the country for sale in another country

Extraterritoriality — the state or privilege of exemption from the laws of local courts, particularly in the case of diplomatic representatives to a foreign country

Fair Deal — the slogan used to describe the domestic program of President Truman

Fascism — a political philosophy, movement, or regime that exalts a nation and/or race above the individual and that stands for a centralized, autocratic government headed by a dictatorial leader, severe economic and social regimentation, and forcible suppression of all opposition. The term Fascist was applied specifically to the regime established by Mussolini in Italy before World War II

Featherbedding — retaining workers on unnecessary jobs, or paying workers more than necessary to do a job, or hiring more workers than necessary to do a job

Federal — the central government or authority as contrasted with state or local government

Federalism — a system of government in which a central authority divides or shares power with its regional parts

Feudalism — the social structure of the Middle Ages, based on the relation of a lord to his vassals, who held land (called fiefs) granted by the lord in return for obedience and loyalty

Fifth Columnist — a traitor who aids the enemy

Filibuster — private imperialistic adventure by unauthorized individuals out for their own profit and in some cases their own sovereignty; extended debate in the U.S. Senate designed to prevent a vote on a bill of which the filibusterer (speaker) disapproves but the majority of Senate members approves

Fourteen Points — Wilson's statement of war aims, delivered to Congress during the course of World War I. Among the points were freedom of the seas, self-determination of subject peoples, reduction of armaments once the war was successfully ended, and, most important, a League of Nations to keep the peace in the postwar world

Frontier — that boundary or border of a country that faces either another country or unsettled land; also the concept of newness or challenge as in John F. Kennedy's New Frontier

Gay Rights — a movement demanding civil rights for gay men and lesbians

Genocide — the deliberate murder, or attempted murder, of a whole people; may be based on racial, ethnic, religious, cultural, or political concepts

Ghetto — place where people of one minority group live together

Glasnost — an opening up in Russian; it refers specifically to both the economic and political opening within the USSR under President Mikhail Gorbachev in the 1980s and the opening in foreign policy that permitted greater contacts with the West and relaxed control over Eastern Europe. Together with peristroika these actions led to the end of the Cold War

Good Neighbor Policy — part of the New Deal's foreign policy, which aimed at strengthening United States ties with Latin America

Great Society — name given to the program of domestic reforms instituted by President Lyndon Johnson

Guerrilla — one who carries on or assists in an irregular war

Guild — an association of persons in the same trade or craft, formed for mutual aid and protection

Hegemony — leadership, paramount influence, or military-economic overlordship of one nation over another, or over other nations or regions

Holding Company — a company that usually does not produce anything or perform any service except to control other companies through the ownership of controlling shares of stock

Holocaust — mass slaughter of European civilians during World War II, especially of Jews, who the Nazis considered to be members of inferior races. Over six million Jews were killed in gas chambers or as a result of forced labor and starvation (see Ethnic Cleansing)

Hostage — a civilian seized by a group or individual and held captive to force an enemy to negotiate and make changes in policy; a form of blackmail

Immigrants — those who come to make their home in a new country

Impeach — to indict a public official for misbehavior; the case is then tried before a jury assigned to the case

Imperialism — a government policy of annexing territory by force or political pressure, or gaining political control over weaker lands

Implied Powers — powers suggested but not specifically listed in the Constitution and exercised by the national government and its three branches

Imports — goods brought into one country from another

Impressment — the practice of the British of forcing American sailors into service on British warships under the assumption that they were escaped British seamen

Inalienable — nontransferable, irrevocable. As associated with rights it means that there are certain rights that humans cannot cancel; they are God-given, or derived from nature

Industrial Revolution — that phase of economic development characterized by a change from home to factory production

Inflation — a large rise in prices due to an increase in the money supply and/or expansion of credit

Injunction — a court order preventing a person or group of people from carrying on some activity; usually applied to an order preventing a union from picketing

Insurgent — a rebel

Integration — bringing together or making as one; unification; applied especially to blacks and whites in a number of social areas

Internationalism — an ideology that emphasizes the unity of the world's peoples, and that deplores restrictive national boundaries and competing national sovereignties

Iran-Contra — name given to the policy followed secretly by the Reagan Administration to sell arms to Iran to help free hostages in Lebanon while using the profits from the arms sales to support the Contras in Central America

Isolationism — a foreign policy that shuns alliances and compacts with other countries

Jim Crow Laws — laws enforcing segregation of African Americans and whites, following the concept of separate but equal

Jingoism — supermilitaristic patriotism

John Birch Society — a pro-American, anti-Communist organization founded after World War II by Robert Welch, an ultraconservative retired businessman from Massachusetts. The Society was organized in semi-secret cells and used vicious and ruthless tactics in its fight against Communism

Journeyman — worker who is learning a craft under a master; such individuals work for a daily wage

Judicial — that branch of government related to the courts and their decisions concerning the legality of laws and acts

Judicial Review — the power of a court to accept appeals of legislative and executive action and decisions of lower courts with the possibility of modifying or nullifying such action as being "unconstitutional"

Jury — a group of people in a court who hear and decide a case

Keynesian Economics — ideas of John Maynard Keynes, British economist. Essentially Keynes believed in government spending during depression periods and retrenching with economy budgets and high taxation during periods of boom

Ku Klux Klan — formed in 1867 by southern whites to help them establish their prestige and power over the freedmen. It was organized in secret groups and terrified the countryside with threats, lynchings, and burnings. It declined after federal laws were passed later in the century but resurfaced in the 1920s as an anti-Communist organization that saw threats to traditional small town American values from Roman Catholics, Jews, and organized labor. It continues as a small, often vocal, anti-minorities organization

Labor Theory of Value — a central part of Karl Marx's scientific socialism. Marx contended that economic value is derived from labor acting on materials of production. The concept was also expressed by John Locke

Labor Union — organization of workers to improve their wages and working conditions

Laissez-faire — noninterference by government in private enterprises

Lame Duck — an elected official (congressperson, etc.) defeated in an election but continuing to serve because his or her successor is not scheduled to take office until a later date

Law and Order — a vaguely defined political concept held by those who oppose violence and anarchy; an important campaign issue in many elections

Legal Tender — any kind of money that is declared official by an act of government

Legislative — branch of government concerned with making laws

Liberal — in politics, an individual who is not tied to tradition or party lines and welcomes experimentation with new ideas; its root is *liber* meaning free

Logrolling — mutual assistance in the passage of legislation so that one member of Congress votes for a colleague's bills in return for similar assistance in his or her desired legislation

Lynching — execution or killing by a mob, with no proper trial

Majority — more than half of the votes, or the larger part of the population

Mandate — a vote of confidence from the people. A mandate also refers to a colony held in trust by a major power under the League of Nations

Manifest Destiny — the belief that it was the destiny of the United States to expand to the natural boundary of the Pacific

Marxism — the economic and political theories of Karl Marx as interpreted by Lenin, Stalin, Mao Zedong, and many others. The main features of Marxism are world revolution, removal of the exploiting class, a dictatorship of the proletariat during the transition period of the "withering away" of the state, and a goal of the classless Communist society where everyone shall contribute according to his or her abilities and take according to his or her needs

Master Craftsman — a worker who has learned a trade and produced a masterpiece to become a member of a guild

Masterpiece — an object produced by a journeyman. If approved of by the guild, the journeyman would be admitted into the guild as a master

Megalopolis — a very large urban region

Mercantilism — the practice of achieving a favorable balance of trade (exports exceed imports) through government acts to benefit the commercial interests of the country (example: English Navigation Acts of the 1680s)

Metropolitan Centers — big cities with smaller cities around them

Middle Class — that part of society between the affluent upper class and the poor lower class

Migrant — person moving from one place to another

Militarism — the overvaluing of the military establishment, its leaders, their aims, and ideals, also, the substitution of military for civilian control of the state

Militarist — one who believes in an aggressive foreign policy backed up with well-prepared armed forces

Military Industrial Complex — a phrase used by President Eisenhower to refer to the relationship between the military and business in the United States; he warned against their power in his Farewell Address to the nation

Monarchy — system of government with a king as ruler

Monopoly — control of the entire supply of some product, giving the power to set prices and/or limit production

Moratorium — a period of suspended activity

Most-Favored-Nation Clause — a common treaty provision that grants to the recipient all privileges granted to any other nation by the granting nation; often applies to trading agreements

Mother Country — the nation that sends out settlers to found a colony and the nation to which that colony owes allegiance

Muckraker — one who exposes, usually in writing, misdeeds in business or political activities, hoping to bring reform

Multilateralsim — (Multinationalism) the concept in foreign policy that nations should work together to achieve political, economic, and social goals. The United Nations, NATO, and Operation Desert Storm are examples of multilateralism. The concept was the basis of U.S. foreign policy from World War II to the inauguration of George W. Bush.

National (or Public) Debt — the sum total of all financial obligations that result from borrowing by a nation-state

Nationalism — ardent and sometimes excessive devotion to national interests and prestige

Natural Law — rules that appear to be true and are argued as true because they are either rational or because they are ordained by God

Natural Right — a right assumed to be protected by natural law

Nazism — the German variation of fascism established by Adolf Hitler in the 1930s. The Nazis considered the Germans a superior race and sought domination over Europe and extermination of those they considered of inferior races such as Jews, gypsies, homosexuals, and East Europeans especially the Slavs of Poland and the USSR

Negotiation — in international affairs, the practice of settling disputes by means other than the resort to armed force, by using judicial or arbitrational or diplomatic mechanisms; in domestic affairs, the settling of disputes by discussion and compromise

Neutral — a country that neither assists nor allies itself with another country at war

Neutralism — a nonpartisan or nonattached view of policy in regard to competing systems or states

Neutrality — the policy of a nation that seeks to maintain impartiality between two opposing states or groups of states, but at the same time to fully protect its own international rights

New Deal — the domestic reform program of President Franklin Roosevelt

New Federalism — President Nixon's domestic program, which centered on returning some power to the states at the expense of the national government under the assumption that the federal bureaucracy had grown too large and unresponsive to local needs; also endorsed by President Reagan

New Freedom — the domestic and foreign policy programs of Woodrow Wilson

New Frontier — the domestic and foreign policy programs of President John F. Kennedy

New Nationalism — slogan for the reform program of Theodore Roosevelt and the Bull Moose Party

Nonviolence — a peaceful kind of protest connected with Gandhi and Martin Luther King, Jr.

Nullify — to cancel or destroy the legal effectiveness of a law, tradition, or agreement

Oligarchy — government by a few

Open Door — American foreign policy in regard to Asia that was initiated by Secretary of State John Hay on September 6, 1899. The policy was to persuade nations having interests in Asia, and particularly having business in China, to deal with China as an equal. The policy sought equal commercial opportunity for all nations and the abolition of restrictive spheres of influence as well as other supranational privileges such as extraterritoriality

Open Shop — factory in which employment is not dependent upon being a member of a union

Ordinance — a rule or regulation issued by a nonsovereign body (usually a city, country, or township)

Panic — financial crisis followed by unemployment and hard times, but not as severe as a depression

Patronage — appointing people to government positions as a reward for political services while disregarding merits such persons might have for the jobs assigned

Peristroika — a rebuilding in Russian; it refers specifically to the rebuilding of the Soviet economic system by President Mikhail Gorbachev in the 1980s. It does not imply any movement towards democracy in the political area but simply a restructuring of the economy

Petition — a written plea from an individual or organized group protesting some wrong, personal or societal, in hopes of gaining a redress

Plebiscite — a vote by the people of the country on some measure submitted to them for acceptance or rejection. It was originally considered an extension of the democratic principle, but has recently been used by dictators to gain support for their autocratic decisions

Plutocracy — government by the wealthy

Police Power — the broad power of government to regulate and restrain the life, liberty, and property of individuals and groups in order to protect and promote peace, order, health, safety, good morals, and general welfare

Policy — the course followed by a government or one of its representatives

Pollution — the fouling of the environment; something unclean or poisonous

Pork Barrel — the money and public works Congress distributes and the spending of public money through logrolling techniques to benefit particular localities and enhance the election possibilities of representatives at the expense of the general public good

Poverty — lack of money or goods; condition of being poor

Precedent — in American and British law, it is a previous ruling in law that is so important it must be taken into account in subsequent cases; these later decisions usually abide by the earlier decision

Prejudice — dislike for a person or group without reason

Pro-choice — the position that abortion should be a woman's choice and not subject to restrictions established by government

Proclamation — a public announcement of official policy

Pro-life — the position that abortion is not a right and the Supreme Court decision of *Roe v. Wade* should be overturned

Propaganda — ideas, beliefs, and information either untrue or exaggerated spread by an organized group or government

Proportional Representation — a system of electing legislators that results in representation approximately proportionate to the strength of each political party as determined in a vote

Proprietary Colony — a colony run and controlled by an individual or group of individuals as their private estate, such as, William Penn's Pennsylvania

Protective Tariff — a tax on imported goods designed to increase their price to the level of similar home-produced goods

Protectorate — a country protected by a more powerful state that shares in its government

Protestant Ethic — the extolling of work and the abhorrence of waste by Calvinists and their descendants; connected in the United States with the Puritans

Purge — to free a state or party of disloyal elements

Quorum — the minimum number of members who must be present in order for a business to be transacted by a group, usually of elected representatives

Racism — the doctrine that some races are inherently superior to others because of supposed cultural and intellectual inheritance

Radical — one who favors basic changes in the structure of society

Ratify — to approve a bill or law

Reactionary — one who favors a return to an older, more conservative way of life

Reaganomics — President Reagan's plan of reduced taxes to stimulate economic activity and cut inflation; supply-side economics

Rebate — a percentage of the cost returned ostensibly for services performed or commodities sold

Recall — a petition signed by a large percentage (usually 25 percent) of the voters that recalls an elected representative from his or her position and thus leaves vacant the office held; the official so removed may run again

Recession — panic or slight depression

Referendum — a petition signed by a small percentage (usually 10 percent) that permits the public to vote on a law the legislature has passed

Religious Right — the conservative, fundamentalist, "born again" side of Protestantism in America first organized in the mid-20th century

Renaissance — a rebirth of interest in culture, especially as applied to art and literature in the 14th to 16th centuries in western Europe. The term has been used for other periods of rebirth such as the 12th-century Renaissance in France or the Harlem Renaissance of the 1920s in New York City

Reparations — payment in compensation for damages, caused usually as a result of war or war-connected activity

Representative — a person elected to represent others; a member of the U.S. House of Representatives or some other legislative body

Republic — a nation in which the people elect representatives to govern; from the Latin *res publica*, or public thing

Resources (natural) — the natural wealth of a country—minerals, farmlands, forests, etc.

Revenue — money a government collects by taxes and duties

Revolution — a sudden end of one government and the start of a new one; any dramatic and somewhat sudden change

Royal Colony — a colony directly controlled by a king and governed by the king's appointed representative

Rule of Law — a fundamental principle of American and British legal systems and constitutional government. It involves three points: (1) the absolute supremacy of law over arbitrary power—no person is above the law, not even the chief executive; (2) equality before the law; (3) the Constitution is the supreme law of the land and the protective force of inherent or natural rights

Satellite — an object orbiting another and commonly used to describe objects sent into space from earth. The term has also been used to refer to nations that are dependent on another country for defense or political direction

Scalawag — contemptuous name for a Southern white who cooperated with Northerners or African Americans during Reconstruction

SDS (Students for a Democratic Society) — a youth group formed in the 1960s to force changes upon American society by political and/or violent means

Secession — withdrawal of a constituent member from a political group

Sectionalism — devotion to the interests of a state or some particular section of it over and above the interests of the country itself

Sedition — actions that encourage disrespect for law and government that fall short of treason but go beyond normal legal and political opposition

Segregation — as applied to African Americans and whites—isolating one group from the other

Serf — in feudal society, a peasant permanently attached to land owned by a lord

Settlers — those who make their home in a new, usually sparsely settled area

Sharecropping — a type of farm tenancy in which the tenant agrees to share part of the crop in lieu of rent and often to receive seed and other necessary capital goods

Silent Majority — a term used by President Nixon to refer to those Americans who opposed the actions of protestors and activists of the late 1960s and supported "law and order"

Social Contract — a theory that primitive societies were first brought into being by a voluntary agreement between the ruled and the elected ruler in order to provide for mutual protection and welfare

Socialism — belief in a society based on government ownership and control of means of production and distribution

Sovereignty — supreme power. In the United States ultimate sovereignty is vested in the people and exercised by the federal government, which they control. Under the Articles of Confederation it was in the hands of several states, and prior to the American Revolution, in the British Crown. In the United States, each level of government exercises degrees of sovereignty, but since the Civil War ultimate sovereignty has rested in the federal government.

Soviet — Russian word for "council"

Specie — money in the form of coins, usually gold or silver

Speculation — legal gambling on stocks, real estate, farm commodities, etc.

Sphere of Influence — a geographic area in which a nation seeks to dominate to the point of securing preferential treatment of a political, economic, and even social nature

Spoils — in politics, the influence and jobs the winning party distributes to its workers

Spoils System — the awarding of government jobs or the granting of favors or advantages by government officials to political partisans and workers

Square Deal — the slogan used to describe the domestic program of President Theodore Roosevelt

Squatter Sovereignty — (similar to popular sovereignty) the professed right of settlers in an area to determine for themselves solutions to key problems affecting them

Status Quo Ante Bellum — the situation as it existed before a war, especially used to refer to the period before the U.S. Civil War

States' Rights — a belief that the federal government should be limited so that the individual states may exercise more power; it supports the concept of state as opposed to federal sovereignty

Statute — a law. One may distinguish four important types of legal restraint that are embodied in American and British legal systems: *Statutory law* is law established by a legislative body with the approval of the executive (or passed over his veto). *Common law* is the so-called unwritten law that has been established by custom, tradition, or precedent. *Constitutional law* is the overriding legal principles embodied in the basic governing document (such as the U.S. Constitution); *ordinances* are rules or regulations established by bodies—cities, counties, townships—not having full sovereignty, but existing as subdivisions of a sovereign body

Strict Construction — philosophy that holds that the Constitution should be narrowly or literally interpreted, which leads to the concept that government should be limited

Strike — walkout by workers, or general refusal to work, in the hope of forcing an employer or government body to offer better contract terms or change policies

Suburb — residential neighborhood at the edge of a city

Suffrage — the right to vote

Surtax — an additional tax; a graduated income tax added to the normal tax depending on a person's wealth

Tariff — taxes, usually referred to as duties, imposed by governments on imports and exports

Tenement — unsafe, unsanitary, and crowded apartment building

Theocracy — a church-ruled government, local, regional, or national

Third World — a term used to designate nonwestern nations that have not industrialized

Totalitarianism — a government whose leadership excludes all opposition and opposing political parties and exercises complete control over all phases of national life

Treaty — a formal agreement between two or more countries

Trust — an organization composed of different companies united under one board of trustees, whose purpose is to eliminate competition and thereby control an industry by creating a monopoly

Underground Railroad — an escape route for Southern slaves fleeing to the North and Canada in the years prior to the Civil War

Unification — as applied to nations, the process of joining different self-governing states into one central government

Unilateralism — the concept in foreign policy that a nation should strive to achieve its national goals without regard to the opinions and concerns of other nations and that a nation should use its power as it sees fit. The Republican administration of George W. Bush switched the basis of U.S. foreign policy from multilateralism to unilateralism. (see Isolationism)

Union Shop — a limited closed shop

Unwritten Constitution — customs, traditions, and practices in government that have become the way of life of a society

Urban — having to do with a city

Vassal — in feudalism, one who swears loyalty to a higher lord in return for protection and privileges

Veteran — one who has served in the military forces

Vigilantes — individuals who band together without the support of the law to enforce a particular code of behavior

Violence — attacks that harm or damage a person or thing. Politically it is usually associated with anarchy and revolution and often is a result of poverty or extreme, either conservative or radical, ideology

Veto — to refuse approval, usually of a bill, law, or motion, or to forbid

Watergate — a term used to refer to the scandals of the Nixon Administration that led to his resignation as president. The scandal began with a break-in at the Democratic Party headquarters in the Watergate Building—a condominium complex—in Washington, D.C.

Whitewater — a term used to refer to the investigation of the activities of President and Mrs. Clinton in a land development scheme in Arkansas. The Whitewater investigation by special prosecutor Kenneth Starr was expanded to include several other suspected scandals, such as Travelgate and the Monica Lewinsky affair.

Women's Liberation — a women's movement stimulated by Betty Friedan's book, *The Feminine Mystique,* which held that middle-class values stifled women; passage of the ERA (Equal Rights Amendment) was a goal

Welfare State — the set of government supports established by law that provide care for the disabled, elderly, poor, and unemployed who are unable for one reason or another to care for themselves in an industrialized society

Writ — a formal written document; an order or mandatory process in writing issued under seal in the name of the sovereign or of a court or judicial officer commanding the person to whom it is directed to perform or refrain from performing an act specified therein

Xenophobia — a fear or hatred of foreigners

Yellow Journalism — used particularly to describe a newspaper style of the 1890s; the style sensationalized the news, especially scandals, to attract readership

Youth Groups — organizations of young people, often for political action

Index

HTP for the AP U.S. History Exam
CD-ROM Minimum Requirements

The following documentation applies if you purchased *HTP for the AP U.S. History, 7th Edition* book with CD-ROM. Please disregard this information if your version does not contain the CD-ROM.

Documentation

MINIMUM HARDWARE REQUIREMENTS

This program will run on Windows with	This program will run on a Macintosh with
Intel Pentium 166 MHz or equivalent	OS 9 or higher
32 MB RAM	Power PC 8600
MS Windows 95/98/NT/2000/XP	32 MB RAM
SVGA (256 color) monitor	SVGA (256 color) monitor
8x CD-ROM drive	8x CD-ROM drive
Keyboard and mouse	Keyboard and mouse

LAUNCHING THE APPLICATION

Barron's HTP for the AP U.S. History CD-ROM includes an "autorun" feature that will automatically launch the application when the CD is inserted into the CD drive. In the unlikely event that the autorun features are disabled, alternate launching instructions are provided below.

Launching Instructions for Windows	Launching Instructions for Macintosh
Click on the CD-ROM icon (My Computer drive) and a window will pop-up with the executable. Click on the file and that will launch the program.	Click on the CD-ROM icon (My Computer drive) and a window will pop-up with the projector files. Click on the file and that will launch the program.